PENG

THE PORTABLE MALCOLM X READER

MALCOLM X was born in Omaha, Nebraska, in 1925 and raised in Lansing, Michigan, where his father was killed in 1931. Malcolm Little moved to Boston to live with his half sister Ella after living briefly with a foster family following his mother's institutionalization in 1939.

Influenced by his siblings as well as personal writings from Elijah Muhammad, Malcolm converted to the Nation of Islam (NOI) in 1948 and assumed the last name X to represent his lost original name. Malcolm quickly became a leading figure within the Nation of Islam and a dynamic media figure, uncompromisingly preaching the Nation's rhetoric of racial separatism and self-determination. However, unresolved tensions within the NOI led to Malcolm's break on March 8, 1964, and the forming of a new orthodox Muslim group, Muslim Mosque, Inc. (MMI). That June he also helped establish the secular Organization of Afro-American Unity (OAAU). Malcolm then traveled again, as he had in 1959, to Africa and the Middle East as a spiritual sojourn and in order to make political alliances. Through the OAAU and alongside other civil rights groups that he had formerly repudiated, Malcolm hoped to transform the issue of civil rights into one of human rights and bring it before the United Nations in a show of Pan-African unity. He was assassinated in the early afternoon of Sunday, February 21, 1965, as he addressed an OAAU rally at the Audubon Ballroom. He left behind his wife, Betty Shabazz, and six daughters. *The Autobiography of Malcolm X*, coauthored with Alex Haley and published posthumously in November of that year, became an international best seller and remains a celebrated classic of twentieth-century American literature.

MANNING MARABLE (1950–2011) was M. Moran Weston and Black Alumni Council Professor of African American Studies and professor of history and public affairs at Columbia University. He was founding director of African American Studies at Columbia from 1993 to 2003 and directed Columbia's Center for Contemporary Black History. The author of fifteen books, Marable was also editor of the quarterly journal *Souls*.

GARRETT FELBER was the key researcher for Dr. Marable's Malcolm X biography, *Malcolm X: A Life of Reinvention*, and is currently a doctoral student at the University of Michigan, Ann Arbor.

The Portable
Malcolm X Reader

Edited by
MANNING MARABLE *and*
GARRETT FELBER

Preface by
GARRETT FELBER

Introduction by
MANNING MARABLE

PENGUIN BOOKS

PENGUIN BOOKS
An imprint of Penguin Random House LLC
375 Hudson Street
New York, New York 10014
penguin.com

First published in the United States of America in Penguin Books 2013

LIBRARY OF CONGRESS CATALOGING-IN-PUBLICATION DATA
The portable Malcolm X reader / edited by Manning Marable and Garrett Felber ;
preface by Garrett Felber ; introduction by Manning Marable.
pages cm. — (Penguin classics)
Includes index.
ISBN 978-0-14-310694-4
1. X, Malcolm, 1925–1965.   2. Black Muslims—Biography.   3. African Americans—Biography.
I. Marable, Manning, 1950–2011 editor of compilation.   II. Felber, Garrett, editor of compilation.
BP223.Z8L57665 2013
320.54'6092—dc23
[B] 2012049159

Printed in the United States of America
3   5   7   9   10   8   6   4

Set in Sabon
Designed by Sabrina Bowers

Contents

II. ORAL HISTORIES

III. ARTICLES

Preface

In 2006 Manning Marable outlined his concept of "living black history," the reconstruction of African Americans' "hidden, fragmented past" into something usable in the present context of color-blind racism, mass unemployment, incarceration, and disfranchisement. "Preserving the past," he wrote, "creates a living legacy that can help shape the future."[1] Preservation, however, is only part of the practice of living black history. In effect, we must all become historians of our past and present—critical interpreters of the many competing narrative streams before us. As Marable noted, "Being true to black history, for me, means accepting and interpreting its totality."[2] Gathered in this reader—in the form of oral histories, newspaper stories, speeches, legal documents, government surveillance, and scholarly articles—is a remarkable record of the life and legacy of Malcolm X. It is, however, merely the raw material with which scholars, activists, and the young will have to critically engage if they hope to make use of it in the ever-changing present.

At a time when students' understanding of the history of civil rights struggle in America appears to be on the decline, it becomes even more imperative to bring forth a fresh and nuanced body of literature on Malcolm X.[3] Malcolm has been invoked by figures and organizations as disparate as Supreme Court justice Clarence Thomas, white Talibanist John Walker

1. Manning Marable, *Living Black History: How Reimagining the African-American Past Can Remake America's Racial Future* (New York: Basic Civitas, 2006), xv.

2. Ibid., xviii.

3. Sam Dillon, "Students' Knowledge of Civil Rights History Has Deteriorated, Study Finds," *New York Times*, September 28, 2011.

Lindh, black youths in Harlem donning "X" baseball caps and T-shirts, the Iranian government of Ayatollah Ruhollah Mussaui Khomeini, and the United States Postal Service. He was even deployed by al-Qaeda during the 2008 election to denounce presidential candidate Barack Obama as a "house Negro." Malcolm X's trenchant critiques of police brutality, American racism, and neocolonialism, as well as his positive message of black unity and cultural pride, remain as relevant, and in many cases radical, as they were during his day. However, as many of these examples demonstrate, his legacy is not only continually relevant but also susceptible to distortions and appropriations. This collection does not suggest a single "meaning" to Malcolm's legacy but rather offers an imperative to continually grapple with his meaning to our past and present.

The first section of the reader, "Documents," historicizes primary materials relating to thirty-five key events in Malcolm X's life. This section grew out of the chronology constructed for Professor Marable's biography, *Malcolm X: A Life of Reinvention* (2011), as well as materials used in his yearly seminar on Malcolm X. Many of these documents provide greater depth to the early life of Malcolm Little portrayed in *The Autobiography of Malcolm X* (1965)—the transcript of the Michigan State Police interview with his father, Earl Little, for example, following the arson of his home in Lansing, Michigan, and a mental health file that documents the financial strain the family felt following the institutionalization of Malcolm's mother, Louise Little. Letters and newspaper articles from Malcolm's years in prison (1946–52) demonstrate his growing politicization as he fought for Muslim prisoners' religious rights within the Massachusetts correctional system. While some documents offer fuller insights into the events in his autobiography, others fill in missing historical gaps. Documents relating to Malcolm's establishment of the Philadelphia temple in the mid-1950s and his popular lecture series in Detroit offer a window into his influence as an orator and organizer within the Nation of Islam (NOI). Sections on the writing of the *Autobiography* with Alex Haley and his travels to the Middle East and Africa in 1959 illuminate obfuscated or missing portions of the book. Debates with Bayard Rustin, James Farmer, and Louis Lomax exemplify the charismatic speaking style that was responsible for much of Malcolm X's exposure and popularity in the 1960s. Rather than position him somehow outside the stream of the civil rights movement, these debates demonstrate the way in which he actively engaged the movement and pushed it toward a more radical posture. Finally, this section offers a historical perspective on the Nation of Islam. Malcolm and the NOI organized against police brutality in Harlem in 1957, in Queens (New York City) in 1958, in Los Angeles in 1962, and in Rochester, New York, in 1963. Throughout 1962 the NOI waged, in the black press, a rhetorical battle with other American Muslims over the organization's religious legitimacy and place in the Muslim world. Documents also cover the NOI's problematic relationship with George Lincoln Rockwell of the American Nazi Party, as well as the NOI's widespread denunciation of Malcolm X after his departure in 1964.

The second section, "Oral Histories," includes excerpts from interviews compiled by Professor Marable in preparation for his biography. Those with James 67X Shabazz (later Abdullah Abdur-Razzaq) and Thomas 15X Johnson (later Khalil Islam) tell complicated stories of loyalty and betrayal in the Nation of Islam. Shabazz left the NOI with Malcolm and offered his services, for a year, to organize the Muslim Mosque, Inc. (MMI). He was one of Malcolm's closest confidants and one of the few people from within his inner circle to speak to scholars over the decades. Johnson served on Malcolm's security detail in the early 1960s, even buying groceries for the family and ensuring that Malcolm had a parking spot at the mosque on Sundays. After the break, however, he denounced Malcolm X and was eventually convicted, in 1966, along with two other NOI members, of his assassination. Johnson was finally paroled in 1987 and maintained his innocence until his death in 2009. The remaining oral histories come from two very different individuals with unique perspectives on Malcolm X's life. Herman Ferguson was an educator-activist and revolutionary nationalist who lived much of his life in exile in Guyana. He first met

Malcolm X through the Rochdale Movement, a community mobilization against a Queens housing development that refused to employ or house blacks. Ferguson joined the Organization of Afro-American Unity (OAAU) in its early stages and became a founder of the group's Liberation School, which offered classes to both children and adults. Gerry Fulcher was a young, white police officer who was quickly promoted to the New York City Police Department's Bureau of Special Services and put in charge of illegally wiretapping the MMI and OAAU offices at the Hotel Theresa in Harlem but became enamored with Malcolm's speeches and ultimately questioned the legitimacy of the surveillance. In his oral history, Fulcher recounts the day of Malcolm's assassination and voices suspicions about the NYPD's handling of the case. These first-person histories represent multiple accounts of Malcolm X—from the point of view of Nation of Islam loyalists and defectors, a secular community activist, and even a government agent.

The final section, "Articles," offers a historical review of the literature that has shaped Malcolm X's legacy. The process of immortalization and subsequent mythologizing began almost immediately after his death in 1965. Eldridge Cleaver's influential memoir *Soul on Ice* featured a chapter on his reactions, while in prison, to Malcolm X's assassination. In 1972 James Baldwin wrote "Malcolm and Martin," one of the first essays to suggest that the political trajectories of two of the most prominent voices of black America in the 1960s were moving toward, not away from, each other.

These foundational articles from the first decade after Malcolm's death were followed by a second wave of scholarship during his reemergence in the early 1990s. Among the most influential was an essay by black feminist scholar Farah Jasmine Griffin that interrogates and rethinks the gender politics of Malcolm X and its relationship to black nationalism. In examining the role of moral respectability and class striving in the Nation of Islam, Robin Kelley's essay on Malcolm X and the black bourgeoisie importantly complicates Malcolm's condemnations of the black elite while at the same time acknowledging the continued significance of his class critique. Ted

Vincent's brief but important article on the Garveyite roots of Malcolm's parents fills a crucial historical gap left by the *Autobiography*, particularly with regard to his mother's political activity in the Universal Negro Improvement Association. Finally, Manning Marable's essay on Malcolm's life after death reveals the deep and sometimes troubling ways in which this icon of twentieth-century black America has been revisited and refashioned. Embodying some of the most formative scholarship on the subject, this selection gives a narrative arc to the historiographic sources on Malcolm X.

Manning Marable invited me to coedit *The Malcolm X Reader* during a lull in the otherwise chaotic summer of 2010. I had worked with Professor Marable for three years as a research assistant on *Malcolm X: A Life of Reinvention*, and we were both in the anxious waiting stages that are part of the back-and-forth of the editing process. Always looking forward to the next project, and never content to rest on his laurels during a lull in a nearly completed one, Dr. Marable proposed a sourcebook that would act as a companion to the biography. Its core would be drawn from a four-hundred-page chronology of Malcolm X's life constructed for the biography, and the book would document significant events in his life as charted by its nearly two thousand daily entries.

Just days after I set upon the task of identifying the key events in Malcolm's life, Professor Marable received a long-anticipated call to undergo a double lung transplant. Despite the severity of the operation, he optimistically anticipated that we would have the sourcebook ready by fall. Within weeks of his surgery, he began reading through my proposals and soon suggested doubling my initial list of twenty key events. I continued to work on the project, but as the biography moved closer to publication and required more of our attention, we decided to table the reader until after the biography's release in the spring. In a tremendous blow to all whom he touched as a husband, father, mentor, scholar, and activist, Manning Marable passed away on April 1, 2011, just days before the publication of the biography of Malcolm X he'd been working on for a decade. Like many who have been fortunate enough to experience Dr. Marable's unmatched generosity, I wanted to continue to usher his intellectual legacy forward. Although *Malcolm X: A Life of Reinvention* has been called a comprehensive biography, Professor Marable saw it first and foremost as an entreaty to scholars and students to critically engage with Malcolm X. Whether as a companion to the biography or as a stand-alone collection, *The Portable Malcolm X Reader* was conceived in the hope that it might act as a valuable resource to those in and outside academia who wish to participate in a deeper dialogue about the life and meaning of Malcolm X.

This project faced multiple challenges, and consequently many thanks are due to those who helped bring it to fruition. Very early in the process I was aided greatly by Kevin Loughran, who helped gather many of the primary materials as I worked from a distance at the University of Michigan. Dr. Marable's assistant, Courtney Teague, was a constant source of support during a hard time for us all. We are greatly indebted to Professor Marable's literary agent, Elyse Cheney, who kindly helped find a home for the manuscript. At Penguin, Wendy Wolf, Kevin Doughten, and Elda Rotor were instrumental in perfecting this work. Many thanks are due to Mason Taub and Brittney Ross for their help with permissions. I cannot thank Dr. Leith Mullings enough for helping me keep this project afloat in the sad and difficult times of the last year. I could not have completed this project without her commitment and support. Finally, the debt I owe to Manning Marable is an unpayable one. The void he left as a mentor, scholar, and activist will remain felt by many. It is my hope that this book sufficiently carries forward his intellectual legacy. It is dedicated to his memory.

GARRETT FELBER
JANUARY 2013

Introduction

Since the assassination of Malcolm X on February 21, 1965, the black leader has come to symbolize the political and cultural awakening of urban black America in the mid-twentieth century. By 2000 the name Malcolm X could be found in the titles or subtitles of nearly a thousand academic articles and several hundred books. Literally hundreds of poems, plays, and even an opera have taken him as their central figure or muse. With the release of Spike Lee's biographical film on him in the early 1990s, the charismatic leader was introduced to a new generation of African Americans, who incorporated him into the galaxy of hip-hop heroes. In 1999 the U.S. government moved to celebrate the legacy of Malcolm X by issuing a commemorative postage stamp with his image.

The most important source for interpreting Malcolm X's life has long been *The Autobiography of Malcolm X*, which he coauthored with the journalist Alex Haley. Published in November 1965, it almost immediately became an iconic text. By the late 1960s, hundreds of colleges and high schools throughout the United States had assigned it as required reading. By the late 1970s, over three million copies had been sold. *Time* magazine, in 1998, named *The Autobiography of Malcolm X* one of the ten most influential nonfiction works of the twentieth century. Indeed, its popularity obscured its contradictions and limitations as a reliable or objective interpretation of the subject's life and history: Characters and many events in the *Autobiography* are fictive. Malcolm excluded major figures who helped to shape his public life. There is surprisingly little information about his political and religious evolution during the critical years of 1963–65.

While *The Autobiography of Malcolm X* largely defined the

popular representation of Malcolm, several anthologies or readers attempted to interpret the black leader's impact upon both black America and America generally. The most comprehensive of the anthologies produced in the initial years after Malcolm's death was John Henrik Clarke's *Malcolm X: The Man and His Times*, published in 1969. Clarke's book featured excerpts from Malcolm X's speeches and writings. The bulk of the book, however, was made up of commentaries and articles by associates and friends who had worked closely with him throughout his public life. There were also articles debating his final transition from the Nation of Islam (NOI) to his independent activities during the years 1964–65. Despite its strengths, the anthology also had its limitations. For example, it did not include perspectives from leaders or members of the NOI who opposed his decision to leave the Nation of Islam. Most notably, these might have included either speeches or articles by NOI leader Elijah Muhammad and Malcolm's chief protégé, Louis Farrakhan. Clarke's reader presented Malcolm X's evolution as a direct transition from black nationalism to Pan-Africanism. There was little if any analysis that explained Malcolm's spiritual journey from the NOI to orthodox Islam and his embrace of the tenets of Sunni Islam. Nothing addressed Malcolm's growing interest in the cause of Palestinian rights or his connections with Arab and Muslim leaders in the Middle East and Africa.

In the years since Clarke's reader was published, other anthologies have made their way into print, but none of them has possessed the range and scope of *Malcolm X: The Man and His Times*. The sole exception, perhaps, is Joe Wood's *Malcolm X: In Our Own Image*, which was published in 1993. Unfortunately, Wood's untimely death only months after its publication meant that the book was not adequately promoted, and it soon went out of print. The reader featured original essays by several of the most prominent black intellectuals of the 1990s; contributors included Angela Davis, Patricia Hill Collins, and Robin D. G. Kelley. As with Clarke's earlier reader, there were limitations to Wood's book. Despite the availability, by the early 1990s, of both oral history and archival materials documenting Malcolm's life, Wood decided not to include any of this new information. Like Clarke, Wood only presented content that advocated Malcolm's point of view, neglecting to include the Nation of Islam and its critical perspective of Malcolm X. Indeed, there is in the literature related to Malcolm X as a historical subject a lack of balance and objectivity, both in the selection of material and in its interpretation of the subject. The overwhelming majority of writing on Malcolm X—unlike that on Martin Luther King Jr., W. E. B. DuBois, or Booker T. Washington—uncritically celebrates its subject and fails to provide a critical, analytic interpretation of his strengths, as well as the errors and weaknesses that sometimes characterized decisions he made in public life. He has all too frequently been presented as a statue, or frozen icon of black liberation, rather than a real human capable of extraordinary growth and courage yet also capable of making mistakes. Serious historians and researchers have consequently passed over research projects involving Malcolm X, who has come to be treated like a secular saint by the many defenders who insist he was perfect and consistent throughout his public career.

In 1987 I began collecting materials related to Malcolm X, with the aim of writing a modest political introduction to his life. While at the University of Colorado Boulder, from 1989 to 1993, I initiated the Malcolm X Project, which collected hundreds of FBI documents and published literature on the subject. When I accepted the position as director of the Institute for Research in African-American Studies at Columbia University in 1993, I set aside my work on the Malcolm X biography for about seven years in order to build the institute. It was only in 2000, as my term as director neared its end, that I reengaged my efforts to complete a full and richly detailed biography of this black leader. During the next several years, I collected primary source materials with the principal goal of compiling a comprehensive chronology of Malcolm's life as he lived it, day by day. I wanted to know exactly what he did during his remarkable and all-too-short thirteen-year public career as a minister and political spokesperson.

Almost immediately I encountered four major problems in telling Malcolm's life story. The first was the embargo on information imposed by the attitude and decisions taken by Malcolm X's widow, Dr. Betty Shabazz. Following her husband's assassination, Shabazz decided not to collect and archive his papers and original documents in preparation for either giving or transferring them to a library or archive. Instead, for more than three decades thousands of pages of correspondence and documents written or issued by Malcolm X, even his Holy Qur'an, were left rotting on the basement floor of her Mount Vernon, New York, home. Shabazz aggressively sued writers and scholars who utilized or reprinted sections of Malcolm's speeches or writings in their published works. For example, when Clayborne Carson produced a volume documenting FBI surveillance of Malcolm X, in the early 1990s, she insisted that he cut a good section of the material because, she argued, it infringed on her ownership of Malcolm's intellectual property.

After Shabazz's death in 1997, one of her daughters, Malikah, transferred, through a series of haphazard errors, nearly all of Malcolm's private papers from her mother's basement to a Florida lockbox. Because she failed to pay the monthly rent in a timely manner, the material was sold to a speculator who immediately saw its value on the market. That speculator offered the Malcolm X memorabilia for $600,000 on eBay, and a national controversy about Malcolm's intellectual property ensued. When a small selection of Malcolm's letters and documents was released prior to the public auction, researchers were shocked by the poor physical condition of these rare materials. The documents were yellowed and brittle, and the Shabazz estate offered no explanation for its negligence in acting to preserve Malcolm X's intellectual legacy. Eventually, in 2002, the pending sale was voided due to a legal technicality, and the materials were returned to the Shabazz estate. In 2005 the New York Public Library's Schomburg Center for Research in Black Culture announced that it had acquired the Malcolm X archives, which had been loaned to it for seventy-five years, under fairly strict conditions, by the Shabazz daughters and estate. The materials became available to the public only in the summer of 2008. These remarkable holdings include a travel diary kept by Malcolm when he visited the Middle East and Africa in 1964 and hundreds of letters he received or answered, both of which provide a stunning window on his personality and political evolution.

The second impediment to researching Malcolm X was the refusal by the majority of the individuals who worked with him to go on record or to be interviewed. Following Malcolm's assassination, several of his key associates either went underground or fled the United States for many years. For example, Malcolm's chief of staff, James 67X Shabazz, relocated to Guyana in the 1970s and 1980s. Lynne Shifflett, the first organizing secretary of the Organization of Afro-American Unity, refused to be interviewed or to say anything on the record from 1966 until her death in 2007. Gradually, as word of mouth circulated about my project, several of Malcolm's associates appeared and agreed to be interviewed. Consequently, by 2008 I had accumulated a number of key oral histories in the form of interviews with members of Malcolm's organizations and his inner circle of supporters.

The third roadblock in developing Malcolm's life story was presented by the Nation of Islam, which since the early 1980s has been led by Louis Farrakhan. After years of effort, I secured a nine-hour interview with Farrakhan in May 2005, which led to a much more comprehensive interview in December 2007. Farrakhan's approval permitted me to interview Larry 4X Prescott, who had been one of Malcolm's assistant ministers in NOI Mosque No. 7 but disagreed with Malcolm's opposition to Elijah Muhammad and refused to leave the sect with Malcolm's departure. I also interviewed Norman 3X Butler and Thomas 15X Johnson, two of the three men convicted of the murder of Malcolm X, both of whom served more than twenty years in prison for a crime they did not commit.

Finally, the greatest challenge in the reconstruction of Malcolm's life has been the continuing suppression of information about the illegal surveillance and disruption of Malcolm and his organizations by law enforcement—specifically the FBI and the New York City Police Department. The FBI collected tens of thousands of pages of surveillance records pertaining to Malcolm during his relatively brief public career. It has made only about half of this information available to scholars and researchers. The remaining surveillance materials are still redacted and unavailable. Similarly, the NYPD maintained a secret investigative Bureau of Special Services (BOSS), which carried out illegal wiretapping, surveillance, and disruption of Malcolm's organization. Despite repeated requests under the Freedom of Information Act, BOSS and the NYPD have to this day refused to turn over sensitive documents related to the surveillance of Malcolm X during the last year of his life. BOSS even refused access to information related to Malcolm's early career in the 1950s and early 1960s that has no direct bearing on the assassination. My way around this was to obtain information on individual BOSS agents. For example, I located Gerry Fulcher, the BOSS detective in charge of the telephone tapping of Malcolm X's office in the Hotel Theresa during 1964 and 1965. Fulcher's oral history provides strong evidence that BOSS and the FBI had infiltrated Malcolm's organizations and knew in advance about plans for the assassination. One of Malcolm's principal bodyguards, Gene Roberts, was a BOSS detective. Evidence of his actions on the day of the assassination suggests that Malcolm's head of security, Reuben Francis, may have been an FBI informant. Fulcher was deliberately kept out of the assassination's investigation, and a narrative was constructed by police officials to deflect scrutiny of the department's activities leading up to Malcolm's murder.

With its publication in 2011, *Malcolm X: A Life of Reinvention* made available a historical narrative grounded in fresh archival and oral documentation, one that presents a new interpretation of this black leader's life and legacy. This collection, *The Portable Malcolm X Reader*, has been designed as a companion volume to the biography. It documents the most important events that defined Malcolm X's life. The initial section, "Documents," addresses in chronological order the significant activities that confronted Malcolm and his family. It begins with documents related to the firebombing of Malcolm's family home in Lansing, Michigan, in November

1929 and the suspicious death of Malcolm's father, Earl Little, in September 1931. Malcolm's career in the Nation of Islam is fully represented in this section. Included are materials related to the police brutality trial of Betty Shabazz and other NOI members in Queens in 1958; Malcolm's initial travels to the Middle East and Africa in July 1959; and the repercussions from Mike Wallace's controversial 1959 television series *The Hate That Hate Produced*, an exposé of the Nation of Islam. The period of the 1960s is fully covered in this section: the debates Malcolm held with civil rights leaders Bayard Rustin and James Farmer; excerpts of Malcolm's key speeches, including the "Message to the Grass Roots" speech, delivered in Detroit on November 10, 1963; the famous "chickens coming home to roost" comment, made following a speech given in New York City on December 1, 1963, which led to Elijah Muhammad's silencing of Malcolm the following day; and Malcolm's close relationship with heavyweight boxing champion Muhammad Ali.

The second section, "Oral Histories," presents excerpts from interviews with important individuals who worked directly with Malcolm X and offer different points of view about his evolution and split from the Nation of Islam. These include interviews with Thomas 15X Johnson, who was convicted in 1966 for his role in Malcolm's assassination; Malcolm's chief of staff, James 67X Shabazz; Organization of Afro-American Unity activist Herman Ferguson; and NYPD BOSS detective Gerry Fulcher.

The third section, "Articles," presents recent scholarship and original articles by researchers on Malcolm X and the Nation of Islam. These materials represent the essential texts necessary for reinterpreting and understanding the complex and textured life of one of America's most remarkable leaders. Malcolm X was a gifted and charismatic figure, but he was not perfect and was capable of making errors. Indeed, one of his great strengths as a leader was his ability to be critical of himself and statements he had made. During his last year of life, for example, he went out of his way to apologize to civil rights leaders like James Farmer for intemperate personal remarks and some of his criticism of the civil rights movement. What Malcolm sought was a broad united front of black Americans—incorporating the spectrum of black opinion from Republican to communist—that could be organized to fight for black freedom and social justice. Internationally, Malcolm had evolved as a Pan-Africanist and black internationalist who pursued a strategy of taking the United States to the United Nations and other international bodies and charging it with suppression of human rights. By the end of his life, Malcolm was recognized in Africa as a virtual head of state, addressing parliaments and presidents across the continent. His life was a remarkable journey of self-reinvention, from poverty to power. Had he survived, his growth might have culminated in new directions for the history of black America. Those who sought to silence him did so with recognition of how dangerous it was to those in power to permit his voice to continue to be heard.

The Portable Malcolm X Reader presents the essential materials necessary for the critical reevaluation and appraisal of this remarkable man's life. I want to thank my coeditor, Garrett Felber, for his tireless efforts in identifying and editing most of the material in this collection. Special thanks also to Elyse Cheney, my agent, who has assisted in representing this work and taking it to publication.

MANNING MARABLE
SEPTEMBER 7, 2010

Chronology

1890 *July 29* Earl Little is born in Reynolds, GA. Note that 1930 census lists Earl's birth in 1891–92 and Malcolm claimed 1889 on his 1959 passport.

1897 Louise Little is born in La Digue, St. Andrew, Grenada. Note that 1930 census lists Louise's birth in 1898–99 and Malcolm claimed 1896 on his 1959 passport.

1925 *May 19* Malcolm Little is born in Omaha, NE.

1926 *December* The Little family moves to Milwaukee, WI.

1929 The Little family relocates to Lansing, MI.

1929 *November 8* The Littles' home is set on fire. Police investigate arson.

1931 *September 28* Earl Little is killed in a streetcar accident.

1934 *May 28* Betty Sanders is born in Detroit, MI.

1938 Malcolm is placed with a black foster family.

1939 *January 31* Louise Little is received at Kalamazoo State Hospital.

1939 *August* Malcolm is placed in Michigan State Detention Home.

1941 *February* Moves in with half sister, Ella Collins, in Roxbury district of Boston, MA.

1943 *June 1* Registers for the draft in Manhattan, wearing a zoot suit and yellow knob-toe shoes.

1944 *November 29* Steals his aunt's fur coat and pawns it for five dollars. Ella calls police, and he is arrested for larceny.

1944 *December 4* Classified as 4-F by U.S. Army.

1945 *March 17* Robs an acquaintance and is arrested for grand larceny in Lansing.

1945 *December 11* Malcolm and his crew of five break into their first home. By January 10, 1946, they have stolen nearly ten thousand dollars in goods and are arrested two days later.

1946 *February 27* Convicted of four counts of breaking and entering. He and Malcolm "Shorty" Jarvis are sentenced to eight to ten years and sent to Charlestown State Prison.

1947 *January 10* Transferred to Concord Reformatory.

1948 *March 31* Transferred to Norfolk Prison Colony.

1948 After much correspondence and visitation by his siblings, Malcolm converts to the Nation of Islam (NOI).

1950 *March 23* Transferred back to Charlestown after refusing a standard typhoid inoculation on religious grounds.

1950 *April* Malcolm and other Muslim inmates demand a menu without pork and cells facing east, gaining the attention of local newspapers.

1952 *August 5* Request to leave state and live with his brother Wilfred is approved; Malcolm is granted parole and his sister Hilda meets him at his release.

1952 *August 31* Meets Elijah Muhammad for the first time and eats dinner at his home in Chicago.

1953 *April* Prepares for the ministry at University of Islam in Chicago.

1953 *June 8* Quits job at Garwood factory after being appointed assistant minister at Detroit Temple No. 1.

1953–54 Helps open Boston's Temple No. 11 in Roxbury and becomes acting minster of Philadelphia temple.

1954 *June* Muhammad appoints Malcolm minister of Harlem's Temple No. 7.

1956 Betty Sanders joins Temple No. 7 in late summer or fall.

1957 *February* Travels to Alabama to legally and spiritually assist a Muslim who beat a sheriff after being harassed at a train station.

1957 *April 26* Johnson X Hinton is beaten by New York City police. Malcolm intervenes and organizes protest outside precinct in Harlem.

1957 *July 6–7* Malcolm hosts the two-day thirty-fourth annual Feast of the Followers of Messenger Muhammad in Harlem. Two thousand attend, including honored guests from the Syrian mission to the UN and the Egyptian attaché. Wallace Muhammad is principal speaker.

1957 *August 14* Lectures for four weeks at Detroit temple.

1958 *January 14* Marries Betty Sanders in Lansing.

1958 *March* Travels to Los Angeles for two weeks to build membership.

1958 *May 14* Home is raided by New York police while Malcolm speaks at Boston temple. All mosque members in duplex, including his pregnant wife, are put on trial.

1958 *August 1* Speaks for second consecutive year at Marcus Garvey Day celebration in Harlem; Hulan Jack and Earl Brown also speak.

1958 *November 16* Betty gives birth to couple's first child, Attallah.

1959 *January 1* Speaks at African-Asian Exposition at Temple No. 7. J. A. Rogers also speaks before sixteen hundred people. Play called *The Trial* is performed by Boston temple.

1959 *March 2–18* Attends wife's and others' trial in Queens, which ends as longest assault trial in New York City's history.

1959 *April 15* Speaks at African Freedom Day and calls for a "Bandung Conference in Harlem."

1959 *May 31* Introduces Elijah Muhammad at Uline Arena in Washington, DC, before seven thousand to ten thousand NOI members bused in from across the country.

1959 *July 3–22* Leaves New York for nineteen-day trip to Middle East and Africa. Travels to Egypt, Saudi Arabia, Sudan, Israel, Nigeria, and Ghana.

1959 *July 13–17* *The Hate That Hate Produced* airs on New York's channel 13.

1959 *November 11* Elijah Muhammad and sons visit Asia and Africa for several months. Malcolm is put in charge during their absence; Louis X (Farrakhan) takes over in Harlem during interim. Upon his return, Muhammad changes name of temples to "mosques."

1960 *May* Malcolm produces a newspaper called *Mr. Muhammad Speaks*, which sells for fifteen cents a copy and is published monthly.

1960 *September 20* Just after midnight, Malcolm meets with Fidel Castro, at the Hotel Theresa in Harlem, during his visit to the UN.

1960 *October 20* Debates NAACP youth secretary Herbert Wright at Yale Law School. Louis X's record is distributed to the crowd.

1960 *October 29* Attends NOI-sponsored African-Asian bazaar with Dr. Mahmoud Shawarbi as surprise guest. This is the first NOI event Shawarbi attends.

1960 *November 7* Debates Bayard Rustin on WBAI radio.

1960 *December 25* Betty gives birth to second child, Qubilah.

1961 *January 28* Malcolm and minister of Atlanta mosque meet with KKK to work out agreement concerning NOI land purchases.

1961 *March 24* Debates Walter Carrington of NAACP at Harvard Law School Forum.

1961 *April 23* Appears on NBC's *The Open Mind* with C. Eric Lincoln, George Schuyler, and James Baldwin.

1961 *June 25* Speaks before eight thousand at Washington, DC's Uline Arena. George Lincoln Rockwell of American Nazi Party attends with ten to twenty supporters.

1961 *October 30* Debates Bayard Rustin at Howard University after his speech earlier in the year was canceled by the university.

1962 *February 24–25* Attends Saviour's Day, where he is described as "heir apparent" and "chief aide" by Elijah Muhammad. Delegation from American Nazi Party attends.

1962 *March 7* Debates James Farmer at Cornell University.

1962 *April 27* Los Angeles mosque is invaded by police; several members are wounded by gunfire, with one paralyzed and another, Ronald Stokes, killed. Malcolm conducts the funeral the following week.

1962 *June 3* After a jetliner crashes in Paris, killing 130 (including 121 people from Georgia), Malcolm calls it a "very beautiful thing" and frames it as divine retribution for Stokes's murder.

1962 *July 22* Third daughter, Ilyasah, is born.

1962 *October 23* Appears on stand at trial of five NOI members at Attica Correctional Facility, charging that the state is violating their religious rights.

1963 *January 11* Leads NOI demonstration at New York County Criminal Court Building, protesting police hostility toward two Muslims who were selling *Muhammad Speaks* in Times Square on Christmas 1962.

1963 *February 13* Leads a demonstration of 230 Muslims in Times Square, protesting police brutality.

1963 *February 26* Master of ceremonies at Saviour's Day since Muhammad absent for health reasons. "Royal family" is resentful and animosity grows.

1963 *March 23* Speaks at Harlem rally to raise money for blacks in Mississippi; Dick Gregory, Adam Clayton Powell Jr., Percy Sutton, and Lewis Michaux also speak.

1963 *August 28* Despite Muhammad's edict that no NOI member attend, Malcolm witnesses historic March on Washington, calling it a "picnic" and "good show."

1963 *November 10* Delivers "Message to the Grass Roots" speech in Detroit, before two thousand people, at King Solomon Baptist Church.

1963 *December 1* Describes Kennedy assassination as a case of the "chickens coming home to roost" despite Muhammad's insistence that he not address the president's death.

1963 *December 5* At monthly meeting with Elijah Muhammad, Malcolm is informed that he has been silenced for ninety days for his comments on Kennedy.

1964 *January 6* Travels to Phoenix, AZ, for a hearing with Muhammad; Raymond Sharrieff and John Ali are also present. This is the last time Malcolm meets with Muhammad.

1964 *January 15–21* Travels with family to visit Cassius Clay in Miami. It is the first vacation he and Betty have taken.

1964 *February 4* Interviewed by two FBI agents at his home; he states he is more devoted to Muhammad than ever before.

1964 *February 26* Sits ringside in Miami as Clay defeats heavily favored Sonny Liston in seven rounds.

1964 *March 9* Having heard formally that he will not be reinstated to the NOI, Malcolm publicly declares his separation and the formation of his new religious group, Muslim Mosque, Inc. The group is officially announced three days later at Park Sheraton Hotel.

1964 *March 26* Visits U.S. Senate gallery to observe civil rights filibuster. He crosses paths with Martin Luther King Jr., and the two are photographed shaking hands. This is their only meeting.

1964 *April 3* Delivers "The Ballot or the Bullet" speech during debate with Louis Lomax in Cleveland.

1964 *April 13–May 21* Departs New York with plans to travel through Cairo, Jeddah, Khartoum, Nairobi, Lagos, Accra, and Algiers while making the hajj. In addition to the religious transformation of the hajj, he spends a portion of his final weeks in Ghana with American expats Maya Angelou, Julian Mayfield, Alice Windom, and Leslie Lacy.

1964 *June 13* Attends meeting in upstate New York with Whitney Young, Clarence Jones, Ruby Dee, Ossie Davis, and Sidney Poitier to discuss future of the civil rights movement.

1964 *June 15–16* Attends and testifies at two-day eviction trial, in Queens, filed against him by the NOI. He is represented by Percy Sutton.

1964 *June 28* First public rally of his second group, the Organization of Afro-American Unity (OAAU), is held at the Audubon Ballroom. Meanwhile, Elijah Muhammad speaks at the nearby 369th Regiment Armory.

1964 *July 3* Lucille Rosary and Evelyn Williams file paternity suits against Elijah Muhammad.

1964 *July 9–November 24* Departs for Cairo via London. Spends over four months traveling throughout Africa and consulting with religious and political leaders.

1964 *December 3* Debates at the Oxford University Student Union.

1964 *December 31* Fourth daughter, Gamilah, is born.

1965 *January 26* Speaks at Dartmouth College before crowd of fifteen hundred.

1965 *February 3–4* Speaks to three thousand students at voter registration drive in Alabama. Addresses activists in Selma the next day with Coretta Scott King and Fred Shuttlesworth. MLK Jr. is in jail.

1965 *February* 9 Flies to Paris, but French government cites his "undesirable presence" and deports him to London.

1965 *February* 14 Home is firebombed. No one is harmed, and despite Betty's wishes Malcolm attends speaking engagement in Detroit.

1965 *February* 20 Looks at a home with Betty and Long Island realtor. Dines with family, Ella and Rodnell Collins, and Sheik Ahmed Hassoun. Stays the night at the New York Hilton Hotel.

1965 *February* 21 Awakened by threatening phone call at hotel. Just after 3:00 p.m., at an OAAU rally at Audubon Ballroom, Malcolm is shot multiple times, in the chest, legs, finger, and chin, with a sawed-off shotgun, .45, and Luger in a plot executed by five men. At 3:30 p.m. he is pronounced dead at Columbia-Presbyterian hospital.

1965 *February* 23 Mosque No. 7 is burned down by firebomb. Malcolm's body is on view at Unity Funeral Home despite multiple bomb threats.

1965 *February* 27 Buried in Ferncliff Cemetery in Hartsdale, NY, after a ceremony by Alvin Childs, bishop of the Faith Temple Church of God in Christ, and a eulogy by Ossie Davis.

1965 *September* 30 Betty gives birth to twin daughters, Malaak and Malikah.

A Note on the Text

Reproductions from primary sources have been kept true to their original form as much as possible. As a source guide for students and researchers, it is important that readers make their own critical evaluations of the texts. While in some instances corrections to spelling and punctuation were made so as not to distract the reader, typos and misspellings that are historically significant have been retained.

PART I

DOCUMENTS

LANSING FIRE

Just after Malcolm's younger brother Reginald was born, the Little family relocated to Lansing, Michigan, purchasing a three-lot property in a largely white neighborhood. Unbeknownst to Earl Little, the small one-and-a-half-story home carried a restrictive racial covenant, and neighbors promptly initiated an eviction process. Prior to the eviction, on the morning of November 8, 1929, the Littles' home was set on fire. Malcolm's newborn sister, Yvonne, was almost lost, and the family escaped with few possessions. As Malcolm later recalled: "I remember being suddenly snatched awake into a frightening confusion of pistol shots and shouting and smoke and flames. My father had shouted and shot at the two white men who had set the fire and were running away. Our home was burning down around us."[1]

Later that day, police officers G. W. Waterman and Charles B. Allen of the state fire marshal's department located the now-homeless Little family at the house of a nearby black family. Waterman and Allen interviewed Malcolm's mother, Louise, and his eldest brother, Wilfred (then nine years old). When Earl's story failed to mesh with those of his wife and son, the officers interviewed a local gas station and store owner, Joseph Nicholson, who had first reported that the fire department

1. Malcolm X and Alex Haley, *The Autobiography of Malcolm X* (New York: One World/Ballantine Books, 1992), 5.

3

refused to respond to his call on the night of the fire. Nicholson claimed that Earl had given him a revolver the night before. He produced the gun, which had five remaining shells and one missing. He also added that Little had purchased two gallons of kerosene the night before the fire; officers then found the can in the basement rubble, beneath a set of bed springs.

Although police were suspicious of possible arson, the district attorney ruled insufficient evidence, and Little was instead arrested on possession of an unregistered handgun and arraigned, with bond set at five hundred dollars. On November 11, Waterman and Allen visited Little in the city jail to secure a statement admitting that he'd fired a shotgun that night. Speculation that Malcolm's father set fire to the home—a theory fueled by the kerosene purchase and the fact that he held a two-thousand-dollar home insurance policy and five hundred dollars in insurance on household contents—has continued to this day. However, Little had allowed his insurance to lapse and even made a payment the following day, hoping to reactivate the policy, leaving these claims largely unsubstantiated.[2] The hearing was postponed several times before the case was finally dismissed on February 26, 1930.

- Interview of Earl Little, November 11, 1929
- Special report, Chas. B. Allen and G. W. Waterman, Michigan State Police, case no. 2155, November 8, 1929

2. Louis A. DeCaro Jr., *On the Side of My People: A Religious Life of Malcolm X* (New York: New York University Press, 1996), 46.

Earl Little, being duly sworn in by Mr. Allen, swears to tell the truth as to the following statement.

Your full name?
Earl Little.

Age?
40

Married?
Yes, sir.

How many children?
Six.

You lived on M 16?
Yes, sir.

Fire occurred at your house, Friday morning?
Thursday night about 2:30.

Well that would be Friday morning, November 8.
How did you discover that fire?
From a noise.

What kind of a noise did you hear?
Blow up.

Well where were you when you heard the noise?
On the bed.

What did you do?
  I jumped up.

What did you do after you jumped up?
  I yelled for everybody to get up, and put on my pants.

What did you do then?
  I went out doors.

What did you do when you went out doors?
  I saw up on the house a blaze.

Whose house?
  My house. I saw the blaze whooping up on my house.

Just what part of the house was this fire in?
  In the rear end where you go down in the basement on the
northwest corner on the west side.

What did you do when you went out there?
  Well I shot?

What did you shoot?
  A single barrel shot gun.

What next did you do?
  I came back in the house.

What did you do then?
  I got my coat and sweater and helped my wife and children
get out. My wife said call the fire department. I went next
door to Mr. Nichols and called a fire department.

Your wife did not get up when you first got up?
  Yes, sir, she got up. I went next door to Mr. Nichols and
called the fire department.

What did you do with the shot gun when you fired it?
I carried it around with me, and came back in the house; where I laid it down in the house, or out in the yard, I am not able to tell.

You did not take the gun when you went over to Nichols?
No.

Did Mr. Nichols come over there then?
Quite a bit later, two or three of the other neighbors were there first.

Is the shot gun, the only one you had in the house
No sir, I did not say that.

Did you have any more guns in the house, besides the shot gun?
I am not able to say.

Did you give anybody a gun over there?
No.

You won't say there wasn't another gun in the house?
No, I would not say that.

Where did you keep this shot gun that you fired?
Behind the trunk at the wall.

Where was this other gun?
I did not say there was another gun in the house.

Well was there another gun in the house?
I say, I would not be positive there was another gun in the house.

Now, did you have another gun in the house?
I did not refuse to say that I had another gun or not.

What kind of gun did you have in the house before that?
  I have a shot gun in the house.

What kind of other gun did you have in the house?
  I had a gun that belonged to my brother, once.

What kind of a gun?
  An automatic.

Was that gun in the house?
  I would not say. I am not able to say.

Did you have any other gun in the house besides the shot gun?
  No, sir, I did not.

Did you have any gun that you had borrowed from your brother?
  No.

Not besides the shot gun?
  No.

You did not give anybody the gun?
  No.

Did you have a 38 calibre colt revolver in the house the night of the fire?
  No, sir not that I know of.

Did you carry one out of the house?
  No, sir.

Did you give a 38 calibre revolver to any one that night?
  No, sir.

Signed. *by Earl Little*

November 11, 1929
M.E.R.

Special Report,
Chas. B. Allen and G. W. Waterman,
Michigan State Police,
Case #2155, November 8, 1929

SPECIAL REPORT

Case #2155.

County Ingham.	Officers Chas B. Allen.
Near Air Port	
Place of Crime on M 16.	G. W. Waterman.
Date of Crime November 8th, 1929.	Investigation started Nov 8th, 1929.
Nature of Crime Suspected Arson.	Investigation closed
Victims People of the State of Michigan.	Persons charged with crime Earl Little. (colored).

Sir:

I have the honor to submit the following special report covering my investigation of the **Suspected Arson** case at **Near Air Port on M 16.** County of **Ingham** showing the result of my investigation in detail and the present status of the case:

HISTORY OF THIS CASE;

At about 2.30 am, Friday November 8th, 1929, the house owned by Earl Little (colored), burned down. Earl Little had secured this property consisting of three lots and a small house, one and a half story, and some small out buildings located on the two east lots. This property is located on the South side of M 16, near the Air Port. Mr Little was unaware of clause in the original deed to this addition prohibiting colored people from living on this property. The neighbors resented the presence of the colored family, and started proceedings for thier removal. Judge Carr had rulled against Earl Little in this litigation a few weeks prior to the fire. This ruling was common knowledge to the residents of this addition.

I was detailed on the above case by Lieut L.W. Morse, at 3.00 p.m., Friday November 8th, 1929. Upon arriving at the scene of the fire, I met Mr Rouse, of the Rouse Insurance Company of Lansing, and a Mr Burr, of the Westchester Fire Insurance Company. I learned from Mr Burr that Earl Little held a two thousand dollar policy on the house with his Company. Mr Rouse informed me that Earl Little held a five hundred dollar police on the contents of the house with his company.

I interviewed Mr Wolf, who lives on the adjoining lot to the south of the Earl Little property. Mr Wolf stated that he and his wife were awakened during the night by an explosion. Mr Wolf got up and went to the north window and discovered that Mr Little's house was afire. The fire was located at the South West corner of the house, and the flames were rising fifteen or twenty feet high. Mr Wolf dressed and went to assist the collored family. Upon going to the front door, he met Mrs Little who was getting the children out. Mr Wolf entered the front bedroom in which Mr and Mrs Little were sleeping, and got a trunk out of the room. Mr Little then came up and told Mr Wolf not to go in the other part of the house. At this time Mr Dennis, who lives on the lot adjoining Mr Little on the East, came and assisted in getting the family out of the house.

I next interviewed Mr Dennis whoes statement was that he and his wife were awakened first by some one knocking on the kitchen door. Mrs Dennis stated that she did not get up, as she thot that if any one wanted them real bad that they would knock again, while awaiting for the person to knock again, she heard an explosion, she and her husband got up and looked out of the west window and saw that the colored family's house was afire, the flames were rising at the south end of the house, and on the west side of the kitchen. Mr Dennis dressed and went to help.

I next interviewed Mr Joseph Nicholson, who runs a gas station and store, located about twenty rds west, and on the north side of M 16. Mr Nicholson stated that some one awakened him by knocking on his window and told him that a house was afire, and to call the fire dept. Mr Nicholson dressed and went to the store to telephone, at this time he discovered that Mr Little's house was burning. Mr Nicholson then called the fire dept, who refused to come. Nicholson then went over to the burning house, Mr Nicholson was impressed by the fact that the fire was burning in a straight line from the wall to the eves of the house, and covered about one third of the south end of the west side of the house.

Upon returning to the scene of the fire, I met Mr Chas B. Allen, of the State Fire Marshall's Dept, we looked over the ruins, it was so hot however, that we were unable to dig about in the basement. We returned home, and at about 6.30 p.m., Allen and my self located the Little family at the home of Herb Walker (colored) at 732 Clark St, Lansing. Mr Little was not at home at the time we arrived, and did not come until about 9.00 p.m. We interviewed Mrs Little and her son who was about ten years of age. Mrs Little informed us that she was awakened by her husband in the night by his telling her that the house was afire, she got the children and some articuls that were handy, out of the house. She claimed that she and the children went to bed at about seven 7.00 p.m., and that her husband came home from town about 9.00 p.m. Mrs Little appeared to be telling the truth as far as she knew. The boy told us that he got up and unlocked the kitchen door for his father the night of the fire, he did not know what time it was that his father returned, however. We talked with Mrs Little until her husband returned, we then met him out side, we all got in Allens car and talked with Mr Little until about 11.00 p.m., as there were several points in his story that did not check with that of his wife and son, we decided to lock Mr Little up for further investigation.

November 9th, Allen and my self interviewed Mr Joseph Nicholson at his place of business. Mr Nicholson told us about his part in the fire, except the part in which Little had passed a revolver to him. after leading him up to this point as near as we could, giving him the opportunity to tell about it without our asking him about it, and he made no mention of the gun, we asked him if Little had given him a revolver the night of the fire. Nicholson answered, well I might as well tell you about it as I guess you fellows know any way. Well the night of the fire, I went over as soon as I had called the fire dept, I was met by Earl Little several rds from the house, Little stepped up close to me and handed a revolver to me, saying, keep this gun for me, will you.

I then asked Nicholson for the gun, which he then produced from the rear room of the store. It was a 38 cal. Colt Revolver (blue finish). One shell had been fired, the other five were loaded and in the chambers. We gave Mr Nicholson a receipt for the revolver, which I turned over to Lieut L.W. Morse, upon my return to the office that afternoon.

Earl Little had told Allen and my self, the night we interviewed him, that he had run out doors when he was awakened by the explosion, with a shot gun, and had fired once with it, then later that night, had given the gun to some one at the fire, he however did not know who the man was. Up to this time, we have been unable to locate the gun, and we have talked with every one at the fire. On November 11th, Allen and my self talked with Mr Little at the Police Station, then we went to the office of the State Fire Marshall, we took a statement from Earl Little relative to his actions the night of the fire. In this statement, Mr Little stated that he did not give the shot gun to any one. Allen and my self then went to the scene of the fire. In digging about in the ruins, we found a two gallon oil can, that Nicholson later identified as the same in which he had placed two gallons of kerosene oil the evening prior to the Little fire, November 7th. This can was found in the basement, south east corner, under a set of bed springs. Mrs Little had told us the night we interviewed her at Herb Walkers, that she had filled the container on the oil stove with the oil which her husband had brought from Nicholsons store the night prior to, or the night of the fire in fact, and then had set the can behind the kitchen door. The kitchen was built on th the south end of the house, and there was no basement under it.

November 11th, Allen and my self drove to 7.32 Clark St, Lansing, for a further interview with Mrs Little, we were informed by Herb Walker that Mrs Little was down town. Allen and my self then went to the City Jail and talked with Earl Little, we then brought him to the office of the State Fire Marshall, where we secured a statement in regard to the firing of a gun, and as to whether it was a revolver or a shot gun. Little stated that it was a shot gun which he fired, and then denied having given the gun to any one at the fire. We then returned Earl to the City Jail. I then secured a warrant charging him with the possession of a unregestered revolver. Earl was then arraigned before Judge McCellen. Earl pled not guilty, and demanded an examination which was set for 9.00 am, November 19th,-29. Bond set at five hundred dollars.

November 19th, 1929. The examination was set over to November 22nd, by John Bird, prosecuting Attorney. During the afternoon, Mr H.F. Springer, agent for the Western Adjustment Co and my self drove out to the scene of the Earl Little fire. We talked with Mr and Mrs Wolf and Mr and Mrs Dennis. While we were at the Dennis home, Earl Little and wife came to look over the ruins of the house. I again questioned them in the presence of Mr Springer, whose business was not known by the Littles. We then called at the home of Jessie Walker, 318 Beaver St, N Lansing, to inquire for Will Jones (colored) who was at the Little house about 9.00 p.m., the night of the fire with two girls. Dennis told us that Will was working on the construction job at the corner of Capitol and Allegon St's. I called at the job and questioned the foreman regarding this Will Jones, the foreman stated that he did not know this man, and further, did not have a colored man on the job.

November 22nd. The Earl Little case was set over to December 3rd, by the Prosecutor.

December 3rd. Examination set over to December 16th.

December 16th. Examination set over to January 15th.

January 15th. The examination held up pending the decision of Judge Carr who was to be interviewed by the prosecutor regarding the decision Carr would make should the case get to Circuit Court. The examination was then set over to February 28th.

February 28th, case dismissed.

Respectfully submitted.

G. W. Waterman
_____
P.S.T.

Approved: ___*R. W.* [illegible copy]___
         Asst. Chief, B.C.I.

EARL LITTLE'S DEATH

Following the destruction of the Littles' home, Earl, who was a carpenter by trade, built a new home for his family on the outskirts of East Lansing. Malcolm's younger brother Wesley was born several years later, putting further strain on Earl's modest income as an itinerant preacher and laborer. Despite the move from a predominantly white neighborhood, the family's Garveyite principles of black economic self-sufficiency and pride still chafed local racists. Just as the Ku Klux Klan (KKK) was enjoying a revitalization in the 1920s, another white hate group, the Black Legion, began to take shape in nearby Detroit. Substituting the iconic white garb of the KKK with black robes, the Black Legion operated in a more clandestine manner, harassing blacks, Catholics, and alleged socialist sympathizers through nighttime raids and beatings.

On September 28, 1931, Earl set out to Lansing's north side to collect money from residents who had purchased his poultry. Hours later, a young police officer, Lawrence Baril, notified Louise Little that her husband had been in a serious streetcar accident a block east of the town's boundary. The accident was gruesome, and Little was dead by the time his wife reached him; he had been run over by the car and his leg had nearly been severed from his upper body. Although the coroner and the local newspaper reported his death as an accident, Malcolm's then eight-year-old brother, Philbert Little, would later remember that "somebody had shoved him under that car."[1] Malcolm wavered throughout his adult life on the question of who was responsible for his father's death, at times calling it an accident and at others attributing it to the Black Legion.[2]

Malcolm also later recalled in his autobiography that the insurance company holding one of Earl's policies refused to pay his mother.[3] Although a thousand-dollar policy was collected, the debts left in the wake of Earl's death quickly erased most of it. From dental bills and the birthing costs of Wesley and Yvonne to land rent and burial costs, the policy's benefits were soon depleted. Louise was doled out the remainder in a "widow's allowance" of roughly eighteen dollars a month. Earl's death left a void in the family both emotionally and economically, and the circumstances of his death would continue to shape Malcolm's racial perspective.

- Debts, estate of Earl Little, file A-4053, Ingham County Probate Court

Further reading:

- "Man Run Over by Street Car," *State Journal*, September 28, 1931
- Notice of Claims Against Estate, *State Journal*, December 17, 1931

1. William T. Strickland and Cheryll Y. Greene, eds., *Malcolm X: Make It Plain* (New York: Viking, 1994), 25.

2. Manning Marable, *Malcolm X: A Life of Reinvention* (New York: Viking, 2011), 31–32.

3. Malcolm X and Haley, *Autobiography*, 14.

Debts, Estate of Earl Little,
File A-4053,
Ingham County Probate Court

LANSING, MICH: January 14, 1932

Earl Little Estate
Judge of Probate.   Mason, Michigan
                  on Account with
                  [illegible copy]
                    Dentist

Balance August 15, 1931		
6 Silver fillings	$12	00
1 Silicate "	3	00
1 Gold "	5	00
2 Gold Bridges	90	00
Treatments on gums	3	00
	$113	00

The above is a claim against the estate of Earl Little,
for Dental services rendered him.

State of Michigan

The Probate Court for the County of Ingham

Estate of   Earl Little   Deceased

To   Louise Little   Dr.

Address   Lansing,   R.F.D. No. 5.

Funeral expenses and other bills of Earl Little, paid by claimant,		
To Buck's Funeral Residence, Inc.	297	36
Burial expense in Georgia	80	00
Dr. Welch, medical expenses	20	00
Sparrow Hospital service	3	00
Note at Lansing Citz. Loan & Inv. Co.	75	40
Bill of Lyle Dune, carpenter	20	00
Bill of Fred Forward, chickens	7	00
Attorney fee, Dewitt Rathbun	150	00
	762	76

State of Michigan
County of Ingham, } ss.

    Louise Little   being duly sworn says: I reside in the

Township of **Lansing**   **Lansing R.F.D. No.5.**

The foregoing statement of account against the estate of **Earl Little** deceased, is a true and correct statement, and said account is a just claim against said estate.

There is now due and unpaid on said claim, over and above all legal set-offs, the sum of **Five Hundred Sixty-two and 76/100** Dollars

Louise Little

Subscribed and sworn to before me this **15th** day of **February A. D. 1932**

Alvin A. Miller

Notary Public, Ingham County, Michigan.

My commission expires **Sept 23 1932**

State of Michigan

The Probate Court for the County of Ingham

Estate of	Earl Little Estate	Deceased
To	John L. Leighton	Dr.
	534 Cherry Street	
	Address Lansing, Michigan	

Jan 1 1931	Rent of Three acres of land in Section 32 Lansing, Township from July 1st 1930 to December 31st 1930.	$ 60	00
	Taxes for year 1930 which were to be paid by Earl Little as to a condition of rental.	33	47
	Total Due	$ 93	47

Note. At session of Ingham Circuit Court in Chancery decree was granted June 27th 1930 to John L. Leighton on his petition for writ of assistance to put him into possession of the above lands. The above agreement for rent of $60.00 and taxes was made so that Earl Little might harvest the crops he had sown on these premises while these proceedings were pending and to which he was a party.

State of Michigan,
County of Ingham, } ss.

_____John L. Leighton_____ being duly sworn says:
I reside in the ___City___ of ___Lansing___

The foregoing statement of account against the estate of **Earl Little** deceased, is a true and correct statement, and said account is a just claim against said estate.

There is now due and unpaid on said claim, over and above all legal set-offs, the sum of ___Ninety three and 47/100th___ Dollars

John L. Leighton

Subscribed and sworn to before me this __16th__ day of __January__ A. D. __1932__

[illegible copy]

Notary Public, Ingham County, Michigan.
My commission expires __June 17 1932__

19

Jan. 26, 1932

Judge L.B McArthur
Judge of Probate Court,
Mason, Mich.

Hon. Judge:

The following is a claim filed against the estate of the deceased Earl Little for professional services rendered

Birth of Yvonne Inez Little Aug. 11, 1929,------------- $40.00
Philbert Little treated for pneumonia, April, 16/17/
    18/20/24/26/28/30, 1931 at $3.00 per call----------- $24.00
Birth of Wesley Little, May 27, 1931 ---------------------$35.00
                                          _____

Total for services rendered-------- $99.00

Very truly yours,

U.S. Bagley, M.D.

State of Michigan

The Probate Court for the County of Ingham

To the Probate Court for said County:

In the Matter of the Estate of __EARL LITTLE__ Deceased.

I, __Louise Little__, respectfully represent that I reside in the __Township__ of __Lansing__ in said county, and am interested in said estate and make this petition as __widow of said Earl Little, deceased.__

I further represent that said deceased died on the __28th__ day of __September__ A. D. __1931__, leaving no last will and testament, as I am informed and believe.

I further represent that said deceased was, at the time of __his__ death, an inhabitant of the __Township__ of __Lansing__ in said county _____ and left estate within said county _____ to be administered, and that the estimated value thereof is as follows: Real estate, $ __none__ or thereabout; personal estate, __Claim for insurance in amount of $ 1,000.00__ or thereabout, as I am informed and believe.

I further represent that the names, relationship, ages and residences of the heirs-at-law of said deceased are as follows:

Name	Relationship	Age	Residence
Louise Little	widow	33	R.F.D.#3, Lansing, Mich.
Wilfred E. Little	son	11	)
Hilda F. Little	daughter	10	)
Philbert N. Little	son	8	)
Malcolm Little	son	6	) R.F.D. #3.
Reginald Little	son	4	) Lansing, Mich.
Yvonne Little	daughter	2	)
Wesley Little	son	4 mos.	)

I therefore pray that the administration of said estate be granted to __Frank R. Robinson__ of the __City of Lansing State of Michigan (609 N. Washington Ave.)__ or to some other suitable person.

Louise Little
P.O. __R.F.D.#3, Lansing, Mich.__

State of Michigan,
  County of Ingham, $\Big\}$ss.

On this __9__ day of __November__ A.D., __1931__ before me personally appeared the above named petitioner, who being duly sworn says, that __she__ has _____ read the foregoing petition by __her__ signed, and knows the contents thereof and that the same is true of __her__ own knowledge, except as to the matters therein stated to be upon __her__ information and belief, and as to those matters __she__ believes it to be true.

Gertrude M. Perkins
Notary Public, Ingham County, Mich.
My Commission expires __March 29 1935__

LOUISE LITTLE'S INSTITUTIONALIZATION

Already burdened with her husband's debts and burial expenses, Louise struggled to support her children and maintain the pride and self-reliance that she and Earl had always valued. The two eldest children, Wilfred and Hilda, took on the tasks of hunting and babysitting, respectively. Despite a pension law that provided three dollars a week per child to poor families with state-approved guardians, Malcolm recalled that "the checks helped, but they weren't enough, as many as there were."[1] In 1938 Malcolm's half brother Robert was born, but the father spurned Louise and left during the pregnancy. That year Lansing welfare agents placed the young teenager in the black Pentecostal foster home of Thornton and Mabel Gohannah.[2]

Although Malcolm enjoyed the older couple's attention and seemed to be excelling in his new school, West Junior High, Louise protested the state's decision to move her son. As food was scarce in the Little household, Malcolm had taken to petty robbery, and welfare workers saw it as a necessary

1. Malcolm X and Haley, *Autobiography*, 16.

2. There are various spellings of the family's last name. It appears as Gohannas in the autobiography, but the couple's 1917 Livingston County marriage certificate spells the name Gohannah.

change of scenery. It was just before Christmas of that year that Louise was found, by police, wandering through the snow with her newborn child. After being examined by Dr. E. F. Hoffman of nearby Mason, Michigan, Louise was diagnosed as having a "paranoid condition, probably dementia praecox" and was committed to Kalamazoo State Hospital, where she would remain for the next twenty-four years.

A state-of-the-art facility when it opened in the mid-nineteenth century, the hospital was perpetually understaffed and over-crowded by the 1930s. Its primary method of treatment was occupational therapy, although electroconvulsive shock was used in select cases as well.[3] Despite her admittance as a "public patient" with no estate available to support her, the hospital later, in 1957, billed her son Reginald nearly thirteen thousand dollars for her care. Reginald seemed an odd choice since he was the fifth-youngest child and had battled with mental illness of his own following his expulsion from the Nation of Islam (NOI).[4] With his mother institutionalized, Malcolm was placed in a juvenile home in Mason in August 1939. It was only in 1941, when his half sister Ella Collins proposed that he move with her to Boston, that his new life began.

- Mental health file of Louise Little, B-4398, Ingham County Probate Court

3. See William A. Decker, *Asylum for the Insane: History of the Kalamazoo State Hospital* (Traverse City, MI: Arbutus Press, 2007).

4. Marable, *Malcolm X: A Life*, 92–93, 122.

Mental Health File of Louise Little, B-4398,
Ingham County Probate Court

Notice from <u>Kalamazoo</u> State Hospital on <u>Jan. 10</u> 19 <u>64</u>

Re:<u>   Louise Little   </u>   File No. <u> B-4398 </u>
Mentally Ill

<u>Nov. 12</u> 19 <u>64</u> Patient placed on convalescent status

State of Michigan

In the Probate Court for the County of Ingham

In the Matter of
Louise Little,   Mentally Incompetent   **PETITION FOR**
REIMBURSEMENT

Now comes   **Thomas M. Kavanagh**   , Attorney General of the State of Michigan, on behalf of the State Commissioner of Revenue, and respectfully shows unto this Court:

1. That as will more fully appear from the records of this Court, the above-named **Louise Little** was duly committed to the **Kalamazoo State Hospital** by this court and was duly admitted to said hospital as a patient, and that said **Louise Little** received care and medical treatment as shown by attached sworn statement of the Michigan Department of Revnue.

2. That said **Louise Little** was ordered to be admitted to said hospital as a public patient and is an indigent person.

3. That the said **Louise Little** has certain relatives who are liable for his/her support and for the expenses paid and to be paid by the State of Michigan and County of **Ingham** for the care and maintenance of said patient in said hospital.

4. That the names of the said relatives, their relationship to the said **Louise Little** , and their last-known addresses are:

NAME	RELATIONSHIP	ADDRESS
Reginald Little	Son	4705 S. Logan, Lansing Michigan

26

5. That your petitioner verily believes that said relatives have been and are possessed of means sufficient and adequate to reasonably enable them to contribute at least in part to the care and maintenance of said patient in said hospital and to reimburse the said State and County for the expenses paid and to be paid by them, but they have neglected so to do.

6. That said relatives are indebted to the State and County in the total amount of $ __13,499.63__ as of __April 30, 1957__ as shown by said sworn statement.

YOUR PETITIONER THEREFORE PRAYS That a citation issue out of this Court directing each of the aforesaid relatives to appear before this Court on a day certain and show cause why an order should not be entered by this Court directing them to reimburse the State of Michigan and County of __Ingham__ for expenditures heretofore made as aforesaid and to be made on behalf of said patient.

Thomas M. Kavanagh
Attorney General

Roland V. Remington
Assistant Attorney General

STATE OF MICHIGAN
COUNTY OF INGHAM } ss
On this __19th__ day of __May__ __1957,__ personally appeared before me __Roland V. Remington__, Assistant Attorney General, who made oath that he has read the foregoing petition by him subscribed for and in behalf of said Attorney General, he being authorized so to do, and that he knows the contents thereof and that the same is true of his own knowledge, except as to those matters stated on information and belief, and as to those matters, he believes them to be true.

[illegible copy]
Notary Public, Ingham County, Michigan
My commission expires __8-4-1958__

September 24, 1940

Hon. John McClellan
Judge of Probate
Ingham County Probate Court
Mason, Michigan

Dear Sir: Re: Louise Little

Our patient, Louise Little, is making some progress. At the present time she is engaging herself in occupational therapy and for the most part cooperates quite well although at times she is disagreeable and resistant. Her physical health is good and she is apparently not suffering any marked delusions at this time.

The prognosis in her case still is not favorable.

Very truly yours,

Medical Superintendent

April 27, 1939

Martha Thayer
Deputy Probate Register
Ingham County Probate Court
Mason, Michigan

Dear Madam: Re: Louise Little

We wish to acknowledge the receipt of your recent correspondence concerning Mrs. Louise Little who is a patient in our hospital.

We have questioned Mrs. Little concerning the guardianship of her baby, Robert Langdon Little and she is very resentful concerning this. When questioned whether or not she would like to have Mrs. McGuire, the guardian of her child, visit her, she became very resentful and in no uncertain terms stated that she did not wish to see Mrs. McGuire. Because of her marked resentment and because of her irritable disposition, we would not advise Mrs. McGuire to visit her and we certainly would not advise that the child be brought down to the hospital to visit the mother.

Very truly yours,

Medical Superintendent

Apr.12, 1939

Kalamazoo State Hospital,
Kalamazoo, Michigan.

Gentlemen:

We are enclosing herewith a notice of hearing to be served on Louise Little in the matter of Robert Langdon Little, her eight months old baby, together with blank proof of service to be filled out and returned to this office.

In the matter of the service of these papers, we anticipate that Mrs. Little may be somewhat disturbed over the situation and we would like to request that if possible, that the person who serves these papers explain to Mrs. Little that this proceeding is necessary in order to give the guardian of the child authority to care for it during the time Mrs. Little is in the hospital.

Also, would it be possible for you to furnish this office with a report on Mrs. Little's present mental condition and if you deem it wise for Mrs. McGuire, the guardian of her children, to visit her at the hospital. If you feel such a visit would not prove harmful, she would undoubtedly arrange to come over some time soon. If she should come, would you feel that it would be all right for Mrs. McGuire to bring the baby above referred to. You would be able to determine better than we, whether Mrs. Little should see her baby in the near future or whether such visit might have a tendency to aggravate her mental condition.

Thanking you for your consideration of the above matters, I am

Yours truly,

Deputy Probate Register

Self-addressed stamped envelope enclosed for reply.

State of Michigan

The Probate Court for the County of **Ingham** .

In the matter of **Louise Little**

Insane

COUNTY OF **Ingham** ,) ss.

I, **Dr. E.F. Hoffman** , do hereby certify that I am a permanent resident of the **City** of **Mason** , in said County, and a graduate of **Medical College, University of Chicago** , an incorporated medical college; that I am registered according to law, and have practiced as a physician **3½** years; that, acting under the direction and by the appointment of said Court, I did on the **3rd** day of **January** A. D. 19**39** personally examine said **Louise Little**

I further certify that in my opinion said **Louise Little** is an **insane** person and **her** condition is such as to require care and treatment in an institution for the care, custody and treatment of such mentally diseased persons, and that the facts and circumstances upon which such opinion is based, are as follows: **Observations: Mrs. Little gives a history of maladjustment over a period of years. Began talking to herself a few years ago following the death of her husband. She has gradually lost interest in family, has had a decided change of personality and has neglected the care of the children to the point of their becoming delinquent. Recently she has given birth to a child. She has had several controversies with various agencies and is extremely suspicious of everyone. She claims people talk about her and point at her when on the street. She claims to have been discriminated against. Diagnosis: The patient is suffering from a paranoid condition, probably dementia praecox.**

The patient is being hospitalized on the recommendation of Dr. J. G. McCarthy of the Kalamazoo State Hospital, who examined her on Dec. 15, 1938.

I further certify that I am not related by blood or marriage to said **Louise Little** person, or to the person applying for this certificate; that I am not a trustee, the superintendent, proprietor, officer, a stockholder, attending physician in, or have any pecuniary interest directly or indirectly, of or in the said

Kalamazoo State Hospital

_____

_____*E. F. Hoffman*_____   M. D.

Subscribed and sworn to before me this_____**3rd**_____ day of

_____**January**_____ A.D. 19**39**   _____*Janette Severance*

Notary Public, Ingham County, Michigan

My commission expires Sept. 7, 1940

Mrs. Louise Little – about 43

On M. 9 – 2 house North of Jolly rd. on east side.
Lansing #1 Jr. S – Pleasant Grove School
Post office address - ?

Children:-

Wilfred	2/12/20	Reginald	8/23/27
Hilda	10/22/21	Yvonne	8/11/29
Philbert	5/4/23	Wesley	5/27/31
Malcolm	5/19/25	infant (?)	8/31/38

Mr. Earl Little was killed in 1931 at the age of 42 in a trolley car accident.

April 10, 1946–
August 7, 1952   March–June 1954   April 26, 1957

ARREST AND PRISON

Malcolm's move to the Roxbury district of Boston opened his eyes to a world drastically different from that of the rural Midwest. Over the next four years, he held a variety of jobs that introduced him to urban nightlife and black celebrities, as well as to dope peddlers and pimps. As a shoe shiner at the Roseland State Ballroom, he met jazz musicians and entertainers; as a cook on the New Haven railroad, he traveled to Harlem, where he worked at the notorious jazz club Small's Paradise and the less glamorous Jimmy's Chicken Shack; he even performed part-time at Abe Goldstein's Lobster Pond in midtown Manhattan under the stage name Jack Carlton.[1] In addition to this string of odd jobs, Malcolm also continued the life of petty crime he had begun in Lansing. His first arrest came at the age of nineteen, when he stole his aunt's fur coat and pawned it for five dollars. For this indiscretion, his sister Ella promptly called the police and turned him in. The following year he brazenly robbed an acquaintance, Douglas Haynes, at gunpoint in Detroit, prompting his brother Wilfred to post a bond of a thousand dollars before Malcolm then fled Michigan and the warrant for his arrest.[2]

What sealed Malcolm's criminal fate, though, was a string

1. Marable, *Malcolm X: A Life*, 43, 51, 63.

2. Kofi Natambu, *Malcolm X* (Indianapolis: Alpha Books, 2002), 90.

of robberies in the Boston area during the Christmas season of 1945. His prison record suggests that he, along with his Armenian girlfriend, Bea Caragulian; her younger sister, Joyce; a third woman, named Kora Marderosian; and two of his friends, Francis "Sonny" Brown and Malcolm "Shorty" Jarvis, robbed as many as eight homes between December 11, 1945, and his arrest on January 12, 1946. They stole a motley assortment of goods, ranging from clocks, jewelry, and fur coats to twenty pounds of sugar and a swig of whiskey, ultimately valued at over ten thousand dollars, from Boston-area homes and resold the wares in New York City. Ultimately, it was Malcolm who was responsible for the group's arrest (with the exception of Brown, who somehow eluded police). He amateurishly took a stolen watch to a repair shop and the police were waiting when he came to pick it up. Since he was carrying a loaded, unregistered gun, the officers agreed to waive the charge if he would turn in the rest of the gang, which he did.

Malcolm and his partner in crime Shorty Jarvis were incarcerated at the oldest penitentiary in continuous use, Charlestown State Prison. The prison, best known for having held anarchists Nicola Sacco and Bartolomeo Vanzetti before their execution, was decrepit and offered few common areas for prisoners to interact. Malcolm later recalled that his first year was spent berating visiting family members and smuggling hallucinogens, such as nutmeg, into his cell. A prison interview from this period deemed him "calculating and cautious . . . has fatalistic views, is moody, cynical, and has a sardonic smile which seems to be affected because of his sensitiveness to his color."[3] In 1947, though, Malcolm met a fellow inmate and former burglar named John Elton Bembry, who encouraged him to use his time in prison for intellectual pursuits. After a brief stay at Concord Reformatory in 1947, Malcolm secured a transfer to Norfolk Prison Colony.

Norfolk was the brainchild of penologist Howard Belding Gill and was considered first and foremost a reformatory. It

---

3. Preliminary record, March 8, 1946, in prison file of Malcolm Little, Massachusetts Department of Corrections.

was arranged like a college campus, with dormitories around a central quadrangle, and allowed inmates to wear normal clothing and use the remarkably well-stocked library.[4] There Malcolm enrolled in and completed courses in elementary German and Latin, also earning superior scores on a psychometric test in "arithmetical ability" and "abstract reasoning ability."[5] Norfolk also allowed Malcolm more flexible visitation and correspondence, of which he quickly took advantage. Likewise, the Little family recognized this new opportunity and set about revealing to Malcolm the tenets of the Nation of Islam, which they had recently joined.

After some initial resistance, Malcolm converted and began an intense correspondence with both the members of his family and Elijah Muhammad, the sect's prophet and leader. He also began a campaign within the prison to convert inmates and incorporated many of the Garveyite notions of racial pride instilled by his parents into his letters to government officials. In 1950 he refused a typhoid inoculation on religious grounds, prompting a transfer back to Charlestown State Prison.[6] He also wrote a letter on behalf of a Muslim being held in solitary confinement at Norfolk for four months. With his small following growing, Malcolm got the attention of the local press when he and fellow Muslims demanded a menu without pork and prison cells facing east; after an initial refusal, the warden consented when Malcolm threatened to appeal to the Egyptian consul.[7]

In 1952, after six years of incarceration, Malcolm was

---

4. Thomas C. Johnsen, "Vita: Howard Belding Gill: Brief Life of a Prison Reformer: 1890–1989," *Harvard Magazine* (September–October 1999): 54.

5. Psychometric test, May 1, 1946, prison file of Malcolm Little, no. 22843, Massachusetts Department of Corrections.

6. DeCaro, *On the Side of My People*, 90.

7. "Local Criminals, in Prison, Claim Moslem Faith Now: Grow Beards, Won't Eat Pork; Demand East-Facing Cells to Facilitate 'Prayers to Allah,'" *Springfield Union*, April 21, 1950.

granted parole and secured a job through his brother Wilfred as a porter at a Detroit department store. It was there, while living with Wilfred's family and attending Detroit's Temple No. 1, that Malcolm became one of Muhammad's most devoted and loyal followers.

- Prison file of Malcolm Little, no. 22843, Massachusetts Department of Corrections

  - Family and personal history, interview with Ella Collins, May 17, 1946

  - Edward Grennan to Elliott McDowell, March 20, 1950

  - Preliminary record, March 8, 1946

  - Out-of-state progress report, February 14, 1953

  - Inmate summary (undated)

- "Four Convicts Turn Moslems, Get Cells Looking to Mecca," *Boston Herald*, April 20, 1950

- "Local Criminals, in Prison, Claim Moslem Faith Now: Grow Beards, Won't Eat Pork; Demand East-Facing Cells to Facilitate 'Prayers to Allah,'" *Springfield Union*, April 21, 1950

- Malcolm X FBI file, summary report, Detroit office, March 16, 1954, pages 3–12

Prison File of Malcolm Little, No. 22843, Massachusetts Department of Corrections

Family and Personal History, Interview with Ella Collins, May 17, 1946

Malcolm Little, M.S.P. 22843

C. Peterson

5-17-46

Mrs. Ella Collins, half-sister.

Family & Personal history.

Subjects half-sister, ██████████████ of ██████████
was interviewed at her home at the above mentioned address.
She is a very sophisticated person, who has obviously elevated
herself to a high standard of living and possesses a great deal of
affectedness. She is a good looking negor who uses cosmetics,
is well groomed and is a smart dresser. She has a nine room
house, very well furnished in taste in a good residential district
of Roxbury, a section in which very few colored families live.

The interview was entirely unsatisfactory due to her refusal
to answer any questions regarding family background to any
extent, giving her reason that she could see no value in having
innocent persons names on records in correctional institutions. The little information she did furnish the investigator
believed little credence could be placed in it, because of obvious discrepancies in her statements.

The following is the only information obtained from ███
██████████

Father—██████████████ was born in Georgia, and died in
Lansing, Mich. in 1931 at the age of 41 years. He was killed
by a Street car. Most of his life he was a Baptist minister. He
married one ██████████ in either Canada or Philadelphia and by
her had 7 children, the oldest 25 years, the youngest 13 years
old. All these children are living in Michigan.

Mother— ██████████ My informer claimed to have seen this woman only once in her life and stated that she considered her colored and not white. ████████████████ would have nothing else to say about ██████████ other than she claims that she is now confined in some hospital suffering from a nervous breakdown and has been there 7 or 8 years.

My informer refused to give the name of her mother, whom subject listed as ████████████████ but did make the slip that she is living some where on the cape.

My informer stated that subject lived with one ████████████████ who operates for sometime after his mothers break down. Subject wrote to his half sister, ██████████ requesting permission to come to live with her. She in turn sent for him and he arrived here in Boston at the age of 13 years. Subject refused to go to school and she got him a job in the Towns Drug Store in Roxbury. He remained there until he got a job on the R.R., traveling between N.Y. and Washington, D.C. Informer claimed subject had a nice group of friends while in Boston, but claims to know nothing about his associates after he left Boston. She admitted that subject never was disciplined to any extent because of the inability of his mother to control him, and since her confinement, subject had his own way pretty much. She believed that subject went as far as the 9th grade. She states that ████████ and ████████████ of ██████████████ are aunts of subjects on the fathers side. ██████████ is a cousin of subject.

Although ████████████████ was questioned a great deal no further information could be obtained from her. She was polite enough and seemed to have an interest in subject. She would answer very few questions.

From a number of her statements it appeared that she believe subject received a much longer sentence than he deserved and laid the blame to racial prejudices in view of the fact that he was keeping company with a white woman.

It would be wise to make an effort to locate her mother on the who perhaps could furnish a more comprehensive picture of this families background. In person would undoubtedly be contacted by ████████████████ and warned not to furnish any information should they be contacted.

The Commonwealth of Massachusetts

Department of Correction

State Prison Colony

Norfolk

March 20, 1950

Elliott E. McDowell, Commissioner
Department of Correction
State House
Boston 33, Mass.   Re: Malcolm Little, SP#22843
                              MR#33428, SPC#8077

Dear Mr. McDowell:

On 2-27-46 the above-named was arraigned in Suffolk Superior Court on four counts of breaking and entering (nighttime) and larceny, and on the same day was sentenced to four concurrent terms of 8-10 years. On 4-10-46, on a writ of habeas corpus, he was taken from State Prison to Norfolk Superior Court where he was charged with three counts of breaking and entering (nighttime) and larceny, for which he was sentenced to three concurrent 6-8 year sentences to be served concurrently with the sentences imposed in Suffolk Superior Court. On 1-10-47 he was transferred to Massachusetts Reformatory, and on 3-31-48 he was transferred to this institution.

Since he has been at this institution he has been unnecessarily race conscious and has taken up the Moslem faith. He has frequently complained about the prejudice of officers and interference in his religious beliefs. On March 19, 1950, he requested an interview with Assistant Deputy Dacey and was interviewed on March 20. He stated that he anticipated we would soon be given typhoid inoculations and that he had recently found out that this was against his religion. Mr. Dacey explained that the water at this institution was not treated water and it was mandatory that every inmate at this institution be inoculated and that should they refuse they are returned to the institution from which they came. Subject stated he was aware of this ruling and did not mind being sent back to State Prison. Accordingly it is respectfully requested that the above-named inmate be returned to State Prison.

Very truly yours,

Edward S. Grennan

DEPUTY SUPERINTENDENT

Preliminary Record, March 8, 1946

PRELIMINARY RECORD

DATE INTERVIEWED: 3-8-46
INTERVIEWER: ▮

INSTITUTION & #: 22843

NAME OF INMATE: Malcolm Little
FULL TRUE NAME: Malcolm Little
ALIASES: Jack Carlton

Sentenced	Admitted	Offense	Sentence	Court
2-27-46	2-27-46	a)b)c) & d) B. & E. nt. dwelling house and Larceny	a) thru d) 8-10 yrs. each concurrent.	Middlesex Superior.

DATE & PLACE OF BIRTH: 5-19-1925. Omaha. Nebraska
CITIZEN OF: U.S.A.
RACE: Negro (Mulatto)

ELIG. PAROLE: 6-26-51   Age: 20
CIVIL STATUS: Single
RELIGION: Protestant

Name		Rel.	Age	Address (If deceased, give year)	Occupation
▮	(Negro)	Fa.		Deceased	Minister
▮	(White)	Mo.	49	Kalamazoo Receiving Hospital, Kalamazoo, Michigan.	Minister
▮	Foster Parents			▮., Lansing, Michigan.	
▮	Foster Parent			▮ Mason, Michigan 1938-1939	
▮	Foster Parent			Mason, Michigan, 3 months 1939.	

Name	Rel.	Age	Address (If deceased, give year)	Occupation
▮	Bro.	27	▮, Detroit, Michigan.	
▮	Sis.	25	▮, Detroit, Michigan.	
▮	Bro.	23	▮Detroit, Michigan.	
▮	Bro.	19	▮Roxbury, Mass.	Merch. Mar. Seam
▮	Sis.	17	▮, Lansing, Michigan.	
▮	Bro.	15	▮, Detroit, Michigan.	
▮	Half-Bro.		Deceased (June–1941, Boston, Poison).	
▮	Half-Sis.	32	▮Roxbury, Mass.	
▮	Half-Sis.	30	▮, Roxbury, Mass.	

FAMILY DATA: (*Important items in health or mentality and in parental or married home life. Subject's last address.*)

Subject's father was previously married to one ▮ and had 3 children by her. He divorced her in Boston, Mass. in 1917 so he could marry subject's mother. Parents very devoted to each other. Both did Missionary work. The father was colored, the mother white of Scotch antecedents. This intermarriage resulted or led to racial prejudices against the family because their missionary activities took them to many cities of the U.S., and homes were either purchased or rented in the most desirable white sections of the communities. After the accidental death of the husband, the mother changed from Baptist missionary to 7th dat Adventist. The racial prejudice and discrimination against her mixed blood (offspring was contributory, if not the main reason, for her breakdown which resulted in her confinement to Kalamazoo Receiving Hospital ▮). Both parents were strict disciplinarians, especially the father. Following the confinement of mother, the children became wards of the State of Michigan, and subject was under the supervision of ▮, Lansing, Michigan from 1936 to 1939.

EDUCATION: (*On aliens, show literacy, when entered U.S., naturaliz. steps, etc.*)
Subject claims 8th grade education in Michigan.
No grades skipped or repeated, no truancies.

EMPLOYMENT:
The following are subject's claims of employment: Odd jobsman; Shoe Shine Boy; Clerk; Warehouseman; Dishwasher; Porter and Messenger; Waiter; Bartender & Drummer; Packer; Butler; Dancer; Mattress maker. Also dancing under name of Rythm Red at ██████ Ballroom and ██████

SPECIAL FACTS FOR DETAILING: (*health, drugs, homosexuality, escapes, enemies, etc.*):
Gonorrhea 1942. No recurrences. Subject admits occasional use of drugs but claims they have [illegible copy]
Occasional use of liquor to excess.
Subject owns share in small farm with other brother and sisters, the resident of the estate of [illegible copy]

CRIMINAL HISTORY: (*See separate sheet for* REPORT FROM MASS. BOARD OF PROBATION.)
No previous record.

SUBJECT'S VERSION OF THE PRESENT OFFENSE: Subject states that early in December, 1945, he arrived in Boston from N.Y. and went to live with his Half-sister, ██████ Roxbury. He had been in Boston but a short time when he met ██████ (missing accomplice sought by Police) whom he had known while working in a Drug Store in Roxbury, and ██████ told him that he was having trouble with his wife and needed some money right away. He suggested to subject that they break into some house and subject agreed. They went to Belmont, where they broke into a ██████ where they broke into a home and obtained, watches, jewelry and other valuables, which were taken to the home of the subject In 1941 subject had made the acquaintance of ██████ age 23 (Co-defendant W.R. 5 yrs.) and her sister ██████ (age 18), both of ██████ at the Tic Toc restaurant, Boston, where he had approached and conversed with them. ██████ husband was in the Army at the time, and subject escorted her to many night clubs over a long period of time. He renewed this acquaintance with her at this time and called on her at the home of her Mother (when the mother was away) on ██████, ██████ age 23, (co-defendant suspended sentence). All of the above named girls were white and where he was introduced to ██████ age 23, (co-defendant suspended sentence). All of the above named girls were white and the men in this case colored. On one of his calls on ██████ subject took ██████ with him, and ██████ and subject went out riding, and stopped at a home in Belmont, which they also broke into. On this occasion the girls did not know what ▆▆▆ and subject were doing. While in the company of the girls, four nights in a row homes were broken into in Arlington, Belmont Brookline, and Walpole, and although girls did not participate by entering these home they were aware what was being done. After breaking into two homes, subject brought ▆▆▆ age 22 (codefendant ▆▆▆) to Arlington with him and introduced him to the girls, and ▆▆▆ accompanied them on all the breaks that occurred at the first two. He had met Malcolm about three years previously, in Roxbury and with various musicians. ▆▆▆ did not know what was happening on the occasion of the break in Arlington the first of many to follow, and told subject that he was not going to get mixed up with the white girls, and stealing, but subject says that he threatened ▆▆▆ by saying, "If I ever get caught I'll tell the police that you were with me."

The procedure of the breaking into these home was always the same. ▆▆▆ would jimmy the back door and allow subject to enter by the front door, and ▆▆▆ would stand watch, the girls remaining in the car. The loot would be taken to the home of the subject or ▆▆▆ and disposed of by subject the following day. Of this subject states that instead of selling the merchandise he was putting it away, so as he could get enought to start a business, and would pay $10. or $12. apiece telling them that he had disposed of the thefts. The accumulated thefts amounted to property around $10,000. in value being stored away by subject and he says that the Police recovered 97% of it. On Dec. 16, the three girls, subject, ▆▆▆ and a friend of ▆▆▆ went to N.Y. and remained there until Dec. 23. While in N.Y. they sold some jewelry and watches for expenses. Upon his return from N.Y. subject gave one of the stolen watches to his ▆▆▆ as a gift for Christmans, and shortly afterwards ▆▆▆ sold the watch to a jeweler for $40. The Jeweler recognized the watch as being stolen and reported it to the police who suspected that subject was responsible and were waiting for him. In January, subject dropped one of the stolen watches that was very valuable and took it to a Jeweler's Store on Warren St., Roxbury. When he returned to get it one week later on Jan. 12, he was arrested by ▆▆▆ of the Boston Police.

At the time of his arrest subject had a gun on him, and the Detectives said that they would drop the gun charges if subject would name his accomplices, and so subject told about the girls, only when he had been assured by the police that they would not be brought into court, and that the charges against them would be dropped. He also told about the activities of ▆▆▆ and ▆▆.

When arraigned on Feb. 27, subject pleaded guilty and was sentenced to 8-10 years. State Prison and the gun carrying charge was placed on file.

Subject felt that inasmuch as this was his first conviction, that he should have received a lighter sentence, and the excessive sentence was because he had associated with white girls.

Subject's Version of the Present Offense, *(continued)*

Subject also said that he had anticipated such a severe sentence that he would have used the gun for armed robbery, and thus attained ready cash.

REMARKS: Subject is a light complexioned mulatto and served calculating and cautious throughout the interview. He has fatalistic views, is moody, cynical, and has a sardonic smile which seems to be affected because of his sensitiveness to his color. To offset this he seems to assume a nonchalant, complacent, superior attitude. He is worldly-wily and amoral and states "I've been heading here a long time." He further says that prior to accepting a life of crime he had weighed the penalty (of what he thought would be a three yr. sentence) against what he hoped to gain. He again says that had he anticipated the 8-10 yrs. sentence that he would have gone in for armed robbery instead of burglary.

NOTE: Subject started using Marihuana at the age of 17. This habit was acquired as was the use of other drugs by subject's associating with people in the theatrical world. Marihuana was the principal drug used because of its easy accessibility, and one stick a week at the beginning to one stick a day just previous to commitment was the amount used by subject. Of the stimulation received by the use of this drug, subject says that it would last a few hours with him, although the same amount taken by others would last a day.

Subject says that he is allergic to needles and the following drugs were taken by him orally, with the exception of Opium, Cocaine, ▇▇▇▇▇

The use of the Opium and Cocaine were confined to the occasional parties that he attended with theatrical people where it was more or less common for it to be used. He says that he never purchased any of these dopes himself and that is perhaps the reason for his not acquiring the habit, as the cost would have been prohibitive. He did have to leave N.Y. on a number of occasion to dissociate himself from those with whom it was habit forming and with whom he was constantly in contact. The use was from three or four times a week to occasional use, but only during the times that he was in New York. 2Yensy" (the scraping of Opium bowls) was taken occasionally by subject when he was in contact with those who used this drug. This was used by dropping Yensy in drinks.

Occasionally subject would use ▇▇▇▇ purchase an inhalant and drop the wrappings in liquor, (occasionally means about once a week or less.)

Subject has had on occasions also used ▇▇▇▇ and ▇▇▇▇ one producing a sleepy effect and the other a stimulating, but the use of all of these drugs was confined to the times that he was in New York with the exception of Marhuana which he has used regularly since he was 17 years of age.

State of Michigan

Division of Pardons,
Paroles & Probation
Lansing, Michigan

Date   February 14, 1953

Attention: <u>Mr. Gus Harrison</u>   Re: <u>Malcolm Little</u>

No: <u>22843-Massachusetts</u>

Reported by: <u>Godfrey G. Agriesti, Parole Officer—Detroit</u>

Reason for Report   <u>Out-State Progress Report</u>

Recommendation

8-7-52	Paroled from Massachusetts.
8-8-52	Arrived in Detroit.
8-9-52	Initial Interview. Will follow through on pre-parole progress. Please refer to REQUEST FOR OUT-STATE PASS REPORT OF 8-28-52.
8-16-52	Reported for work at the Cut Rate Furniture Company, 8940 Oakland Avenue as a part time salesman and porter.
8-26-52	Home Call. The sister-in-law gave favorable reports. Subject working every day and she is certain that he has good intentions. Is taking an interest in their church.
8-29-52	Report. Listed earnings of $36.52. No time lost.
9-15-52	Home Call. Sister-in-law reported no changes. Made trip to Chicago without incidents. Has not gone out once without being accompanied by either herself or her husband. Stays home evenings.
9-23-52	Report. Earned $164.00. No time lost. Said he has ▅▅▅▅▅▅▅▅▅ condition that needs immediate attention. Lacks funds for an ▅▅▅▅▅ Was sent to Receiving Hospital.
9-28-52	Telephone call. Brother said subject will have to take time off from work for an operation. Had a ▅▅▅▅▅▅▅▅ at the institution in Massachusetts. ▅▅▅▅▅▅▅▅▅▅
10-27-52	Telephone call. Subject said he is scheduled for an operation

at Receiving Hospital. Took temporary lay off from job. Has to obtain welfare order permitting entrance in hospital.

11-2-52   Home Call. Sister-in-law said subject has been given the run around at Receiving Hospital. Was told to report four days in succession for admission and was sent home each time. Subject cannot eat. Is extremely nervous. Said he has no associates outside of the family. Asked P.O. to help subject in being admitted into hospital.

11-6-52   Job check. Manager of the Cut Rate Department Store said subject hasn't worked this week. Said it was obvious that subject tried hard but he was ill.

11-18-52   Telephone call. Subject said he was admitted at the hospital on 11-12-52 and released on 11-16-52. Has been ███████ ███████ Was told to report back for checkup in two weeks. P.O. advised him to report ███████

12-8-52   Job check. Manager said subject hasn't returned to work yet but has been contacting them frequently. Understands that subject has been keeping himself in spending money by making leather billfolds, bags, etc.

12-23-52   Report. Still convalescing. Plans to work in a factory. Wrote to Omaha, Nebraska for birth certificate. Subject didn't look very well. Lost considerable weight. Looked anemic.

1-9-53   Telephone call. Subject claims that he is too ill to work yet. Has consulted a private doctor.

1-15-53   Telephone call. Obtained a job at Lincoln Mercury today, assembly line, $1.80 per hour. Badge number #61-70, day shift.

1-26-53   Home Call. Subject said he was fired from Lincoln Mercury after working one week. Just couldn't keep up on the assembly line. Job was to guide automobile bodies on the chasis. Put in an application at Garwood Industries in Wayne. Expects to be called this week. Said he still is not strong enough to do heavy work.

1-27-53   Report. Earned $69.00 at Lincoln Mercury. To report to work at Garwood Industries on 1-29-53, as a grinder, day shift. Did not receive his badge number yet. Debts total $143.00, mostly for board and room.

EVALUATION

The subject continues to reside with his brother and sister-in-law, ███████ and ███████ Michigan and is now employed at Garwood Industries as a grinder. The subject has had considerable difficulty in making an adjustment through no fault of his own. At first, P.O. suspected him of malingering but it was very obvious by his physical appearance that he was actually ill. He has lost considerable weight and has a tired, weary, run-down look. P.O. is reasonably assured that the subject has good intentions. So far he has shown no inclinations to return to his former pattern of living. He does not appear to have any associates outside of the family and has been developing an interest in church activities. He lives in a very religious home and undoubtedly his brother and sister-in-law are a good influence. Prognosis in this case appears favorable at the present time. It is noted that the subject is eligible for discharge on 5-4-53 with good behavior.

Cc: Central Office

Detroit Office

State of Massachusetts   Godfrey G. Agriesti, Parole Officer

Inmate Summary [undated]

Name   Malcolm Little   No. 22843   True Name Malcolm Little
Alias   "Detroit Red"; "Rythm Red"; Jack Carlton.

POLICE AND COURT DATA

(7-23-46 John T. Herstion)

Sentenced	Admitted	Offense	Sentence	Court	Plea Charge	Judge
2-27-46	2-27-46	a)b)c)d)B.&E. dwelling in nt. & L.	a)b)c)d) 8–10 yrs on ea. conc.	Midd. Sup	Guilty	Buttrick
6-10-46	(on habeas)	a)b)c)B.&E.nt.&Larc.	6–8 yrs. on conc. w/above	Norf. Sup	Guilty	Collins

Par. elig. 6-26-51   Min. 2-26-54   G. C. rel.   Max 2-26-56   Trans. to S. P. C.
Arrest off. Detective Manning, Boston Police Department.   Def. Atty. None

Claimant or Victim

Codefendants   ███████████████   at large;

Warrants on file #A-29931 – 3-19-45 – Criminal Warr. from Recorder's Court of the City of Detroit Michigan.

PERSONAL DATA

Birthdate 5-19-1925   Birthplace Omaha, Nebraska   Race Negro (mulatto)
Citizen of U.S.A.   Naturalization data   Religion Protestant
Civil Status Single   Mar.____   Place ____   Div. ____   Place ____

Occupations: (1) Mattress-maker   (2) Entertainer   (3) Train-boy cook

FAMILY DATA

Name	Rel.	Nativity	Date Birth	Address or Date of Death
▉	Fa.	Georgia	1890	Deceased 9-28-1931, Lansing, Mich.
▉	wife (Divorced)			
▉	Mo.	D.W.T.	1890	▉, Kalamazoo, Mich.
▉	H/bro	Boston	1912	Deceased 1941, Boston
▉	H/sis	Boston	1914	▉ Roxbury, Mass.
▉	H/sis	Boston	1916	▉ Roxbury, Mass.
▉	bro	Phila, Pa.	1919	▉, Detroit, Mich.
▉	sis	Omaha, Neb.	1921	▉, Detroit, Mich.
▉	bro	Omaha, Neb.	1923	▉, Detroit, Mich.
▉	bro	Mil, Wisc.	1927	▉ Roxbury, Massachusetts
▉	sis	Lansing, Mich.	1929	▉, Lansing, Mich.
▉	bro	Lansing, Mich.	1931	▉, Detroit, Mich.

**To be notified in case of emergency.

EDUCATIONAL HISTORY

From	To	Grade Compl.	School and Address
v. 1931	10-27-38	5th (was in 6th)	Pleasant Grove School, Lansing, Michigan. "Poor scholastic rating, poor attitude".
v. 10-27-38	6-17-39	7th	West Junior High School, Lansing, Michigan. "Poor scholastic rating; in considerable difficulty"
v. Sept. 1939	1-5-41	8th	Mason High School, Mason, Michigan.

From	To	Employer	Address		Wage	Reason Terminated
unv. 6-7-40	9-7-40	Leo Kelly, Oak St., Mason, Mich.	Chauffeur			To come to Boston
v. 5-10-39	2-7-41	Dr. Gertrude Sullivan, 207 Nash. St., Mason, Michigan, "honest, would rehire"	house worker			
v. 6-27-41 1-4-42 3-1-43	9-13-41 10-6-42 3-18-43	New Haven R.R., Boston, dining service "careless & troublesome."	trainboy		28.56	Discharged for insubordination.
unv. 11-1942	12-1942	Shaw's Jewelry Store, Lansing, Mich	Porter & Messenger		$30.	Quit Job
unv. 1942	Oct. 44	Jimmy's Chicken Shack, 763 St. Nicholas Ave., New York City.	Waiter		$50. to $80.	Permanent & occasional work.

From	To	Employer Address		Wage	Reason Terminated
v. July-44	Sept. 44	Abe Goldstein, 152 42nd St., N.Y.C., proprieter of "lobster Pond" "A bit unstable & neurotic but under proper guidance a good boy".	Bar & entertainer		
v. 10-20-44	11-10-44	Sears Roebuck Company, Brookline Ave., Boston "would not rehire subject".	warehouseman	$29.00	Walked off the job
v. 1944	1944	Paul Lennon, 5 Arlington St., Boston "Fairly dependable, honest".	Butler & occ. houseworker	3.75 hr.	Temp. work
v. April	7-5-45	Capitol Bedding Co., 207 N. Cedar St., Lansing, Mich. "Would be rehired" Also did dancing under name of Rythm red at various ballrooms and night clubs.			

RESIDENCES

From	To	Address	With whom living
1925	1929	Various address in Omaha, Neb.; Milwaukee, Wisconsin; Albion, Michigan.	With parents.
1929	1937	, Lansing, Mich.	Foster parents
1938	1941	Various addresses, Mason, Mich	Foster parents
1941	1942	Roxbury, Mass.	Sister
		Roxbury, Mass.	
		Roxbury, Mass.	
11-1942	12-1942	Lansing, Mich.	Boarding House of
1943	1945	, NYC	
		Roxbury, in 1944	
4-1945	7-1945	Lansing, Mich	Brothers and sisters.
1945	1-12-46	Roxbury, Mass.	Sister

DATE 1952	TYPE OF REPORT	
8-26-52		Letter to Michigan advising that subject's good conduct discharge date is May 4, 1953. SG
8-27-52		Letter received from Michigan advising of subject's arrival and further advising that he reported to Parole Officer Agriesti. SG
2-14-53		Cooperative report received from Michigan submitted by Godfrey G. Agriesti.
8-7-52		Paroled from Massachusetts and arrived in Detroit on 8-8-52.
8-9-52		Initial Interview. Will follow through on pre-parole program.
8-16-52		Reported for work at Cut Rate Furniture Co., 8940 Oakland Avenue, as a part time salesman and porter.
8-26-52		Home call. Sister-in-law gave favorable reports. Subject working every day and she is certain he has good intentions. Is taking an interest in their church.
8-29-52		Report. Listed earnings of $36.52. No time lost.
9-15-52		Home call. Sister-in-law reported no changes. Made trip to Chicago without incidents. Has not gone out once without being accompanied by either herself or her husband. Stays home evenings.
9-23-52		Report. Earned $164. No time lost. Said he has serious ▮▮▮▮▮ condition that needs immediate attention. Lacks funds for operation. Was sent to Receiving Hospital.
9-28-52		Telephone call. Brother said subject will have to take time off from work for an operation. Had ▮▮▮▮▮▮ at the institution in Massachusetts.
10-27-52		Telephone call. Subject said he is scheduled for an operation at Receiving Hospital. Took temporary lay-off from job. Has to obtain welfare order permitting entrance in hospital.

DATE 1952	TYPE OF REPORT	
11-2-52		Home call. Sister-in-law said subject has been given the run-around at Receiving Hospital. Was told to report four days in succession for admission and was sent home each time. Subject cannot eat. Is extremely nervous. Said he has no associates outside of family. Asked P.O. to help subject in being admitted to the hospital.
11-6-52		Job check. Manager of the Cut Rate Department Store said subject has not worked this week. Said it was obvious he tried hard but was ill.
11-18-52		Telephone call. Subject said he was admitted to the hospital on 11-12, and released 11-16. ▮ Was told to report back for checkup in two weeks. P.O. advised him to ▮ report immediately.
12-8-52		Job check. Manager said subject has not returned to work yet, but has been contacting them frequently. Understands subject has been keeping himself in spending money by making leather billfolds, bags, etc.
12-23-52		Report. Still convalescing. Plans to work in a factory. Wrote to Omaha, Nebraska for birth certificate. Subject did not look well. Lost considerable weight and looked ▮
1-9-53		Telephone call. Claims he is too ill to work. Has consulted private doctor.
1-15-53		Telephone call. Obtained job at Lincoln Mercury, assembly line, $1.80 per hour. Badge number 61-70, day shift.
1-26-53		Home call. Subject said he was fired from Lincoln Mercury after one week. Just couldn't keep up on the assembly line. Job was to guide automobile bodies on the chasis. Put in an application at Garwood Industries in Wayne. Expects to be called this week. Not strong enough to do heavy work.

[illegible copy]:

  Assigned at SPC:

    4-9-48   Laundry

    6-19-48 Transferred to Kitchen – Kettleman – Average
             worker

    7-12-48 Transferred to Laundry – Hand finisher – below
             average worker.

             1-1-49 Work report – lazy

             6-30-49 Work report – below average worker –
             destest work in any [illegible copy]

             1-4-50 Work report – below average worker –
             accepts and performs given work seemingly in
             silent disgust

Education:

  Library: 7 fiction; 10 nonfiction

  Academic: 6-12-48 to Elem. English & Rhetoric – 7 of
             10 assignments completed—[illegible copy] of
          good plus

          8-7-48 to 1-15-49 Junior High—average
             student—dropped for being disturbing
             influence

          9-12-49 to 1-4-50 Senior High—average
             ranging from 60 to 95. Attitude poor—
             dropped at own request

          2-15-50 Latin Part I—3 assignments turned
             in—average of excellent

          Great Books Discussion Group—attended 15 of
             17 meetings—quit active discussion—had his
             own ideas but was OK

Spare Time Activities:

  Recreation: reading, writing letters, walking yard,
              chatting with other inmates

  Avocation: 7-7-48 Plaster work. 10-5-48 Dropped because
              of lack of interest and no activity

  Community: None

  Religion: Studies Moslem faith

Medical:
> 8-22-50, Up-to-date medical summary.
>>   4-15-49 Hinton negative.
>>   Had several admissions in the hospital ▮▮▮▮▮▮▮▮
>> ▮▮▮▮▮▮▮▮▮▮▮▮▮▮▮▮▮▮▮▮▮▮▮▮▮▮▮▮▮▮▮▮
>> ▮▮▮▮▮▮▮

Mental:
> 5-1-46 MSP, I.Q. 101, average intelligence
> 9-26-49, SPC, Psychiatric note by Dr. Weisman. No psychiatric
>>   diseases ▮▮▮▮▮▮▮▮▮▮▮▮▮▮▮▮▮▮▮▮▮▮▮
>> ▮▮▮▮▮▮▮▮▮▮▮▮▮▮▮▮▮▮▮▮▮▮▮▮▮▮▮▮▮

Conduct:
> Present term: at MSP: 11-12-46, Shirking, detention
>>   3 days, work changed
>>   at MR: 3-6-47, Shirking, poor, work,
>>   adjusted.
>>   4-29-47, Suspicion of possessing
>>   contraband—adjusted.
>>   9-4-47, Disturbance in shop,
>>   shirking, poor work—adjusted
>>   12-18-47, Shirking, poor work—
>>   adjusted.
>>   at SPC: No infractions reported.
> Prior Conduct: No reports.

Personality:
  Subject is reported to be a shrewd and cunning individual.
One who complains about prejudice of officers and interference with his religious beliefs (Moslem). He appears unnecessarily race conscious and is outspoken about the superiority of
his race.

"Four Convicts Turn Moslems, Get Cells Looking to Mecca," *Boston Herald*, April 20, 1950

Four convicts who were transferred recently from the state prison to the Norfolk prison colony were back at the prison yesterday, having become Moslems in the meantime, according to their own assertion. They demanded a special diet, special jobs and special quarters facing East, in accordance with the Moslem practice.

The last demand was satisfied. They were placed in standard cells whose barred windows happen to look toward Mecca. Warden E. Lawrence Spurr said there was no basis for a report that several other convicts had proclaimed themselves fetish worshippers and demanded hacksaws in their cells.

"Local Criminals, in Prison, Claim Moslem Faith Now: Grow Beards, Won't Eat Pork; Demand East-Facing Cells to Facilitate 'Prayers to Allah,'" *Springfield Union,* April 21, 1950

The two bearded Springfield brothers, and a pair of equally hairy convicts from Boston continue peacefully pursuing the dictates of the Moslem faith from their cells at the Massachusetts State Prison, but have made no further requests, Warden John J. O'Brien told The Union yesterday afternoon.

Warden O'Brien said that he had absolutely no idea who or what converted the quartet, pointing out that they first announced their decision to pray to Allah at the Norfolk Prison Colony.

The warden pooh-poohed reports that the four, who hold the distinction of being the first Islam adherents at the prison, have been granted any special privileges by him. He admitted they do have cells that face eastward, but declared that they are "just regular cells." Furthermore, he said that it was the job of the deputy warden to assign quarters.

The four are Osborne Thaxton, 26, and Leroy Thaxton, 23, both of Springfield, and Malcolm Jarvis and Malcolm Little of Boston. The older Thaxton, along with Jarvis and Little were confined at the Norfolk Colony, but were transferred back to the State Prison for disobeying regulations. Later they converted Leroy Thaxton.

The four have grown beards and mustaches, refused to submit to typhoid fever inoculations, and will not eat pork. The guards have proven co-operative in granting religious freedom, but are keeping the four under close surveillance.

They have announced their intentions of turning their faces eastward at sundown to pray to Allah. "He will help us and protect us from evil," they told their astonished jailers. Local police said that the Springfield boys displayed little interest in religion before going to prison.

Yesterday the warden said simply "they have been no trouble."

Leroy Thaxton, who lived at 95 Westminster St., was sentenced to a 10 to 12-year term in Superior Court last Jan. 13 on a charge of assault with attempt to rape.

Osborne was given from seven to 12 years on Jan. 7, 1949, for a series of house breaks in the Walnut St. section.

Malcolm X FBI File, Summary Report, Detroit Office, March 16, 1954, 3–12

Assistant United States Attorney KENNETH W. SMITH, Detroit, Michigan, declined prosecution in this case inasmuch as Subject complied with regulations of the Selective Service Act of 1948 by registering with Local Board 102, Plymouth, Michigan.

E. Identification Record

1. FBI No. 4282299

The following arrest record was furnished by the FBI Identification Division:

CONTRIBUTOR OF FINGERPRINTS	NAME AND NUMBER	ARRESTED OR RECEIVED	CHARGE	DISPOSITION
PD, Boston, Mass.	Malcolm Little #05213	11-29-44	Larceny fur coat 250	
PD, Lansing, Mich.	Malcolm Little #15686	3-17-45	Grand Larceny	TOT Detroit Mich PD
PD, Detroit, Mich.	Malcolm Little #74831	3-18-45	G.L.	4-28-47 no prosse

CONTRIBUTOR OF FINGERPRINTS	NAME AND NUMBER	ARRESTED OR RECEIVED	CHARGE	DISPOSITION
PD, Milton, Mass.	Malcolm Little # —	1-15-46	B. and E. in N.T. and larc.	
Norfolk Co. H. of C., Dedham, Mass.	Malcolm Little #1898	not given FP 1-31-46	B.E. and larc. (N.T.)	
St Prison, Charlestown, Mass.	Malcolm Little #22843	2-27-46	B & E in N.T. and larc. 4 cts.	4 conc. sent. 8–10 years each
SRef., West Concord, Mass.	Malcolm Little #33428	1-10-47 in trans from St. Pr. Charlestown, Mass.	4 cts B. and E. nt. and larc. 3 cts. B. nt and Larc	8-10 yrs 4 cts. 6-8 yrs. 3 cts (7 conc.
SOS Army	Malcolm Little #30-GML	applicant 11-17-42		
SOS Army	Malcolm Little #30-GMA	laborer 12-23-42		

2. Additional Criminal Records

The following additional arrest records were obtained from the Massachusetts State Board of Probation, Boston, Massachusetts, the central repository for all arrest records in the commonwealth of Massachusetts:

DATE	OFFENSE	COURT	DISPOSITION
11/30-44	Larceny	Roxbury	3 months House of Correction SS 11-30-45-Filed M.R.ss 1-15-47
1-15-46	Carrying firearms	"	
1-16-46	Breaking & Enter. Larceny	Quincy	1/2-Grand Jury
2-27-46	Breaking & Enter. Larceny	Middlesex Superior	8/10 years State Pris
"	"	"	"
"	"	"	"
2-27-46	Conspiracy, Break. and Entering	"	Filed
4-10-46	B & E and Larc.	Norfolk	6–8 years SP Conc.
3-7-46	"	Newton	Dismissed
2-7-52	Paroled 4 5/4/53	State Prison	

███ Subject was sentenced to serve 8 to 10 years on a charge of breaking and entering in the night time and that he began this sentence February 27, 1946. ████████████

████████████████████ Subject was eligible for parole May 29, 1951 but was denied parole at that time.

On September 23, 1953 ████████████████████

███████████ Norfolk Prison Colony, Massachusetts, stated Subject is a former inmate and had been paroled in care of Michigan parole authorities on August 7, 1952.

The records of the Detroit Police Department and the Wayne County Sheriff's Office, as reviewed by SE JAMES C. KRAUS on February 8 and 9, 1953, reflect no arrests in addition to those reported above.

F. Employment
Traveling minister, Muslim Cult of Islam (present);
Garwood Industries, 1953

G. Residences
Receives mail at 18887 Keystone, Detroit Michigan (present);
4336 Williams Street, Inkster, Michigan (1952–1953)

II. CONNECTIONS WITH THE COMMUNIST PARTY AND RELATED GROUPS

A. Connections with the Communist Party

The Communist Party (hereinafter referred to as the CP) has been designated by the Attorney General of the United States pursuant to Executive Order 10450.

████████████████████████████

excerpts from letters written by Subject. ████████████
these excerpts were not quotes but rather notes jotted down
██████████████████ on the contents of these letters.

On June 29, 1950, the Subject ████████████████ letter
████████████████████████████

"Tell ████████████████████ to get in shape. It looks like

another war. I have always been a Communist. I have tried to enlist in the Japanese Army, last war, now they will never draft or accept me in the U.S. Army. Everyone has always said ████████████████████ MALCOLM is crazy so it isn't hard to convince people that I am."

In January, 1952 ████████████████ that Subject had been visited by ████████████████ ████████████████████████ a member of the Crispus Attucks Club of the American Youth for Democracy.

The American Youth for Democracy (hereinafter referred to as the AYD) has been designated by the Attorney General of the United States pursuant to Executive Order 10450.

B. Muslim Cult of Islam

that the Muslim Cult of Islam (hereinafter referred to as the MCI), which is also known as the Allah Temple of Islam, is a religious cult whose members regard ALLAH as their supreme being and claim to be the direct decendants of the original race on earth. The members fanatically follow the teachings of ALLAH as interpreted by ELIJAH MOHAMMED, the "true prophet of ALLAH" entitled titular head of the Muslim Cult of Islam in the United States and believe that any civil law which conflicts with the Muslim law should be disobeyed. The members disavow their allegiance to the United States and pledge their allegiance only to ALLAH and do not consider it their duty to register for Selective Service or to serve in the United States Armed Forces as they cannot serve two masters. According to the teachings of ELIJAH MOHAMMED and the cult's ministers, the members of a minority race in the United States are not citizens of this country but are merely slaves of this country and will continue to be slaves until they free themselves by destroying non-Muslims and Christianity in the war of "Armageddon."

████████████████████ the cult teaches that the Korean war is a futile effort by the United States to prevent the coming Asiatic conquest of the world and the defeat of the United States in Korea is a prelude to the "resurrection" when North America and Great Britain will be doomed and the original man, led by ALLAH, will reign supreme.

████████████████████████████████ the following information taken from another letter of Subject dated January 29, 1950:

"It is better to be jailed by the devil for serving ALLAH than it is to be allowed by the devil to walk free. The black man has been enslaved. The time is coming for the devils to be destroyed."

On September 23, 1952 ████████████████████████

██

provided SA ████████████████ with three letters, one of which is addressed to him ████████████████████

██

letters are set out below in their entirety. The following is a letter ████████████████████████████████

"In the name of Allah, the All-Wise True and Living God, the One who is giving us a Knowledge of ourselves which alone will save us from the coming destruction . . . and in the name of His Last messenger, the One who is sounding a warning to all of we Black people so we can pull ourselves away from the ways of the leperous devil and escape his disaster, the one whom the Highest devils in the government fear, but can't touch, our great Leader and Teacher, the Honorable Mr. Elijah Mohammed.

As. Salaam Alaikum"

"Dear Brother,

"You must have been thinking I had forgotten you. I can never forget those who believe in Allah and desire to follow his way by casting aside the ways of the devils.

"I had dinner in Chicago last week with our Leader. He is All-Wise. The words which flow from His Lips prove that Allah is the Best-Knower, and that Allah Himself taught our Leader. The very fact that he stands in the midst of hell, teaching against the very boss of Hell (satan) and the devil can't stop Him proves that the devils time is up and they have no more power.

"All over the World the Dark Peoples know that the devils time is up, and these Dark Peoples want to sweep down like a huge Tidal Wave and wash the devils from this planet . . . Allah Himself is holding them back, but only long enough to let all of us hear the Truth that His Messenger is Teaching. When we have all have **heard** and had a chance to accept or reject it and have chosen which side we'll be on . . . then Allah will Allow His 'Sea of Black Soldiers' to sweep out of the East and make this entire hemispere a 'sea of blood' (red sea) . . . but this sea will part and let those of us pass by who are for the Truth . . .

"We are living in the Bible **today**. While reading it, bear this in mind and all will be clear. No matter how the devil acts, don't be fooled by him. He knows what is taking place. He knows he can't escape destruction, so he's going to try and drag many of us down with him. We must make the choice ourselves. This is the Day of Chosing (Separation.)

"Tell all Bros who will to please write to me. If I can't answer myself, I'll have some one here at the Temple to do so.

"A civilized man is a man who **knows himself**. The First duty of a civilized man is to civilize his Brother. **All Black People are Brothers.** Today, our motto must be: **Each One teach one**!!!

"All here send the greeting to all there
As Salaam Alaikum
Your Brother
Malachi Shabazz

"P.S.
"Tell me where you are working and the type you're doing."

The following is a letter ███████████████████
████████████

                                    ███████████████

"In the Name of Allah, the Great God of All the World, who came all the way here to hell just to free His long lost people from the clutches of the devil. And in the Name of

His Messenger, who is Teaching us that the white man is the devil and that America is hell. This Truth is so strong and clear that not even the white man himself will deny it once he knows we know . . . and to prove that the white mans time is up on this earth, the Honorable Elijah Mohammed is here in the white man's strongest country teaching this truth, and still they can't stop him. Allah is God. He has let the devil rule us long enough, now He Himself has come to reclaim us.

As Salaam Alaikum"

"My brother, never stop feeling in Allah, for we are so near the Day of Total Destruction there is no time to take a chance of putting the time to stop sinning off. By sinning I mean trying to be white instead of trying to be ourselves.

"Stick close to the Muslims. Many who don't believe will redicule you, but they also ridiculed Noah when he warned them of the approaching storm. . . . tis better to be laughed at and be safe from the storm, than to be caught in the storm just because you didn't want to be laughed at.

"Allah is going to open the prison doors pretty soon now. The devil knows he can't survive much longer. The country is in worse shape than you could ever imagine but the devil is a master of deceit and has everyone still thinking he is god. He is through! Done! Finished!! He's not even master in his own land anymore. In fact, he has no more land. Next few months will see them driven out of all parts of the world. This will be the only country where a pale face will be seen . . . then shortly afterwards they will all be destroyed, and be no more . . . all of this they know. The bible itself tells of it.

"Keep in close touch with me, and whenever I can I'll write. When I can't, some of the other Bros will. All the Bros here send the Greeting to all of you there.

As Salaam Alaikum
Your Brother
Malachi Shabazz

"Stick close to the Muslims, and tell all the Muslims to stick close to each other."

The following is a letter ████████████████

"January 9, 1951

████████████████

"Indeed you are an excellent judge of character. Your experience in dealing with a great variety of personalities has quite evidently enabled you to understand the subconcious workings of a man's mind better than the man understands himself.

"Why do I say this? Well, you once told me that I had a persecution complex. Quite naturally I refused to agree with you. The illusions by which I was at that time obsessed would not allow me to see how true your diagnosis was; and I was too beset with the idea that I knew something to realize that I knew absolutely nothing.

"I was guided by hate, envy and the craving for revenge . . . deluded by my own vanity and self-esteem; I was blinded with my own ignorance and false-sense of reasoning. In my effort to justify my many **self-inflicted** wrongs I placed the blame upon everyone except the one who was mainly responsible for all of my troubles . . . myself.

"There is nothing that can now be said in my behalf; I offer no excuse, no **deffense**.

"However, even though I greatly mis-led myself, you will admit that I was sincere. I thought that I was being motivated solely by the earnest desire to think, speak and act in the manner that all Muslims should. Well, I was wrong!

"Most fortunately, during the recent holidays I received an enlightening visit from my family in Detroit, and my many past errors were then made known to me. I am not, and never shall be, too proud to admit when I am wrong . . . and with great remorse I now think of the hate and revenge that I have been preaching in the past. But from here on in my words shall all be of Love and Justice.

"I only pray that it is not too late to make amends, and to take steps toward rectifying my many mistakes. I thought that I was doing right, and was sincere in all that I advocated. Now that the Way has been made clear to me my sole desire is to re-place the seeds of hate and revenge that I have sown into the hearts of others, with the Seed of Love and Justice . . . and to be Just in all that I think, speak and do.

"This humble message is a note of thanks and sincere appreciation to you for the kind understanding and patience that you and your subordinates have so often exercised in my behalf, and it is also a humble apology for the unrest and misrepresentation of the Truth for which I was responsible for fomenting while under your jurisdiction.

"If my present sincerity is doubted, tell me of just one time that I have not always spoken from my heart just what I felt. You always spoke frankly to me, and treated me with squareness . . . so how could I ever be any other way except square and frank with you?

Very sincerely
/s/ Malcolm X. Little"

███████████████████████████████████ Subject was present at a meeting of the Temple of Islam, MCI, ██████████ 1474 East Frederick Street, Detroit, Michigan. At this meeting, ████████████████ a minister ████████████████ stated, "I do not care about Russia but any enemy of my enemy is my friend."

██████████████████████ Subject attended and made a short speech at the Temple of Islam █████████████████

██████████████████████ Subject attended, and spoke at a meeting of the Detroit Temple of Islam ██████████████████ at 1474 East Frederick Street.

██████████████████████ Subject presided over a meeting of the Temple of Islam ████████████████████████████████ Subject might start another Muslim Temple in Inkster, Michigan.

██████████████████████ Subject attended and spoke at a MCI meeting held ██████████████████ at 1474 East Frederick Street, Detroit, Michigan.

██████████████████████ Subject attended and conducted a Temple of Islam meeting █████████████████

MALCOLM X IN
PHILADELPHIA

Although he only joined Detroit's Temple No. 1 in August 1952, Malcolm quit his job as a grinder at Gar Wood Factory less than a year later, after being appointed one of several assistant ministers in Detroit. He had planned to establish a temple of his own near his brother Wilfred's residence in Inkster, Michigan, but Malcolm was soon sent to Boston to recruit members. Exploiting connections in his old teenage haunt, Malcolm was able to establish the new Temple No. 11 in Roxbury by February 1953. By March 1954, Malcolm was given the difficult task of removing the minister and Fruit of Islam (FOI) captain from Philadelphia's temple and inserting himself as "acting minister." In Philadelphia, Malcolm was reunited with Joseph Gravitt, a World War II veteran Malcolm had converted after finding him in a Detroit alley, addicted to drugs and alcohol. Gravitt acted as captain of the temple's FOI and spoke in Malcolm's place during the many absences necessitated by his need to maintain a foothold in both Boston and New York.

The two men presented a contrast not only in their physical presences (Malcolm at six foot three and 170 pounds, Joseph at a stout and muscular five foot six) but also in their rhetoric. Malcolm was well spoken and didactic in his sermons, while Joseph was terse yet pugnacious. However, both men had the reputation of being a strict disciplinarian. During one of Malcolm's absences, Captain Joseph informed the temple that it was the "duty of Muslims to take the heads of four devils for which they will win a free trip to Mecca." During a series of lectures sometime in early 1954, Malcolm delivered several ultimatums to the temple. First he criticized the lack of women in the group, attributing it to internal quibbling: "If a sister talks about another sister she will be put out of the temple . . . I'd rather put all of the sisters out for bickering and go out and get a lot of prostitutes. That sounds harsh but I cannot stand this disunity." He then mandated that members be weighed twice a week; those who were overweight would be given two weeks to lose ten pounds or be suspended. "Is there anyone who wants to question me or doesn't think I am being fair?" he asked. When no one did, he added, "Good thing you didn't because you would have gotten out of the temple." Finally, he added that any women attracting men by "display of their bodies . . . were as common as the dog we see chasing the other dog in the streets."[1]

Malcolm's tenure in Philadelphia, although brief, established him as a prominent NOI minister not only on the East Coast but also at the national level. The following year he was called to the Midwest for a three-week registration drive at the Chicago headquarters. Between his move to Boston in 1953 and the end of 1955, he had turned New York's membership of several dozen into over two hundred; the NOI had grown at the national level from twelve hundred to roughly six thousand.[2] And, although Gravitt and Malcolm maintained an efficient and amiable relationship during these years, the two men would soon be at odds in an event that foreshadowed the adversarial climate of the NOI in the mid-1960s.[3]

1. Malcolm X FBI file, summary report, New York office, January 31, 1956.

2. Marable, *Malcolm X: A Life*, 123.

3. Captain Joseph was tried within the temple in September 1956 for beating his wife and was "silenced," or put out of the community, for three months. Malcolm, as minister, led the trial and administered the punishment before the congregation. See Marable, *Malcolm X: A Life*, 125–126.

- Malcolm X FBI file, summary report, New York Office, January 31, 1956, pages 6–11

Further reading:

- Malcolm X FBI file, memorandum, Detroit office, April 12, 1954
- Malcolm X FBI file, memorandum, Philadelphia office, April 30, 1954
- Malcolm X FBI file, summary report, Philadelphia office, November 18, 1954, page 2
- Joseph Gravitt FBI file, summary report, Philadelphia office, November 19, 1954, pages 4–5, 8
- Joseph Gravitt FBI file, summary report, New York office, March 28, 1955, pages 11–12

ACTIVITY IN PHILADELPHIA, PENNSYLVANIA

████████ at the Temple of Islam, 1043 North Bailey Street, Philadelphia. ████████████████████████████ after the
regular meeting for new members and visitors, a special meeting of registered Muslims was held.

████████████████████████ the group was advised that the 19th of May was MALCOLM LITTLE'S birthday and a discussion took place as to the type of present which
should be presented to him. ████████████ it was decided
that all members would go together and buy a present for
LITTLE rather than give him presents individually.

at a meeting held by the Philadelphia Temple of the MCI
████████████████ the subject was the principal speaker and
stated:

> "You hear us talking about the white man and you want to go
> away and tell him we have been subversive. Here is a man who
> has raped your mother and hung your father on his tree, is he
> subversive? Here is a man who robbed you of all knowledge of
> your nation and your religion and is he subversive? Here is a man
> who lied to you and trick you about all things, is he subversive?

Today E. MOHAMMED is subverting him. He is pulling the covers off this snake and giving us his true identity. This is a man who the Almighty God Allah is subversive against. Black man all over the planet are subversive to this devil and you come in here and get mad at us. You's better listen or you will be taken off the planet along with the devil. This wicked government must be destroyed and those of you who want to follow after the serpent and commit evil also. This is a warning to you that you are living in the last day and you must decide tonight whether you want to survive the war of Armageddon. That lying preacher tells you that this is a war that will be fought between the God and the devil at the end of time. How do you think two spirits can have a war. All things are here on earth. Come out of the sky. As soon as I say heaven, your mind leaps above the sun, moon, and stars. You are here to learn the truth tonight. You are all God's children. The white man tells you this all the time but he has made you so blind and deaf that you are unaware of what goes on around you. North America is already smothering with fire. You think you are so hep and Jack you can't even smell the smoke. We have been a basard people until the God came to the hells of North America and raised up from out of our midst one and last prophet E. MOHAMMED. Is not this what a child is called who does not know his father. So do you not know your father. Your mother is a prostitute when you are not respecting women ———— you might as well say this because this is what is proven by your actions. A black man goes back and tell his great white father what we say here but when you do this he will tell you everything you are saying he already knows. When you are against your own people he knows he cannot trust you so he will soon turn you into our hands and we are going to chop your head right off. The FBI follows me all over the country and they cannot do anything about this teaching unless it is the will of Allah. The devils have lost their power now and the only thing they can do is try to frighten the black men who are still dead. You want to kill us when you come in here but we are not afraid of you. The kuran teaches us your nature "and we search you before you come in here. And we have two of the baddest guards standing here so the only thing you can do is listen and try to learn something in your empty head. Everything is reality. You are not going any place after you die so you might as well realize it now and get away from this wicked Christianity. Heaven is in the East and this North America is hell. When the Bible speaks of hell, this is the land they are referring to and not to any place under the ground. ELIJAH MOHAMMED is the Jesus of today. All the stories you read of what Jesus did is not telling you about the old history but what E. MOHAMMED is doing today and will do before the total destruction. We are a subversive people and all the prophets were subversive in order to free their people, MOSES, NOAH, etc. Islam is mathematics. Four and four is eight and Islam can be added up in the same way. In this day everything that has any bearing on your life must add up or you need not bother with it. Remember that when the people had the lambs blood on their doors they were saved from being killed and this is the same today. DANIEL in the Lion's Den and the children who unfearfully walked into the fiery furnace were subversive against the government but they were unafraid because they knew God was on their side, and the proper name for God is Allah. You have sung his praises every time you sing Hallelulia, which only means praise be to Allah. This is not your flag, but it was designed by a black man for G. WASHINGTON. Since the black man was the first and will be the last on the scenes the red stripes depict the black man's existence. The red stripes in between are for the few crumbs the devils will hand us from their table. Do you know what D. C. means in the roman numeral? They tell you this stands for the district of Columbia. The blue "in this flag means the devil is untrue and was this color for that purpose. The white flags stand for the color of him, the pale skin, unhealthy serpents. Once the devils said every one had a flag except the coon. Today the so called coon is the only one who has a flag. Your flag represents the entire universe. It stands for freedom, justice and equality. After this victory all the black nations all over the planet began to wake up and chase the devil out of their country in order to separate themselves from the enemy. Every black man is awake except this man on the tree who is still a mental slave. I talked to a Jew in a restaurant around dead brothers in New York yesterday and he beared witness after I had tricked him into admitting it, that the black man was the first on the scene. The dead do not listen to us as much as they do the white man. Masons do not need to pay for a few secrets now, continue coming here and you will be all wise free, also you will be encouraged to tell all you come in contact with, because when the sun is shining the candle under the table is not needed. You are thinking that all white people are not devils. I will prove it to you in the Bible that God said none of them are good both Jews and Gentiles. They all are looked upon the same by the all wise Allah. A farmer does not allow weeds to continually grow among roses. He plucks them up, even the little ones because they will choke that beauty out of the rose also. The devil babies, born and unborn will be destroyed. Get unto your own kind before you are destroyed with them.

"First I want to tell you that we have a new sister, Sister HAT-TIE who received her X today Look on the books yoursef and you will find out the brothers are bringing in lost founds and the sisters are not. Our job is to wake up the dead and this we must do. Just get the sisters in here and make her feel welcome.

There is something very wrong that sisters are not coming in. Brothers are in complete unity and Allah has blessed them. If a sister talks about another sister she will be put out of the temple for . . . time. I'd rather put all of the sisters out for bickering and go out and get a lot of prostitutes. That sounds harsh but I cannot stand this disunity. The sisters in New York are in complete harmony and are progressing while helping to rise up the dead. There is from now on a new MGT. ALMETA is the 1st lieutenant and ELIZABETH is the second lieutenant. Does anyone have any objections? Give time out of the time for the sisters causing trouble.

I want you to buy scales and weigh the members on Mon. and Thurs. Those who are overweight will be given two weeks to lose ten pounds or will be given time out. Be strict to enforce this rule. Tomorrow night the ministers will speak in Jersey City. The entire MGT in New York are going. They stick together in everything. I know this is the best temple on the East Coast but there is always room for improvement. I do not want anyone to talk about me. I'd better not hear anyone mentioning my name in criticism or I will give them indefinite time out of the temple and might keep you out of here for good. Is there anyone who wants to question me or doesn't think I am being fair? Raise your hand. Good thing you didn't because you would have gotten out of the temple. I spend seven days a week teaching and traveling all over the country. If you want to talk about me and I think I am right you will have to suffer the penalty. There must be a stop to this lateness. You will be excused if you are working but must have proof. Sisters must become more friendly. I noticed tonight that they were not sitting next to each other. When you come in here and see an empty seat beside a sister, sit there. Don't forget tomorrow night—Jersey City. There must not be a Muslim drawing unemployment compensation. Get out and get a job. A brother who does not try to help himself is not any help to the temple. We worked on the waterfront when we first opened the temple here and that was hard work and we were on time in the temple."

At the meeting, the subject spoke and stated that the things that are happening in the world today are the result of colored peoples all over the world telling the white man to get out. He related how this has happened in China, Japan, Iran, Egypt and all over the planet Earth, where the white man has no business. He stated:

"There are only two kinds of people, the white and the black, so if you are not white you must be black."

He told the group that in masonry every step of wisdom they give is paid for dearly, but in the Temple of Islam it is all a free gift, and in masonry you are forbidden to relate anything you learn even to your own son or daughter or wife, whatever the case may be, while in Islam you are required to tell all of your brothers and sisters and give them what Allah has given you.

He stated that they "had been taught to go around the world and fight for their name, but not to cross the street to defend a brother or sister."

JOHNSON X HINTON

Perhaps no single event catapulted Malcolm X into the public eye more than the police beating of Johnson X Hinton. Malcolm had quickly risen through the ranks of the Nation of Islam since his release from prison, becoming a permanent fixture in Philadelphia before being appointed as the head minister of Harlem's Temple No. 7 in 1955. However, both the minister and the NOI maintained a low public profile and were regarded by most as little more than a fringe religious cult. This changed on April 26, 1957, when police intervened in a scuffle between a man and woman at 125th Street and Lenox Avenue in Harlem. Hinton and several local mosque members came across the police beating the man. When Hinton and his companions were ordered to leave the scene, they refused and responded, "You're not in Alabama—this is New York." Hinton was then placed under arrest and subsequently beaten with a nightstick by patrolman Mike Dolan, receiving what was later described as "multiple lacerations of the scalp" and a "subdural hemorrhage."[1]

Malcolm X was quickly notified and marched with mosque members to the nearby Twenty-Eighth Precinct station house. With a few telephone calls, in less than half an hour fifty members

---

1. James L. Hicks, "Riot Threat as Cops Beat Muslim: 'God's Angry Men' Tangle with Police," *Amsterdam News*, May 4, 1957.

of the NOI's paramilitary group, the FOI, stood in formation outside the station. There Malcolm demanded that Hinton be admitted for treatment at Harlem Hospital, while the crowd outside swelled to nearly two thousand. More impressive than the size of the silently protesting crowd was the orderliness and simplicity with which it was dispersed. Assured that Hinton had received the proper care, Malcolm approached the crowd, raised his arm, and gave a signal. One bystander described it as "eerie, because these people just faded into the night. It was the most orderly movement of four thousand to five thousand people I've ever seen in my life—they just simply disappeared—right before our eyes." Malcolm's silent command also left a strong impression on the New York City police. The chief inspector at the scene turned to *Amsterdam News* reporter James Hicks and said, "No one man should have that much power."[2]

The event garnered media attention for both the Nation of Islam and for Malcolm individually, earning him the reputation as the one man who "could stop a race riot—or start one."[3] Of course, not merely the Harlem public but also the NYPD took notice. The chief inspector quickly released a series of urgent inquiries to police departments and government agencies in Michigan and Massachusetts, requesting Malcolm's criminal background. Malcolm also became a primary concern for the department's newly formed surveillance unit, the Bureau of Special Services (BOSS). The NOI eventually filed three lawsuits, the largest for one million dollars. And although the sum eventually granted Hinton was sizably less, the seventy thousand dollars in damages was the largest award the city had ever paid in a police brutality case and was granted by an all-white jury. Ultimately, the legacy of the Johnson X Hinton case was not merely Malcolm X's explosion onto the local and national scene but also the strong precedent set by

2. Hicks, "Riot Threat as Cops Beat Muslim."

3. Malcolm X and Haley, *Autobiography*, 359.

the NOI in fighting against police brutality through litigation and public protest.

- James L. Hicks, "Riot Threat as Cops Beat Muslim: 'God's Angry Men' Tangle with Police," *Amsterdam News*, May 4, 1957
- Malcolm X FBI file, summary report, New York office, April 30, 1958, pages 76–79
- Malcolm X to Stephen Kennedy, NYPD, Bureau of Special Services (BOSS), November 2, 1957

Further reading:

- "400 March to Score Police in Harlem," *New York Times*, April 29, 1957
- "Moslem Announces $ Million NY Suit," *Pittsburgh Courier*, November 9, 1957
- "City Gives Muslim $70,000 Award," *Amsterdam News*, July 1, 1961
- Evelyn Cunningham, "Moslem Cop Victim on 'Critical List,'" *Pittsburgh Courier*, May 4, 1957
- Malcolm X FBI file, summary report, New York office, April 30, 1958, page 59

James L. Hicks, "Riot Threat as Cops Beat Muslim:
'God's Angry Men' Tangle with Police,"
Amsterdam News, May 4, 1957

Harlem was teetering on the brink of a serious race riot Tuesday as a member of the Moslem faith battled for his life in Sydenham Hospital after having his skull crushed by a policeman in what appeared to be a flagrant case of police brutality.

The injured man was Johnson Hinton of 409 W. 140th St., a member of the Muhammad Temple of Islam at 102 W. 116th St.

Dr. Thomas W. Matthew, director of neurosurgery at Coney Island Hospital, told the Amsterdam News that Hinton is suffering from a "subdural hemmorhage" (blood clot on the brain), that he has "multiple lacerations of the scalp" and a "contusion of the brain."

Hinton landed in Sydenham Hospital at 4 p.m. Saturday afternoon—about 16 hours after his skull had been cracked open by a policeman's nightstick when he became the central figure in the nearest thing to a race riot Harlem has seen since war days.

This is the story.

It started innocently enough at 125th Street and Lenox Avenue where a man named Reese V. Poe of 120 W. 126th St. was found by police beating an unknown woman who escaped in the confusion that followed.

BITES COPS

When Ptl. Ralph Plaisance sought to arrest Poe he allegedly put up a fight and bit the officer in the scuffle. As they scuffled

Ptl. Plaisance was joined by Ptl. McMananon who was also allegedly bitten in trying to subdue Poe.

Meanwhile the officers were working over Poe with their night sticks and it was at this point that Hinton, a Moslem, intervened.

Hinton was in the company of another Moslem, Lypsie Tall, 28, of 349 W. 121st St. and Frankie Lee Pots, 25, of 2099 Eighth Ave.

According to police the three Moslems refused to move when ordered to do so. Instead, police charged, they taunted police for beating Poe and remarked "You're not in Alabama—this is New York."

Ptl. Mike Dolan, who had arrived on the scene by this time, then attempted to place Hinton under arrest for failure to move. He charged that Hinton resisted arrest and that he had to hit him with his nightstick. In this fracas the cops drew their guns but did not fire them.

Hinton and the others finally were arrested and taken to the 28th Precinct station house.

A woman who had witnessed the incident, then rushed to the Moslem restaurant on Lenox Avenue and told the Moslems that one of the brothers had been beaten by a policeman.

MOSLEMS GATHER

A group of Moslems, led by their spiritual leader Minister Malcolm X then went to the station house and asked to see their brother. Mr. X claims that police first told him that they did not have such a man in the station.

But as the word passed through Harlem the Moslem crowd swelled around the station house and finally police admitted that they did have the Moslems inside.

The Moslems asked to see their brother. Mr. X was permitted to see Hinton. He claims that Hinton told him that when he had been brought into the station house he was suffering from the blows of the nightstick and that in his pain he fell down on his knees to pray.

HIT WHILE PRAYING

He told Mr. X that when he was on his knees praying in the station house the lieutenant in charge came upon him and hit him across his mouth with a nightstick and also hit him on his shins with the stick.

Mr. X demanded that Hinton be sent to a hospital for attention. Police finally agreed and sent him to Harlem Hospital.

While he was being treated there the Moslems, joined by a group of Nationalists and other Harlemites, congregated into a crowd of 2,000 outside the hospital.

As the crowd grew, police rose to the emergency and all acailable cops were pressed into duty with Deputy Inspector McGowan taking command.

Then to the surprise of all, Hinton was released from Harlem Hospital and taken back to the 28th Precinct where he was placed in a cell.

MOSLEMS FOLLOW

The Moslems followed. They formed a solid line a half block long in front of the 123rd St. station house and waited orders from their leaders. Their discipline amazed police and more than one high ranking officer expressed growing concern.

By this time Mr. X was in the station house with his attorney Charles J. Beavers of 209 W. 125th St. They arranged bail for Pots and Tall and then asked to see Hinton.

When Attorney Beavers saw Hinton's condition he immediately asked that he be sent to the hospital, charging that he was in no condition to remain in jail.

But police flatly refused saying that he had already been to the hospital. They said Hinton must remain in a cell for arraignment in court Saturday morning.

REFUSE PILLOW

Beavers, then in a small but humanitarian gesture, asked police to at least provide a pillow in the cell for the wounded man who at this point could not rise to his feet.

When police refused this, Beavers asked that the man's topcoat be folded under his head as a pillow. Police permitted this and the cell door clanged shut on the seriously wounded man. It was 2:30 a.m. by this time. But the Moslem followers were still in front of the station house. Mr. X left the station house gave one brief command to his followers and they disappeared as if in thin air.

One amazed policeman on seeing this said "no one man should have that much power."

This reporter, who had been called from his bed to the riot scene, followed the Moslems to the restaurant which they own on Lenox Avenue.

There they assembled at four o'clock in the morning and talked over events of the evening. On orders of Mister X they agreed not to appear at the arraignment in Felony Court on Saturday.

BAILED WITHOUT LAWYER

Mr. X was there however along with Mr. John, another Moslem, and Attorney Beaver. This writer was also present.

Here again police irritated the Moslems by attempting to arraign Hinton without his lawyer being present. Actually they did put him under bail while Attorney Beavers was in Judge Baers court on another case.

After bail was set at $2,500 without Hinton's lawyer being present, the Moslems quickly put up the bail money and stood outside where they were told Hinton would be delivered to them.

But instead of Hinton being delivered to them he was turned loose in the building to find his way out alone.

MOSLEMS ENRAGED

He came out of the jail staggering, bleeding and alone. This enraged the Moslems.

They then rushed him in a car to Dr. Leona Turner in Long Island. She took one look at him and ordered him to the hospital at once. Back sped the car across the island to Manhattan and Hinton was finally admitted to Sydenham.

There it was found that he had a clot on the brain, that he was bleeding internally. Hospital authorities gave him a 50-50 chance to live.

As he battled for his life the Moslems gathered again Sunday. This time in daylight in the square opposite Sydenham Hospital. They marched around the square protesting and police soon discovered that they had been joined by Moslems from Boston, Hartford, Baltimore, Washington and Wilmington.

ORDERLY PROTEST

Though they were stern in their protest they were as orderly as a battalion of Marines.

With the crowd growing around the hospital, the Moslems were joined by some teen agers carrying zip guns. As soon as this was learned Mr. X once more dismissed his followers and sent them home. He stated that it was not their intention to start any violence.

But Monday, as Hinton's life hung in the balance, reports spread through Harlem that if Hinton died there would be a riot in Harlem Monday night.

Police prepared for the worst. High police officials arranged a meeting with Mr. X at an uptown location.

In the meeting he openly stated that his followers were ready to die when mistreated. But he insisted that they were not "looking for trouble."

"READY TO DIE"

"We do not look for trouble," he told police officials. "In fact we are taught to steer clear of trouble. We do not carry knives or guns. But we are also taught that when one finds something that is worthwhile getting into trouble about he should be ready to die, then and there, for that particular thing."

Excellent public relations work on the part of police persuaded the Moslem leader that every effort was being made to correct any wrongs on the part of police and the meeting ended with the implied, though not expressed, promise that the Moslems would not cause any trouble Monday night.

At the meeting it was brought out that the Moslems have a witness, Harry Buffins, who is prepared to testify that an officer wearing shield number 2775 said in front of Harlem Hospital Friday night: "I'd have shot the nigger but the other cops kept getting in my way."

The witness will also testify that an officer pointed at Mr. X and said "We should break that bastard's head because he is their leader."

HARDING IN KEY ROLE

One of the things that added to the tension Friday night was that all officers involved in the Lenox Avenue fracas were white.

The case is certainly to end in the courts in a civil suit.

It is the firm belief of this reporter that, had it not been for detective Sergeant James Harding who was off duty and chanced by, there would have been a serious riot Friday night.

Under the tension, many white officers appeared to be doing all the wrong things at the wrong time, particularly for Harlem.

▉▉▉▉▉▉▉▉▉▉▉▉▉▉▉▉▉ 1957, ▉▉▉▉▉
▉▉▉▉▉▉▉▉▉▉▉▉▉▉ the New York Temple of the
NOI held ▉▉▉▉▉▉▉▉▉ 1957. ▉▉▉▉▉▉▉▉ advised that
MALCOLM LITTLE was in attendance at this meeting.

▉▉▉▉▉▉▉▉▉▉▉▉▉▉▉▉ 1957, advised that he had
▉▉▉▉▉▉▉▉▉ a meeting of the NOI, New York City, held on
▉▉▉▉▉▉▉▉ 1957, at which time MALCOLM LITTLE
spoke about the feast to be held by the Pittsburgh, Pennsylvania, Temple on ▉▉▉▉▉▉▉▉▉ 1957. ▉▉▉▉▉▉▉ also advised that LITTLE mentioned that JOHNSON HINTON,
NOI member injured while being arrested by the New York
City Police Department will sue the City of New York for a
million dollars.

The "New York Amsterdam News," November 9, 1957,
edition, carried an article captioned "Moslems Ask Kennedy
to Fire Two Cops," which read as follows:

"Harlem's Moslem sect this week demanded that Police
Commissioner Stephen Kennedy remove from the police force
two white policemen who beat up one of their members last
April 26 in an incident which set off a near riot and left the
Moslem in the hospital with a brain concussion.

"The demand was made in a telegram sent to the Commissioner by Minister Malcom X, spiritual leader of Muhammad's Temple 9 in mid Harlem.

"It came a few days after a grand jury had refused to indict
the Moslem victim, Johnson X, on charges by the police
officers that Johnson was disorderly and resisted arrest, making it necessary to forcibly restrain him.

"Dismissal of the complaint by the grand jury was seen by

the Moslems as paving the way for the half million dollar suit which Hinton has filed against the city as a result of the beating.

"POWDER KEG

"In his telegram to Kennedy, Minister X said Harlem is a 'potential powder keg' and that if the officers are allowed to remain on duty in the Harlem area their presence is 'not only a menace to society but to world peace.'

"Minister X reminded the Commissioner that on April 29, Commissioners Robert Mangun and Walter Arm had promised the Moslems a fair and impartial investigation of the beating and that 'justice would be done' if it was found that the beating given Hinton was 'unwarranted.'

"RECALLS PROMISE

"The telegram suggested that the grand jury action proved that the beating was unwarranted and said, 'We respectfully trust that the confidence imposed in the promise of your representative will not be shaken by your allowing these prejudiced white men, disguised as police officers . . . to remain on active duty.'

Commissioner Walter Arm, commenting on the telegram, said, "In my capacity as commissioner in charge of community relations, I did promise an immediate investigation into the matter. We asked the attorneys to supply us with the names of some of the witnesses in the case—and were politely turned down.

"Our investigation was then discounted, pending the outcome of the grand jury's action. Now that the grand jury has finished with the case, our investigation will be continued since we can get all names from the grand jury's records.

"UP TO KENNEDY

"It would have to be judged as to whether the police officers exceeded their authority or not. When the investigation is completed, the results will be turned over to the Commissioner (Stepher P. Kennedy), who decides on all transfers or suspensions."

████████████████████████ 1957, ███████

████████████████████████████ Temple #7, New York City, held on ██████████████ 1957, at which MALCOLM LITTLE was one of the principal speakers.

The "Pittsburgh Courier," November 9, 1957, edition, carried an article captioned "Moslems Announce Million Dollar New York Suit," which reads as follows:

"NEW YORK-Echoes of a near-riot involving members of the Moslem sect of Prophet Elijah Muhammad and New York City police were revived here when Malcolm X announced that a million-dollar suit was being filed against local patrolmen.

"Mr. Malcolm X announced that the suit was being filed by one Johnson X who was said to have been beaten into insensibility by arresting officers.

The suit, according to Malcolm X, was filed after a General Sessions Court decision ruled for the dismissal of all charges against Johnson X, who had been accused of felonious assault.

"Johnson X was defended by Atty. Edward M. Jacko, along with three other individuals, two of whom were given suspended sentences and the third an acquittal.

"One of the men who received a suspended sentence, Lloyd Young, is suing for $50,000 in damages from the beating allegedly inflicted on him by officers said Malcolm X. The acquitted man, Frank Lee X, a Temple of Islam member, is seeking $75,000 in damages, Malcolm X announced.

"According to Malcolm X, Johnson X is accusing officers with false arrest, false imprisonment, malicious and criminal prosecution among sundry other charges.

"Malcolm X said, 'Johnson X, who suffered severe and permanent brain injuries, had to undergo four major brain operations performed by Dr. Thomas W. Matthews, director of neurosurgery at the Coney Island Hospital.

"A sizeable silver plate had to be inserted in Johnson's head to replace a major portion of the bone which the police had destroyed in their savage battering of his skull. He will be permanently disabled, scarred and crippled for life, and he should be amply and adequately compensated."

"The ruckus involving Johnson X occurred last May when police moved in on a disturbance between a man named Reece V. Poe and an unknown woman. When police began beating Poe, Johnson X intervened and a near riot resulted."

■■■■■■■■■■■■■■■■■■ 1957, ■■■■■■■■■■■
■■■■■■■■■■■■■■■■■■■■■■■■the New York City Temple of the NOI ■■■■■■■■■■ 1957. ■■■■■■■■advised that it was announced that MALCOLM LITTLE was in San Diego, California, and sent his regards to the members of the New York Temple.

Malcolm X to Stephen Kennedy, NYPD, Bureau of Special Services (BOSS), November 2, 1957

New York NY Nov 2

Commissioner Stephen P. Kennedy, Police Dept of New York City

Report delivery 240 Centre St NYK

Commissioner S. P. Kennedy:

Members of Muhammad's Temple of Islam here in Harlem are greatly disturbed. Our religion is Islam, the religion of peace. Our spiritual leader and teacher, Messenger Elijah Muhammad, teaches us to respect and obey all laws and law enforcement officers.

Our record shows that all of us who have accepted his divine guidance immediately become better citizens. He makes us conservative, clean-living, peaceful, law-abiding citizens. Through his spiritual guidance we have learned how to abstain from smoking, using drugs and alcohol, adultery, stealing, and all acts of aggression.

We do not try to force ourselves upon or among people who are not our own kind; whose record and history is sufficient proof that they don't want our kind around them. We are taught not only to avoid trouble, but to avoid even the people whose presence creates trouble.

On April 26, 1957 one of our most peaceful members, ▇▇▇ was the victim of one of the most savage beatings ever inflicted upon an innocent human being since the days of slavery. The bone structure of his skull was shattered by the blows of two white sadistic policemen of the 28th precinct.

On April 29, 1957 in the office of Mr. James L. Hicks, editor of the New York Amsterdam News, in the presence of attorneys T. A. Chance, and Charles Beavers, we met with representatives from your office: Commissioners Walter Arm, Robert Mangum, and Police Captain Eldridge.

Speaking for your office and in your name, they promised us that an immediate and complete investigation would take place and that justice would be done in the form of disciplinary action against the open and unwarranted acts of criminal brutality by these demented white members of the police department.

Investigation to date discloses that the brutal assaults by these prejudiced white officers of the 28th precinct, inflicted against this helpless black man were willful, atrociously inhuman, beast-like, and showed utter disregard and contempt for the black citizens of Harlem.

Also, these biased white police officers, by beating their helpless victim in the mouth with their nightsticks while he was praying to allah, showed contempt not only for his dark skin but also for his god and the religion of islam. This outrageously inhuman act incenses not only our fellow citizens of the Harlem area, but also ignites great concern in the hearts of 600 million sons and daughters of Allah throughout the Moslem World, which stretches from the China Seas to the shores of West Africa.

To justify and hide their own criminal acts, these same guilty officers charged mr ▮▮▮▮▮▮▮▮▮▮▮▮▮▮▮▮ with resisting arrest, and with felonious assault against them.

On October 27, 1957 after hearing all witnesses involved, including a number of police officers, the grand jury refused to indict ▮▮▮▮▮▮▮▮▮▮▮▮▮▮ on the false accustions of the guilty police officers, clearing him of all their charges and setting him completely free.

Since the grand jury has established ▮▮▮▮▮▮▮▮▮ innocence, and this innocent man has had his skull crushed by these police officers, you must realize that their heartless acts were without just cause, and criminally wrong.

Therefore we respectfully trust that the confidence imposed in the promise of your representatives will not be shaken by your allowing these prejudiced white men, disguised as police officers, who are responsible for this inhuman act of brutal savagery, to remain on active duty.

Harlem is already a potential powder keg. If these ignorant white officers are allowed to remain in the Harlem area, their presence is not only a menace to society, but to world peace.

Pending all further investigation, their immediate suspension and removal from the police force is advised, requested, urged and demanded.

Respectfully,
Minister Malcolm X.
Muhammad's Temple of Islam
No. 7.

DETROIT LECTURE SERIES

With the Johnson X Hinton affair generating publicity for the Nation of Islam, Malcolm continued to lecture at various East Coast temples. News of Hinton's beating also traveled quickly within the NOI, and the FBI reported that Detroit's Temple No. 1 was encouraging members to write Malcolm letters of support. Soon after, for four weeks in mid-1957, Malcolm returned to the temple, where he spent his first year out of prison delivering a series of guest lectures. Described in the *Amsterdam News* as a "32-year-old, 6'3" bachelor [who] devotes twenty-four hours daily spreading Muhammad's messages," Malcolm further solidified his position as the organization's public face and foremost disciplinarian during his time in Detroit.[1]

Upon arrival, he ordered that the temple be cleaned and renovated in preparation for a visit from Elijah Muhammad. Malcolm also took the opportunity during his visit to promote his older brother Wilfred to minister of the Detroit temple, replacing the current minister, whom he described to Muhammad as "inefficient."[2] Malcolm later suggested this model of

1. "Malcolm X Returns; Detroit Moslems Grow," *Amsterdam News*, October 26, 1957.

2. Malcolm X FBI file, summary report, New York office, April 30, 1958.

familial advancement to Muhammad, a notion that would
work against him when many of the "royal family" became
hostile to Muhammad's prized minister.

Within the first week of lectures, Malcolm was already
drawing capacity crowds of four thousand Muslims and non-
Muslims to the temple. He encouraged journalists to attend
the meetings, and soon black newspapers from both coasts
were reporting on the NOI. By the end of his monthlong tenure at the temple, membership had tripled and the NOI had
purchased properties for religious services and a private school.[3]
One newspaper reported that Detroit had not seen such growth
in an organization "since the days of Marcus Garvey." Another noted that "since [Malcolm X's] arrival here, things have
really begun to hum in the Moslem World."[4] With Detroit
buzzing over his electrifying speeches, Malcolm returned to
New York in late October, and the temple expected a capacity
crowd to welcome home its celebrity minister. Although he
needed to be admitted to New York's Sydenham Hospital several days later, for symptoms related to stress and exhaustion,
Malcolm X had managed to transform Detroit's somewhat
sleepy temple and to solidify his prominence among Harlem's
ministerial elite.

- "Malcolm X in Detroit for 2 Weeks," *Amsterdam News*,
  August 31, 1957

- "Malcolm X Making Hit in Detroit," *Amsterdam News*,
  September 7, 1957

---

3. "Malcolm X Returns" *Amsterdam News*; and Marable, *Malcolm X: A Life*,
102.

4. "Detroit Moslems Continue Growth," *Pittsburgh Courier*, November 2,
1957; and Malcolm X FBI file, summary report, New York office, April 30,
1958, 31.

- "Malcolm X Returns; Detroit Moslems Grow," *Amsterdam News*, October 26, 1957

- Malcolm X FBI file, summary report, New York office, April 30, 1958, pages 18–31

Further reading:

- Raymond Sharrieff FBI file, summary report, Chicago office, July 10, 1958, page 49

"Malcolm X in Detroit for 2 Weeks," *Amsterdam News*, August 31, 1957

DETROIT—Muhammad's Detroit Temple of Islam, 5401 John C. Lodge, was filled to capacity Sunday, Aug. 18, to hear Malcolm X, "the fiery disciple" of Messenger Elijah Muhammad, minister of Muhammad's New York Temple.

It was the unity and fearlessness displayed by the New York Moslems in April, when one of their members was brutally beaten by the New York police that enabled the Moslems to capture the attention and admiration of the other Harlemites, which greatly increased their membership, and also won them the "respect" (if nothing else) of that city's police force, said Malcolm X.

Citing the failures on the part of all others to solve the problems of the so-called Negroes, Malcolm X pointed out that Messenger Elijah Muhammad has a "Mathematical Solution" that removes all fear and enables him alone to take a "firm stand, with no compromise."

HITS LEADERS

Wild applause broke out when he declared that "if the present political and religious leaders of the so-called Negroes don't unite soon and take a firm stand, with positive steps designed to eliminate immediately the brutal atrocities that are being committed daily against our people . . . and if the so-called Negro intelligentsia, intellectuals and educators won't unite to help alter this nasty, most degrading situation . . . then the little man in the street will begin to take matters into his own hands.

"It is the little man in the street today who is fed up with the empty promises of the white man, and with the ignorance and greed that has been causing our own political and religious leaders to sell us out.

"And this little man in the street is the one who is turning away now from the political and religious system of the white man, and coming into the Temple of Islam to try Messenger Elijah Muhammad's uncompromising solution," he said.

Malcolm X will be at the Detroit Temple for two more weeks.

"Malcolm X Making Hit in Detroit,"
Amsterdam News, September 7, 1957

DETROIT Muhammad's Detroit Temple of Islam was again packed to capacity Sunday, August 25, to hear Malcolm X, "the fiery disciple" of Messenger Elijah Muhammad, and minister of Muhammad's New York Temple.

"Black people all over America who are hearing Messenger Muhammad's message of naked truth are awakening, rising, and coming into Messenger Muhammad's fold faster than we can get Temples set up to teach and train them into the knowledge of themselves," said Malcolm X.

Asked why Messenger Muhammad's teachings seem to be attracting so many young people, Mr. X declared that "Islam removes all juvenile delinquency; it dignifies the black man, unites us, removes our former fears and uncertainties, and gives us security."

ASKED ABOUT POLICE

Asked by local reporters concerning the recent clashes between the police and Moslems, that seems to be spreading to other cities, Malcolm X stated:

"Messenger Elijah Muhammad teaches us that Islam is the religion of peace. Our people must awaken and realize that these displays of brutal savagery by the police throughout the country are not directed against any particular group among the so-called Negroes.

"These inhuman attacks against our people follow a general pattern, and are directed against all elements of our people here in America.

"The rest of the trouble, and center of the arena is in Washington, D.C., where Pharaoh's modern day Magicians are putting on a great show, fooling most of the so-called Negroes, by pretending to be divided against each other, fighting in behalf of our rights, but always it is a well-planned losing battle, with the Master Magician, the modern Pharaoh, too busy playing golf to speak out.

"And when he does speak out, with the expert timing of the Master General, the Master of the Show, he seems to make certain that his words will always be too late.

"Our own political and religious leaders are too blind, too afraid, or have already sold us out," said Malcolm X.

"Messenger Elijah Muhammad is the Spiritual Teacher, Leader, and Spokesman for the fastest-growing group of Freedom-seeking Black people in America today. His Divine Wisdom, coupled with fearlessness, makes him well-qualified to speak out in our behalf today with no compromise."

Malcolm X has one more week in Detroit before returning to New York. Already his lectures have been a great hit with the general Detroit Public.

"Malcolm X Returns; Detroit Moslems Grow," *Amsterdam News*, October 26, 1957

Messenger Elijah Muhammad, the Spiritual Leader of America's growing group of Moslem converts, sent his fiery New York Minister Malcolm X to represent him here in Detroit two months ago.

During the past two months the Detroit Moslems have tripled their membership and attendance and have purchased the properties at 5401 John C. Lodge, for the Detroit Branch of Muhammad's Temples of Islam and to house the private school for their Moslem children.

The fanatically zealous followers of Muhammad have been busily cleaning and renovating the Temple, and preparing better facilities for their rapidly expanding University of Islam.

IN MAGAZINE

Featured in the October isssue of a national magazine the story states that Elijah Muhammad and his followers are rapidly becoming a power to be reckoned with, and that even biased observers are forced to admit that he is getting the "cream of America's young Negroes" to follow him and has molded them into the "Fastest-growing, best disciplined" black organization in America . . . whose "unto the death" devotion and obedience to Muhammad's "Divine Message" is causing "whispers of concern" in highest national and international circles.

One of Muhammad's most devoted followers is Malcolm X, minister for the Moslems in New York City. This 32-year-old, 6'3" bachelor, devotes twenty-four hours daily spreading Muhammad's messages among the Negroes of America and organizing his fanatic followers into well disciplined, "fearless warriors for Allah."

Having directed the progress of the Detroit Moslems successfully for the past two months, Minister Malcolm is returning to the New York Temple, 102 W. 116th St., Sunday, Oct. 27 where a capacity crowd is expected.

ACTIVITY IN DETROIT, MICHIGAN

███████████████████████████ 1957 advised that at a meeting of the Detroit Temple Number 1 of the NOI held on ████████████████████ 1957, it was announced that MALCOLM LITTLE would visit the Detroit Temple the following week.

████████████ 1957, ████████████ advised that at a meeting of the Detroit, Michigan Temple of the NOI held on ████████████ 1957, an incident involving the New York Police Department NOI member was discussed. HAROLD D. GOINS, Captain of the Detroit Michigan Temple, told all in attendance that they should write letters to MALCOLM LITTLE, Minister of the New York City Temple "so that he would know that the Muslims were behind him 100 percent." ████████████ advised that LITTLE'S address was then furnished to all those in attendance.

The Pittsburgh Courier, a weekly Pittsburgh newspaper, August 17, 1957 edition carried an article captioned "MALCOLM X Will Lecture Four Weeks at Detroit Spot." This article read as follows:

"Malcolm X, disciple of Messenger Elijah Muhammad, and minister of Muhammad's Temple of Islam, 102 W. 116th St., New York City, will start a four week series of lectures Wednesday, Aug. 14, at Muhammad's Detroit Temple of Islam, 5401 John C. Lodge, corner of Kirby.

"Attorneys for the New York Temple recently filed a 'million dollar suit' against the city of New York for the brutal beating inflicted by the New York Police upon Johnson X, a New York Moslem, at which time a near riot was almost triggered by the Moslems when they marched into the 28th Precinct 'to get their Moslem brother.'

"Asked by local reporters concerning the recent clashes between the police and the Moslems that seem to be spreading to other cities, Malcolm X stated:

"Islam is the religion of peace. Our people must awaken and realize that these displays of brutal savagery by the police throughout the country are not directed against any particular group among the so-called Negroes. These inhuman attacks against our people follow a general pattern, and are directed against all elements of our people here in America.

"The root of the trouble, and center of the arena is in Washington, D.C., where the modern day 'Pharoah's Magicians' are putting on a great show, fooling most of the so-called Negroes, by pretending to be divided against each other, fighting in our behalf but always it is a 'well planned' losing battle—with the 'Master Magician' too busy playing golf to speak out—and with the expert timing of a master general, when he does speak out, it is always too late.

█████████████████████████ 1957 advised that a meeting of the Detroit Temple of the NOI was held in Detroit, Michigan on ██████████ 1957. ███████████████ advised as follows:

"Today's meeting opened at 2:00 O'clock as is the custom only today it was done with much more gusto. Everyone was in his place and at the appointed time the ministers were marched to the speakers stand and seated, after which Brother MALCOLM headed the group in prayer. MALCOLM in fact took over the meeting and led from here on out.

"The crowd was large every seat being filled. The overflow was seated in the school building and they heard the talks by loud speaker. MALCOLM gave greeting from the Messenger and thanked all the persons in the group for coming to the meeting he assured them that they would not regret having attended the meeting.

"Each person who had been given a part in the meeting went through his part and by the time MALCOLM came on to speak the group had been well informed as to the views of the people who believed in Islam. MALCOLM spoke for over an hour and he blasted everything American. This was wrong. That was wrong. The flag 'was wrong etc. The only thing right in America was the movement of Islam. He showed that by reasoning anyone could see that the only right thing for the Black Man in America was Islam."

████████████ 1957 advised that a meeting of the Detroit Michigan Temple of the NOI was held on ████████ ████████ at which MALCOLM LITTLE spoke. According to ████████ LITTLE told those in attendance that Christianity is a lie and that black ministers who preach that religion are stooges of the devil white man. ████████████ advised that after his speech, LITTLE dismissed the visitors to the Temple and held a special meeting for registered NOI members at which time a discussion was held on the finances of the Detroit Temple.

The New York Amsterdam news of September 7, 1957 carried an article captioned "MALCOLM X Making Hit In Detroit" which reads as follows:

"Muhammad's Detroit Temple of Islam was again packed to capacity Sunday, August 25, to hear Malcolm X, 'the fiery disciple' of Messenger Elijah Muhammad, and minister of Muhammad's New York Temple.

"Black people all over America who are hearing Messenger Muhammad's message of naked truth are awakening, rising, and coming into Messenger Muhammad's fold faster than we can get Temples set up to teach and train them into the knowledge of themselves,' said Malcolm X.

"Asked why Messenger Muhammad's teachings seem to be attracting so many young people, Mr. X declared that 'Islam removes all juvenile delinquency; it dignifies the black man, unites us, removes our former fears and uncertainties, and gives us security.'"

ASKED ABOUT POLICE

"Asked by local reporters concerning the recent clashes between the police and the Moslems, that seems to be spreading to other cities, Malcolm X stated:

"Messenger Elijah Muhammad teaches us that Islam is the religion of peace. Our people must awaken and realize that these displays of brutal savagery by the police throughout the country are not directed against any particular group among the so-called Negroes.

"These inhuman attacks against our people follow a general pattern, and are directed against all elements of our people here in America.

"The rest of the trouble and center of the arena is in Washington, D.C., where Pharoah's modern day Magicians are putting on a great show, fooling most of the so-called Negroes, by pretending to be divided against each other, fighting in behalf of our rights, but always it is a well-planned losing battle, with the Master Magician, the modern Pharoah, too busy playing golf to speak out.

"And when he does speak out, with the expert timing of the Master General, the Master of the Show, he seems to make certain that his words will always be too late.

"Our own political and religious leaders are too blind, too afraid, or have already sold us out," said Malcolm X.

"Messenger Elijah Muhammad is the Spiritual Teacher, Leader, and Spokesman for the fastest-growing group of Freedom-seeking Black people in America today. His Divine Wisdom, coupled with fearlessness, makes him well-qualified to speak out in our behalf today with no compromise."

"Malcolm X has one more week in Detroit before returning to New York. Already his lectures have been a great hit with the general Detroit Public."

██████████████████ 1957 advised that MALCOLM LITTLE spoke at a meeting of the Detroit Michigan Temple held on ████████████ 1957. LITTLE told those in attendance that in the near future ELIJAH MUHAMMAD would visit the Temple to speak to them about the organization of the Temple and a new organization. MALCOLM stated that Detroit would have to clean its Temple if and when the messenger came and stated that a cleanup organization would be instituted to make the Temple fitting for the messenger.

████████████████████████████████████

1957 advised that MALCOLM LITTLE spoke at a meeting of the Detroit Michigan Temple of the NOI on ██████████████ ██████████████████ 1957. ████████████ advised that LITTLE spoke along the usual subject of the "black man being owner of the earth and the white man is the only real devil on the planet earth." ████████████████ advised that LITTLE referred to the United States as the "hell of North America."

████████████████████████████████████

1957 advised that at a meeting of the Detroit Michigan Temple held on ████████████████ 1957, MALCOLM LITTLE was the principle speaker.

████████████████████████████████████

1957 advised that MALCOLM LITTLE is attempting to have his brother WILFRED LITTLE made minister of the Detroit Michigan Temple and has represented the former minister EDWARD HENRY ANDERSON as being inefficient to ELIJAH MUHAMMAD. ████████████████ advised that LITTLE should be considered as one of the top men in the higher echelon of the NOI organization.

████████████████████████████████████

1957 advised that at a meeting of the Detroit NOI Temple on ████████████████ 1957, MALCOLM LITTLE said "IKE" (President EISENHOWER) and FAUBUS (Governor of Arkansas) are laughing at the negroes. Publically they pretend to be angry with each other, but behind closed doors, they behave like close friends. IKE has no love for the so called negro and pretends to be acting in their behalf now, but that is because he and North America do not have any choice.

The entire black world is watching the events and incidents going on in North America. Russia had a large cartoon depicting NIXON with his arm around ALTHEA GIBSON and FAUBUS with a bayonet attacking small children. This is intended to embarrass the United States. "I was in New York last week and visited the United Nations Headquarters. While there, I witnessed the diplomats from the dark countries as they took the rostrum to condemn this white government for the way it is treating the so called Negro. Each one of the little black men who took the rostrum said "shame." American Diplomats thought the foreign diplomats were taking the rostrum to condemn Russia for its action in Hungary. They would have if the Little Rock attacks had not captured world-wide notice.

"It has been prophesied that in the last day there would be plagues, strife and catastrophe. It was also prophesied that God would raise up out of the midst of a lost people a leader like unto them to lead them out of captivity. The Honorable ELIJAH MUHAMMAD is the little Lamb spoken of in the prophesy. He is the one standing up in the strongest government in the world and condemning it. He is the only true prophet. Today there are many false prophets. The black Christian Ministers are the false ones. They are the ones like in the days of MOSES who are trying to keep our people in slavery for a few pieces of silver. They are using all the magic they possess to keep the minds of the so called Negroes enslaved.

"It is these black ministers who should be whipped for fooling our people. They teach that after we die we are going off in the sky some place. We all know that when you die you go down in the ground and remain there. They teach the so called Negro to call on JESUS when they are in difficulty. JESUS has not come to ones rescue in all the four hundred years that the so called Negro has been here. How can a dead JESUS help anyone? He couldn't help himself. These lying black ministers will be burned up along with the rest of North America.

"How can a black Christian Minister help the so called Negro? He can't even help himself. Who is it today being beaten up and lynched more than so called Christian Negro Ministers? Who is it that is lynching and beating the black Christians? Other white Christians are attacking the so called Negro Christians. No white person loves a black man. It is against his nature. Many white men have pretended to love the so called Negro. You think ABRAHAM LINCOLN loved the Negro.

(MALCOLM read from a book but he never gave the title or author. The passage he read purportedly were quotes from LINCOLN. He stated there was no hope for the black man in America. It also stated LINCOLN was much disturbed by the presence of black folks in the Country and he suggested they go back to Africa because they could never achieve an equal status here.) EISENHOWER has a caddy he calls "Cemetery." The name is quite appropriate because that Negro is mentally dead." MALCOLM said America has not seen anything yet. He said when ELIJAH gets through there won't be anything left of this government."

The "Los Angeles Herald Dispatch," August 22, 1957, edition, carried an article captioned "Negroes, No Compromise On Civil Rights' Malcolm X," which read as follows:

"DETROIT, Michigan – (Special to the Herald Dispatch) More than 4,000 Moslems and Non-Moslems filled Muhammad's Detroit Temple of Islam to capacity to hear young Malcolm X, the fiery disciple of Messenger Elijah Muhammad, explain the 'mathematical solution' that removes all fear and enables the black man to take a firm stand for civil rights without compromise.

"It was the unity and fearlessness displayed by the New York Moslems last April when one of our members was brutally beaten by the New York Police, which enabled us to capture the attention and admiration of all Harlemites, which greatly increased our membership and won the respect of the New York City Police force,' Mr. X told his audience. Citing the many failures on the part of others to solve the problems of the so-called Negro, Mr. X pointed out that Messenger Elijah Muhammad has a mathematical solution which removes all fears and has enabled him alone to take his stand with no compromise. This mathematical solution, he stated, is available to all members of the Moslem faith.

"The brilliant young Mr. X delivered, without fear, a message from Messenger Elijah Muhammad which is enabling to so-called Negro to see and understand what is going on around us for the first time since we were kidnapped and brought to America 400 years ago to become slaves for the

white man. 'No country,' he said, 'has ever risen so high, become so rich and powerful in such a short period of time as the
United States of America. America is regarded as the strongest
country on earth today,' he added. 'The President has powers
that affect people even in the most remote part of the planet,
Earth. He, himself, referring to President Eisenhower,' he continued, 'is like a god.' His powers "are so great. Small wonder,
then, that every four years the eyes of the entire world are
turned toward America wondering who will be our next 'god.'

"Launching into a bitter criticism and recrimination against
those who are playing with the lives and the rights of the
Negro people in blocking effecive legislation on Civil Rights,
Mx. X said 'It is not American Foreign Policy that decides
who will get the 'chair,' but rather her Domestic Policy. In this
great drama, he continued, 'the Negroes play the leading role
and are being posed a serious problem. The position the American Negro occupies is both strategic and unique. For, although the Negroes are deprived of most of their voting
powers yet their diluted vote will swing the balance of power
in the Presidential or any other election in this country. What
would the role and the position of the Negro be if he had a full
voting voice?'

"'No wonder, then,' he continued, 'the freedom or equal
rights struggle of the Negro people is so greatly feared by his
enemies.' Standing applause greeted the brilliant young orator
as he declared, 'If the present leaders of the so-called American Negro don't unite soon and take a firm stand with positive
steps designed to eliminate immediately the brutal atrocities
that are being committed daily against our people; and, if the
so-called Negro intelligentsia, intellectuals and educators
won't unite to help alter this nasty and most degrading situation; then,' he said, 'the little man in the street will henceforth
begin to take matters into his own hands. As an example,' he
continued, 'the struggle led for Negro job rights by a beautiful
young Negro woman in Los Angeles, California. Miss Helen
Smith, will multiply 10,000 fold through the width and breath
of this land. Beacause, the little man in the street today is
fed up with the empty promises of the white man, and the

ignorance, and greed that has been causing our own political and religious leaders to sell out.'"

On ███████████████████ 1957, ███████████████ advised that at a meeting of the Detroit, Michigan, Temple of the NOI held on ████████████████ 1957, MALCOLM LITTLE advised those in attendance that the so-called Negro had really been taken for a ride by accepting a religion which teaches that there is life after death. He said the very phrase "life after death" is self-revealing if put in its proper prospective. He told those in attendance that they should immediately dispense with this false religion which is a throwback of the days of slavery and accept Islam which "is the religion of the black man."

███████████████ went on to say that LITTLE continued by saying that Muslims should not brag about their association with the NOI, for it is letting their enemies know who they are and what they believe. He stated that Muslims should not deny their connection with the NOI, but should avoid being braggarts for then the Christians will not know who they are when they ask questions and if they do not know who they are they will not know how to attack their questions when asked. ███████████████ advised that this was in reference to those occasions when Muslims visit Christian churches and ask questions in an effort to discredit the Christian religion.

The "Los Angeles Herald-Dispatch," a weekly Los Angeles, California, newspaper, October 17, 1957 edition, carried an article captioned "Malcolm Scores US 'Too Late Policies,'" which read as follows:

"Malcolm X disciple of Messenger Elijah Muhammad; and Minister of Muhammad's Temple of Islam, No. 7, 102 W. 116th Street, New York City concluded a four weeks series of lectures here this week at the Muhammad's Detroit Temple of Islam, 5401 John C. Lodge.

"Mr. X told a battery of newsmen that attorneys for the New York Temple recently filed a 'million dollar suit' against the city of New York for the brutal beating inflicted by the New York police upon Mr. Johnson X, a member of the New York Temple. A near riot was averted at the time, triggered by

the Moslems when they marched into the 28th Precient 'to rescue their Moslem Brother.'

"Asked by the newsmen concerning the recent clashes between the police and the Moslems that seem to be spreading to
other cities, Mr. X stated, 'Islam is the reliigon of peace. Our
people must awaken and realize that those displays of brutal
savagery by the white police throughout the country are not
directed against any particular group from among the so-
called Negroes. These inhuman acts of violence against our
people follow a general pattern, and are directed against all
elements of our people here in America.'

"'The roots of the trouble,' he continued, 'and center of
the arena is in Washington, D.C., where the modern day
"Pharoah's Magicians" are putting on a great show, fooling
most of the so-called Negroes by pretending to be divided
against each other, fighting in our behalf . . . but always it is a
well planned losing battle with the Master Magician too busy
playing golf to speak out and with the expert timing of a master general, when he does speak out, IT IS ALWAYS TOO
LATE.' 'And,' he said with a grin, 'our own political and religious leaders are too blind, too afraid, or have already sold us
out, to speak up.'

"Messenger Elijah Muhamad is the Spiritual Teacher,
Leader, and Divine Spokesman for the fastest-growing, and
most respected group of freedom-loving and freedom-seeking
Black people in America today. His wisdom, plus his fearlessness makes him well-qualified to speak out in our behalf without compromise, Mr. X said explaining the principles of Islam
teachings.

"Mr. X invited the newsmen to attend and report firsthand
on the teachings practices and aims of the Moslems who follow Messenger Elijah Muhammad. In the Detroit area these
teachings are more necessary than anywhere on earth he said."

The "New York Amsterdam News" on October 26, 1957,
carried an article captioned "Malcolm X Returns; Detroit
Moslems Grow," which read as follows:

"Messenger Elijah Muhammad, the Spiritual Leader of
America's growing group of Moslem converts, sent his fiery

New York Minister, Malcolm X to represent him here in Detroit two months ago.

"During the past two months the Detroit Moslems have tripled their membership and attendance and have purchased the properties at 5401 John C. Lodge, for the Detroit Branch of Muhammad's Temples of Islam and to house the private school for their Moslem children.

"The fanatically zealous followers of Muhammad have been busily cleaning and renovating the Temple, and preparing better facilities for their rapidly expanding University of Islam."

IN MAGAZINE

"Featured in the October issue of a national magazine the story states that Elijah Muhammad and his followers are rapidly becoming a power to be reckoned with, and that even biased observers are forced to admit that he is getting the 'cream of America's young Negroes' to "follow him and has molded them into the 'Fastest-growing, best disciplined' black organization in America . . . whose 'unto the death' devotion and obedience to Muhammad's 'Divine Message' is causing 'whispers of concern' in highest national and international circles.

"One of Muhammad's most devoted followers is Malcolm X, minister of the Moslems in New York City. This 32-year-old, 6'3" bachelor, devotes twenty-four hours daily spreading Muhammads message among the Negroes of America and organizing his fanatic followers into well disciplined, 'fearless warriors for Allah.'

"Having directed the progress of the Detroit Moslems successfully for the past two months, Minister Malcolm is returning to the New York Temple, 102 W. 116th St., Sunday, Oct. 27 where a capacity crowd is expected."

The "Pittsburgh Courier" on November 2, 1957, carried an article captioned, "Detroit Moslems Continue Growth," which read as follows:

"Messenger Elijah Muhammad, the spiritual leader of America's fastest-growing group of Moslem converts, and considered even by many non-Moslems to be the most outspoken, uncompromising black leader ever to appear among Negroes of America, sent his fiery New York minister, Malcolm X to represent him in Detroit.

"And since his arrival here, things have really begun to hum in the Moslem World."

MARRIAGE TO
BETTY X SANDERS

As 1957 drew to a close, Malcolm X was traveling for weeks at a time to establish temples around the country and monitor the progress of those already formed. Marriage seemed a distant thought to the young bachelor, and he was careful not to encourage the fondness of sisters in the Nation of Islam or sacrifice what he called the "good work" that still needed to be done. However, despite the chaste perception surrounding the minister, he had in fact proposed marriage twice in the previous year: to teenage sweetheart Evelyn Williams of Boston and to Betty Sue Williams, likely the sister of the Buffalo minister Robert X Williams.[1] Both proposals were apparently retracted, though information in the cases is unclear. Whatever the reason, another woman who had recently joined Temple No. 7's intimate community, Betty X Sanders, had caught his eye.

Sanders also grew up in Michigan, living with a foster family in nearby Detroit and briefly attending Tuskegee Institute in Alabama before settling in New York at the Brooklyn State College School of Nursing. After noticing the twenty-three-year-old, who had begun teaching as a health instructor in the NOI's General Civilization Class, Malcolm summoned the courage to ask Betty out, inviting her to visit the Museum of Natural History under the

---

1. Marable, *Malcolm X: A Life*, 140–41.

pretext that the exhibits could help her teach her courses. Shortly after their first date, Malcolm consulted with Elijah Muhammad at their monthly meeting in Chicago. Betty was then invited to what was ostensibly a national training meeting but was actually an assessment of her suitability. With Muhammad's approval secured, Malcolm soon proposed to Betty over the telephone from a gas station in Detroit on the morning of January 12, 1958.[2]

The two were married two days later, before Malcolm's brothers Philbert and Wilfred, by a justice of the peace in Lansing. Not only did the announcement surprise Betty's foster parents, the Malloys, who were skeptical of the older Muslim man, but black newspapers in Pittsburgh and New York published the unexpected news. Likewise, Malcolm recalled that many brothers in the NOI looked at him upon his return as if he had betrayed them; Evelyn Williams reportedly ran from the temple, screaming, when the marriage was announced.[3] Although the newlyweds spent their first night in a hotel, Betty would soon learn the burden of Malcolm's schedule and the expectations of a minister's wife. She flew home to New York the following day for her classes.[4]

- "Malcolm X Married!" *Pittsburgh Courier*, January 28, 1958
- "Malcolm X Wed: It's a Surprise," *Amsterdam News*, January 25, 1958

Further reading:

- Betty Shabazz FBI file, summary report, New York office, June 30, 1958, pages 3, 5–6

---

2. Russell Rickford, *Betty Shabazz, Surviving Malcolm X: A Journey of Strength from Wife to Widow to Heroine* (Naperville, IL: Sourcebooks, Inc., 2003), 69.

3. Marable, *Malcolm X: A Life*, 146.

4. Rickford, *Betty Shabazz*, 75.

"Malcolm X Married!" *Pittsburgh Courier,* January 28, 1958

LANSING, Mich.—Malcolm X, widely known minister and leader of the New York Temple of Islam 7 of the Moslem movement, was married in a surprise wedding ceremony here last week. The bride is Betty X, a New York medical student, and a member of the Harlem Temple over which her husband presides.

Attending Malcolm X were his two brothers, Philbert X, minister of Temple 16 here in Lansing, and Wilfred X, minister of Temple 1 in Detroit, Mich. The wedding was attended by a few close friends and relatives of the couple.

"Malcolm X Wed; It's a Surprise,"
Amsterdam News, January 25, 1958

DETROIT—Messenger Elijah Muhammad's widely traveled minister and representative, Malcolm X, surprised both Moslems and non-Moslem friends this week.

The 32-year-old long-time bachelor married 23-year-old Betty X, a Moslem medical student. The beautiful young bride is a member of the New York Temple and a firm follower of Messenger Muhammad.

The quiet ceremony was performed in Lansing, Michigan, Tuesday, January 14.

The hard-working leader of Harlem's fiery young Moslems said no one but Allah and His Messenger had advance knowledge of his "carefully laid" plans,—the bride herself didn't know until the last day.

Minister Malcolm X is scheduled to return to New York this Sunday and speak at 2 p.m. at the Temple, 102 W. 116th St.

POLICE BRUTALITY
IN QUEENS

Malcolm had actively thrust himself into the Johnson X Hinton affair in 1957, gaining public prominence for the Nation of Islam. The following year, however, police violence came to him. While Malcolm spoke at Boston's Temple No. 11, two New York police detectives, Joseph Kiernan and Michael Bonura, forced their way into the East Elmhurst, Queens, home he and his wife shared with two other Muslim couples (including future NOI national secretary John Ali). Allegedly searching for a mail fraud suspect, the officers were rebuffed at the door by twenty-seven-year-old Yvonne Molette when they failed to produce a search warrant. The officers were furious about the lack of cooperation and returned shortly with a federally issued warrant, which was checked at the door by Molette's husband, who had rushed home from work. He claimed police then kicked him and shoved him aside, smashing glass in an attempt to enter. Meanwhile, another officer had climbed a rear stairway leading to Malcolm and Betty's upstairs rooms; he then fired several shots into the home, just feet below six women and children. One of the women, seventeen-year-old Audrey Rice, was six months pregnant, as was Betty, with the couple's first child, Attallah.

Malcolm returned to a home scarred by bullet holes and shattered windows. His wife and five others had been arrested.

Although significantly smaller than the crowd protesting the Hinton beating, a group of forty was quickly assembled to picket the Astoria precinct house. As he would do in later police brutality cases, Malcolm drew parallels between the well-publicized southern police tactics and the ongoing mistreatment of northern blacks by government officials: "Negroes in Mississippi could not have their civil rights as openly violated and stomped upon any worse than has been done here in Queens County Courthouse."[1]

The trial had a life of its own, lasting several weeks and featuring dramatic testimonies and evidence. The five on trial, including Betty, faced five years and thousand-dollar fines each. John Molette testified to being beaten, kicked, and dragged out of the home, and his wife, Yvonne, gave such a stirring account that defense attorney Edward W. Jacko Jr. began crying and had to excuse himself from the courtroom. The Nation of Islam had a remarkable presence at the trial, filling the court daily with hundreds of followers. Surely due in part to Malcolm's impeccable appreciation for details, as well his understanding of how to gather the sympathies of a crowd, the NOI also submitted a stack of photographs of the home and several scale drawings by John Ali; it also produced the front door as evidence before the court, replete with signs of struggle and gunfire. In fact, as one paper reported, the NOI provided its own court stenographer and even controlled who could enter the courtroom, its orderly presence so noticeable that one white court attendant remarked, "We should put their officers on our payroll. They do a better job that [sic] we do."[2]

Although the Nation of Islam is often understood as standing apart from the civil rights movement, due in large part to Elijah Muhammad's reluctance to involve what he saw as an economically pragmatic religious movement in political matters, Malcolm X had begun as early as 1959 to involve the organization in such

1. "Moslems' Ten Day Trial: Lawyer Breaks Down in Tense Courtroom," *Amsterdam News*, March 21, 1959.

2. Ibid.; and Al Nall, "Moslems Accuse Cops: Bring Their Own Steno to Court," *Amsterdam News*, March 14, 1959.

discussions. Despite thirty-one outright acquittals and the edict of a mistrial, Malcolm charged that the court refused to see the case as a civil rights matter, despite clearly being a case of "Force of Authority vs. the Rights of People."[3] And although the police involved were never charged, city officials felt heat from the case and eventually agreed to pay a small settlement in response to a lawsuit filed by Betty Shabazz.[4]

- "Moslems' Ten Day Trial: Lawyer Breaks Down in Tense Courtroom," *Amsterdam News*, March 21, 1959
- Al Nall, "Moslems Accuse Cops: Bring Their Own Steno to Court," *Amsterdam News*, March 14, 1959
- Report of trial, BOSS, March 27, 1959

Further reading:

- "Three Moslems Seized as Police Fighters: Home of 'X' Group's Leader Site of Battle," *Amsterdam News*, May 24, 1958
- "Moslems Charge False Arrests in N.Y.," *Pittsburgh Courier*, May 24, 1958
- Al Nall, "Moslem Trial Begins: Right to Defend Life Is Stressed," *Amsterdam News*, March 7, 1959
- Memorandum, Detective William K. DeFossett to BOSS commanding officer, BOSS, May 27, 1958
- Malcolm X FBI file, summary report, New York office, May 19, 1959, pages 48–50

3. Al Nall, "The Moslem Trial," *Amsterdam News*, March 28, 1959.

4. Rickford, *Betty Shabazz*, 114.

"Moslems' Ten Day Trial: Lawyer Breaks Down In Tense Courtroom," *Amsterdam News,* March 21, 1959

"There was a crash of glass at the back door and he (Detective Kiernan) stuck his gun in the door and fired point blank. I felt the bullet pass my leg. I turned and ran back to get my (four) children out of the way.

"Detective Bonura came in and took me out in the driveway. They had lined John (her husband) up against the wall in the driveway. His face was bleeding, his eyes swollen and his clothes ripped off.

"Detective Kiernan had a gun on him and he said:

"'You yellow-bellied bastard. I should shoot you right now!'"

Thus went the testimony of Mrs. Yvonne Mollette, 27, one of the four Moslems on trial for alleged assault against two white detectives, Joseph Kiernan and Michael Bonura, who tried to enter their East Elmhurst home last May 14, with a search warrant, while seeking a Mrs. Margaret Dorsey, who later turned out to be at that same time living in the Bronx.

"THEY KICKED ME"

John Mollette, 27, testified that when he heard someone fumbling at his door he stepped outside and questioned their right to search his house without a warrant:

"They started beating and kicking me. They knocked me down and kicked me in the groin and side. They hit me in the mouth and jaw and tore my clothes off."

Mollette said that when he stumbled back into the side door of his house and locked the door, Kiernan shot twice through the glass panels and then broke the door open, dragging him out.

Defense attorney Edward W. Jacko, Jr., 271 W. 125th St. introduced both the shattered door and the bullet into evidence along with the torn bloody clothing worn that night by Mollette.

COURT ROOM WEEPS

Most dramatic moment of the trial occurred on the 10th day when Mrs. Minnie Simmons, 25-year-old wife of Moslem Secretary John X. tearfully described how she and 13-year-old Barbara Crosby, barricaded themselves along with Mrs. Betty Little, 24 (wife of Malcolm X), behind the locked doors of the Moslem minister's bedroom to escape police officers.

Weeping beyond control, the young mother said Detective Kiernan threatened to throw the minister's pregnant wife down the glass littered back staircase because she was not moving fast enough.

Mrs. Simmons said: "When they broke into our home I had been in the midst of bathing my five-months-old baby and with my still naked baby screaming in my arms, I pleaded with them not to drive me out into the cold with my naked baby in my arms."

LAWYER CRIES

Touched by her testimony Attorney Jacko stood in the middle of the courtroom with tears flowing down his cheeks, unable to continue his role. The spectators wept. Judge Peter T. Farrell called a recess to give the attorney and the spectators time to regain composure.

CALL DA

Kiernan had testified early in the trial that Margaret Dorsey was one of the women he had recognized in the house assaulting him with bottles. Under cross-examination by Jacko, Kiernan was asked why, if the police knew Margaret Dorsey was really in the Moslem home that night, assault charges were not placed against her when she was finally apprehended in the Bronx.

Kiernan claimed he tried to place charges against Margaret Dorsey but the District Attorney's office and his police superiors would not allow him.

DID NOT ASK SUMMONS

Using Moslem Captain Joseph X as his process-server, Jacko subpenaed Assistant D. A. Bernard M. Patton to take the stand. Under the questioning of Jacko, Patton admitted that Kiernan had never requested that his office accept assault charges against Margaret Dorsey.

A summons was also issued the county clerk, but when he took the stand Judge Farrell barred Jacko from initiating testimony that these same white police officers had once faced the same Grand Jury on criminal charges brought against them by the Moslem defendants.

HITS JUDGE

After sitting through 10 days of the trial, Moslem minister Malcolm X stated:

"Negroes in Mississippi could not have their civil rights as openly violated and stomped upon any worse than has been done here in Queens County Courthourse, in Judge Farrell's courtroom, and by Judge Farrell himself."

Throughout the three-week trial the Moslems virtually

controlled the courtroom. No one could enter without passing them. They had their own doorman, ushers and guards. One white court attendant was heard to remark:

"We should put their officers on our payroll. They do a better job that we do."

Al Nall, "Moslems Accuse Cops: Bring Their Own Steno to Court," *Amsterdam News*, March 14, 1959

"You yellow-bellied bastard, I should shoot you right now!"

This was the statement attributed to Det. Joseph Kiernan by Mrs. Yvonne Mollette Monday as the assault trial of four Moslems went into its second week.

Mrs. Mollette, a tall, handsome woman whose hair remains neatly tucked beneath a white bandana, is currently one of the defendants in the second-degree assault action before Queens County Court Judge Peter T. Farrell.

The stately, 27-year-old woman unemotionally unfolded her version of the incident which occurred in her home last May 14, when she was jailed along with her husband, John and two other women, also on trial.

The defense, handled by Atty. Edward Jacko, had John Mollette on the stand Tuesday.

PRIVACY IS ISSUE

The Moslems, who hold that the privacy of their home and house of worship was invaded both because of their race and religion, have shown a diligence in court that has kept all that attend the hearings, both curious and confused.

They have brought their own court stenographer into court—with the blessings of their messenger Elijah Muhammad in Chicago.

They have filled every seat in the courtroom daily, but in a quiet and orderly manner.

They have had admitted into evidence a stack of photographs and two scale drawings of their home at 35–45 99th St., East Elmhurst, Queens.

They have even brought to court the green door which once hung at the front of their home and bears the marks of struggle and gunfire which they claim were suffered at the hands of two detectives.

The whole case, which is being considereed by an all-male jury of 10 whites and three Negroes, drew out of the incident of last May 14, when the two detectives—Kiernan and Michael Bonura came with postal inspector Herbert Hall in search of one Margaret Dorsey—who the Moslems claim was never there.

The defense charges that the two officers shot up their home, then hauled Mollette and the women to jail—after viciously beating Mollette, who offered no resistence.

The officers and the postal inspector all testified on the stand that they were bombarded by bottles, hurled from an upstairs window by the women.

6 WITNESSES

Assistant DA Moses Z. Yam, who is prosecuting the case, brought a total of six witnesses on the stand, all policemen except one who was a doctor.

He finished his case Monday and Jacko started off with John Simmons, secretary of Muhammad's Temple of Islam, who identified the pictures and expert drawings.

Throughout the hearings a tone of diligence has also been noted on the part of both Yam and Judge Farrell. Yam was permitted to introduce evidence of a civil suit Tuesday, which the religious group has brought against the city.

But Judge Farrell vehemently refused to permit Jacko to initiate any testimony that the officers once faced the Grand Jury on criminal charges brought by the defendants.

Report of Trial,
BOSS, March 27, 1959

Date and Time of Occurrence	A.M.
May 14, 1958	**P.M.**
Crime or Offense Reported	
Assault on Police Officers	
Crime or Offense Changed to	
Investigation	
Investigating Officer's Signature	
Ernest B. Latty	
Investigating Officer's Name (Typed)	
Ernest B. Latty	
Rank **Det.** Shield No. **1373** Command **B.S.S.**	
Signature of C.O. of Investigating Officer	
Lt. Francis M. Sullivan	

Rank	Name	Command

Date of

This Report   **March 27, 59**

SUBJECT: THE TRIAL OF 4 MEMBERS OF THE MUSLIM CULT, FOR ASSAULT.

1. "If any of those on trial are convicted, we should all go to jail." These words were uttered by one of the Muslim leaders in Philidelphia. News of this statement was relayed to this department by the F.B.I.

By noon of March 16th, 1959 at Queens County Court, silent, protesting members of the Muslim Cult had swelled to over Four-Hundred in number. Due to the backlog of cases that had accumulated since this case began on March 2, 1959 court was adjourned until 9:30 A.M. the next day.

Det. Robert Byristricky #1494 and Det. Frank Bianco # 101 and the writer were assigned to Queens County Court on March 17, 1959 to observe, report and assist in maintaining order. The courtroom and corridors were again filled with Muslims by about 2:00 p.m.

At 2.30 p.m. the jury went into deliberation. A tense 13 hour vigil by the N.Y. Police Department had now begun. This time was spent observing and trying to understand what makes this people function.

2. Through questioning and observing certain incidents were made known to the writer.

a. One unidentified white man, curious about the type of case in progress attempted to enter the courtroom. An unidentified Muslim intercepted him and told him that this was not a public trial. He was denied admission.

b. Det. Joseph Kiernan, one of the arresting officers, complained about being shoved aside, in the court corridor, by one of the Muslims and told to allow a woman, cult member, to pass. He decided to let the incident pass rather than to worsen an already serious situation.

c. "What more do you expect from a nigger cop ?", was heard by the writer, as I passed a group of young Muslims on the sidewalk. The statement was delibrately spoken for my benefit.

d. Anyone who entered the court corridor on the first floor had his picture taken by one of three roving Muslim photographers. They patrolled the streets in the immediate area of the court, snapping pictures of any one who met their fancy.

e. The "Fruit of Islam" or the supposed judo experts could be distinguished by their closely shaven heads, white shirts and scarlet ties. A button (white in color) was worn on the left lapel of all male members. The women wore white kerchiefs over their heads.

There was indeed a disturbing calm.

3. At approximately 2:30 AM March 18th 1959 the jury had reached the following finding.

Two defendants ████████████ and ████████████ ACQUITTED.

Two defendants ████████████ and ████████████ ACQUITTED ON ½ OF THE COUNTS. HUNG JURY ON THE REMAINING COUNTS.

Judge Peter Farrell ordered retrial for April 17, 1959.

The jurors were escorted through a rear door, under guard, to the subways as all of the 300 stolid Muslims gathered on the front stairs of the courthouse From the top of the stairs Mr. Malcolm Little known as Malcolm X, leader of the Muslims in N.Y. City addressed the throng

In essance he served a warning on the N.Y. Police Department that they had better be right in dealing with the Muslims. "Any Policeman who abuses you belongs in the cemetary." "Be peaceful firm and aggressive but if one of them so much as touch your finger, Die." He was interrupted by frequent shouts of approval and applauds.

4. Plate numbers were taken and are in the process of verification the area was cleared by about 4:30 AM.

MIDDLE EAST TRAVELS

One of the most foundational periods in Malcolm X's early religious and political development is also one of the most obscure. Along with gaining greater visibility among both black and white Americans, the Nation of Islam had by 1959 also intrigued emerging Muslim states in Africa and the Middle East. Following the NOI's support for the first Afro-Asian People's Solidarity Conference, held in Cairo, Egypt's president Gamal Abdel Nasser extended an invitation to Elijah Muhammad. Muhammad turned to his most trusted lieutenant, Malcolm X, to travel abroad first and make the necessary preparations. Although he intended to make the hajj, a requirement of the five pillars of Islam, Malcolm was delayed and started his trip from New York on July 3, 1959. Seeing him off from the airport was the Egyptian attaché to the United Nations, Ahmed Zaki el-Borai. Borai's presence provided a preview of the royal treatment Malcolm would soon come to appreciate; for three weeks he traveled and stayed with heads of state and luminaries of the Muslim world.

The first eleven days of Malcolm's trip were spent in Cairo, where he met several times with Anwar el-Sadat and heads of Cairo's Al-Azhar University. Despite a personal invitation from Nasser, Malcolm declined as the mere "forerunner and humble servant of Elijah Muhammad."[1] Although he enjoyed the

1. Account by Abdul Basit Naeem, BOSS, August 5, 1959.

pleasures of being an esteemed guest abroad—staying at the Kandara Palace Hotel in Jeddah, Saudi Arabia, and the Grand Hotel in Khartoum, Sudan—Malcolm was also laid up for several days with dysentery, suffered from the excessive heat, and felt increasingly embarrassed by his meager knowledge of orthodox Muslim rituals. After traveling to Ghana briefly, he returned home on July 22.

Malcolm's trip to the Middle East was of great interest not only to Nasser and the Egyptian government, who reportedly viewed the Nation of Islam as an important "minority pressure group," but also to BOSS.[2] Abdul Basit Naeem, a Pakistani Muslim who acted as a consultant to the NOI and made Malcolm X's travel arrangements, updated BOSS on the trip. In his report he noted that Malcolm encouraged Muhammad to move the sect toward greater accordance with orthodox Islam. Malcolm advised that Muhammad study Arabic before going to Egypt and planned to return himself in six months. Perhaps due to Malcolm's advice, or to his own experiences in the Middle East in early 1960, Muhammad did in fact move the NOI in this direction: the temples were renamed mosques, Arabic instruction was instituted, and his son Akbar was sent to study at Al-Azhar University. For Malcolm personally, the trip introduced him to the possibility of finding a place for the NOI within the *ummah*, or world community of Islam. It also offered him even greater prominence within the organization; just days after leaving for Cairo, it was announced at Temple No. 7 that Malcolm would need a home of his own in the future, to "welcome distinguished visitors."[3]

- Malcolm X, "Africa Eyes Us," *Amsterdam News*, August 22, 1959

- Malcolm X, "Arabs Send Warm Greetings to 'Our Brothers' of

2. Abdul Basit Naeem, "Malcolm X as Nasser's Guest," BOSS, July 23, 1959.

3. Malcolm X FBI file, summary report, New York office, November 17, 1959, 2, 32.

Color in U.S.A.: Malcolm X Finds Africans, Arabs Fret More about Us Than Selves," *Pittsburgh Courier*, August 15, 1959

- "Malcolm X as Nasser's Guest," BOSS, July 23, 1959
- Account by Abdul Basit Naeem, BOSS, August 5, 1959

Further reading:

- Malcolm X FBI file, memo, FBI director to New York office, July 21, 1959
- Malcolm X FBI file, summary report, New York office, November 17, 1959, pages 31–32
- "Malcolm X Off to Tour Middle East," *Amsterdam News*, July 11, 1959

Malcolm X, "Africa Eyes Us," *Amsterdam News,* August 22, 1959

Sir: Racial troubles in New York occupied prominent space on the front pages here and in other parts of Africa yesterday. Everyone here seems aware of America's color problems.

Africans appear more concerned with the plight of their brothers in America than in their own conditions here in Africa. Many are aware that for the industrial development of Africa, foreign economic aid and technical assistance will be necessary.

Thus, Africans consider American's treatment of Black Americans a good yardstick by which they can measure the sincerity of America's offers of assistance here, and many young Africans are openly stating that what America practices at home, does not coincide with what she preaches abroad, and are thus suspicious of her overtures here.

The African finds it difficult to understand why in a land that advocates equality, twenty million Black Americans are without equality.

Why, in a land classing itself as leader of the free world, twenty million Black Americans are not free; why in a land of schools, colleges and all forms of educational opportunities, twenty million Negroes need Army escorts to accompany them to many of these institutions.

And they are asking why so many American Negroes suffer unemployment, bad housing, slum conditions and poverty.

New York is the world's largest city and international metropolis. It is the capitol of the world, the home of the United

Nations. Thus, news of racial trouble there quickly spreads abroad.

Here in Africa, the all-seeing-eye of the African masses is upon America.

Malcolm X
Khartoum, Sudan

Malcolm X, "Arabs Send Warm Greetings to 'Our Brothers' of Color in U.S.A.: Malcolm X Finds Africans, Arabs Fret More About Us Than Selves," *Pittsburgh Courier*, August 15, 1959

KANDARAH PALACE HOTEL, Saudi Arabia—The people of Arabia are just like our people in America in facial appearance. They are of many differing shades, ranging from regal black to rich brown, but none are white. It is a safe postulation to say that 99 per cent of them would be jim-crowed in the United States of America.

The people of Arabia know more about the color problem, and seem even more concerned and angered by the injustices our people receive in America than the so-called Negroes themselves.

The predominant religion of Southwest Asia, Arabia and Africa, of course, is Islam. Since the Pittsburgh Courier is the first newspaper in America to carry Mr. Muhammad's column, it is the most widely read of the American journals. News about the rapid increase of Moslems in America, plus other extensive news items on Africa and Asia, make your sheet very important for Arabians.

The majority of this Arabian population cannot be distinguished from the people of Africa. In fact, the darkest Arabs I have yet seen are right here on the Arabian peninsular. Most of these people would be right at home in Harlem. And all of them refer warmly to our people in America as their "brothers of color."

There is no color prejudice among Moslems, for Islam teaches that all mortals are equal and brothers. Whereas the white Christians in the Western world teach this same thing without practicing it. Here in the Moslem world not only is it taught, it is actually "a way of life."

Even the white Christians are forced to admit, in this area, that Moslems have the truest (and most intelligently conceived) form of devotion to the One True God—the Supreme Being, whose proper name is Allah.

I am leaving Arabia without visiting the Holy City, Mecca; an experience which would break the average Moslem's heart; but if it is Allah's will, I shall return with Mr. Elijah Muhammad, spiritual head of the American Moslems when he comes to this area during the fall.

Something I ate just before leaving Cairo gave me a serious seige of upset stomach (diarrhea), a bacilliary exposure which made it impossible for me to travel 60 miles into the desert, through 110-degree temperatures, beneath a pitiless sun.

Bad plane connections from Jeddah, to my regret, mean that if I miss my plane this morning, I will have to cancel my tour to Africa.

So, I am postponing my journey to Mecca, cancelling my stay in Aamaro (Eritrea) and Addis Ababa (Ethiopia), and going southwards, straight to Khartoum (Sudan) and Lagos (Nigeria).

I regret the fact, because I should have felt the pulse of as many of the African masses as possible before returning to the United States.

Africa is the land of the future . . . definitely the land of tomorrow, and the African is the man of tomorrow. Only yesterday, America was the New World, a world with a future—but now, we suddenly realize Africa is the New World—the world with the brightest future—a future in which the so-called American Negroes are destined to play a key role.

Traveling in these lands, seeing and speaking with our people here, I, myself, am getting an even broader vista of "things yet to come." One can even more fully appreciate the vital role being played by Mr. Elijah Muhammad and his work among our people in America.

Sincerely,
MALCOLM X

"Malcolm X as Nasser's Guest,"
BOSS, July 23, 1959

About two months ago an invitation to visit Egypt came from the U.A.R. government to Elijah Muhammad. At first he wanted to go himself but after discussing it with his associates he selected Malcolm X to go in his place. Elijah chose him because Malcolm X goes all out in lauding Elijah and attributing devine power to him. Malcolm X would be the emissary who would pave the way for a subsequent visit by Elijah himself a few months from now. (Possibly in November.)

Travel arrangements for Malcolm X were made with Hilton Hill inc. A Negro travel agency at # 55 W 42nd St. Mr. Hill told the writer that he arranged the plane trip but did not arrange for hotel accomodations in Cairo. Naeem, who went out to Chicago at Elijah's request and expense to discuss the trip with him tells the writer that Malcolm was invited to be the guest of the government while in Egypt. It is not known who paid the plane fare. Naeem showed the writer a letter received from from Malcolm X that he received July 21, mailed from Saudi Arabia. In substance the letter said "I spent 9 days in Cairo and met very important people." (the names were not specified but Naeem said included-positively from advance arrangements meeting Deputy Premier Anwat el-Sadat and probably Nasser.) "I was laid up two days with dysentary & now I an well again and have come on to Saudi Arabia. From here I will go to Khartoum then to Kano and then to Ghana and home. Owing to delay I am cutting out a couple of places."

Malcolm X was dubious about the kind of reception he would receive from authentic Moslems, knowing that much of Elijah's ritual would be regarded as blasphemy by the devout. Malcolm X was assured by BORAI, an Egyptian diplomat and others that he would receive a cordial reception.from the U.A.R. government people.

These pseudo-Moslems sects are regarded askance by the Moslems. The devout are shocked by the illiteracy and cheap pagentry and the disregard for the dogma of the Koran. Nasser however has confirmed the importance he attaches to American Nationalist Negroes to serve as a minority pressure group. The Egyptian diplomatic people have been instructed to show courtsies to Negro Nationalists. BOARI who previously established close contacts with Elijah and with Malcolm X has come back to N.Y.C. and is extending these contacts. Nassers diplomatic people, who normally would not associate with Temple type low-class Negroes, now go out of their way to flatter them. They also are more politican than Moslem and close their eyes to the ridiculous dogma deviations in the Temples sect.

DAWUD, leader of a rival pseudo-Moslem sect. in Philadelphia has also just made a similar Cairo Mecca pilgrimage receiving much attention in Egypt.

HILL, a negro from Bermuda who ordinarily specializes in business to the Carribean, has hired NAEEM as an assistant to develop this Negro Nationalist type of business to the Middle east.

Account by Abdul Basit Naeem,
BOSS, August 5, 1959

This is Abdel B. NAEEM'S account of Malcolm X's visit to Egypt. Naeem made all of the travel arrangements and has had several long talks with Malcolm X since his return. Early this year Elijah Muhammad received an invitation from BORAI and one or two other Egyptians to be the guest of the Egyptian government in Cairo. Elijah was first inclined to go but his disciples advised him to send one of them in his place. and look over the ground and if he liked it prepare the way for Elijah's visit. Malcolm X was chosen. Elijah paid Naeem's trip to Chicago to work out the travel details. Hilton G. Hill travel bureau with which Naeem is associated worked out the trip. Malcolm X paid for the trip ommiting to ask for hotel reservations in Cairo where he was to be entertained. Naeem thinks the temple paid the plane fare. Malcolm X took out his passport under the name of Malik L SHABAZZ. Boari Naeem and a delegation from the temple saw him off at the airport. He was met by government people upon his arrival in Cairo He was first to stay a couple of nights with a professor from the University of Cairo. Several prominent people put him up in turn. An architect offered to prepare plans gratis for any temple Elijah may choose to build in this country. Many Egyptians did'nt identify him as negroid because of his color until they saw him closer. Malcolm X had a message of greeting as "a fellow African coming back to his real home and a Moslem, eager to pray at the seat of the one true religion."

The Egyptian government people had Malcolm X constantly in hand. He was given considerable time by Anwar el Sadat who also plays on his color and he met all of the top people in the Moslem congress. He was cordially received by the Ulemas of Al Azhar. They took the Temples on it's face value as a Moslem sect and had no idea that even the name SHABAZZ is part of Elijah's blasphemy.

Malcolm X said that he was given an opportunity to meet NASSER, but declined because he made it clear that he was just the forerunner and humble servant of Elijah Muhammad. From early morning until late at night Malcolm was taken from one party to another. Tables were laden with food. As a result he developed acute indigestion, the usual dysentary coupled with excessive eating He remained in Cairo about 3 days longer than he planned. Malcolm X was in bad shape when he went on to Jidda in route to Mecca. He was given friendly welcome by the Moslem travel director a jet black African who insisted that this was the color of the authentic original Arab. Felled with dysentary in the 120 degree heat Malcolm X had but one desire, to go home. He also had the responsibility of setting up a spectacular welcome for Elijah in New York. Lucious, his principal rival, had arranged a tremendous ovation for Elijah in Washington

Naeem has been a consultant on Moslem ritual and etiquette to Elijah and his associates for several years now. Malcolm X who claims that Arabic was their original language and has been conducting Temple ritual in a jibberish reportedly Arabic, confessed to Naeem that he was extremely embarrassed going through the prayers 5 times a day in Egypt. He did not know the Arabic and had only a sketchy notion of the ritual. He was obseverant and thinks he got by mumbling. On this point he has advised Elijah that he should do some homework in Arabic before he goes to Egypt. Malcolm X also intends to do some studying with the idea of returning to Egypt in about 6 months. In Egypt Malcolm X did a combined job of building up the importance of the Temples movement & picturing his fellow blacks as oppressed by the arrogant American whites. The Egyptians loved it. He also took along pictures of their gatherings. Malcolm X is so delighted with his trip that he persuaded Elijah to go and is now promoting visits to Egypt among the Temples congregation. Up until recently Elijah discouraged his followers from reading the Koran and above all against visiting the Middle east.

THE HATE THAT HATE PRODUCED

By 1959 the Nation of Islam had become recognizable to the general public, although it was viewed by many as a marginal "hate" group not unlike George Lincoln Rockwell's American Nazi Party. Among those interested in the burgeoning group was C. Eric Lincoln, a young doctoral student who began research on his work *The Black Muslims in America*, which would become a seminal text on the NOI. Another upstart, black journalist Louis Lomax, pitched the idea of a documentary series on the NOI to media personality Mike Wallace. While Malcolm X was out of the country on his first trip abroad, the series aired in New York July 13–17, 1959, in five half-hour increments. More than the Johnson Hinton affair or any of Malcolm's previous public appearances, *The Hate That Hate Produced* introduced the NOI to a mass audience.

Unfortunately for the Nation of Islam, the primary thrust of the broadcast—encapsulated in its name—was from an integrationist perspective. The series threatened white liberal viewers by portraying the sect as a vengeful and reactionary answer to racism in America. Eager to distance themselves, civil rights leaders quickly denounced the NOI, and the public perception of Malcolm X and Elijah Muhammad as black demagogues was further solidified. Despite this negative publicity, the series acted as a springboard for all those involved. Mike Wallace would go on to cover the 1960 presidential campaign and eventually land on CBS's *60 Minutes*. Lomax continued to maintain a relationship with the NOI and published several books in which the group served as a major topic. For the Nation of Islam, the series was yet another introduction to a wider audience and showed the possibilities for growth that such publicity offered. After putting out the flames ignited by the documentary, Malcolm X began working, over the next couple years, to produce a monthly newspaper, *Mr. Muhammad Speaks*, which would spread the word of Elijah Muhammad to both a Muslim and non-Muslim audience. Although the lesson in public affairs served Malcolm well, by garnering more attention for the NOI, it also exacerbated feelings at Chicago headquarters that such publicity was driven primarily by vanity and self-promotion.

- "Moslems Fight Back; Bar White Press," *Amsterdam News*, August 1, 1959
- Malcolm X FBI file, memo, New York office, July 16, 1959
- Memorandum, Detective Thomas G. Hains to BOSS commanding officer, July 14, 1959
- Memorandum, Detective Ernest B. Latty to BOSS commanding officer, July 16, 1959

Further reading:

- "TV Show Hits Black Groups," *Amsterdam News*, July 25, 1959
- Malcolm X FBI file, summary report, New York office, November 17, 1959, pages 36–46
- Malcolm X FBI file, memo, New York office, July 21, 1959

"Moslems Fight Back; Bar White Press,"
Amsterdam News, August 1, 1959

Daily newspaper writers, television newsmen, and magazine writers seeking to cover the St. Nicholas Arena rally for Messenger Elijah Muhammad Sunday found a new twist in New York City coverage when the Moslem security officers hung out a "Whites Barred" sign.

No white reporters were allowed to enter nor were any white persons permitted as guests. White reporters, including one for a Negro weekly newspaper, security officers for the St. Nicholas Arena, and a Catholic priest who sought to enter.

John X secretary of the New York Muslims, told newsmen that "I had instructions to bar all white reporters." Asked for further comment, John refused.

MIKE BARRED TWICE

Mike Wallace, TV commentator who last week had run a TV series on the Moslem group, was barred twice and at first threatened to take the case to SCAD, but later said he would not press his actions any further.

A police official on the scene said while such actions would be in violation of city laws if it were a public meeting, who the Moslems termed it a religious meeting, they would "discretion as the better part" in handling the situation.

One Negro policeman who was assigned to check on the rally was forced to go through the Moslem's security check on all persons who enter their religious meetings.

Oddly enough, Negro reporter Louis Lomax, for the Mike Wallace show, was allowed to enter, but James Boyack, white reporter for the Pittsburgh Courier, which carries the Muhammad column was barred.

Negro newsmen in addition to Lomax who were allowed to enter included writers for the Amsterdam News, Journal and Guide, Radio Station WLJB, and several news photographers.

Much national attention was centered around the Moslems in recent weeks since the Wallace TV shows which led to national news writers attempting to cover Sunday's rally.

DAKOTA IN ACT

Last week Singer Dakota Staton, whose husband is Talub Dawud, leader of another group of Moslems, criticized the Wallace shows as "vicious misrepresentation of the religion of Islam."

She said that her religion is that "there is no line of demarcation racially, so far as Moslems are concerned." She denied any connection between her group and Elijah Muhammad.

MUHAMMAD ANSWERS

More than 6,000 persons filled St. Nicholas Arena and lined the streets Sunday as Elijah Muhammad, who claims to have more than a quarter-million black Moslems in the U.S., answered what he termed "charges" leveled at him.

OFFICE MEMORANDUM   UNITED STATES GOVERNMENT

TO   : DIRECTOR, FBI (25-330971)   DATE: 7/16/59

FROM   : SAC, NEW YORK (105-7809) (412)

SUBJECT : NATION OF ISLAM
          IS – NOI
          (oo: CHICAGO)

ReNYairtel, 7/14/59.

As the Bureau has been advised, MIKE WALLACE on his News Beat show on WNTA-TV, Channel 13, NY, 6:30 p.m.–7:00 p.m., during the week of 7/13–17/59, is showing a five-part report which he calls "The Hate That Hate Produced."

The following is a substantially verbatim account of the first part of this report which was shown on 7/13/59.

Copies of this letter are designated for Detroit in view of the fact that NOI parochial schools in Chicago and Detroit were mentioned.

Tonight, a special report assembled by News Beat reporters and camera crews in New York and Washington; a fully documented story of the movement for black supremacy among a growing and well-organized minority of American Negroes. The leaders of this movement are crafty, resourceful men who know what they are about. Their followers are Negroes who find in the cause of black supremacy an answer to centuries of persecution. We call our story "The Hate that Hate Produced" and you'll see and hear that story in just a few minutes. But first lets look at todays news.

WALLACE: Tonight we begin a five part series which we call "The Hate that Hate Produced"; a story of the rise of Black Racism, of a call for black supremacy among a growing segment of American Negroes. While city officials, state agencies, white liberals and sober-minded Negroes stand idly by, a group of Negro dissenters are taking to street corner step ladders, church pulpits, sports arenas and ballroom platforms across the nation to preach the gospel of hate that would set off a federal investigation if it were to be preached by Southern whites. What are they saying?

Listen—

I charge the white man with being the greatest liar on earth. I charge the white man with being the greatest drunkard on earth. I charge the white man with being the greatest . . . on earth. Yet the bible forbids it. I charge the white man with being the greatest gambler on earth. I charge the white man, ladies and gentlemen of the jury, with being the greatest murderer on earth. I charge the white man with being the greatest . . . on earth. I charge the white man with being the greatest adulterer on earth. I charge the white man with being the greatest robber on earth. I charge the white man with being the greatest deceiver on earth. I charge the white man with being the greatest troublemaker on earth. So therefore ladies and gentlemen of the jury I ask you to bring back a verdict of guilty as charged.

WALLACE: The indictment you've just heard is being told over and over again in most of the major cities across the country. This charge comes at the climax of a morality play called "The Trial." The plot, indeed the message of the play, is that the white man has been put on trial for his sins against the black man. He has been found guilty. The sentence is death. The play is sponsored, produced by a Negro religious group who call themselves the Muslims. They use a good deal of the paraphernalia of the traditional religion of Islam. But they are fervently disavowed by orthodox Muslims. Negro American

Muslims are the most powerful of the black supremacist group. They claim a membership of ¼ of a million Negroes and our search indicates that for every so-called card carrying black supremacist there are perhaps 10 fellow travelers. Their doctrine is being taught in 50 cities across the nation. Let no one under-estimate the Muslims. They have their own parochial schools like this one in Chicago where Muslim children are taught to hate the white man. Even the clothes they wear are anti-white man, anti-American like these two Negro children going to school. Wherever they go the Muslims withdraw from the life of the community. They have their own stores, supermarkets, barber shops, restaurants. Here you see a progressive modern air conditioned Muslim department store on Chicago's South Side.

Their story of hatred is carried in many Negro newspapers. Here you see their Minister MALCOLM X proudly displaying five of the biggest Negro papers in America. Papers published in Los Angeles, New York, Pittsburgh, Detroit and Newark and Negro politicians, regardless of their private beliefs, respectfully listen when the leaders of the black supremacy movement speak. Here you see Borough President HULAN JACK shaking hands with ELIJAH MUHAMMAD, who is the leader of the Muslims and here you see NAACP Director ROY WILKINS greeting Minister MALCOLM, the heir apparent to ELIJAH MUHAMMAD. Four or five times a year the Muslims assemble in one of America's major cities to hear their leader, ELIJAH MUHAMMAD. Here you see them arriving at Washington's Uline Arena for a meeting held only five weeks ago. Every devout Muslim attends these rallies, for some time between now and 1970 and at just such a rally as this, the Muslims expect that ELIJAH will sound the death knell of the white man. Every precaution is taken to protect their leader. As you will shortly see the Muslims, men and women both, submit to a complete search before entering the meeting hall. Some 10,000 persons attended the rally that you see here, all of them searched like this man. This began almost three hours before the meeting started.

They are waiting now for ELIJAH MUHAMMAD, founder and spiritual leader of their group. And here he comes. He is actually ELIJAH POOLE of Georgia. During World War II, MUHAMMAD was arrested and charged with sedition and draft dodging. The Department of Justice finally dropped the charge that he advocated defeat of the white democracy and victory for the colored Japanese, but MUHAMMAD and his followers did serve time in the federal penitentiary for refusing to register for the draft.

Here you will hear ELIJAH MUHAMMAD introduced by Minister MALCOLM X, the Muslims' New York leader and ambassador at large for the movement. The good news that Minister MALCOLM X will talk about here is the coming rise of the black man and the fall of the white man.

MALCOLM: Everyone who is here today realizes that we are now living in the fulfillment of prophesy. We have come to hear and to see the greatest and wisest, the most fearless black man in America today. In the church we used to sing the song "Good News, the Chariot is coming." Is that right or wrong? But what we must bear in mind that what's good news to one person is bad news to another. While you sit here today knowing that you have come to hear good news, you must realize in advance what's good news for you might be bad news for somebody else. What's good news for the sheep might be bad news for the wolf.

WALLACE: Good news for the black man is that he is on the verge of recapturing his position as a ruler of the universe. The bad news for the white man is that his long and wicked reign will shortly be over and then ELIJAH MUHAMMAD spoke.

MUHAMMAD's speech was inaudible and interrupted numerous times by applause.

WALLACE: But of more interest to New Yorkers is Minister MALCOLM X, the Muslims' New York Minister, who you will shortly see. This is a remarkable man, a man who by his own admission to News Beat was once a procurer and a dope peddler. He served time for robbery in the Massachusetts State

Penitentiary. Now he is a changed man. He will not smoke or drink. He will not even eat in a restaurant that houses a tavern. He told News Beat that his life changed when the Muslim faith taught him no longer to be ashamed being a black man.

Reporter LOUIS LOMAX asks Minister MALCOLM X to further explain MUHAMMAD's teachings. The conversation you will hear took place as LOMAX and Minister MALCOLM X were discussing the teachings of ELIJAH MUHAMMAD.

LOMAX: That the same context that Mr. ELIJAH MUHAMMAD teaches that his faith, the Islamic faith, is for the black man. The black man is good. He also uses the Old Testament incident of the serpent in Adam and Eve in the Garden of Eden and he sets up the proposition there that this is the great battle between good and evil and he uses the phrase devil and he uses it almost interchangeably and synonymously with the word snake. Now what does he mean there?

MALCOLM: Well number 1 he teaches us that this individual was a real serpent.

LOMAX: It was not a real serpent.

MALCOLM: That one in the garden.

LOMAX: What was it?

MALCOLM: But as you know the bible is written in symbols, parables and this serpent or snake is the symbol that is used to hide the real identity of the one that this actually was.

LOMAX: Well who was it?

MALCOLM: The white man.

LOMAX: I want to call your attention Mr. MALCOLM to one paragraph in this column. He says and I quote him "that only people born of Allah are the black nation of whom the so-called American Negroes are descendents."

MALCOLM: Yes

LOMAX: Now is this your standard teaching?

MALCOLM: Yes. He teaches us that the black man by nature is divine.

LOMAX: Now does this mean that the white man by nature is evil?

MALCOLM: By nature he is other than divine.

LOMAX: Well does this mean that he is evil. Can he do good?

MALCOLM: By nature he is evil.

LOMAX: He cannot do good?

MALCOLM: History is best qualified to reward all research and we don't have any historic example where we have found that they collectively for the people have done good.

LOMAX: Minister MALCOLM, you now, in Chicago and Detroit, have universities of Islam, have you not?

MALCOLM: Yes sir, in Detroit and Chicago.

LOMAX: And you take your parishioners, you take children from the kindergarten ages and you train them right through high school. Is this true?

MALCOLM: Yes sire, from the age of 4 up.

LOMAX: And you have a certified parochial school operating in Chicago?

MALCOLM: In Chicago.

LOMAX: And in Detroit?

MALCOLM: And in Detroit.

LOMAX: And kids come to your school in lieu of going to what we call regular day school?

MALCOLM: Yes sir.

LOMAX: What do you teach them there?

MALCOLM: We teach them the same things that they would be taught ordinarily in school minus the Little Black Sambo story and things that were taught to you and me when we were growing up to breath an inferiority complex in us.

LOMAX: Do you teach them what you just said to me that the white man is somewhat evil?

MALCOLM: You can go to any small Muslim child and ask him where is hell or who is the devil and he wouldn't tell you that hell is down in the ground or that the devil is something invisible that you can't see. He'll tell you hell is right where he has been catching it and he'll tell you the one who is responsible for him having received this hell is the devil.

LOMAX: And he will say that this devil is the white man?

MALCOLM: Yes.

WALLACE: These then are the Muslims and these are the things they are saying, preaching and teaching their youngsters. They are the most powerful of the black supremacist groups, and later this week we will hear more from the Muslims.

Now let us look at another group. Every night when the weather is good, knots of people gather in Harlem at 125th

Street and Seventh Avenue in front of the Theresa Hotel to hear the speakers for the United African Nationalist Movement spread their gospel of black nationalism. We made a film of one of those meetings. The lighting was poor and it was almost impossible to get good sound quality. The man you are about to hear is JOHN DAVIS, a paid orator for the United African Nationalist Movement. You will hear him attack liberals, ELEANOR ROOSEVELT, PEARL BUCK and then he will go on to say some rather surprising things about the NAACP and its leader, ROY WILKINS.

FILM CLIP: And now you got what they call so-called white liberals . . . and the white liberals go around claiming that they are against discrimination, they are against lynching. . . . Lots of brutal liberals like phoney Mrs. ROOSEVELT, the African white goddess . . . They got another one by the name of PEARL BUCK and the one who wrote the "Imitation of Life." Oh all of those phoney liberals. Then you got the NAACP—The National Association for the Advancement of some colored folks and you got . . . ROY WILKINS.

WALLACE: This almost any night at the corner of 125th Street and Seventh Avenue in New York. The leader of the United African Nationalist Movement is JAMES R. LAWSON, some times public relations man and black nationalist. The man who says he has authorization to bring greetings from the United Arab Republic's President NASSER to black nationalist groups in the United States. News Beat asked Mr. LAWSON to explain the nature of the organization and its aims.

LAWSON: United African Nationalist Movement—it is an organization of people of African descent here in America, however, we have associated organizations throughout the Caribbean, Africa and the Middle East.

LOMAX: Can a non-African or non-Negro person join your organization?

LAWSON: He cannot.

LOMAX: He cannot. Why not?

LAWSON: Because this is an organization of people of African blood or descent.

LOMAX: Are you anti-white?

LAWSON: Well I think you ought to ask white people are they anti-black.

LOMAX: But are you anti-white?

LAWSON: I don't think I'm anti-white, but I'm pro-black.

LOMAX: Do you favor integration?

LAWSON: No.

LOMAX: Do you favor the NAACP?

LAWSON: No

LOMAX: Do you think ROY WILKINS is a good leader of his people?

LAWSON: ROY WILKINS is not the leader. ARTHUR SPENGAR [Spingarn] (PH) is the leader.

LOMAX: And what is ARTHUR SPENGAR [Spingarn] (PH)?

LAWSON: A Zionist Jew.

LOMAX: Mr. LAWSON, were you present at the meeting when Dr. RALPH BUNCHE of the United Nations go up to introduce Prime Minister . . .

LAWSON: Sure I was. Don't you remember. I was with my family—my wife and two children.

LOMAX: But as I recall the incident, Dr. BUNCHE was booed when he stood up. Is that correct?

LAWSON: That is true.

LOMAX: Mr. LAWSON, who booed RALPH BUNCHE and why?

LAWSON: I think the people booed him. That's what it looked like to me.

LOMAX: Do you know any of the people who booed him?

LAWSON: Sure.

LOMAX: Do you know why they booed him?

LAWSON: I don't know exactly why, but I have a hunch.

LOMAX: What's your hunch sir?

LAWSON: My hunch is that black people—those of African descent in this country-considered RALPH BUNCHE a sort of GEORGE WASHINGTON of Israel—a man who made a million people that are closely related to their . . . and haven't done a cockeyed think for the black man.

LOMAX: Now you say the black people believe that. Do you JAMES R. LAWSON believe that RALPH BUNCHE is a GEORGE WASHINGTON of Israel?

LAWSON: Well I know he is.

WALLACE: These black supremacists, Muslims and United African Nationalists, are not practioners of hate just for hate sake. They didn't grow up in a vacuum. Rather theirs is a hate that hate has produced: the hate that some Negroes are returning for the hate that all Negroes have received in the past 300 years. The burden of being a black man in America has proved more than some of them can bear and now they are fighting back with the same weapons that were used to subjugate them. They are finding it increasingly difficult to identify with America. They have lost faith in the honesty of American law enforcement agencies when it comes to protecting their individual rights. Many of them have abandoned christianity. They name it a dogma of enslavement. Even those who have not abandoned it are preaching that Jesus was not white. Jesus was not white like the men who lynch and discriminate against Negroes, but that he was a black man. JAMES LAWSON shows the black supremacist concept of Jesus and notice how much the Jesus in the painting and JAMES LAWSON resemble one another.

LOMAX (Film Clip)

In conjunction with your remarks that the Negro needs a vanguard or at least some image he can identify I wonder if you could tell me what this picture is? What it is all about?

LAWSON: Well we don't . . . a black god. We know that God is a spirit, but this is a painting, concept of an artist, of Jesus in the Garden of Gethsemane and we know SOLOMON himself said look not upon me because I am black and somewhere else is clear I think in Revelations where it says his hair is like a lamb's . . . and his feet like polished brass. Therefore we feel that we are on sound ground . . . After all Jesus was of the Tribe of Judah.

WALLACE: Tomorrow night we will continue our report on the rise of Black Racism among a segment of the American Negro population, as we examine the role that christianity has played in this disturbing drama. You will hear Muslim leaders charge that christianity is a white man's religion, that it has failed the Negro. You will hear black nationalists say that before the Negro can come into his own he must get rid of Jesus and will hear the Rev. ADAM CLAYTON POWELL charge that christianity has been dragging its feet on the race issue, that there is more segregation at 11:00 on Sunday morning then at any other time of the week.

I'll be back with a conversation with News Beat reporter LOUIS LOMAX, the man who has done virtually all of the research four our special report, in just a moment right after this message.

* * * * * *

Reporter LOUIS LOMAX, who enabled News Beat to bring you the alarming story of a rising cult of black supremacy which you have just heard, is here with us tonight and you will see him throughout the remainder of this week as we bring you further reports on "The Hate that Hate Produced."

WALLACE: LOU, first of all we talked about perhaps 250,000 people who are involved in movements for black supremacy.

LOU: Yes.

WALLACE: Is that an accurate figure?

LOU: Well it's a debatable figure. This is what the Muslims claim. I wouldn't be surprised if you took the hard core people and then added in the fellow travelers that you wouldn't find something approaching this figure. However, I think it should be underscored that most Negroes are not this way and that most Negroes don't feel this way. But the important thing is that a sizable segment and more important a vocal segment of the Negro population is doing and saying this and it needs to be looked into.

WALLACE: Is the Negro community aware of what is going on with these movements?

LOU: Yes and I think they have been guilty to a large degree of sweeping it under the rug.

WALLACE: Why?

LOU: I don't think they want to face it. It has a lot of ramifications that we'll get into as the week goes on. But the Negro leadership has been hesitant to talk about this thing. We've had an awful lot of trouble trying to get them to talk about it and I think that now that it is out in the open it is time to talk about it forthrightly.

WALLACE: Perhaps the most significant thing which we brought out tonight is the existence of so-called parochial schools in Chicago and Detroit to teach these Muslim youngsters to hate the white man.

LOU: Yes I think this is quite true.

WALLACE: When you were around New York and Washington digging for facts on this story did you run into trouble.

LOU: Twice—when we did the film with Mr. DAVIS up on the street corner where we got into a little hassle—it could have led to trouble and in Washington. I was all right because the leaders had cleared me, but I had a white camera crew with me and I had to stay with them throughout the meeting because some of the people don't take too kindly to white men running around.

WALLACE: Thank you LOU. We'll be talking to you again tomorrow night and throughout the week on News Beat. Tomorrow night another installment of "The Hate that Hate Produced."

Memorandum, Detective Thomas G. Hains to BOSS Commanding Officer, July 14, 1959

July 14, 1959

From: Det. Thomas G. Hains # 718 Bureau of Special Services

To : Commanding Officer of the Bureau of Special Services

SUBJECT: MIKE WALLACE PROGRAM THIS DATE FROM 6:30 p.m. to 7:00 p.m. CONCERNING THE "BLACK SUPREMACY GROUP"

1. This was number two in a series by the program. The first speaker was Louis Lomax, a newsbeat reported for the program, who referred to the incident at the 28th Pct. S.H. last night as one of confusion. He stated that the demonstration was a spontaneous one and did not represent any one group. The reason he gave for the demonstration was that the word was passed that a negro woman was being beaten in the S.H. by a white man. This concluded Mr. Lomax's appearance.

2. Film clips were shown of a Mr. John Davis alleged to be a paid speaker of this "hate group." This was on film and Mr. Wallace did not say when the speech had been made. Mr. Davis called Christianity the religion of enslavement, stating that "you have all been brainwashed about Jesus, and this heaven stuff." He then spoke of the Mack Parker lynching, and told his listeners to "get rid of the white mans religion."

3. Film clips of Mr. Elijah Muhammad, spiritual leader of Muslim Cult Islam, were shown of previous interviews. Mr. Muhammad said that the white mans religion was not for the negro. He also said that the Christian relaigion had

failed the negro, he said that Christianity was the religion of enslavement and that when the negro was brought to this country as a slave the first thing the white man did was to make Christians of them. Mr. Muhammad referred to the Islam religion as the maternal religion and the natural one for negroes. He stated he had converted hundreds of thousands to his religion but did not know if all were still practicing. At the conclusion of this film clip Mr. Wallace stated that the members of Islam religion did not associate themselves with this cult and stated that there religion was open to all persons regardless of race or national origin and did not preach hate.

4. Adam Clayton Powell was the final person interviewed and when asked the question, is the Protestant religion the friend of the negro? answered, Christianity has been "dragging its feet" and had been detrimental to the segregation problem. He also included the Catholic religion. This was the conclusion of the program as it related to the subject.

<hr>

Det. Thomas G. Hains # 718 B.S.S.

Memorandum, Detective Ernest B. Latty to BOSS Commanding Officer, July 16, 1959

July 16, 1959

From : Det. Ernest B. Latty, Shield # 1373, B.S.S.
To   : Commanding Officer, Bureau of Special Services
Subject: MIKE WALLACE, T.V. SERIES, "THE HATE THAT HATE PRODUCED."

1. July 15, 1959, 6:30 p.m.–7:00 p.m. W.P.I.X. series #3. "Today we will see how Adam C. Powell, Hulan Jack and Earl Brown accept political support from these racist, "Black Supremists Groups."

Louis Lomax, Newsbeat reporter, stated on May 18, 1959, Hulan Jack, highest elected Negro Official in the City of New York was booed off of the Harlem Streets. The incident took place at a N.A.A.C.P. street meeting. "This, stated Mr Lomax, was an organized movement." It started as had been pre-arranged when Malcolm X stepped through a revolving door. Other Negroes who were in attendance joined in the booing which was led by Moslems. Immediately after that incident Mr. Hulan Jack hired a public relations man. He also invited Elijah Muhammad to N.Y. He wooed the Moslems.

2. Reporter, Louis Lomax interviewed James R. Lawson, president of the United African Nationalist Movement.

Q. *Do you and members of your organization participate in Harlem politics?*
A. Yes.

Q. *Do you support candidates?*
A. Yes.

Q. Do you support A. C. Powell?
A. Yes.

Q. What does Mr. Powell think of you?
A. I do not know, you will have to ask him. At our Africa Freedom Day rally, he could not attend. He did write a tribute to the United African Nationalist Movement.

Q. What did he say about you? about the organization?
A. He said we were doing a great job for the liberation of Africa and for those africans at home and abroad.

3. In a filmed interview Mr. Lomax then asked Adam Clayton Powell

Q. Do you approve of what Mr. Lawson is doing and saying?
A. No I do not believe in extremist movements but I do believe in freedom of speech.

4. The interview was then switched back to James R. Lawson and he was asked if he supported Hulan Jack?

A. Yes I support Jack, After all we are all members of the same order.

Q. What order is that?
A. The order of The Star of the Ethepoian Flag.

FIDEL CASTRO IN HARLEM

Malcolm's exposure to postcolonial and third-world revolutionaries continued the year after his trip to the Middle East, but this time it was a domestic affair. When Fidel Castro, premier of the new Cuban regime, attended the United Nations General Assembly in September 1960, he and his entourage became incensed over the bill at New York City's Shelburne Hotel. Castro proposed that his delegation would sleep in Central Park if necessary: "We are mountain people. We are used to sleeping in the open air."[1] Malcolm, as a member of Harlem's welcoming committee, quickly saw an opportunity and invited Castro to stay at the Hotel Theresa, just blocks from Mosque No. 7 and the Shabazz luncheonette. The two men met at slightly past midnight, in the premier's suite. Castro's move to Harlem was clearly a political one, and many criticized him for such obvious pandering. Likewise, Malcolm's late-night meeting with the Cuban revolutionary also appeared tactical and was met by criticism; yet Malcolm's critics, unlike Castro's, were largely from within his own organization.

The meeting itself lasted less than an hour and was attended by *Amsterdam News* journalist James Booker and staff photographer Carl Nesfield, who captured the meeting. Malcolm

---

1. Max Frankel, "Fidel Complains to U.N.: Angry Castro Quits Hotel in Row over Bill: Moves to Harlem," *Los Angeles Times*, September 20, 1960.

was accompanied by Captain Joseph and John Ali according to Ralph Matthews, another black journalist allowed to attend.[2] Malcolm's close assistant Benjamin 2X Karim later claimed that Malcolm tried to "fish" Castro to the NOI.[3] In general, though, Malcolm tried to remain noncommittal in his support of Castro's regime and reportedly turned down an offer to visit Cuba. Although this may have been an attempt to uphold the NOI's public policy of political disengagement, his order that the Fruit of Islam be deployed on twenty-four-hour alert to "assist Castro in the event of any anti-Castro demonstrations" implied that he still viewed the meeting as an opportunity to bolster the NOI's domestic and international reputation.[4] Cubans also saw the possibilities of joining forces with black militant groups in the U.S. and quickly renamed Havana's pricey Riviera Hotel in honor of the Hotel Theresa.[5] Conversely, Elijah Muhammad saw the entire event as a political charade and unnecessary public display of partisanship. Although strong discord between Muhammad, his family, and Malcolm X was still several years away, the meeting with Castro was an early warning sign of the conflicting political strategies of Muhammad and the soon-to-be-named national spokesman of the NOI.

- "Malcolm X Explains Wee-Hour Visit to Castro at Theresa," *Pittsburgh Courier*, October 1, 1960
- Malcolm X FBI file, summary report, New York office, November 17, 1960, pages 18–20

2. Ralph D. Matthews, "Going Upstairs—Malcolm X Greets Fidel," *New York Citizen-Call*, September 24, 1960.

3. "Fishing" was a term used by the Nation of Islam to refer to the recruitment of new members. Robert L. Jenkins, ed., *The Malcolm X Encyclopedia* (Westport, CT: Greenwood Press, 2002), 144.

4. Malcolm X FBI file, summary report, New York office, August 22 1961, 27.

5. "Cuban Hotel Now the 'Theresa,'" *New York Times*, September 21, 1960.

- Ralph D. Matthews, "Going Upstairs—Malcolm X Greets Fidel," *New York Citizen-Call*, September 24, 1960

Further reading:

- "Castro Leaves an Unruffled Harlem," *Amsterdam News*, October 1, 1960
- James Booker, "Castro Talks: Bars White Press; He Calls Himself 'African American,'" *Amsterdam News*, September 24, 1960
- Vincent Butler, "Castro Helps One Harlemite, The Hotelman," *Chicago Daily Tribune*, September 21, 1960
- "Castro Walkout Termed a Stunt," *New York Times*, September 21, 1960
- "Cuban Hotel Now the 'Theresa,'" *New York Times*, September 21, 1960
- "Fidel Calls Harlem 'an Oasis in Desert,'" *Baltimore Afro-American*, October 1, 1960

NEW YORK—"Fidel Castro has denounced racial discrimination in Cuba, which is more than President Eisenhower has done here in America," Minister Malcolm X, head of the Harlem Muslim Temple, told The Courier last week.

The statement was made by Malcolm X in the course of explaining his post-midnight meeting with the Cuban Premier.

He said he went to the Theresa Hotel to see Castro in his capacity as a member of the 28th Precinct Committee Council. The council had formed a reception committee to greet prominent United Nations members who visited Harlem.

WHILE DISCLAIMING any connection with Premier Castro, Malcolm X said he would not apologize for the meeting. He said he would rather be seen with Castro than "some prominent white people here in the United States."

Malcolm X said: "Premier Castro has also come out against lynching, which is also more than Eisenhower has done. Castro has also taken a more open stand for civil rights for black Cubans. I went to see Castro as a Muslim."

He said no outside man can help the "so-called" American Negro. No outside force, no outside power. It takes God to correct the situation here because it is so complicated. Muhammad represents that God. That's why I am with Muhammad.

Malcolm X said the "white press" and other media of public information have been trying to make his visit to Castro "suspicious" because he was a Muslim.

B. Subject's Contact with Cuban Premier FIDEL CASTRO,
at New York, New York, September, 1960

███████████████████████████████████████

███████████████████████████████████████

███████████████████████████████████████

██████████████████

████████████ advised on September 21, 1960, that in con-
versation with subject on that date, subject stated that he had
visited with CASTRO for approximately 30 minutes in his
Hotel Theresa room. The source advised that LITTLE stated
that during this visit he told CASTRO, in reference to CAS-
TRO himself, that usually when one sees a man whom the
United States is against, there is something good in that man.
To this CASTRO replied that only the people in power in the
United States are against him, not the masses. LITTLE further
expressed the opinion that any man who represented such a
small country that would stand up and challenge a country as
large as the United States must be sincere.

██████████████████████████ further stated that LITTLE denied that the meeting with CASTRO was pre-arranged and
LITTLE further stated that the NOI was not allied with CAS-
TRO or with any foreign power on earth. LITTLE stated that
the NOI was allied with God in whom they believe, hence,
they cannot be affiliated with Communism since it is atheistic.

████████████████████████ stated that in explaining his
reason for the visit, LITTLE stated that he was on a committee which was formed to meet and greet any of the African
delegates to the United Nations when they came to Harlem,
and when he heard that CASTRO had moved to a hotel in

Harlem, he felt that as a representative of this committee he should greet CASTRO. LITTLE also stated he was the only member of the committee available at the time of the visit, hence, he went to the meeting with CASTRO accompanied by three NOI members and two members of the Negro press.

The "New Jersey Herald News," a weekly newspaper published in Newark, New Jersey, for the week ending, September 24, 1960, contained an article datelined New York City, September 20, 1960, which reflected that Cuban Premier FIDEL CASTRO had moved into the Hotel Theresa in Harlem at 12:29 a.m. on September 20th. He was shortly followed and visited by MALCOLM X, leader of the New York Muslim population, who in his role as a member of the 28th Precinct Community Council constituted a one man welcoming committee.

The "Pittsburgh Courier," a weekly newspaper published in Pittsburgh, Pennsylvania, dated October 1, 1960, New York edition, contained an article headlined "Malcolm X Explains Wee-hour Visit to Castro at Theresa." This article reflected that subject stated that he went to see CASTRO in his capacity as a member of the 28th Precinct Community Council which had been formed to greet prominent United Nations members who visited Harlem.

This article further reflected that subject denied any connection with CASTRO, and subject also stated, according to the article: "Premier CASTRO has also come out against lynching, which is also more than EISENHOWER has done. CASTRO has also taken a more open stand for civil rights for black Cubans. He wants to see CASTRO as a Muslim."

Earlier in the article, subject was quoted as saying: "FIDEL

CASTRO has denounced racial discrimination in Cuba which is more than President EISENHOWER has done here in America."

This same "Pittsburgh Courier" in their New York edition dated October 15, 1960, contained an article which reflected that subject had tendered a bitter resignation from membership on the Welcoming Committee of the 28th Precinct Community Council, which committee had been designated by the 28th Precinct of the New York City Police Department to welcome ruling heads of state to Harlem during the General Assembly session of the United Nations for the purpose of avoiding any embarrassing incidents.

Ralph D. Matthews, "Going Upstairs—Malcolm X Greets Fidel," *New York Citizen-Call*, September 24, 1960

To see Premier Fidel Castro after his arrival at Harlem's Hotel Theresa meant getting past a small army of New York City policeman guarding the building, and past security officers, U.S. and Cuban.

But one hour after the Cuban leader's arrival, Jimmy Booker of the *Amsterdam News,* photographer Carl Nesfield and myself were huddled in the stormy petrel of the Caribbean's room listening to him trade ideas with Muslim leader Malcolm X.

Dr. Castro did not want to be bothered with reporters from the other daily newspapers, but he did consent to see two representatives from the Negro press.

Malcolm X gained entry when few others could because he had recently been named to a welcoming committee for visiting dignitaries set up by Harlem's 28th Police Precinct Council.

We followed Malcolm and his aides, Joseph and John X down the ninth floor corridor. It was lined with photographers, disgruntled because they had no glimpse of the bearded Castro, and writers vexed because security men kept pushing them back.

We brushed by them, and one by one were admitted to Dr. Castro's suite. He rose and shook hands with each one of us in turn. He seemed in a fine mood. The rousing Harlem welcome still seemed to ring in his ears.

Castro was dressed in green army fatigues. I expected them to be as sloppy as news photos tended to make. To my surprise, his casual attire, just the same was immaculately creased and spanking clean.

His beard by dim room light was dark brown with just a suggestion of red.

After introductions, he sat on the edge of the bed, bade Malcolm X sit beside him and spoke in his curious brand of broken English. His first words were lost to us assembled around him. But Malcolm heard him and answered, "Downtown for you, it was ice, uptown it is warm."

The Premier smiled appreciatively. "Aahh yes, we feel very warm here."

Then the Muslim leader, ever a militant, said, "I think you will find the people in Harlem are not so addicted to the propoganda they put out downtown."

In halting English, Dr. Castro said, "I admire this. I have seen how it is possible for propaganda to make changes in people. Your people live here and are faced with this propaganda all the time and yet, they understand. This is very interesting."

"There are 20 million of us," said Malcolm X, "and we always understand."

Members of the Castro party spilled over from an adjoining room, making the small quarters even more cramped. Most of the Cubans smoked long cigars and when something amused them, they threw their heads back and blew smoke puffs as they laughed.

Castro's conversational gestures were unusual. He would touch his temples with extended fingers as he made a point of tapping his chest as if to see if they were still there.

His interpreter would translate longer sentences from Malcolm X into Spanish and Castro would listen alertly and smile courteously.

During their conversation, Cuba's Castro and Harlem's Malcolm covered much political and philosophical ground.

On his troubles with the Shelburne Hotel, Dr. Castro said: "They have our money—$14,000. They didn't want us to come here. When they knew we were coming here, they wanted to come along."

(He did not clarify who "they" were in this instance.)

"On racial discrimination, we work for every oppressed

person." But he raised a cautioning hand. "I did not want to interfere in the inner policy of a country."

And then in a slight voice of warning, still on the general theme of racial inequity, Dr. Castro said, "I will speak in the Hall" (referring to the United Nations General Assembly).

On Africa:

"Is there any news on Lumumba?" Malcolm X smiled broadly at the mention of the Congolese leader's name. Castro then raised his hand. "We will try to defend him (Lumumba) strongly. I hope Lumumba stays here at the Theresa."

"There are 14 African nations coming to the Assembly. We are Latin Americans. We are their brothers."

On American Negroes:

Castro is fighting against discrimination in Cuba, everywhere.

"You lack rights and you want your rights."

"Our people are changing. Now we're one of the most free people in the world."

"Negroes in the U.S. have more political consciousness, more vision than anyone else."

On U.S.-Cuba relations:

In answer to Malcolm's statement that "As long as Uncle Sam is against you, you know you're a good man," Dr. Castro replied, "Not Uncle Sam. But those here who control magazines, newspapers . . ."

On the UN General Assembly:

"There will be a tremendous lesson to be learned at this session. Many things will happen in this session and the people will have a clearer idea of their rights."

Dr. Castro tapered the conversation off with an attempted quote of Lincoln. "You can fool some of the people some of the time . . ." but his English faltered and he threw up his hands as if to say, "you know what I mean."

Malcolm, rising to leave, explained his Muslim group for a Cuban reporter who had just come in. "We are followers of Muhammad. He says that we can sit and beg for 400 more years but if we want our rights now, we will have to . . . " Here he paused and smiled enigmatically. "Well . . . "

Castro smiled. He smiled again as Malcolm told him a parable. "No one knows the master better than his servants. We have been servants ever since we were brought here. We know all his little tricks. Understand? We know what he is going to do before he does."

The Cuban leader listened to this being translated into Spanish, then threw his head back and laughed heartily. "Sí," he said heartily, "Sí."

We said our adios and then walked down the crowded hall, took the elevator to the street where outside the crowds still milled around. Some excited Harlemite then shouted into the night, "Viva Castro!"

GEORGE LINCOLN
ROCKWELL AND THE NOI

Although George Lincoln Rockwell, founder of the American Nazi Party (ANP), may have seemed ideologically incongruous with the attitudes and theology of the Nation of Islam, in the early 1960s both he and Elijah Muhammad found reasons to coordinate and discuss strategies of racial separation. In one of the more bizarre pairings since Marcus Garvey sat down with Ku Klux Klan (KKK) imperial wizard Edward Young Clarke in 1922, Rockwell and the NOI had a standing relationship for the better part of two years, during which he and other ANP members attended several meetings and wrote articles supporting the black separatist group. Although Malcolm X was always uncomfortable with the relationship, Rockwell had little trouble finding common ground; just a year after Malcolm's assassination, in an interview with Alex Haley, Rockwell pronounced, "Malcolm X said the same thing I'm saying."[1]

The détente between the ANP and NOI was not without precedent. Earlier in 1961, Malcolm and minister Jeremiah Shabazz secretly met with the KKK in Atlanta, just as Garvey had done nearly forty years earlier. The meeting's purpose was

1. Alex Haley, "Interview with George Lincoln Rockwell," *Playboy* 13, 4 (April 1966): 71–72, 74, 76–82, 154, 156.

to secure farmland in the south for NOI business ventures while forming a nonaggression pact with the local Klan. The formal declaration of the ANP's relationship with the NOI came at a "Freedom Rally" in Washington, DC, at Uline Arena before a crowd of eight thousand. Rockwell and twenty "storm troopers" gathered to hear Malcolm X deliver a speech entitled "Separation or Death." Rockwell stated that "Muhammad has a solution for his people, and I have a solution for my people."[2]

In January 1962, Rockwell wrote to his followers in the party's newspaper, *The Rockwell Report*, that Elijah Muhammad "has gathered millions of the dirty, immoral, drunken, filthy-mouthed, lazy and repulsive people sneeringly called 'niggers' and inspired them to the point where they are clean, sober, honest, hard working, dignified, dedicated and admirable human beings in spite of their color."[3] The following month, Rockwell was invited to attend the NOI's yearly convention, Saviour's Day, in Chicago. There, in full Nazi regalia, he addressed the crowd of twelve thousand, stating that "no American white desires to intermix with black people." He then contributed twenty dollars to a collection plate being passed around; when Malcolm X asked who had given the money, one storm trooper shouted, "George Lincoln Rockwell." Rockwell then stood to recognize a smattering of applause. Malcolm chided, "You got the biggest hand you ever got."[4] Rockwell's appearance at NOI functions dwindled, but he was spotted in May of 1963 at the Los Angeles trial following the death of mosque member Ronald Stokes. Certainly the affinity between the NOI and the ANP was not well conceived, and Malcolm X used the meeting with the KKK as leverage against

2. "Separation—or Death: Muslim Watchword," *Amsterdam News*, July 1, 1961.

3. George Lincoln Rockwell, "The Jew: Moment of Lies in the South," *The Rockwell Report*, January 3, 1962.

4. William H. Schmaltz, *Hate: George Lincoln Rockwell and the American Nazi Party* (Washington, DC: Batsford Brassey, 1999), 120–21; and "Separation—or Death," *Amsterdam News*.

Elijah Muhammad once their relationship had soured. But the continued negotiations with white racists, during a time when blacks in the South were being beaten, harassed, and murdered, is one of the most disturbing facts in the history of the NOI and Malcolm X's career.

- "Separation—or Death: Muslim Watchword," *Amsterdam News*, July 1, 1961

- George Lincoln Rockwell, "Black Muslims Hear U.S. Nazi," *The Rockwell Report*, April 1, 1962

Further reading:

- "Muslims Heading for Washington," *Amsterdam News*, June 17, 1961

- "Muslims' Defense Opened on Coast," *New York Times*, May 12, 1963

- Raymond Sharrieff FBI file, summary report, Chicago office, February 8, 1962, pages 17–18

"Separation—or Death: Muslim Watchword," *Amsterdam News*, July 1, 1961

In striking contrast to the non-violent civil rights movement to completely and peaceably integrate Negroes in all spheres of th national life, the nation's black Muslims served notice Sunday on the Government at a mass rally in Washington, D.C., that they would "not turn the other cheek" in their quest for separation of the races.

The Muslim ultimatum for "Separation or Death" was issued by Malcolm X, Harlem minister of Muhammed Temple No. 2 at W. 116th St. and Lenox Ave., and Wallace D. Muhammed, son of Elijah Muhammed and minister of Philadelphia Muslims, at the Uline Arena.

Muslim officials estimated that 10,000 black Muslims from all sections of the nation met at the arena, but other sources gave the number as about 7,500.

The rally was described as a "Freedom Rally" to urge the Government to separate the Muslims and the nation's Negroes, rather than integrate them as the southern Negro sit-ins are seeking.

"We don't intend to turn the other cheek," Muhammed's son said at the rally which unofficial sources said included 30 to 40 whites.

"We are a peaceful people, but we can cause a great deal of trouble," Muhammed said. He added that the nation's black Muslims can cause the deaths of "1,000 persons a minute for every minute that we last," in any showdown between their forces and the "forces of oppression."

Muhammed spoke in place of his father, leader of the nation's black Muslims, who was said to have been sick in Chicago. He He was to be the leadoff speaker at the three-hour rally.

Muhammed's son also said that the Muslims are tired of the white man's efforts to integrate Negroes, for whom integration can only be another one of the many pills given them to put them into a deep political stupor.

He suggested that separation of the races was the Negro's only salvation.

Malcolm X, who was also a key speaker at the rally which was assertedly attended by 3,000 Muslims from the New York area, said there were no known high governmental officials at the rally, but added that he knew other governmental officials, as well as FBI agents, had attended the mass confab.

"Any Negro trying to integrate is actually admitting his inferiority, because he is also admitting that he wants to become a part of a 'superior' society," Malcolm X said.

Commenting on the rally, he said that the "white man was surprised that so many black people would show up in support of complete separation, rather than for integration."

According to the Harlem Muslim, 31 bus loads of Muslims left New York Sunday morning for the rally.

The biggest delegations, he said, came from Newark, which sent 13 bus loads, Philadelphia, which sent 16 bus loads, Chicago, which sent 8, Boston, which sent 7, and Hartford, which sent 5. He said a large delegation also was sent from California.

Malcolm X said that Elijah Muhammed will speak at another rally which will be held sometime in August, either at Madison Square Garden or at the 369th Regiment Armory in Harlem.

George Lincoln Rockwell, the American Nazi fuehrer, who was banned from Alabama and Mississippi during the height of the Freedom Riders tour through those two states, assertedly contributed $20 to the Muslims Sunday because "Muhammad has a solution for his people, and I have a solution for my people."

Malcolm X described the Sunday meeting in the nation's capital as quiet, without any disturbances. He commended the police for their courteous cooperation.

George Lincoln Rockwell, "Black Muslims Hear U.S. Nazi," *The Rockwell Report*, April 1, 1962

On February 25, 1962, I stood up in full Nazi uniform before 12,500 Black Muslims and gave an all-out speech calling for the geographical separation of the races, with America's "foreign aid" going to our own Negro people rather than to Red and "neutralist" nations which hate us, shoot up and imprison our citizens and spit in our faces.

Again and again my speech was interrupted by applause and cheers from these thousands of Black men and women who, we are told in our Jew-ized press, are "hate" people, bent on murder and massacre. At the end, I gave a Nazi salute and shouted "Heil Hitler!"—and got first applause, and then some Boo's.

Then a rich, well-fed Negro with a Phi Bete key dangling from his gold watch got up and said he was from the NAACP. He raved and ranted at Elijah Muhammad for allowing me to speak. He got so worked up he began to scream unintelligibly, so that nobody could even understand a word he said! His face was PURPLE with HATE, all the while he was blasting the Muslims and the Nazis for being "hate people."

Following him, a man who said he was an Arab, but whom I suspect was a Jew, got up and told the WORST lies I have ever heard. He told that audience of Black Men that Africa had been full of goose-stepping Nazis before the War, and that these awful Nazis marched all over Africa torturing and murdering innocent Negroes! Some of the audience believed him and applauded these horrible lies.

I wondered what Elijah Muhammad would say about all this. Every other leader in America had RUN A WAY from me when I stood up and told the simple TRUTH. Now they were calling this Black Leader a "Nazi" for letting me tell the SAME TRUTH HE IS PREACHING. What would he do?

The Honorable Elijah Muhammad stood up, and hush fell over the vast sea of people. Then this black leader showed why he is destined to lead the Black people out of bondage and into their OWN DIGNITY AND FREEDOM.

"The German Nazis are not Hypocrites!," he said (he meant American Nazis) "—they tell you the truth! The White Man does not want to mix! And the Black Man want to be HIM-SELF, not somebody else. HE does not want to MIX! Only the boot-licking so called 'Negro' comes to another race begging to 'mix'! I TAKE MY HAT OFF TO ANY WHITE MAN WHO WANTS TO STAY WHITE!"

"Why should you not applaud this White Man for telling you the same truths I tell you?" asked this courageous Black Leader—and he was swamped with ten thousand cheers.

Here was the most smashing, dramatic possible refutation of the Jew lie that the Muslims and Nazis are "hate" groups; here was the leader who was supposed to want to kill all white men actually praising and "taking his hat off" to not only a white man but an ALL-OUT white man fighting for the survival and dignity of the White Race.

BAYARD RUSTIN DEBATE
AT HOWARD UNIVERSITY

Despite some trepidation on the part of Elijah Muhammad, who viewed forays into the public intellectual sphere with skepticism, in the early 1960s Malcolm X undertook a series of college debates with significant figures in the civil rights movement. One of these was with longtime civil rights activist Bayard Rustin at the prominent black institution Howard University. The events leading up to the debate illustrate the divisive position Malcolm and the NOI held within the black community. After inviting him to speak as part of Negro History Week in February 1961, the campus chapter of the NAACP could not secure approval from the Student Activities Office. The students then rescheduled at New Bethel Baptist Church, but the church later balked, saying that the expected audience was too large for the venue.[1]

How the lecture finally came to fruition as an October debate with Bayard Rustin is still mysterious. It is possible that E. Franklin Frazier, who had been associated with the university since the mid-1930s, intervened, convincing the school that an integrationist voice like Rustin's be present to counterbalance Malcolm X's separatism. According to Rustin, Malcolm first broached the subject of the canceled lecture, and Rustin replied that he could convince Howard if Malcolm

---

1. "Muslim Malcolm X Out as Howard U. History Speaker," *Pittsburgh Courier*, February 25, 1961.

agreed to his terms: "You'll present your view, and I'll present a view which says that you're a fraud. You have no political, no social, no economic program for dealing with the black community and its problem."[2] Malcolm allegedly took the challenge, and Rustin wrote to Howard University's president, who supported the debate. Rustin claimed that the university was reluctant to have Malcolm alone because it could jeopardize its federal funding.

The debate took place before a capacity crowd of fifteen hundred, with five hundred left outside Cramton Auditorium. Eager to avenge a debate on WBAI radio the year before, in which he had been outmaneuvered by Rustin, Malcolm rallied the crowd by speaking not as "a Republican, Democrat, Christian or Jew, and certainly not as an American," but as a "BLACK MAN!"[3] Although Rustin pressed against what many viewed as the NOI's weak point, the unlikelihood of a separate state, Malcolm captured the support of the more radical student audience and left Howard University's old guard teetering. One professor left the auditorium saying, "Howard will never be the same. I feel a reluctance to face my class tomorrow."[4] Malcolm X and Rustin continued to cross paths over the next several years, both in debates and at the 1963 March on Washington—Rustin as a chief architect of the march, and Malcolm as an observer and critic.

- "Muslim Malcolm X Out as Howard U. History Speaker," *Pittsburgh Courier*, February 25, 1961

2. Reminiscences of Bayard Rustin: Oral History, 1987, Columbia University Oral History Research Office.

3. Howard University lecture, October 30, 1961, Malcolm X Collection, Box 5, Folder 15, Schomburg Center for Research in Black Culture, New York Public Library.

4. "1500 Hear Integration–Non-segregation Debate," *Chicago Defender*, November 11, 1961.

- Reminiscences of Bayard Rustin (1987), on pages 217–19 in the Columbia University Center for Oral History Collection (hereafter CUCOHC)

Further reading:

- "Malcolm X at Howard as Speaker," *Amsterdam News*, February 11, 1961
- "Malcolm May, May Not Talk at Howard," *Amsterdam News*, February 25, 1961
- "1500 Hear Integration–Non-segregation Debate," *Chicago Defender*, November 11, 1961
- Malcolm X FBI file, summary report, New York office, May 17, 1962, pages 18–19

"Muslim Malcolm X Out as Howard U. History Speaker," *Pittsburgh Courier*, February 25, 1961

WASHINGTON, D.C.—The Howard University student chapter of the National Association for the Advancement of Colored People had to withdraw its invitation for Malcolm X, New York leader of the Black Muslims, to address the students on the campus during Negro History Week.

The students originally planned Mr. X's appearance on the campus for Tuesday, Feb. 14, for Negro History Week, but when the Howard University officials learned that the guest speaker was to be the "controversial" Mr. X, the students were immediately notified that Malcolm X's appearance "had not, as prescribed, been registered in advance with the Student Activities Office."

School officials "explained" that the faculty Committee on Student Organizations and Activities must approve in advance all student programs.

Officials then pointed out that the committee "did not have time" to meet and decide whether to clear the program in time for Mr. X's scheduled appearance.

The student chapter then obtained the use of New Bethel Baptist Church, Ninth and S Sts., NW, but Douglas Jones, program chairman of the chapter, decided to cancel the program completely because "the church was not large enough for the many students planning to attend."

Minister Malcolm X, New York representative of Muslim spiritual leader Elijah Muhammad, has lectured and debated at some of the nation's leading educational institutions, including Yale and Boston Universities, and Hunter, Queens, Clark and Morehouse Colleges.

He also has an invitation to address the Harvard Law School Forum this spring.

Mr. Jones said the NAACP students' chapter still hopes to bring Malcolm X to the Howard campus, and Carl Anderson, director of student activities, said his office and the committee would consider the proposal when it is properly presented.

"We don't try to tell the students whom to invite or not to invite," Anderson said. "If we feel that what the speaker will have to say is pertinent to American life, we certainly permit the invitation."

Meanwhile, the unperturbed Malcolm X has been invited by the New York City College students chapter of the NAACP to debate "Islam vs Christianity" with Rev. C. Lawrence on the CCNY campus at noon, March 2.

The Muslim minister is scheduled to debate TV writer Louis E. Lomax, on "Separation or Integration" over Radio WINS on March 10, and has also been invited to Clark College in Atlanta on March 17 to debate Rev. Samuel Williams, famed Morehouse theology and philosophy professor.

RUSTIN: Oh yes. I had met with Malcolm several times. Malcolm and I were very good friends. One of the reasons Malcolm and I became good friends is that when Malcolm came to me and told me that he had been refused the right to go to Howard University to lecture, after the students had invited him, I said, "Well, that's absolutely ridiculous. If you want to go, I can make it possible for you to go—but you've got to go on my terms." He said, "What are your terms?" I said, "You go, and we'll have a debate. You'll present your view, and I'll present a view which says that you're a fraud. You have no political, no social, no economic program for dealing with the black community and its problem." He says, "Okay, I'll take you up on that." So I wrote to the president of Howard University, Mordicai Johnson, and I said—was it Mordicai then? Well, whoever it was. I said, "I would like to appear in a debate at Howard University. Malcolm X." Now Howard University had no objection to Malcolm coming on campus. What they had objection to was the fact that they didn't want to run in to members of the Senate and the House about having him there, when they have to go like no other college in the United States. Howard University is the only college in the United States which gets its appropriation from the Congress of the United States. Did you know that?

Q: No, I did not.

RUSTIN: Well, that goes all the way back to the Freedmen's Bureau. Howard University grew out of the Freedmen's Bureau. It's the only college that gets its money from the Congress of the United States. So the president, of course, is terrified that somebody told them about their having Malcolm. But if they were justified in saying that he was debating someone, they were safe. So Malcolm was very appreciative of my opening up that possibility, because I said to Malcolm, "Once you speak at Howard, which is supported by the federal government, the rest of these black colleges will be afraid not to have you," which turned out to be the case.

So I had talked with Malcolm any number of times. I said, "You know Malcolm, you're not going to do yourself any damn good coming down in Washington denouncing something like the march. What Malcolm did was not denounce the march, but something equally naughty. When they came to him after King's speech, "I have a dream," on the ground there and said to Malcolm, "Well, Dr. King's speech 'I have a dream' was a great speech, wasn't it." He says, "You may think it was a great speech, but I can tell you his bloody dream will turn in to a nightmare." [laughter] Malcolm always had the last and the most exciting words.

Now, I never had any trouble with Malcolm, and Randolph was greatly respected by Malcolm because when Randolph set up in 1961 an economic conference, something called the Harlem Economic Conference, that was simply a meeting in Randolph's office which took place once a month where all the blacks met, for Randolph's trying again to prepare them for the fact that once we have won the right to vote, the right to public accommodations and all these other rights under law, the trouble just begins. Because then you're going to be up against the economic question, same thing that I was saying his analysis was of the March on Washington. When the black Christian leadership of Harlem said to Mr. Randolph, "If that Malcolm X is coming, we will not come to these meetings of the economic summit." Mr. Randolph said, "I am very sorry. Malcolm X is welcome, as any of you are welcome." While three or four of the black leaders from the churches refused to come, most of them did come, and Malcolm also came. Malcolm never forgot Mr. Randolph for having done that.

JAMES FARMER DEBATE
AT CORNELL UNIVERSITY

Malcolm X continued his string of college debates with a 1961
appearance at Cornell University, where he took on Congress
of Racial Equality (CORE) executive director James Farmer.
Sponsored by the Cornell Committee Against Segregation, the
speech was on a familiar theme: separation or integration? Although the pitting of a prominent integrationist against Malcolm's separatist views had become a familiar strategy, the
black nationalist leader was caught off guard by Farmer's
and CORE's stance, which was significantly more militant
than the attitudes of the NAACP he had previously argued
against. Later that year the Freedom Riders would make significant strides in the South, further challenging Malcolm's
position that integration was an untenable position. Despite
Malcolm's attacks on integration as a solution promoted only
by the black middle class, Farmer challenged him to create a
better solution: "We know the disease, physician, what is your
cure? What is your program and how do you hope to bring it into
effect?"[1] Ultimately, Malcolm resorted to the charge that Farmer
was married to a white woman. However, despite the inef-
fectiveness of many of his arguments at the debate, Malcolm
continued to make inroads among CORE's constituents and
other more activist-oriented movements. Malcolm's position,

1. Malcolm X and James Farmer, "Separation or Integration: A Debate," *Dialogue* 2, 3 (May 1962): 14–18.

however, continued to be complicated by Elijah Muhammad's insistence that he remain silent on political matters. The following year Muhammad wrote his national spokesman: "When you go to these Colleges and Universities to represent the Teachings that Allah has revealed to me for our people, do not go too much into the details of the political side . . . speak only what you know they have heard me say or that which you yourself have heard me say."[2] The debate with Farmer was emblematic of Malcolm's tenuous position within the NOI and foreshadowed greater challenges he would face in the coming years. It also anticipated his growing appeal to a younger generation of activists within the civil rights movement.

- Joe Matasich, "2 Negroes with Opposing Views Debate Segregation-Integration," *Ithaca Journal*, March 8, 1962

Further reading:

- Malcolm X and James Farmer, "Separation or Integration: A Debate," *Dialogue* 2, 3 (May 1962): pages 14–18; also reprinted in August Meier, Elliott Rudwick, and Francis Broderick, eds., *Black Protest Thought in the Twentieth Century* (Indianapolis: Bobbs-Merrill, 1971), pages 387–412

- Malcolm X FBI file, summary report, New York office, May 17, 1962, page 23

2. Elijah Muhammad to Malcolm X, February 15, 1962, Malcolm X Collection, box 3, folder 8, Schomburg Center for Research in Black Culture, New York Public Library.

Joe Matasich, "2 Negroes with Opposing Views Debate Segregation-Integration," *Ithaca Journal*, March 8, 1962

Fanatical Malcolm X, top sergeant for Elijah Muhammad's Black Muslim movement, attacked everything except motherhood here Wednesday night in a fireball debate with James Farmer, national director of the Congress of Racial Equality (CORE).

And time and his Allah permitting, Mr. X would probably have done that too.

In presenting his argument for complete separation of blacks and whites and the creation of an independent black nation, Malcolm X rattled off insults against the federal government, all whites, Negroes who don't agree with the Muslims, and even found time to take a poke at Christianity—ironically on Ash Wednesday night.

Farmer, one of the founders of CORE and leader in the non-violent civil rights movement, labeled the Muslim's views as impractical and supported his argument with the claim that non-violence is the key to common humanity.

Both men presented their arguments in 20 minute presentations, 10-minute rebuttals, cross-examined each other's views for another 10 minutes, and answered questions from the floor.

A turn-away crowd in the Myron Taylor Moot Courtroom applauded the speakers, and many times hissed the Muslim spokesman. Sponsored by Dialogue magazine, "Which Way Civil Rights: Separation or Integration?" the debate was moderated by the Rev. L. Paul Jacquith, director of Cornell United Religious Work (CURW). It was be aired at 5 p.m. Sunday over WVBR-FM Radio.

JAMES FARMER: MASSES TIRED
OF SEGREGATION

Farmer, first leader of the "Freedom Ride," to Jackson, Miss., described the race problem as a disease that has affected and crippled the Negro and the white man.

Speaking eloquently and maintaining complete composure even when Malcolm X made several remarks about Farmer's wife being a white woman, the director of CORE spoke against the racists who claim Negroes are inferior to whites.

This has resulted in four problems and he described them as psychological, economic, social and political.

"One tenth of the population of the people who could produce are being denied work. We share the guilt for the system of segregation and its existence. He said the Negroes are as much to blame as the whites since they have been supporting and perpetuating segregation in the South.

"I myself did this at one time when as a young man in Texas I would sit in the balcony of the theater because Negroes were not allowed anyplace else."

Farmer said the masses are tired of putting up with segregation and Negroes want to solve their own problem.

"The time has come when the little man can be involved in this fight. We no longer have to wait for the law." Farmer reminded the audience of lunchcounter integration in 150 cities.

Farmer, who spent 40 days in several Mississippi and other southern jails in "Freedom Ride" demonstrations said, "the rides, by and large, have been successful."

"We're not looking for the pie in the sky, but things are being done. And we'll be eating our Easter dinner in any restaurant we want on Rte. 40 between Wilmington and Washington.

Farmer consistently peppered Mr. X as to the exact plan of the Black Muslims and their black nation project.

In his rebuttal to Malcolm, Farmer said, "If you think the Negro should be allowed to go back to where he came from

(Africa) then we should give this land back to the Indians, and so on."

Farmer defended remarks made about his marriage and answered Mr. X with, "I have so much faith that I don't think virtue will be corrupted by association."

Farmer disagreed with Mr. X that the black man has patterned his life after the white. "I don't know about that. Whites imitate the kinky hair style, copy our jazz and (with a brush of his hand over his face) there's even Man Tan. (a tanning lotion)"

Farmer said Negro integrationists come solely from the middle class. "We have many unemployed workers among our groups."

Mr. X said the majority of CORE's sit-in demonstrators were whites, but Farmer volleyed back that he was incorrect, that the majority was composed of Negroes.

Farmer pointed out that he visited Africa three years ago and said, "Culture in Africa is very different. We have much more in common here."

The integrationist claimed Americans refuse to practice freedom, democracy and equality although they believe in it. He described this as a split personality, a double-edged sword of prejudice.

Farmer said CORE and other integrationist groups are shooting for the day when Negroes will enter all professions.

"We must achieve this through non violent demonstrations," Farmer said.

Farmer repeatedly put the issue at the feet of Mr. X by asking the exact plans of the Muslims in their black nation movement.

And when he finally got the answer, Farmer rolled his eyes and smiled, saying, "Oh, I see. You mean Allah hasn't decided yet and it's all a big secret."

Midway through the debate the speakers started calling each other "brother." This term was quickly picked up by those asking questions.

Farmer often referred to quotes and sylogisms.

When Malcolm repeated that Muslims want to "get out of the house of the white man and discontinue forcing ourselves on the white man," Farmer said:

"I remember a sylogism as a college freshman that went something like—I have a dog, my dog has spots, therefore all dogs have spots."

MALCOLM X: WHITE IS WHITE; BLACK IS BLACK

Malcolm X, born in Iowa, the son of a slave woman, for 30 minutes of debate, dodged Farmer's question: How, when and where will the Black Muslims set up their own nation?

The bespectacled leader of one of the fastest growing mass movements in the United States was finally pinned in the cross examination period and answered that the Muslim's Allah has not decided when these events will take place. "No followers of the honorable Elijah Muhammad know what he has in mind. When the federal government makes up its mind about this and tells Allah is when the Black Muslims will know," Mr. X explained.

Mr. X, who denounces Christianity, once got excited in answering a question from the floor and shouted, "My God-given rights."

Mr. X explained he had taken only the first name, that given by his slave mother, and dropped the last name, Little, because, "I don't know my last name. The white man has robbed me of it like he has other blacks." And he further explained, in answering the question of a student from Africa, that his Muslim name is Malik Shaboz, the one he uses in traveling.

Malcolm, whose slender physique and glasses give him the appearance of a young student, claims conversion to Islam while serving a prison sentence in Concord, Mass.

While he shouted and excitedly stuttered out his anti (which he claims are not anti) charges, one of the members of the

"Fruit of Islam" guards sat about 15 feet away. The "Fruit of Islam" is the elite Muslim para-military organization.

Mr. X explained that Muslims work to rehabilitate the "so-called Negro" who has fallen under the influence of the "blue-eyed devil." The cult's tactics include establishing the Negro's self-sufficiency, restoring family life under a strict moral code, and finally the complete separation of the black and white races.

"We don't spend money on night clubs, liquor, narcotics and women like we did when we were Christians," hollered out Mr. X. The finely-dressed Malcolm said the group's emphasis is on frugality.

Mr. X, in explaining why the cult calls itself Muslim, and not Moslems, waved his hand and said, "Moslems are Muslims and Muslims are Moslems."

"The white man is making us something different . . . a monster . . . completely robbed of his culture. The black man doesn't know who he is. He has a white heart, white brain, but is black on the outside and white on the inside. And then he wants your way of life, your job, your home and your women too."

Hissing and boos interrupted the fired-up Mr X at this point, and he cracked, "That's okay, the serpents hissed in the garden too." The leader of some 100,000 Negroes in America said the teachings of Allah predict the separation of the black and white races.

Malcolm repeated many times that the racial issue has not, and cannot be solved through workings of non-violent groups, that government and laws have failed to do anything, and that the Black Muslims feel the only solution to the problem is complete separation.

"What we want is some of that money and energy to show us how to do the things whitemen have done so that we can do those things ourselves."

"And we're not going to get it through a cup of coffee. I'll never take part in a sit-in because if someone forces me with a club or attacks, I would have to rely on my equality, my God-given rights, and use the same force in retaliation."

To this Farmer said, "And we don't want you either."

The Muslims use as their motto, "an eye for any Eye, a tooth for a tooth," and although they preach against aggression, they support active retaliation in the event they are attacked.

Malcolm said the white man is a hypocrite and supported his claim by referring to the Constitution and the Supreme court ruling on desegregation eight years ago.

"We don't want to integrate with someone who says one thing and preaches another." Mr. X referred to the change in the secretarial and presidential positions the past two years in the United Nations, both formerly held by white Christians, now held by the black man.

"While the white world is getting more quiet, the black world is getting more loud. We're living in an era of great change."

At the outset Mr. X went so far as to go along with integration, "if it restores human dignity," as he put it. "But if it doesn't, out the window with integration and let's get another method."

Mr. X tossed a few barbs at what he called the "bourgeois" group of Negroes, the middle and upper class, who believe in the American dream of integration. "We call it a nightmare."

"We've been giving slave labor for 400 years and we're not going to get sufficient repayment through any Jackie Robinsons, Marian Andersons or a cup of coffee."

The cultist criticized intermarriages, and after Farmer brought up the point that the Muslims have attack him for marrying a white woman, Mr. X expounded his and the Muslim beliefs of black and white marriages.

And before he was through, Malcolm predicted that the teachings of Muhammad predict the eventual destruction of the white man.

When an 18-year-old Negro girl asked Malcolm if she should go to a black nation (as he suggested) and change her way of life after living in a society she knows and likes, Malcolm advised, "If that's what you like and want, you don't change. We feel there's no skin lost there."

RONALD STOKES'S MURDER

Having already battled against police brutality in the case of Johnson X Hinton and in his own Queens home the following year, it was in late April of 1962 that Malcolm X faced what many cite as the greatest tragedy during his tenure with the Nation of Islam. In what journalist Peter Goldman termed "a sort of *volte-face* version of the Johnson parable," Los Angeles police hassled several Mosque No. 27 members who were unloading dry cleaning from their car.[1] The officers were suspicious, due to a series of clothing store burglaries in the area, and confronted the men. A scuffle ensued, the details of which are still confused. However, after what the *Los Angeles Times* later dubbed a "blazing gunfight" (despite the fact that none of the Muslims were armed), seven mosque members were shot, many through the back. One was paralyzed, another five were injured, and most dramatically, Korean War veteran and mosque secretary Ronald X Stokes was shot and killed at close range while walking toward an officer with his hands raised.[2]

The day before conducting Stokes's funeral before nearly two

---

1. Peter Goldman, *The Death and Life of Malcolm X*, 2nd ed. (Urbana: University of Illinois Press, 1979), 97.

2. For a full account, see Frederick Knight, "Justifiable Homicide, Police Brutality, or Governmental Repression? The 1962 Los Angeles Police Shooting of Seven Members of the Nation of Islam," *Journal of Negro History*, 79, 2 (Spring 1994): 182–96.

thousand mourners, Malcolm held a press conference at the Statler-Hilton Hotel in Los Angeles. There he framed the crime in racial rather than religious terms, attempting to mobilize the black civil rights groups and leaders he had often publicly criticized. A telegram from Roy Wilkins was read at the press conference and reprinted in the NOI's official organ, *Muhammad Speaks*, in which the NAACP leader assured full support. Malcolm appeared on a Pacifica Radio show, alongside James Farmer and William Worthy, to discuss the "crisis of racism." He then spoke at the local Second Baptist Church before a joint meeting organized along with local ministers and politicians.[3]

In addition to his participation in rallies featuring a cross-section of black civic and religious organizations, Malcolm continued to downplay religious differences and stress the need for a black united front. At a protest rally sponsored by the Los Angeles County Civic League, he urged the heads of all black organizations to meet and pursue a unified strategy, stating: "Police brutality must end before something happens that can't be stopped. We must come together against the common enemy. Remember all of us are black. It's not a Muslim fight. It's a black man's fight."[4] Even Elijah Muhammad, who generally shied away from the political sphere, called for a united black coalition. "In these crucial times," *Muhammad Speaks* editorialized, "we must not think in terms of one's religion, but in terms of justice for us poor black people. This means a United Black Front for justice in America."[5]

Where Muhammad and Malcolm X differed drastically was not in their rhetorical but their physical responses to the attack. Malcolm saw the brutality at Mosque No. 27 as more than a basic violation of human rights and dignity. He had personally organized the mosque in the late 1950s and knew several of the victims intimately, including Ronald Stokes.

3. Malcolm X FBI file, summary report, New York office, November 16, 1962.

4. Ibid.

5. "Muhammad Calls for United Black Front!" *Muhammad Speaks*, June 1962.

Malcolm felt that Stokes's death called for immediate retribution, and before leaving for Stokes's funeral, he anticipated organized retaliation: "I got to go out there now and do what I've been preaching all this time."[6]

Conversely, Muhammad took an apocalyptic and prophetic approach to the events, even privately criticizing the mosque members for allowing an "aggressor to come into their mosque."

Despite Malcolm's readiness to bring retaliatory violence to Los Angeles, Muhammad advised him to "cool it" and asked his followers to "hold fast to Islam."[7] Perhaps most difficult for Malcolm was bringing the news back home to Harlem. Before a crowd of several thousand in Harlem Square, he had to publicly justify Muhammad's stance and advise that they "play it cool, calm, and collected. And leave it in the hands of God."[8] Over a year and a half before the public split between Malcolm X and Elijah Muhammad, the Stokes incident provided what would come to be regarded as the most illustrative example of the two men's diverging religious and political visions.

- "Muslims and Police," *Amsterdam News*, May 12, 1962
- Lois Saunders, "L.A. Negro Community Unites in Defense of Black Muslims," *The Militant*, May 21, 1962

Further reading:

- "Cultist Is Slain Battling Police," *New York Times*, April 29, 1962
- "Study Shows Los Angeles Police Were Investigating Muslims at Time of Riot," *Amsterdam News*, May 12, 1962

6. Goldman, *Death and Life*, 98.

7. Claude Andrew Clegg III, *An Original Man: The Life and Times of Elijah Muhammad* (New York: St. Martin's Griffin, 1997), 171.

8. "Malcolm X: Make It Plain," directed by Orlando Bagwell for *American Experience*, PBS Video, 1994.

- "Police Criticized in Muslim Slaying," *Amsterdam News*, May 12, 1962

- "Cops Slay Muslim on Coast," *Amsterdam News*, May 5, 1962

- "Charge Muslim Was 'Murdered,'" *Amsterdam News*, May 5, 1962

- "Muhammad Calls for United Black Front!" *Muhammad Speaks*, June 1962

- "Malcolm X Raps Trial of 14 Muslims in L.A.," *Chicago Defender*, December 5, 1962

- Malcolm X, interviewed by Dick Elman, May 1, 1962, Pacifica Radio Archives, BB0541

- Malcolm X FBI file, summary report, New York office, November 16, 1962, pages 15–23

- Raymond Sharrieff FBI file, summary report, Chicago office, August 19, 1963, page 6

"Muslims and Police,"
Amsterdam News, May 12, 1962

The following is the reprint of an editorial which appeared in the California Eagle after police shot and killed an unarmed Muslim and seriously wounded six others:

The killing of one man and the wounding of six others last Friday in a wild burst of gunfire that came as the aftermath of a routine police shakedown of an automobile and a pair of burglary suspects was the almost inevitable outcome of an ever mounting hostility between police and residents of the Negro community. In a sense, it had to happen.

It had to happen because relations between Negroes and the police have been stretched to the breaking point where only a trifling incident was needed to set off a conflict. Negroes, as James Baldwin has pointed out, look upon the police with the same distrust with which a conquered people views an army of occupation. In their proper turn, police officers, fed on a steady diet of statistics seeming to prove Negro criminality, tend to regard all Negroes as opponents and potential lawbreakers.

Friday's incident got out of hand more readily because the police were confronted with a Muslim group. Muslim distrust of the police rests on Muslim doctrine that all Whites are the Negroes' natural enemies and on repeated police denunciation of the cult. The police attitude toward the Muslims is a compound of hate and fear—hatred of the Muslim anti-white doctrine, fear of the Muslims as their enemies. The stage was set for violence.

The fact that the dead man and the six wounded were all Muslims does not excuse the police for the wild shooting spree that ensued. The evidence is irrestible that the Muslims were not armed and that they had no arms in their meeting place. The melancholy truth is that the police lost their heads and fired on their opponents out of vengeance and fright. It takes a lot of shooting to kill one man and wound six others.

Armed police officers who can't quell an unarmed group of fifty persons without that much bloodshed either lack the training or the desire to do so. Every Negro who looked at newspaper photos of the dead and wounded lying in the sidewalk after Friday's affray must have shuddered to himself that there but for the grace of God he lay, or his son lay.

We do not condone Muslim teaching that whips up promiscuous hatred of white persons. We have said so many times. We reiterate it now. We think that the Muslim way, like that of white groups such as the Klan and the White Citizens Councils, is more than mistaken; it's dangerous and beckons Negroes into a blind alley of frustration and despair.

On the other hand we know that guns will not meet, or defeat, Muslim arguments. Friday's bloodshed will only arm them with new arguments that "White Devils" are out to defend racial discrimination with bullets and blackjacks.

It seems to us that the bloody incident requires a thorough investigation by a disinterested agency such as the attorney general's office, an investigation that will lay bare the reasons for the deteriorating relations between Negroes and police officers and offer suggestions for remedies.

Unless there is a thorough investigation Friday's incident will fester and nourish a whole new set of conflicts between Negro citizens and police that will finally build up into a riot that will make last week's incident seem like child's play.

Lois Saunders, "L.A. Negro Community Unites in Defense of Black Muslims," *The Militant*, May 21, 1962

LOS ANGELES, May 12—The police shooting of unarmed Muslims April 27 has created the sharpest division ever witnessed here between the Negro community and the city authorities.

Immediately after the shooting, in which one man was killed and six others wounded, Police Chief William H. Parker issued statements blaming the Black Muslims, in an obvious attempt to deprive them of community support.

As it became apparent that this maneuver was failing, city authorities extended their fire to the local branch of the NAACP and other groups accusing the police of brutality.

Coming in for special criticism is Mayor Samuel W. Yorty, who told his press conference last Wednesday that he is "100 per cent behind Chief Parker." In last year's elections, Negroes gave impressive support to Yorty, largely because they believed he would "do something" about police brutality.

Indicating his administration intends to use the shooting as an excuse for trying to smash the local Muslim movement—and to show the Negro community who is boss—Mayor Yorty said he plans to ask Attorney General Robert Kennedy to place the Muslims on the subversive list. Such a listing, he reportedly stated, would enable police to take drastic measures, close down Muslim meeting places, seize their literature and force a curtailment of their activities.

The mayor also scored local NAACP officials for branding the shooting an extreme example of police brutality and said the demand for a Police Review Board to investigate charges against police officers is "Communist inspired."

After the shooting, 17 Muslims, including the six wounded, were arrested and charged with assault with intent to commit murder. These charges have now been reduced to assault with intent to commit great bodily harm, but may again be modified following a grand jury hearing scheduled for May 15.

May 13—An outpouring of 3,000 Negroes, filling the Second Baptist Church to overflowing, gave notice here today that the Negro community is resolved to call a halt to the Gestapo-like police terror rampant in minority areas here.

The rally, called by Negro leaders, emphatically gave the lie to statements by Mayor Yorty and his police chief, Parker, that the Negro community is divided about support of the unarmed Black Muslims who were shot down in an unprovoked assault April 27.

The meeting passed unanimous resolutions condemning police brutality in Los Angeles and calling for investigations of the police department by local, state and national bodies.

Learning of the presence in its midst of Malcolm X, a national leader of the Muslims, the audience called him to the speaker's stand. He urged solidarity of Negro, Mexican-American and other minority groups to combat police terror. "Today, it is our temple," Malcolm X warned, "but tomorrow it will be your churches, your lodges and your synagogues."

A collection of more than $900 was taken for the purpose of continuing the action begun by today's meeting. Another mass rally, called by the Muslims, will be held May 20.

NOI ANSWERS
MUSLIM CRITICS

By the time Malcolm X had been named its national spokes-man in 1961, the Nation of Islam had come under public scru-tiny from groups ranging from conservative whites to civil rights leaders. However, after trips to the Middle East by Mal-colm X and Elijah Muhammad in 1959, as well as the organ-ization's increased public profile, another group joined the chorus of criticism: orthodox Muslim organizations in the U.S. The NOI was preceded by other predominantly African American Muslim groups, such as Noble Drew Ali's Moorish Science Temple and the Ahmadiyya Movement in Islam (AMI). Just as the NAACP scrambled to distance itself from the NOI in the aftermath of *The Hate That Hate Produced*, the AMI and orthodox Muslims launched attacks charging that the NOI's religious heterodoxy in fact crossed into heresy.

Talib Dawud, a jazz trumpeter and prolific proselytizer asso-ciated with the Moslem Brotherhood of America, Inc., first at-tacked the NOI in 1959 with a series of articles in the black Chicago newspaper the *New Crusader*. The most scathing was a photograph of NOI founder W. D. Fard, whom the group be-lieved to be Allah in person, paired with the headline: "White Man Is God for Cult of Islam."[1] The NOI found the article so

1. "White Man Is God for Cult of Islam," *New Crusader*, August 15, 1959.

disturbing that the Chicago and New York mosques worked to purchase and destroy as many copies of the issue as possible. Along with jazz pianist Ahmad Jamal, Dawud and his wife, Dakota Staton (Aliyah Rabia), also slandered the NOI by claiming that Elijah Muhammad could not perform the hajj in 1959 because the Saudi Arabian government had banned him as an inauthentic Muslim. Eventually, Dawud's monopoly on the *New Crusader* disintegrated, and bitterness between the groups peaked in 1962 when Dawud sued Muhammad, enjoining a district court to disallow the terms "Islam" or "Muslim" in association with the sect. Malcolm finally unleashed his assault against Staton, a jazz vocalist: "Even the non-Muslim public knows that no Muslim sister who follows Mr. Muhammad would think of singing sexy songs, half-naked in a nightclub where people are getting drunk and expect people to respect her as an 'example' of religious piety."[2] Malcolm then turned the rhetorical war toward Dawud, implying that his suit was an attempt to reinvigorate his lackluster career.

Another voice echoing Dawud's sentiments was a Sudanese Muslim student at University of Pennsylvania, Yahya Hawari, who wrote a letter to the editor of the *Pittsburgh Courier* that same year, challenging Elijah Muhammad's hajj as being out of season. Malcolm responded to Hawari (consistently misspelling his name Hayari) in a private letter and again publicly in the *Pittsburgh Courier*, challenging the student to settle the dispute "in private, not in public." He downplayed the differences between the NOI and the Islamic *ummah* and lamented that Hawari suffered from a "colonial mentality" and sounded like a "brainwashed, American Negro."[3] Ironically, for all his work as a religious apologist for the NOI, Malcolm later employed a strategy similar to Dawud's and Hawari's as he at-

2. DeCaro, *On the Side of My People*, 148–50.

3. Malcolm X to Yahya Hawari, September 1, 1962, box 3, folder 4, Malcolm X Collection, Schomburg Center for Research in Black Culture, New York Public Library; and "What Courier Readers Think: Muslim vs. Moslem!" *Pittsburgh Courier*, October 6, 1962.

tempted to discredit Elijah Muhammad and place himself distinctly within the world of orthodox Islam.

- Malcolm X, "What Courier Readers Think: Muslim vs. Moslem!" *Pittsburgh Courier*, October 6, 1962

- Yahya Hawari, "What Courier Readers Think: A Blast at Muhammad," *Pittsburgh Courier*, October 27, 1962

- Malcolm X, "Pulse of New York's Public: No Compromise," *Amsterdam News*, December 1, 1962

Further reading:

- Mohd Yakub Khan, "White Man Is God for Cult of Islam," *New Crusader*, August 15, 1959

- "Moslems Denounce US 'Muslims,'" *Amsterdam News*, October 22, 1960

- "Muslims a Fraud, Dakota, Hubby Charge," *Chicago Defender*, June 8, 1962

- "Dakota Staton, Hubby File Suit Against Mr. Muhammad," *Pittsburgh Courier*, June 9, 1962

- "Singer's Husband Issues Muhammad Debate Challenge," *Pittsburgh Courier*, June 23, 1962

- Alfredo Graham, "'Suit Against Muhammad Ridiculous; Is Publicity Stunt,' Says Malcolm X," *Pittsburgh Courier*, June 23, 1962

- "Pakistan Moslem Blasts Muhammad," *Pittsburgh Courier*, July 21, 1962

- "Charges Muhammad Was Not at Mecca," *Pittsburgh Courier*, August 25, 1962

- "Malcolm X Fires Salvo at Dakota," *Pittsburgh Courier*, September 22, 1962

Malcolm X, "What Courier Readers Think: Muslim vs. Moslem!" *Pittsburgh Courier,* October 6, 1962

To the Editor:

Your "letters-to-the-editor" section has been allotting much space to almost anyone who wishes to attack Hon. Elijah Muhammad, the spiritual leader of the fastest growing, best disciplined religious group among the American so-called Negroes. One of the latest "hate Muhammad" letters was written by a Yahya Hayari, who says he is a Sudanese Muslim. It is difficult to believe this man is a Muslim, and even more difficult to believe he is a Muslim from the Sudan. In 1959 I visited Khartoun and Omdurman in the Sudan, and also visited the Muslims in Nigeria, Ghana, Egypt and Arabia. I was impressed the most by the Muslims of the Sudan. Their religious piety and hospitality are unmatched anywhere. I really felt in heaven and at home there. If this Mr. Hayari is really a Muslim and is from the Sudan, then he has been in Christian America too long, and already sounds like a Westernized, brainwashed American Negro. At least our people in America have an excuse for our "westernized-thinking" because we have spent 400 years here in the hands of our slavemaster, over 9000 miles from our own people. I don't know what Mr. Hayari uses as his excuse. No real Muslim will ever attack another Muslim just to gain the friendship of Christians. As it says in the Holy Quran: "Oh you who believe, take not the Jew and the Christians for friends. They are friends of each other. And whoever amongst you takes them for friends he is indeed one of them. Surely Allah guides not the unjust people." (Chapter five, verse 51).

This man can't be a real Muslim. He probably is an American Negro who is a Christian, but is posing as a Muslim just to lend "authenticity" to his attacks upon Messenger Elijah Muhammad. How can we tell? If real Muslims have difference they settle their differences in private, but never to the public delight of Jews and Christians. The followers of Messenger Elijah Muhammad never let themselves be used by Christians to makes statements against other Muslims, no matter how much disagree with those Muslims. The policy of the enemies of Islam has always been "divide and conquer." This was the only real weapon the colonial powers ever had . . . their ability to use one of our people against the other. Some who still suffer from this "colonial mentality" are too quick to let themselves be used to argue and dispute with their own kind to the delight of the enemy. The Europeans are still in the Congo because the Congolese have been kept busy fighting each other, they are in Algeria because the Algerians have been fighting each other, they are still in the Middle East because the Arabs are fighting each other. Surely Muslims have learned a lesson from this! It would be quite foolish for Muslim students to come here from the Sudan or any other part of Africa and allow themselves to be used to attack us in a Christian country, a white country, a country in which over 20 million of their own "Darker Brothers" are yet being held as Second Class Citizens, which is only a modified form of "20th Century Colonalism." So don't let these "Negro Uncle Toms" use foreign-sounding names just to disguise their real identity when they attack Mr. Muhammad. One can always spot the "thought-pattern" of an "americanized" black man no matter what name he hides under . . . for he thinks and writes just like the white man, and will always waste much time an energy attacking the Hon. Elijah Muhammad because Mr. Muhammad is the only Black Man in America with sufficient nerve, wisdom and "following" to be independent of the white man and hit him where it really hurts in the struggle for the freedom of the people.

Malcolm X

New York City, N.Y.

PS: Since Mr. Hayari wrote from Philadelphia, I'd like to

inform him that Mr. Muhammad will be speaking at the Philadelphia Arena, Sunday, Oct. 7. His subject will be "Islam vs Christianity." Anyone who wishes to challenge his religious authenticity is welcome to come out at that time and do so.

Yahya Hawari, "What Courier Readers Think: A Blast at Muhammad," *Pittsburgh Courier*, October 27, 1962

To the Editor:

My name is Yahya Hawari and I wrote you concerning the "Pilgrimage to Mecca" of Mr. Elijah. For this someone called Malcolm X felt it necessary to comment on my letter. I hope you will allow me the privilege to reply as I have since found out more about Mr. Elijah. Since Mr. X has decided to defend Mr. Elijah, he must bear his punishment also. Neither Mr. X nor Elijah will be allowed to visit Sudan again.

Since my letter I have had a chance to read Mr. Elijah's paper and talk to some of his members. All true Muslims accept the Holy Quran as the liberal, verbal word of the Almighty God revealed to the Holy Prophet Muhammad 1400 years ago. It is the last book revealed by God and it is for the guidance of all mankind. The entire life of Muslims is based upon it and it is for all times and for all the activities of men. Mr. Elijah does not believe in or teach Islam. What he teaches in the name of Islam is the own social theory.

Only deep study of the Holy Quran will answer the problems of mankind and unless the followers of Mr. Elijah study the Quran they will never know the truth about Islam. If you do not study medicine you cannot be a doctor. If you do not study the Quran you cannot be Muslim. Brothers and Sisters! The proof of Allah's guidance is never based on numbers but on spiritual purity. "Surely the best of you in the eyes of Allah is he who is most righteous."

I visited the Muslim Brotherhood and became acquainted with Hajji Dwaud. He said that he had challenged Mr. Elijah three times to a public debate on the Religion of Islam. Why has not he accepted these challenges?

Hajji Dawd also said, "Will he agree to a prayer-duel with me?" The Holy Quran says, "If you are truthful wish for death! Also that, "you cannot live for 23 years and say that Allah has sent you and die a natural death," "Would Elijah be willing to make the statement that Allah sent him, that Allah speaks to him, and that he is a prophet or messenger from Allah—would he be willing to state this publicly?"

If Mr. Elijah does not do these things all those that follow him should know that they are being led straight to Hell. Surely Allah is with the truthful. In such a case, protection comes only from Allah, the True. He is the Best in respect of reward, and the Best in respect of consequence."

To Malcolm X my only reply is, "Astaghfiru-llaha Rabbi min kulli dhanbin wa atubu ilaihi." Allahu Akbar.

YAHYA HAWARI
Philadelphia, Pa.

Malcolm X, "Pulse of New York's Public: No Compromise," *Amsterdam News*, December 1, 1962

Sir: I'm surprised to see so much space provided by the press for hip-swinging, blues singing Dakota Staton to continue her insanely jealous attack on Messenger Elijah Muhammad.

Mr. Muhammad is the spiritual head of the fastest-growing, and best disciplined group of Muslims in the Western Hemisphere. Even his most bitter critics admit that he speaks out boldly and without compromise against the injustices done to ALL so-called Negroes in America.

Whenever Negro "leaders" and other publicity-seeking "celebrities" find their own popularity is fading, they know the best way to get the type of "national press coverage" that will put them back on the front pages is by attacking Mr. Muhammad and his young Muslim followers, and the fading Miss Staton is no exception.

Dakota Staton actually has the audacity to think her religious beliefs are keeping her from getting bookings, and causing her records to lose sales value; and she blames the public for mistaking her to be a follower of Mr. Elijah Muhammad.

How absurd can Miss Staton be? It isn't her religious beliefs that have stopped the public from buying her records. Ever since she changed her "tunes" and started "singing" against Mr. Muhammad, her popularity has been on the downturn.

She is over-rating herself and underestimating the intelligence of the public if she thinks they really mistake her for a follower of Mr. Muhammad.

Even the non-Muslim public knows that no Muslim sister who follows Mr. Muhammad would think of singing sexy songs, half-naked in a night-club where people are getting drunk and expect people to still respect her as an "example" of religious piety. The Sisters who follow Mr. Elijah Muhammad's religious guidance wouldn't even think of entering a night-club or any, other place where alcohol is served . . . much less singing in one to entertain a bunch of drunks.

Miss Staton really wants her own husband (Talib Dawud) who is also a fading musician, to be recognized as a Muslim religious leader, and spokesman for the Muslim World. Who is Talib Dawud?? If he wasn't married to his once-famous jazz singer he'd still be unheard of. Even now his name appears in print only when he attacks Mr. Elijah Muhammed.

If Talib Dawud is a religious leader, where are his followers? If he is a Muslim spokesman, where is his audience?

When Messenger Elijah Muhammad speaks, millions listen . . . but when Talib Dawud speaks, only Dakota Staton listens; she is his follower, his audience . . . he is her leader, her spokesman.

In other words, all of Dawud's combined followers can fit into the front seat of his station wagon. Why should Mr. Muhammad waste his time over the "Yapping" of a little puppy.

A dog can bark at the moon until doomsday, and no one will even notice the foolish yapping of the dog unless the moon answers back.

Miss Staton also complains that the words "Muslim," and Islam" and "Allah" have become synonymous with the name Elijah Muhammad. This is naturally as it should be, for if it was not for the success God has granted Mr. Muhammed in spreading truth among our people, the Religion of Islam would still be unknown to the American so-called Negroes.

Miss Staton condemns Mr. Muhammad's teachings about the white man, classifying it as "hate teaching." She contends that oppression is the common enemy of all mankind. She is wrong.

It is not oppression, but rather it is the OPPRESSOR who is the enemy of mankind. We can't condemn oppression and exclude the role of the WHITE oppressor, nor can we condemn exploitation and ignore the role of the WHITE exploiter. How can we claim to be against CRIME and ignore the CRIMINAL who is committing the crime? How can one claim to be against slavery, and yet not take an uncompromising stand against the WHITE ENSLAVER of our people here in America?

Malcolm X

MALCOLM X SPEAKS AT MICHIGAN STATE

In early 1963 the Nation of Islam continued to fight against police brutality and was involved in litigious battles over confrontations with police in Times Square and Rochester, New York. Meanwhile, Malcolm X built upon his nascent following of radical youth by continuing his college speaking circuit at Michigan State University and University of Pennsylvania. His speeches emphasized the growing divide between the approach of the older generation and the more youthful politics of groups such as CORE and the Student Nonviolent Coordinating Committee (SNCC). The fact that his talk at Michigan State on January 23, 1963, was sponsored by the campus NAACP signaled that even the traditionally more conservative black organization had been radicalized by its younger members. Before a crowd of more than one thousand, almost half of whom were white, Malcolm delivered a speech entitled "The Black Muslim and the American Negro." This speech was subsequently given in Philadelphia as "The Old Negro and the New Negro." These speeches were among the earliest iterations of what would become one of Malcolm X's most notable rhetorical devices: the "house Negro and the field Negro."

Malcolm characterized a house Negro as one who "dressed like his master. He wore his master's second-hand clothes. He ate food that his master left on the table. And he lived in his master's house . . . [and] always identified himself in the same sense that his master identified himself." On the other hand, the field Negro was in the majority. "When the master got sick, they prayed that he'd die. If his house caught on fire, they'd pray for a wind to come along and fan the breeze."[1] Just eight months before the March on Washington, Malcolm was already drawing sharp attention to the fissure emerging within the civil rights movement by articulating early tenets of the Black Power ideology he, among others, came to inspire. Malcolm also distanced himself from the rhetoric of Yacub's history and the Asiatic identity preached by the NOI, instead stressing the cultural similarities of black Americans to Africans: "The man that you call a Negro is nothing but an African himself."[2] The address, so close to his boyhood home, also marked one of the few times Malcolm spoke of his father's death as an accident rather than a malicious murder.

- "Muslim Leader Is Anti-integrationist," *State News*, January 24, 1963

Further reading:

- "Muslim Leader Asks Negro Nation in U.S." *Chicago Defender*, January 26, 1963
- Malcolm X FBI file, summary report, New York office, May 16, 1963

1. Malcolm X, "Twenty Million Black People in a Political, Economic and Mental Prison," in Bruce Perry, ed., *Malcolm X: The Last Speeches* (New York: Pathfinder Press, 1989), 25–57.

2. Ibid.

"Muslim Leader Is Anti-Integrationist,"
State News, January 24, 1963

The only solution to the race problem is complete separation of whites and Negroes, Minister Malcolm X, spokesman for the Muslims in America, said Wednesday.

The majority of the Negroes do not want integration, and they do not want segregation, Malcolm X said. They want separation that allows them to control their own economy, government and affairs.

"We should be given part of this country, and the government and economy," he answered when asked how the separation would be possible.

The country owes a debt to the Negroes for having kidnapped them and enslaved them, he said.

Segregation he said, is unsatisfactory because the Negro is controlled from the outside by the whites.

Two types of Negroes exist in America, he said, and to solve the race problem the difference between the two must be seen.

The "Uncle Tom" Negro originated with the house slave who completely identified himself with his master copying his every characteristic.

The new type of Negro springs from the field slaves who scorned their master and saw him only as an oppressor.

The 20th century Uncle Tom has been brainwashed into thinking of himself as white; he identifies himself with everything in the white man's world, Malcolm X said.

It is the Uncle Toms that are pushing for integration and they are only the minority of the Negroes in America.

The new type Negro does not want to identify with the white man, he said, instead they want something of their own. This group is represented by the Muslims.

The Uncle Toms, he said, will not attack a white man, instead they will reject their fellow Negroes because they do not want to be connected with anything black.

The new type Negro thinks on a broader international scale, he said. They see the majority of the people in the world as dark, and, therefore, no longer speak as the underdog.

The Muslims reject the white Christian religion and have adopted Islam.

The new type Negro does not turn the other cheek to anyone. He believes in law and order, he said, but he reserves the right to strike back if attacked.

White Americans if the race problem is to be solved, must stop thinking that they are doing the Negroes a favor by giving them a little freedom through token integration, Malcolm X said.

Once they recognize the new type Negro and realize that they are not doing the Negroes a favor, then a start can be made toward the solution of the race problem.

Integration can never work, he said, because one man cannot be forced to love another. Advocates of integration are hypocrites for while they cherish the liberal idea they would be the first to move out if a Negro moved into their neighborhood.

In reality neither the white man or the Negro wants integration.

The Kiva and the lobby of the education building were packed. Campus police guarded every door, but the crowd was quiet.

Malcolm X is a tall, light-skinned Negro, formerly of Lansing. He is presently a leader of the New York Temple of the Muslims.

The speech was the first of a series of lectures jointly sponsored by the African Student Association and the NAACP.

POLICE RAID ROCHESTER MOSQUE

During the trial of Muslims in Los Angeles after the police raid in 1962, it came to light that the LAPD had already identified the group as a concern and hassled mosque members peddling *Muhammad Speaks* in a Safeway supermarket parking lot. In a similar chain of events the following year, the NOI would also be subject to police targeting, this time on the East Coast. Just weeks after two Muslims were arrested for selling *Muhammad Speaks* in Times Square on Christmas Day, a mosque in Rochester, New York, was raided by two policemen. On January 6, 1963, Rochester police received an anonymous tip that a man attending a religious service above a nearby casino was carrying a firearm, and they attempted to enter the mosque without a warrant. The officers were met with strong resistance by a man at the door, and a brawl ensued when eight to ten other members appeared at the top of the staircase. Another ten policemen and a police dog were called in to settle the disturbance. Although only two men were initially arrested, the incident sparked a related skirmish a month later, which resulted in the arrest of over a dozen members, including the mosque's minister, for "third degree assault" and "inciting to riot."[1]

Clearly the murder of Ronald Stokes had exacerbated the

---

1. Malcolm X FBI file, summary report, Buffalo office, March 7, 1963.

relationship between police enforcement and the organization; mosque members reportedly shouted, "Don't let them in, no [p]olice allowed," citing the shooting in Los Angeles as evidence of police brutality.[2] Elijah Muhammad's edict that Muslims prevent white law enforcement from entering a place of worship, even at cost of life, had clearly been heard. After the first disturbance in January, Malcolm flew to Rochester and filed a protest with both the State Human Rights Commission and Rochester Public Safety Commission. "We allow no intrusion of our religious services," he stated. "We will give our lives if necessary to protect their sanctity."[3]

Just four days after the incident in Rochester, Malcolm led a demonstration outside the New York County Criminal Court Building, where the two Muslims charged with assault while selling *Muhammad Speaks* in Times Square were being held. He then sent telegrams to New York City's mayor, Robert Wagner; district attorney, Frank Hogan; and police commissioner, Michael Murphy. After the February 8 disturbance in which Rochester minister Robert James X Williams and a dozen other mosque members were arrested, the indicted Muslims waged a partial hunger strike to protest being served commercial bread, mashed potatoes, and pork. Though a physician determined that the inmates would not die from the way they were eating, Malcolm X made a public statement that they had not eaten in eight days and would fast until they die. "Rochester," he stated, "will be better known than Oxford, Mississippi, [and] . . . may be a precedent-setting city for police hostility towards Muslims."[4]

Although the Nation of Islam was viewed by many as a religious entity that kept its distance from the stream of civil rights politics and public disobedience, Malcolm X continued to protest acts of police brutality. He led a crowd of over five

2. Ibid.

3. "Muslims Protest Rights Violation by Police," *Chicago Defender*, January 10, 1963.

4. Malcolm X FBI file, summary report, New York office, May 16, 1963.

hundred through Rockefeller Center in Manhattan and wired President Kennedy concerning the incident in Rochester, demanding an "immediate investigation at the federal level . . . into the criminal use of political power and political office in Rochester, N.Y. to suppress the civil rights and the human rights of the Negro community in general, and the religious rights of the Muslims in particular."[5] Further inserting the NOI into the discourse of the civil rights movement, Malcolm spoke in Rochester the following day at a rally sponsored by the NAACP, CORE, the Monroe County Non-Partisan Political League, and the Rochester Civil Rights League. The event drew nearly a thousand people and was deemed by local observers the "most spectacular display of Negro unity ever witnessed in Rochester."[6]

- "Racial Tension Causes Aired by 3 Panelists," *Rochester Democrat and Chronicle*, March 7, 1963

- William Vogler, "The Rochester Image Two-Faced? Angry Voices Raised by Opposing Groups," *Rochester Democrat and Chronicle*, March 13, 1963 (excerpt)

- "Trial Set for 15 on Riot Charge," *Rochester Times-Union*, February 28, 1963

- Memorandum, William Lombard, Rochester Chief of Police, to Inspector John Kinsella, BOSS, February 19, 1963

Further reading:

- "Muslims Protest Rights Violation by Police," *Chicago Defender*, January 10, 1963

5. Malcolm X FBI file, summary report, Buffalo office, March 7, 1963.

6. "NAACP Atty. Defending 'Black Muslims,'" *Pittsburgh Courier*, March 2, 1963.

- "NAACP Atty. Defending 'Black Muslims,'" *Pittsburgh Courier*, March 2, 1963

- "13 Black Muslims Being Fed Monks Bread in Rochester Jail," *Chicago Defender*, February 16, 1963

- "Rochester NAACP Aid Asks Unity with Muslims Against Cop Abuses," *Chicago Defender*, February 19, 1963

- Malcolm X FBI file, summary report, Buffalo office, March 7, 1963

- Malcolm X FBI file, summary report, New York office, May 16, 1963, pages 16–20

"Racial Tension Causes Aired by 3 Panelists," *Rochester Democrat and Chronicle,* March 7, 1963

Rochester, an unlikely city to have racial disturbances, has reached its recent crisis primarily because of a "lack of alert, aroused understanding of the deepening crisis facing all Northern cities," according to a Colgate Rochester Divinity School professor.

Dr. Prentiss L. Pemberton, professor of Christian social ethics and sociology of religion, said, "My thesis is that we face an increasing breakdown of communication between the white and non-white in Northern cities. This leads to a deepening mood of suspicion which is shattering our traditional Northern ways of handling racial problems, through patient negotiation . . ."

Dr. Pemberton and two others discussed basic forces underlying recent racial tensions here at a public meeting in the divinity school. About 75 persons attended. The other speakers were Sidney J. Lindenberg, executive director of the Baden Street Settlement, and Dr. Walter Cooper, research chemist at Eastman Kodak Co. and chairman of the community affairs committee of the National Association for the Advancement of Colored People.

BOARD SAID "CONCRETE STEP"

In answer to a question, Pemberton termed the proposed Advisory Citizen's Review Board "the most concrete step we can take" to create new channels of communication.

Lindenberg called the proposed board "water to put out the fire," but called for long-term, creative attention to community tensions, "not just police tensions."

In his talk Lindenberg described evidences of tensions that settlement house workers have observed, and criticized "an awful lot of people (who) talk about an area (such as Baden-Ormond) without much knowledge of it."

The Negro community is being motivated to draw together by "the same things that drew the Jewish group together at the time of Hitler—fear, and hopelessness," Lindenberg said.

BRUTALITY "SYMPTOM"

He praised city officials for trying to correct the situation, but called for a wider understanding among the average citizens of the community. He called police brutality a symptom rather than a basic cause of racial unrest and urged attention to housing, jobs, education and relationships of minority groups.

"If we don't do something, groups like the Black Muslims are going to slide in and take control," he added.

Dr. Cooper said criticism of liberal groups by so-called "freedom now" Negro leaders has arisen because "liberals see the Negro as a symbol . . . but not as a man.

"The black American cannot be assimilated until the majority group is willing to accept the humanity of the black man."

He said there is more segregation in Northern cities now than there was 20 years ago and that "the plight of the Negro in urban Northern communities is like backward countries."

William Vogler, "The Rochester Image Two-Faced?
Angry Voices Raised by Opposing Groups,"
Rochester Democrat and Chronicle,
March 13, 1963 (excerpt)

Rochester, like the mythological Narcissus, looked at its reflected image and generally liked what it saw.

Rochester, said the Rochesterian, was a nice community to
raise children in. It had a high-employment, skilled-worker economy. Generally speaking, its politics were clean—certainly
there was no local equivalent of Frank Hague or James Curley.
And it was "culture" conscious—witness the Eastman School of
Music, the Civic Music Association, the Memorial Art Gallery.

But Narcissus, trapped by his own vanity and tricked by
pagan gods, had been fascinated by an illusion. So, in a sense,
had Rochester's "image" been illusory. And, as illusions will,
Rochester's broke down recently.

The Flower City, never shy about setting up a committee or
holding a meeting, suddenly found itself caught in an angry
swirl of meetings, sit-ins and debates that produced a blizzard
of statements on "current racial tensions."

BABBLE OF VOICES

A babble of voices rose in an uneven chorus: "Police brutality," some said: "Force necessary to affect arrest," others replied. "Discrimination," some said. "Irresponsible minorities,"
came the reply.

One thing was certain. The Rochester image wasn't what it
used to be. But then the image of the body politic as a unified
entity is at best a convenient fiction. People have a tendency
now and then to break ranks.

If it's a healthy body politic, the ranks will re-form after a while and march, though not everyone will be in step, in a different direction. Rochester is now searching itself to determine what that direction will be.

Well, what about it? Is there a crisis, or is it just another ripple in the pond?

ATTEMPT TO ANSWER

What follows is an attempt to answer that question in terms of the feelings in the non-white community, as indicated in meetings, through statements and through conversations with some of those directly involved in recent events.

While the sentiments of both the white and non-white communities are germane to the present situation, more emphasis has been focused here on feelings in the city's two predominantly non-white areas, probable locale of any explosion that may occur.

Is the potential for a blow up exaggerated? Not according to Mrs. Constance Mitchell, Third Ward Democratic supervisor, who said recently:

"It would take only a minor incident to start a race riot . . . This is not something that started with A.C. White."

INDICATIONS CITED

These were some of the indications, cited by Mrs. Mitchell and others, that the present mood of friction and unrest had been building for some time.

—A 204 per cent increase in this city's Negro population between 1950 and 1960, that saw the Negro community in the city increase from 7,845 in 1950 to 24,228 in 1960.

—The Baden-Ormond urban renewal project that led to the relocation of many people into already crowded areas on the fringe of Baden-Ormond and in the 3rd Ward.

—A meeting between city officials and representatives of

the Negro community in August 1961. One of the top points on the agenda was the use of police dogs in minority group areas.

—A man living in the 3rd Ward, speaking of everyday frustrations, commented over a cup of coffee:

"We can't make a living. We can't go to certain places unless we want to risk direct or implied discourtesies. And we can't even break the law and get the same treatment that other people do."

—Rabbi Allan Levine of Temple Emanu-El, and one of several key figures in the current swirl of events, had this to say about people's awareness of their community:

"Many people in Rochester live utterly isolated from the problems of the central city therefore, when complaints of injustice arise, they dismiss them as utterly baseless."

That the blinders have been discarded by at least part of the community is evidenced by recent events.

For one thing, a group of more than 100 clergymen—interracial and interfaith—from many Monroe County communities, believe the current situation is a crisis involving the total community and they have demonstrated a high degree of unanimity in suggesting possible solutions, immediate and long-range, to the present condition.

HIGH-LEVEL MEETINGS

Some of the clergymen also participated in high-level meetings with city officials dealing with allegations of police abuse of authority. Out of those meetings emerged the promise by the city to consider proposals for an independent agency to review complaints of alleged unnecessary and excessive use of force by police. The city administration has drawn up an ordinance for City Council consideration to accomplish this purpose.

The clergy group can be more than matched in size by laymen, acting through organizations or as individuals, who have a similar concern with the current situation.

But back to the crisis, that mishmash of fact, rumor and, above all else, feelings.

The impression gained from attending scores of meetings, and from discussions with dozens of people familiar with the situation is that the feeling exists that unequal law enforcement is meted out to non-whites and that this could be the spark that could touch off an explosion.

That feelings concerning alleged unequal law enforcement are not isolated from other problems such as housing and employment will become evident later.

STRESS PAINT

One thing cannot be stressed too strongly, even though it has been said again and again: The Police Bureau as a whole is not being indicted. Those pointing the finger, point it at a few policemen, whose names, according to the accusers, crop up repeatedly in incidents of alleged harassment or unjustified use of force.

People from the Third and Seventh Wards, refuting the bromide that "a cop is a cop," cited policemen who have won the confidence of people in those areas.

These policemen, according to the Third and Seventh Warders, have been able to walk into the midst of an excited crowd in Joseph Avenue, ask "what's it all about" and with a few words and/or actions take the heat out of the situation.

For the moment, that is. Memories of A.C. White, Rufus Fairwell and the arrest of 15 men following a clash with police at a meeting of the Black Muslinms could provide the potential for the possible riot envisioned by Mrs. Mitchell and other observers.

OUTSTANDING POINTS

Two things stand out in discussions of these cases. One is a strong feeling of identification among Negroes with White, Fairwell and the 15 men. The other, especially strong in the

Fairwell case, is a sense of bewilderment and sometimes anger over the explanations of the three cases which have been made public.

Fairwell, a 28-year-old service station attendant, was arrested last August on charges of assaulting two policemen, who, Fairwell charged, assaulted him. A grand jury subsequently cleared Fairwell and the two officers.

Fairwell has filed a $125,000 suit against the city for "damages for personal injuries and indignities" suffered because of what he described as the negligence and wilfull misconduct of the city and its employees.

White, 46, of 383 Joseph Ave., is facing County and City Court trials on charges of driving while intoxicated, resisting arrest, third degree assault, driving without an operator's license and without proper registration in connection with his arrest Jan. 26.

Four patrolmen involved in his arrest were suspended pending the outcome of a Police Bureau investigation of the White arrest, in which White suffered injuries that required hospitalization. The policemen were later reinstated with reprimands.

White later filed and then withdrew charges against three of the four policemen involved in his arrest. According to his attorney, White withdrew the charges to concentrate on his upcoming trials.

MUSLIM MEETING

Those arrested in connection with the Jan. 6 scuffle with the police at the Black Muslim meeting on Jan. 6 face trial on charges of riot and third degree assault. Police said they went to the meeting to investigate an anonymous report that a man with a gun was at the meeting place.

Malcolm X, a national leader of the Muslims, later protested that police had tried to force their way into a religious meeting.

These matters have previously been reported, but since all three cases are now before the courts this is not the place to argue the merits of the cases. However, one can select a few from many available illustrations to indicate the feelings of the Negro community about the cases.

The weekend that began with the evening of Feb. 8 saw the suspension of the four officers in the White case and the arrest of 13 men on charges stemming from the Jan. 6 clash with police at the site of the Muslim meeting. Two other defendants involved in that incident were arrested earlier, and all 15 are free in bail.

Dr. Walter Cooper, chairman of the community affairs committee of the Rochester Branch, National Association for the Advancement of Colored People, recalled that he was one of several people who circulated in the city's two predominantly Negro areas that weekend.

"What we tried to do that weekend was to visit bars and barbershops and try to bring some sanity to people who had become more than emotionally involved," Dr. Cooper said.

"GOING TO FIGHT BACK"

Typical of the comments he heard were: "I've had enough. If I get hit, I'm going to fight back."

The tour left the impression, according to Dr. Cooper, that "this was not just idle talk."

At a Feb. 18 meeting called by integration groups to protest alleged police abuses of Negroes, several things significant to the entire community emerged.

The meeting, which was called on very short notice, drew an audience of about 600, all Negro except for a sprinkling of whites. The issue that attracted them was alleged misuse of authority by police. Most were people who almost never attend regular meetings held by traditional protest groups.

Malcolm X, although not a scheduled speaker, talked during the question period and was received enthusiastically.

Furthermore, integration groups, while rejecting the separatism of the Muslims, indicated at the meeting and since then that they would stand by the Muslims to help defend the civil rights of Rochester Negroes.

FEELING PERSISTS

While many of the actions of the integration groups in the current situation can be interpreted as moves to counter the local impact of the Muslims, on the issue of alleged abuse of authority by police the feeling persists that, as a speaker at the Feb. 18 meeting said: "We are black folks first."

In discussing the significance of the Feb. 18 meeting with those close to the situation, two different assessments were heard. According to one, any leader of national stature with a reputation for plain talk would have received a favorable response.

Challenging this, others said Malcolm X has a stronger appeal to the Negro masses than some other Negro leaders. Malcolm X, these people asserted, can get people to identify more easily with him because "he says what the masses of Negroes want to hear."

The strength of the Muslim movement is not something other Muslim leaders care to discuss. Locally, estimates range from about 25 to about 200. Nationally, C. Eric Lincoln, author of "The Black Muslims in America," wrote "in recent years their membership has spiraled to at least 100,000—some estimates would triple that figure—with more than 50 temples in major cities from Boston and Miami to San Diego."

LESS SIGNIFICANT

However, those conversant with the movement state that numerical strength is less significant than the number of people who, while declining to join the Muslims, nevertheless, share many of the criticisms of the American scene made by the Muslims.

This poses a challenge for believers in integration and a paradox for the Muslims. The recent coalescing of integration forces demonstrates that these groups have accepted the challenge.

In addition to a closer degree of cooperation recently evidenced between traditional protest groups such as the NAACP and the Congress of Racial Equality, the recent past has seen the organization of new groups such as the United Action Committee for Rufus Fairwell, the Integrated Non-Violent Committee (the group that negotiated with city officials on cases of alleged police brutality) a group which staged sit-ins at police headquarters, known simply as the supporters of the non-violent committee and the organization of more than 100 clergymen of all major faiths.

Two things should be noted about the new groups, according to those close to them. For one thing there is the aspect of interlocking membership; members of the NAACP and/or CORE and other established groups also belonged to the Fairwell Committee and the non-violent group.

A distinction also is made between NAACP, for example, which is termed a permanent group with the broad goal of equal justice, and the Fairwell group, which is seen as a committee set up for a specific limited purpose.

NEWER GROUPS

Secondly, the newer groups are causing people, who though previously intellectually committed, to speak out and take an active part in the struggle.

Discussing the future of the Muslim movement, Lincoln saw the Muslims caught in a dilemma: whether to retain their present militant, anti-white, anti-Christian pose or modify it to win followers now repulsed by these Muslim themes.

At their Feb. 26 Chicago national convention, the Muslims made a bid for cooperation with traditional protest groups. National leaders of the NAACP and CORE reiterated their distaste for Muslim separatism, but indicated the possibility a limited degree of cooperation on such issues as police brutality.

"Trial Set for 15 on Riot Charge,"
Rochester Times-Union, February 28, 1963

Trial of 15 men on charges of riot and third-degree assault was set today for March 18 in County Court.

They were arrested after a clash with police at a Black Muslim meeting Jan. 6.

The trial was scheduled by Judge John P. Lomenzo after assignment of additional counsel for the defense.

While the defendants were in court for the proceedings, three men carrying signs walked up and down in front of the Court House. The signs proclaimed: "Black Man Political Tool No More," "Rochester Police State" and "We Worship Allah."

An attempt by the "pickets" to enter the courtroom before the riot case was called was blocked by court attendants. They then went to the Main Street sidewalk in front of the building.

In court, the 15 defendants lined up stiffly in front of Judge Lomenzo.

"I notice you are all standing at attention," he said. "At ease. You're not in the Army. You're in a court of law."

Standing with the defendants were court-assigned attorneys Reuben K. Davis, Robert L. Brenna and Charles B. Kenning. Davis asked that additional counsel be assigned. Upon the individual request of each defendant, Judge Lomenzo assigned two more counsel—Alan J. Underberg and Mervyn M. Kroll.

CITY OF ROCHESTER
NEW YORK

DEPARTMENT OF PUBLIC SAFETY
BUREAU OF POLICE

Feb. 19, 1963

Inspector John L. Kinsella
Bureau of Special Services
56 Worth St.
New York City, Manhattan
New York

Dear Sir:

Your file 2817/FC, BOSS,
Letter of Feb. 15, 1963.

Trouble with Muslims in the City of Rochester.

On Jan 6, 1963 about 8:15 p.m. our police telephone operator received an anonymous call of "a man with a gun over
Buddy's Casino on North Street." The caller immediately hung
up the 'phone without identifying himself. Two uniformed
officers were dispatched to the scene and were met at the door
by an unidentified Negro who stated that the police could not
enter. They explained to the door man the nature of their
complaint and started up the stairs. The door man yelled the
police are coming and as the two patrolmen reached the top of
the stairs they were met by two more door men who were later
identified as ███████████, and ████████████ The two
patrolmen were assaulted by the door men who also yelled
the police are coming. About ten or twelve more men converged
from the room at the top of the stairs and started assaulting the
patrolmen and tried to throw them down the stairs. Other police responded to the call, order was restored, and the names of

236

all Muslim members were taken. The two original officers on the scene were treated at the hospital for injuries.

On Jan. 7th, ███████████ and ███████████ were arraigned in City Court for assault, to which they pleaded not guilty and their cases referred to the Grand Jury. Malcolm White (Malcolm X) Chief Lieutenant of Elijah Poole (Elijah Muhammad) was present and made statements to the press, radio and T. V. stations. The hall on North Street was kept under surveillance and on Jan. 13th about 8:45 p.m. fire engines responded to a an anonymous call of a fire over Buddy's Casino. On arrival at the hall the firemen were blocked from entering the building by a group of Muslims who blocked the entrance way leading upstairs.

John B. Strickland (John B. X) of Mosque, #23, Buffalo, N. Y. was the spokesman for the group that was blocking the door. There was no indication that any fire was in progress so the firemen left. On February 8th, after the Grand Jury had heard the assault and resisting arrest charges against ███████████ and ███████████ it indicted sixteen members who were present on January 6th for inciting a riot and assault third degree. All of the warrants were served with the exception of two who could not be located; ███████████ and ███████████

On Feb. 15th the defendants were released on $500. bail, each, bail was posted by Malcolm X White and their attorney. Malcolm X real name is Malcolm Little, born in Omaha, Neb.

This group started its activities in Rochester in the middle 50's and at present have about 15 to 20 hard core members. We also have the names, addresses and some photographs of other members and ex-members of this group. If we come across any information which we feel you might use we will send it to you.

Enclosed please find a list of the Muslims who were in attendance at the meeting on Jan. 6th and also photos and records of the persons arrested.

Very truly yours,

William M. Lombard
Chief of Police.

By: *James J. Cavoti*
Detective Captain.

MALCOLM X ATTENDS
MARCH ON WASHINGTON

Whether at college lectures, debates with civil rights leaders, or in television interviews, Malcolm X struggled in the early 1960s to uphold the subdued political stance of Elijah Muhammad. In 1962 Muhammad stressed the need for less incendiary political rhetoric to Malcolm, who had hoped to attend a discussion concerning the civil rights bill. "If you care to visit the discussion," Muhammad wrote, "you must remember how we must steer away from being classified as an actual political party under the disguise of religion."[1] Muhammad was concerned in part because of the tax benefit given the group for its incorporated religious affiliation. However, he was also a deeply practical leader who saw radical social action as an obstacle to the class aspirations of his economic and spiritual program.

As much as he appreciated the publicity garnered by sociological studies such as C. Eric Lincoln's *The Black Muslims in America* and E. U. Essien-Udom's *Black Nationalism: A Search for an Identity in America*, Muhammad disagreed with the thesis that the NOI was essentially black nationalism

1. Elijah Muhammad to Malcolm X, September 18, 1962, box 3, folder 8, Malcolm X Collection, Schomburg Center for Research in Black Culture, New York Public Library.

masquerading as religion. Amid these concerns, Muhammad strictly forbade all NOI members from attending the March on Washington to be held August 28, 1963. At a meeting at Mosque No. 7 earlier that month, Malcolm informed the audience that anyone attending the march would receive a ninety-day suspension. If anyone belonged to a union that required their participation, Malcolm admonished, they had better "get sick."[2]

As the date of the march approached, Malcolm continued to staunchly represent Muhammad's stance and was quoted just days before it in the *Los Angeles Times* as saying, "No Muslim will be involved. Neither directly nor indirectly."[3] However, on the evening after the march, a reporter for the socialist newspaper *The Militant* encountered the Muslim leader, who admitted to witnessing the events from the sidelines. Malcolm chided it as being "a good show—like the Rose Bowl," but added that revolution is not a halfway process, "You are either free or you aren't free."[4] Journalist Peter Goldman also recalled being led by Louis Lomax to a prominent cocktail party that night, where they witnessed a crowd gravitating toward Malcolm. Although it may have been to keep an eye on Malcolm, Elijah Muhammad's son Herbert also attended the march after securing a press pass as the NOI's photographer.[5]

The NOI went to lengths to cast Malcolm's participation in the march as a premeditated critique, rather than blatant disregard for Muhammad's instructions. An article in *Muhammad Speaks* recounted a speech at Los Angeles' Embassy Auditorium in which Malcolm called the march a "'farce . . . subsidized by white liberals' and stage-managed by President

2. Malcolm X FBI file, summary report, New York office, November 15, 1963, 27.

3. "NAACP Official Says 250,000 Will March," *Los Angeles Times*, August 26, 1963.

4. "How Malcolm X Viewed March," *The Militant*, April 16, 1963; and Malcolm X FBI file, summary report, New York office, November 15, 1963, 27–28.

5. Herbert Muhammad FBI file, memo, Chicago office, August 29, 1963.

Kennedy."[6] In reality, though, Malcolm disobeyed strict orders not to attend the March on Washington, and his address in Los Angeles foreshadowed the public critique of President Kennedy that would cement his formal ousting from the Nation of Islam.

- "How Malcolm X Viewed March," *The Militant*, vol.27, no.32, April 16, 1963

- Interview of Malcolm X, Edwin Cooper to BOSS commanding officer, August 8, 1963

- Transcript, Peter Goldman interview, July 12, 2004, Malcolm X Project

Further reading:

- "Muslim Leader Plans to Join Washington March," *Chicago Defender*, August 10, 1963

- "NAACP Official Says 250,000 Will March," *Los Angeles Times*, August 26, 1963

- "'No Muslims in DC March': MX," *Chicago Defender*, August 26, 1963

- William Raspberry, "Rights Leaders Reaffirm Belief That Marchers Will Be Orderly," *Washington Post*, August 26, 1963

- "'Whites Made Washington March a Farce,' Declares Malcolm X," *Chicago Daily Defender*, October 10, 1963

- "Minister Malcolm Exposes 'Farce' of D.C. 'March,'" *Muhammad Speaks*, October 25, 1963

- Malcolm X FBI file, summary report, New York office, November 15, 1963, pages 27–28

---

6. "Minister Malcolm Exposes 'Farce' of D.C. 'March,'" *Muhammad Speaks*, October 25, 1963.

- Raymond Sharrieff FBI file, summary report, Chicago office, February 19, 1964

- Herbert Muhammad FBI file, memorandum, Chicago office, August 29, 1963

- Reminiscences of Bayard Rustin (1987), on pages 215–19 in CUCOHC

"How Malcolm X Viewed March," *The Militant*, vol. 27, no. 32, April 16, 1963

Encountering Malcolm X in Washington, D.C., the evening of the Aug. 28 March, a *Militant* reporter asked him for a statement.

Of the March itself, the Black Muslim leader said, "It was a good show—like the Rose Bowl."

He remarked that the present Negro leadership was talking about a "civil-rights revolution." But revolution is not a half-way process, he added. "You are either free or not free." There was, he said, a revolutionary tradition in this country—from George Washington to the Abolitionists. Because the Muslims are independent of the white power structure, they are, he declared, in the tradition of these revolutionaries. "That is why we are the most slandered organization in the U.S."

Interview of Malcolm X, Edwin Cooper to BOSS Commanding Officer, August 8, 1963

August 8, 1963

From: Patrolman Edwin B. Cooper, Shield #20096, B.S.S.

To: Commanding Officer, Bureau of Special Services

Subject: INTERVIEW OF MALCOLM X RE: MARCH ON WASHINGTON ON AUGUST 28, 1963

1. On Wednesday, August 7, 1963, Detective William K. DeFossett, Shield #631, of this command, accompanied by the undersigned, visited the Muslim Restaurant, 113 Lenox Avenue, Manhattan and interviewed Malcolm X relative to the subject matter listed above.

2. Malcolm X stated that his organization will not take part in this mass demonstration in Washington on August 28, but that he would be in Washington at this time holding a religious ceremony in connection with the opening of a new Mosque in Washington.

3. Minister Malcolm X further stated that when the "White Man" heard about this mass demonstration in the beginning which was to consist of sit-in's etc. on the White House lawn, airports and other public grounds, he decided to control it. This was done by large contributions of money by the white liberals, such as the $800.00 by the Taconic Foundation, to keep the so called Negro leaders in a Strait-Jacket. He believes that the white liberal with large sums of money invested are calling the "shots" in connection with this march, not the so called Negro leaders.

4. He stated in closing of this interview that he does not see how, and I Quote, "these so called Negro leaders can state that there will not be any incidents in connection with this march."

5. The conditions in the Harlem area, so far as they pertain to this command, will receive continued attention and new developments will be reported.

Edwin B. Cooper
Ptl. #20096 BSS

GOLDMAN: That, to me, is the key, that he was, just as a po-litical figure, was a person of truly—and I deal with main-stream political figures all the time. That's been my specialty for twenty-seven years. And Malcolm would put most of them to shame. He was a figure of such complexity and sophistica-tion of political thought. That doesn't mean it always came out right for him. In fact, I think some of it didn't, but in those cases, I'm not sure what the right answer would have been. You know, I fluctuate between days of hope and days of de-spair, and in my days of despair, I begin to think there was no way out for Malcolm. And I wonder if we'll ever, ever solve the questions that Malcolm was addressing. In my days of hope, I think yes.

[Begin Tape 1, Side B]

GOLDMAN: At the march, the march, I think, was—I tell the story in my book about Louis Lomax spotting me in the lobby there. Lomax and I were pretty good friends. Lomax loved hanging out with people from the national press. He liked feel-ing part of that, but he also liked being as knowing as he was. He was a guy who was always wired to all the gossip. Mal-colm, himself, recognized it. He said, "All I know is when I see Lomax going somewhere, I'm going to follow him." Lomax I was very fond of.

Anyway, he saw me, and he said, "Come with me." He didn't tell me what, where, who, what, when, or why, but I fol-lowed what I would later discover was Malcolm's rule, and followed Louis. And we went up the elevator into a hotel room.

It was a suite, actually. There must have been fifty or so—I think I was the only white guy in the room. And these were upper middle-class black folks who had come down for the march and were quite passionate about being there, that that was where you had to be.

And there was Malcolm, and until I saw him, I had no clue that was what Lomax was leading me to. His attitude, his public attitude toward the march was that this is a picnic, it's a circus, it's meaningless. "The Farce on Washington" he called it and so on. He was doing a very much muted version of that. He wasn't addressing them. It was more kind of a cocktail party setting. Indeed, there were a lot of bourbons splashing, including into my glass. [Laughs] I tried to put it down when I was talking to Malcolm.

It was more like a cocktail party and cocktail party conversations, and since he had a great deal of figurehood/celebrity, there's always one power center at a cocktail party, and he was it. And he was doing a muted version—the same rap, but a much muted version. He was respecting their need to be there and to feel part of this day.

Q: But he was not supposed to be there.

GOLDMAN: He was not supposed to be in town.

Q: No, no. I mean within the NOI. He was not supposed to be there.

GOLDMAN: That's what I mean.

Q: Right.

GOLDMAN: No, he wasn't supposed to be in town, let alone at the headquarters hotel of the march, talking to marchers and taking a position one way or the other. He was just not—they were—this was just not happening. I think, as far as Chicago is—

Q: That's right. Roger Wilkins saw him standing under a tree the next day as the march was progressing outside of the mall, not far from the Justice Department, where Roger was working at the time. So his engagement was very much the way you describe in '62 and '63, on the margins, watching something transpire, but he desires to engage, and it's hard for him to stay away.

GOLDMAN: Oh, I mean, it just radiated that kind of hunger. He knew. I write in the book, and I believed then and believe now, he knew that that was the capital, that was the epicenter of black America on that day. And the people in the room had to be there, these sort of bourgeois people who were not doing sit-ins and were not marching in the streets or anything, but they had to be there. He had to be there, and that was transparent, even though he was saying, "It's a Farce on Washington."

In the room, as I say, he was doing a more muted version. I got into this silly little thing with him about—he said, "Name me one of these so-called American Negro leaders who's truly nonviolent." And it was a pop quiz, and the first name that flew out of my mouth was Bayard Rustin. And I think, you know, Bayard was not spiritually nonviolent, as some of the SCLC people were, but Bayard was profoundly tactically nonviolent.

Q: That's right. He's not Jim Lawson.

THE AUTOBIOGRAPHY OF
MALCOLM X

Alex Haley, having just retired from twenty years as a cook
and journalist in the U.S. Coast Guard, was living in San Francisco when he began writing freelance in 1959. He met Malcolm X the following year while composing an article on the
Nation of Islam for *Reader's Digest*. After several other articles on Malcolm X and the NOI for the *Saturday Evening
Post* and *Playboy*, Haley approached Malcolm about the possibility of an autobiography. Haley later recalled that "it was
one of the few times I have ever seen him uncertain."[1] With
Elijah Muhammad's approval secured, Malcolm conceived of
the book as a testament to the spiritual and moral teachings of
the Nation of Islam; all proceeds would be donated to the organization. For Haley, a staunch conservative and integrationist who had political misgivings about Malcolm X, the book
would serve as a warning of integrationist failings and might
prove a popular success that could help launch his still nascent
career. In March 1964, for instance, Haley excitedly wrote
Ken McCormick about its commercial possibilities: "For this
man is <u>so</u> hot, so HOT, a subject, I know you agree . . . this
book is <u>so</u> pregnant with million or more sale potential . . . that
it will be simply <u>criminal</u>, from all of our points of view, if

1. Malcolm X and Alex Haley, *Autobiography*, 444.

248

every effort isn't exerted in our respective areas to see it on the bookstands by fall."[2]

Correspondence between Alex Haley, his literary agent Paul Reynolds, and Doubleday editor Ken McCormick provides insight into the production of the most influential and enduring representation of Malcolm X. Haley's initial September 1963 outline of the book foreshadows the difficulty he would later face when Malcolm X broke with the NOI. Where the original scheme featured a series of Malcolm's ruminations of a variety of subjects, as well as a section entitled "Questions That I Get Asked," the finished product would hurriedly try to sum up the tumultuous final year of Malcolm's life. The first three chapters of this early draft follow the final version closely. However, in a later chapter, "What the Black Ex-Slave Is Costing America," Malcolm planned to discuss the issue of public assistance from slavery through Reconstruction and excoriate the Urban League for its public statement that the "Negro is costing this country $28 billion every year." He would return to this theme in the chapter "Why Are We Attacked," calling for the Nation of Islam to be subsidized by the government for providing—through its social and moral programs—a positive welfare that contrasted with the "negative" welfare of the government. Another chapter would reproach liberal whites in what Malcolm would later rework in his famous folk metaphor of the fox (white northern liberals) and the wolf (southern racists). Malcolm would also spend a chapter denouncing police brutality, for if "there is one thing that every black in America has in common with all the rest, it is that he has at some time or another been exposed to the whims of the police. And this, to untold millions, has symbolized what the white man means by his Bill of Rights—for the black man."[3] Several essay chapters were also eventually cut from the final book after Malcolm's death, including three mentioned in Haley's

2. Alex Haley to Ken McCormick and Paul Reynolds, March 21, 1964, folder 37, box 1, Ken McCormick Collection of the Records of Doubleday and Company, Manuscript Division, Library of Congress (KMC).

3. Alex Haley book outline, 1963, folder 37, box 1, KMC.

January 1964 letter: "The Negro," "The End of Christianity," and "Twenty Million Black Muslims."[4] Perhaps more important for readers of the *Autobiography* who have wondered about the conspicuous absence of Malcolm's impressions of African decolonization, one of the final chapters was scheduled to be entitled: "What the Emergence of Africa Did for the Black Man." And finally, anticipating the well-known Black Panther Party's Ten-Point program of the late 1960s, Malcolm would lay out the NOI's central tenets in a section called "What We Muslims Want . . . What We Believe."[5]

Haley also noted changes in Malcolm's disposition, quoting from what he described as the most intimate letter he ever received from Malcolm, a description of a trip he and his brother made to Kalamazoo, Michigan. "It may shock you to learn that two weeks ago," Malcolm wrote, "I had dinner with my mother for the first time in 25 years and she is now home and residing with my brother Philbert in Lansing, Michigan." Malcolm described the catharsis of visiting his mother and how it loosened him to Haley's probing questions: "It was only after opening up and speaking quite freely about her to you during the interview that the subconscious block I had erected was removed, enabling me to remember many things that I had actually blocked out of my mind."[6] Haley's letters not only revealed Malcolm's shifting sensibilities, but also his own motivations. According to Haley, Malcolm agreed to an unchecked afterword by his coauthor. Here, Haley hoped to "hit very hard, speaking from the point of view of the Negro who has tried to do all of the things that are held up as the pathway to enjoying the American dream, and who (if not I personally, so many are) so often gets dissolusioned [*sic*] and disappointed." While frustrated with the glacial pace of change, Haley clearly did not see the NOI as an answer but

4. Alex Haley to Ken McCormick, Tony Gibbs, and Paul Reynolds, February 18, 1964, folder 37, box 1, KMC.

5. Alex Haley book outline.

6. Alex Haley to Ken McCormick, Tony Gibbs, and Paul Reynolds, November 19, 1963, folder 37, box 1, KMC.

rather a product of democratic failings. "I plan to look at America and at the society which has produced the Black Muslims," he wrote. "And I am going to give some courses that every American and every Christian needs to subjectively wrestle with."[7]

Unfortunately, around the time of Malcolm's assassination, many of the provocative essay chapters were removed. Moreover, while Haley had excitedly noted Malcolm's commercial potential the previous year, following his death, he had in fact become too "hot" for the publishers at Doubleday. Amid threats to the lives of Elijah Muhammad and Muhammad Ali as well as the burning of Mosque No. 7, Ken McCormick regretfully wrote Alex Haley that in "a policy decision at Doubleday, where I was a minor, contrary vote, it was decided that we could not publish the Malcolm X book." The editor described calling Paul Reynolds and instructing him to shop the manuscript elsewhere the "hardest thing I ever had to do."[8] The decision would go down as one of the most disastrous marketing moves in Doubleday's history, as the book sold over 6 million copies for Grove Press by 1977, establishing itself as one of the most important autobiographical works in American history.

- Ken McCormick to Alex Haley, March 16, 1965, folder 37, box 2, KMC

Further reading:

- Paul Reynolds to Ken McCormick, September 19, 1963, folder 37, box 1, Ken McCormick Collection of the Records of Doubleday and Company, Manuscript Division, Library of Congress (KMC)

- Alex Haley book outline, 1963, folder 37, box 1, KMC

7. Alex Haley to Ken McCormick, Tony Gibbs, and Paul Reynolds, February 18, 1964, folder 37, box 1, KMC.

8. Ken McCormick to Alex Haley, March 16, 1965, folder 37, box 2, KMC.

- Alex Haley to Ken McCormick, Tony Gibbs, and Paul Reynolds, November 19, 1963, folder 37, box 1, KMC

- Alex Haley to Ken McCormick, Tony Gibbs, and Paul Reynolds, January 19, 1964, folder 37, box 1, KMC

- Alex Haley to Ken McCormick, Tony Gibbs, and Paul Reynolds, February 18, 1964, folder 37, box 1, KMC

- Alex Haley to Ken McCormick and Paul Reynolds, March 21, 1964, folder 37, box 1, KMC

Ken McCormick to Alex Haley, March 16, 1965,
Folder 37, Box 2, Ken McCormick Collection of the
Records of Doubleday and Company, Manuscript
Division, Library of Congress

March 16, 1965

Dear Alex:

I think the hardest thing I ever had to do was to call Paul
Reynolds and ask him to show THE AUTOBIOGRAPHY OF
MALCOLM X to other publishers. In a policy decision at
Doubleday, where I was a minor, contrary vote, it was decided
that we could not publish the Malcolm X book. I want you to
know how much I respect the enormous energy and inspiration you poured into that book. I'm sorry we arent' going to
have the privilege of publishing it, but I hope it doesn't mean
the end of the relationship between us. I loved the book you
described in the restaurant that day, and I hope we'll have the
privilege of publishing that.

Best personal wishes.

Yours,
Ken McCormick

Mr. Alex Haley
Box 110
Rome, New York

KMcC/pw

MALCOLM X IN CALIFORNIA

Elijah Muhammad's bronchial asthma was upgraded to acute in 1961, and he subsequently made his permanent home in the arid climate of Phoenix, Arizona. His absence furthered the schism in leadership that came to a head at the 1963 Saviour's Day convention. There Malcolm acted as master of ceremonies in lieu of the ailing figurehead, only exacerbating tensions between him and the already hostile Muhammad family. After attending the March on Washington in August, Malcolm embarked on a speaking tour of California, marking his first extended visit to the state since the Stokes murder in April 1962. Not surprisingly, Muhammad found the trip unnecessary and suggested that his national minister was traveling too frequently; however, with speaking engagements already secured, he accepted that it was best for Malcolm to follow through on his commitments. For nearly two weeks, in what would be his last West Coast tour, Malcolm stopped in cities such as San Diego, Los Angeles, Fresno, Santa Barbara, Sacramento, Oakland, and San Francisco.

Malcolm's speeches ranged from a guest lecture combined with musical guests Richard "Groove" Holmes and Teddy Edwards in Los Angeles to a panel discussion at University of California, Berkeley. He did not hesitate to criticize the Los Angeles police about the 1962 police brutality case, nor did he spare popular civil rights leaders, adding that although "the white man is our first and main enemy. Our second enemy are [*sic*] the 'Uncle Toms' such as Martin Luther King and his turn the other cheek method."[1] Despite making the usual perfunctory references to Elijah Muhammad and his economic and religious program, Malcolm's speeches also began to incorporate a secular political tone.

In the most significant of his speeches on the West Coast, Malcolm delivered an address entitled "America's Gravest Crisis since the Civil War," to a crowd of four thousand at Berkeley. In Richmond he claimed that where civil rights would fail because it was a "government-controlled" revolution, the black revolution of the NOI would succeed since it was controlled by God.[2] He also delivered his "Farce on Washington" speech before two thousand at Los Angeles' Embassy Auditorium before returning to New York on October 18 to give a report to Mosque No. 7 on the condition of blacks on the West Coast.[3] While many aspects of Malcolm's California tour represented the old rhetoric of religious apocalypse and racial separation, his biting political criticism of the "Catholic administration . . . which offered a civil rights bill, but no civil rights" continued to anticipate his fateful comment concerning Kennedy's assassination in the coming months.

- James Dufur, "Malcolm X Tells Negroes: Quit Integrating, 'Get Off Welfare,'" *Fresno Bee*, October 5, 1963

- "Malcolm X Tells About White Fox," *Hartford Courant*, October 13, 1963

1. Malcolm X FBI file, summary report, New York office, November 15, 1963, 16.

2. Malcolm X FBI file, summary report, New York office, June 18, 1964, 17–19.

3. "Malcolm X Back, Will Speak Fri.," *Amsterdam News*, October 19, 1963.

Further reading:

- Display ad 58 (untitled), *Los Angeles Sentinel*, October 3, 1963

- "Malcolm X Back, Will Speak Fri.," *Amsterdam News*, October 19, 1963

- Title unknown, *ACLU News*, November 1963

- Malcolm X FBI file, summary report, New York office, November 15, 1963, pages 16–17

- Malcolm X FBI file, summary report, New York office, June 18, 1964, pages 7, 9–10, 16–19

- Joseph Gravitt FBI file, summary report, New York office, January 27, 1964, pages 11–12

James Dufur, "Malcolm X Tells Negroes: Quit Integrating, 'Get Off Welfare,'" *Fresno Bee*, October 5, 1963

Malcolm X, the No. 2 national leader of the Black Muslims, last night called on Fresno Negroes to stop trying to integrate the city's schools and neighborhoods. Instead, he said, they should concentrate on doing away with crime, vice and promiscuity in their own community, be polite and "get off welfare."

In a speech before 250 persons during a dinner and fund raising rally in the Edison Social Club—and during a press conference in the Hotel Californian—the Muslims' New York City leader also accused Fresno and Los Angeles of religious persecution because of the court cases involving Muslims in the two cities.

30 WHITES ATTEND

In the audience at the dinner and rally were about 30 whites, including a dozen Fresno State College sociology students. The whites were required to sit separate from the Negroes.

Malcolm X was alternately soft spoken, fiery and even inflammatory but never lost his composure. He was detained for more than an hour after his talk at the rally for an informal question and answer session with both whites and Negroes. Some whites became argumentative but Malcolm X's quick and broad smile kept the tension to a minimum. Plainclothes policemen were in attendance but there were no incidents.

During his press conference his talk and the informal discussion, Malcolm X contended:

1. The white man will not give up his job to a Negro without violence. "The white man hasn't enough jobs for himself." If Negroes try to take white men's jobs, "it may lead to a race war." Instead, Negroes should start their own businesses and industry and create their own jobs.

2. Muslims "must never be the aggressor but if (the white man) puts a hand on us we will fight and we don't care what the odds. A murderer of a Muslim must be murdered. An eye for an eye. A tooth for a tooth. Life for life. If it's his (the Muslim's) price of freedom, he won't hesitate to pay the price (his life). The day is past when the Negro will turn the other cheek." These statements drew the heaviest applause at the rally.

3. The Muslims want to "return" to Africa but would accept "as an alternative" a part of the United States as a separate black nation. "However, we don't want to separate because we hate him (the white). We want to separate because he's doomed. We see doom ahead for America. We want to swim out. We religiously believe America is doomed."

Elijah Muhammad, the Muslims' leader, is a "minor Moses" who will lead the 20 million American Negroes to Africa or to their own nation. When they have their own nation, the Negroes would continue to trade and communicate with whites but would not integrate with them.

4. The Negro and the white are biologically different. The black man was created first Malcolm X implied but would never say the black man is superior.

5. "The American white man is the most hated man on earth. He even hates himself. Maybe the country should be given back to the Indians. We can go back to Africa. But the white man can't go back to Europe. They don't want him."

6. The "masses" of the Negroes are "fed up with the white liberal. The white liberal points out what is going on in the south but tries to hide what is going on in the north. The white fox in the north is even more cruel than the southern wolf. (The white person) uses integration for infiltration. By joining, he strangles your militancy."

7. Negroes should not celebrate the Fourth of July "because it was not your independence."

8. The National Association for the Advancement of Colored People "has done some good and we're thankful for what they have done. But they are outdated. The are a white head on a black body. They don't speak for the masses. They speak for the upper class Negro. Even if you solve every problem of the upper class, you haven't solved the Negro problem."

9. "The March on Washington was a farce." The militant Negroes who had planned to go, did not go. The Kennedy administration (identified as white liberals) took over control of the march, dictating where the marchers would march, also when they would arrive, when they would leave, what signs they would carry and even what they would sing.

10. Tension between the Negroes and the whites "is going to get worse before it gets better." The government should talk with—and listen to—Elijah Muhammad instead of the Negro leaders it talks with now.

MAKES INTRODUCTION

Malcolm X was introduced by Otis T. Morrow, who identified himself as Otis X, the minister of Muhammad's Mosque at 420 Fresno Street. He is on trial in the municipal court on a charge of contributing to the deliquency of a minor.

Malcolm said "the city" is practicing religious persecution by taking Morrow to court for encouraging two teenage boys to attend services. Law enforcement officers accuse Morrow of encouraging the boys to attend against the wishes of the boys' parents.

A collection was taken to assist in paying legal fees for Morrow's case and other court cases, including the recently concluded trial in Los Angeles involving Muslims who were in a fight with the police. One Muslim was shot and killed by the police and others were injured.

Malcolm X said six of the jurors who heard the trial in Los Angeles complained later the Muslims did not get a fair trial.

Hugh Wesley Goodwin, a past president of the Fresno Branch of the NAACP and the attorney who is defending

Morrow in the trial, spoke briefly. He said "umpteen proposals" are being offered Fresno Negroes as solutions to their problems, and concluded:

"Fear and distrust plague the Negro community today. This should be eliminated by discussing every theory. This fear, this distrust, to a great extent, may result from misunderstanding."

"Malcolm X Tells About White Fox,"
Hartford Courant,
October 13, 1963

BERKELEY, Calif. (AP)—Malcolm X, a leader in the Negro Black Muslim movement, Friday told 4,000 University of California students the parable of the "white fox of the North" and "the white wolf of the South."

The "white fox," he said, is a symbol of "the so-called white liberal who strangles Negro efforts by infiltrating our groups and posing as our friends."

At least, he said, the Negro knows where he stands with the "white wolf" of the South.

Malcolm said the only way to avoid bloodshed in America's racial crisis is to establish a separate Negro nation—at the expense of the federal government.

"This country got 310 years of free labor from Negro slaves—they should pay to set the Negroes up on their own now," he said.

"MESSAGE TO
THE GRASS ROOTS"

Although he could not possibly have anticipated it, the last two months of 1963 would come to define the trajectory of Malcolm X's final year. First Malcolm dined with his mother for the first time in twenty-five years; she was then released from Kalamazoo State Hospital into the care of his brother Philbert, in their hometown of Lansing, Michigan. A week later Malcolm delivered one of his most legendary speeches, "Message to the Grass Roots," to nearly two thousand listeners at the Northern Negro Grass Roots Leadership Conference held at Detroit's King Solomon Baptist Church. Considered to be one of the top hundred American speeches of the twentieth century, Malcolm's address unified many of the strands of black nationalism, Pan-Africanism, and third-world revolutionary thought that had been emerging in his ideas for years.[1] Scholar Richard Brent Turner has described the address as a "classic black nationalist speech . . . [that was] an important

---

1. "Top 100 American Speeches of the 20th Century," opinions of 137 leading scholars of American public address compiled by researchers at the University of Wisconsin–Madison and Texas A & M University, last modified September 19, 2011, http://www.news.wisc.edu/misc/speeches/.

signal to insiders and outsiders that Malcolm X had outgrown the political conservatism of the Nation of Islam."[2]

Indeed, sponsored by Albert Cleage's Freedom Now Party, the speech was recognized by many outside the NOI as a move toward the radical left. Detroit activist Grace Lee Boggs later recalled having a similar impression of the speech: "His speech was so analytical, so much less nationalist and more internationalist than Malcolm's previous speeches, that I whispered in the ear of Rev. Cleage, who was sitting next to me on the platform, 'Malcolm's going to split with Elijah Muhammad.'"[3] Likewise, Gloria Richardson, who first met Malcolm X at the speech and went on to collaborate with him in the civil rights organization ACT, remembered: "That was when I really wondered how long it would be before he broke with [the NOI]."[4]

The rhetorical markers that to many signaled an ideological shift were Malcolm's connections between anticolonialism and the struggle of blacks in the U.S. He drew heavily upon aspects of his "Farce on Washington" speech, and "Message to the Grass Roots" has become his most well-known excoriation of the so-called Big Six (Martin Luther King Jr., James Farmer, John Lewis, A. Philip Randolph, Roy Wilkins, and Whitney Young) and the March on Washington, which he derided as a "picnic" and a "circus." Again using the parable of the house Negro and the field Negro, Malcolm distinguished between a "Negro" and "black" revolution, as he had done in the previous month on the West Coast. He claimed that a revolution centered on nonviolent activism was not revolutionary at all: "Revolution is bloody, revolution is hostile, revolution knows no compromise . . . If you're afraid of black

2. Richard Brent Turner, *Islam in the African-American Experience* (Bloomington: Indiana University Press, 1997), 208.

3. Grace Lee Boggs, "Let's Talk about Malcolm and Martin," presented at the Brecht Forum, New York, NY, May 4, 2007; see also Grace Lee Boggs, *Living for Change: An Autobiography* (Minneapolis: University of Minnesota Press, 1998), 129.

4. James Cone, *Martin and Malcolm and America: A Dream or a Nightmare* (Maryknoll, N.Y.: Orbis Books, 1991), 114.

nationalism you're afraid of revolution. And if you love revolution, you love black nationalism."[5] Ultimately, giving such a speech in Detroit, the center of labor activity and black working-class radicalism in the 1960s, opened Malcolm X to an entirely new audience from that of the NOI.

- Malcolm X, "Message to the Grass Roots," in George Breitman, ed., *Malcolm X Speaks: Selected Speeches and Statements* (New York: Grove Weidenfeld, 1990), pages 4–17

Further reading:

- "Black Muslims Join New Militant Northern Negro Organization," *Chicago Defender*, November 21, 1963, 16
- Malcolm X FBI file, summary report, New York office, June 18, 1964, page 15

5. "Message to the Grass Roots," November 10, 1963, in George Breitman, ed., *Malcolm X Speaks: Selected Speeches and Statements* (New York: Merit Publishers, 1965), 3–17.

"Message to the Grass Roots," in George Breitman, ed., *Malcolm X Speaks: Selected Speeches and Statements* (New York: Grove, Weidenfield, 1990), 4-17

Of all our studies, history is best qualified to reward our research. And when you see that you've got problems, all you have to do is examine the historic method used all over the world by others who have problems similar to yours. Once you see how they got theirs straight, then you know how you can get yours straight. There's been a revolution, a black revolution, going on in Africa. In Kenya, the Mau Mau were revolutionary; they were the ones who brought the word "Uhuru" to the fore. The Mau Mau, they were revolutionary, they believed in scorched earth, they knocked everything aside that got in their way, and their revolution also was based on land, a desire for land. In Algeria, the northern part of Africa, a revolution took place. The Algerians were revolutionists, they wanted land. France offered to let them be integrated into France. They told France, to hell with France, they wanted some land, not some France. And they engaged in a bloody battle.

So I cite these various revolutions, brothers and sisters, to show you that you don't have a peaceful revolution. You don't have a turn-the-other-cheek revolution. There's no such thing as a nonviolent revolution. The only kind of revolution that is nonviolent is the Negro revolution. The only revolution in which the goal is loving your enemy is the Negro revolution. It's the only revolution in which the goal is a desegregated lunch counter, a desegregated theater, a desegregated park, and a desegregated public toilet; you can sit down next to white folks—on the toilet. That's no revolution. Revolution is based on land. Land is the basis of all independence. Land is the basis of freedom, justice, and equality.

The white man knows what a revolution is. He knows that the black revolution is world-wide in scope and in nature. The black revolution is sweeping Asia, is sweeping Africa, is rearing its head in Latin America. The Cuban Revolution—that's a revolution. They overturned the system. Revolution is in Asia, revolution is in Africa, and the white man is screaming because he sees revolution in Latin America. How do you think he'll react to you when you learn what a real revolution is? You don't know what a revolution is. If you did, you wouldn't use that word.

Revolution is bloody, revolution is hostile, revolution knows no compromise, revolution overturns and destroys everything that gets in its way. And you, sitting around here like a knot on the wall, saying, "I'm going to love these folks no matter how much they hate me." No, you need a revolution. Whoever heard of a revolution where they lock arms, as Rev. Cleage was pointing out beautifully, singing "We Shall Overcome"? You don't do that in a revolution. You don't do any singing, you're too busy swinging. It's based on land. A revolutionary wants land so he can set up his own nation, an independent nation. These Negroes aren't asking for any nation—they're trying to crawl back on the plantation.

When you want a nation, that's called nationalism. When the white man became involved in a revolution in this country against England, what was it for? He wanted this land so he could set up another white nation. That's white nationalism. The American Revolution was white nationalism. The French Revolution was white nationalism. The Russian Revolution too—yes, it was—white nationalism. You don't think so? Why do you think Khrushchev and Mao can't get their heads together? White nationalism. All the revolutions that are going on in Asia and Africa today are based on what?—black nationalism. A revolutionary is a black nationalist. He wants a nation. I was reading some beautiful words by Rev. Cleage, poining out why he couldn't get together with someone else in the city because all of them were afraid of being identified with black nationalism. If you're afraid of black nationalism, you're afraid of revolution. And if you love revolution, you love black nationalism.

To understand this, you have to go back to what the young brother here referred to as the house Negro and the field Negro back during slavery. There were two kinds of slaves, the house Negro and the field Negro. The house Negroes—they lived in the house with master, they dressed pretty good, they ate good because they ate his food—what he left. They lived in the attic or the basement, but still they lived near the master; and they loved the master more than the master loved himself. They would give their life to save the master's house—quicker than the master would. If the master said, "We got a good house here," the house Negro would say, "Yeah, we got a good house here." Whenever the master said "we," he said "we." That's how you can tell a house Negro.

If the master's house caught on fire, the house Negro would fight harder to put the blaze out than the master would. If the master got sick, the house Negro would say, "What's the matter, boss, *we* sick?" *We* sick! He identified himself with his master, more than his master identified with himself. And if you came to the house Negro and said, "Let's run away, let's escape, let's separate," the house Negro would look at you and say, "Man, you crazy. What you mean, separate? Where is there a better house than this? Where can I wear better clothes than this? Where can I eat better food than this?" That was that house Negro. In those days he was called a "house nigger." And that's what we call them today, because we've still got some house niggers running around here.

This modern house Nego loves his master. He wants to live near him. He'll pay three times as much as the house is worth just to live near his master, and then brag about "I'm the only Negro out here." "I'm the only one on my job." "I'm the only one in this school." You're nothing but a house Negro. And if someone comes to you right now and says, "Let's separate," you say the same thing that the house Negro said on the plantation. "What you mean, separate? From America, this good white man? Where you going to get a better job than you get here?" I mean, this is what you say. "I ain't left nothing in Africa," that's what you say. Why, you left your mind in Africa.

On that same plantation, there was the field Negro. The

field Negroes—those were the masses. There were always more Negroes in the field than there were Negroes in the house. The Negro in the field caught hell. He ate leftovers. In the house they ate high up on the hog. The Negro in the field didn't get anything but what was left of the insides of the hog. They call it "chitt'lings" nowadays. In those days they called them what they were—guts. That's what you were—gut-eaters. And some of you are still gut-eaters.

The field Negro was beaten from morning to night; he lived in a shack, in a hut; he wore old, castoff clothes. He hated his master. I say he hated his master. He was intelligent. That house Negro loved his master, but that field Negro—remember, they were in the majority, and they hated the master. When the house caught on fire, he didn't try to put it out; that field Negro prayed for a wind, for a breeze. When the master got sick, the field Negro prayed that he'd die. If someone came to the field Negro and said, "Let's separate, let's run," he didn't say "Where we going?" He'd say, "Any place is better than here." You've got field Negroes in America today. I'm a field Negro. The masses are the field Negroes. When they see this man's house on fire, you don't hear the little Negroes talking about "*our* government is in trouble." They say, "*The* government in in trouble." Imagine a Negro: "*Our* government"! I even heard one say "*our* astronauts." They won't even let him near the plant—and "*our* astronauts"! "*Our* Navy"—that's a Negro that is out of his mind, a Negro that is out of his mind.

Just as the slavemaster of that day used Tom, the house Negro, to keep the field Negroes in check, the same old slavemaster today has Negroes who are nothing but modern Uncle Toms, twentieth-century Uncle Toms, to keep you and me in check, to keep us under control, keep us passive and peaceful and nonviolent. That's Tom making you nonviolent. It's like when you go to the dentist, and the man's going to take your tooth. You're going to fight him when he starts pulling. So he squirts some stuff in your jaw called novocaine, to make you think they're not doing anything to you. So you sit there and because you've got all of that novocaine in your jaw, you suffer—peacefully. Blood running all down your jaw, and you don't know what's happening. Because someone has taught you to suffer—peacefully.

The white man does the same thing to you in the street, when he wants to put knots on your head and take advantage of you and not have to be afraid of your fighting back. To keep you from fighting back, he gets these old religious Uncle Toms to teach you and me, just like novocaine, to suffer peacefully. Don't stop suffering—just suffer peacefully. As Rev. Cleage pointed out, they say you should let your blood flow in the streets. This is a shame. You know he's a Christian preacher. If it's a shame to him, you know what it is to me.

There is nothing in our book, the Koran, that teaches us to suffer peacefully. Our religion teaches us to be intelligent. Be peaceful, be courteous, obey the law, respect everyone; but if someone puts his hand on you, send him to the cemetery. That's a good religion. In fact, that's that old-time religion. That's the one that Ma and Pa used to talk about: an eye for an eye, and a tooth for a tooth, and a head for a head, and a life for a life. That's a good religion. And nobody resents that kind of religion being taught but a wolf, who intends to make you his meal.

This is the way it is with the white man in America. He's a wolf—and you're sheep. Any time a shepherd, a pastor, teaches you and me not to run from the white man and, at the same time, teaches us not to fight the white man, he's a traitor to you and me. Don't lay down a life all by itself. No, preserve your life, it's the best thing you've got. And if you've got to give it up, let it be even-steven.

The slavemaster took Tom and dressed him well, fed him well and even gave him a little education—a little education; gave him a long coat and a top hat and made all the other slaves look up to him. Then he used Tom to control them. The same strategy that was used in those days is used today, by the same white man. He takes a Negro, a so-called Negro, and makes him prominent, builds him up, publicizes him, makes him a celebrity. And then he becomes a spokesman for Negroes—and a Negro leader.

I would like to mention just one other thing quickly, and

that is the method that the white man uses, how the white man uses the "big guns," or Negro leaders, against the Negro revolution. They are not a part of the Negro revolution. They are used against the Negro revolution.

When Martin Luther King failed to desegregate Albany, Georgia, the civil-rights struggle in America reached its low point. King became bankrupt almost, as a leader. The Southern Christian Leadership Conference was in financial trouble; and it was in trouble, period, with the people when they failed to desegregate Albany, Georgia. Other Negro civil-rights leaders of so-called national stature became fallen idols. As they became fallen idols, began to lose their prestige and influence, local Negro leaders began to stir up the masses. In Cambridge, Maryland, Gloria Richardson; in Danville, Virginia, and other parts of the country, local leaders began to stir up our people at the grass-roots level. This was never done by these Negroes of national stature. They control you, but they have never incited you or excited you. They control you, they contain you, they have kept you on the plantation.

As soon as King failed in Birmingham, Negroes took to the streets. King went out to California to a big rally and raised I don't know how many thousands of dollars. He came to Detroit and had a march and raised some more thousands of dollars. And recall, right after that Roy Wilkins attacked King. He accused King and CORE [Congress Of Racial Equality] of starting trouble everywhere and then making the NAACP [National Association for the Advancement of Colored People] get them out of jail and spend a lot of money; they accused King and CORE of raising all the money and not paying it back. This happened; I've got it in documented evidence in the newspaper. Roy started attacking King, and King started attacking Roy, and Farmer started attacking both of them. And as these Negroes of national stature began to attack each other, they began to lose their control of the Negro masses.

The Negroes were out there in the streets. They were talking about how they were going to march on Washington. Right at that time Birmingham had exploded, and the Negroes in Birmingham—remember, they also exploded. They began to stab the crackers in the back and bust them up 'side their head—yes, they did. That's when Kennedy sent in the troops, down in Birmingham. After that, Kennedy got on the television and said "this is a moral issue." That's when he said he was going to put out a civil-rights bill. And when he mentioned civil-rights bill and the Southern crackers started talking about how they were going to boycott or filibuster it, then the Negroes started talking—about what? That they were going to march on Washington, march on the Senate, march on the White House, march on the Congress, and tie it up, bring it to a halt, not let the government proceed. They even said they were going out to the airport and lay down on the runway and not let any airplanes land. I'm telling you what they said. That was revolution. That was revolution. That was the black revolution.

It was the grass roots out there in the street. It scared the white man to death, scared the white power structure in Washington, D.C., to death; I was there. When they found out that this black steamroller was going to come down on the capital, they called in Wilkins, they called in Randolph, they called in these national Negro leaders that you respect and told them, "Call it off." Kennedy said, "Look, you all are letting this thing go too far." And Old Tom said, "Boss, I can't stop it, because I didn't start it." I'm telling you what they said. They said, "I'm not even in it, much less at the head of it." They said, "These Negroes are doing things on their own. They're running ahead of us." And that old shrewd fox, he said, "If you all aren't in it, I'll put you in it. I'll put you at the head of it. I'll endorse it. I'll welcome it. I'll help it. I'll join it."

A matter of hours went by. They had a meeting at the Carlyle Hotel in New York City. The Carlyle Hotel is owned by the Kennedy family; that's the hotel Kennedy spent the night at, two nights ago; it belongs to his family. A philanthropic society headed by a white man named Stephen Currier called all the top civil-rights leaders together at the Carlyle Hotel. And he told them, "By you all fighting each other, you are destroying the civil-rights movement. And since you're fighting over money from white liberals, let us set up what is known as the

Council for United Civil Rights Leadership. Let's form this council, and all the civil-rights organizations will belong to it, and we'll use it for fund-raising purposes." Let me show you how tricky the white man is. As soon as they got it formed, they elected Whitney Young as its chairman, and who do you think became the co-chairman? Stephen Currier, the white man, a millionaire. Powell was talking about it down at Cobo Hall today. That is what he was talking about. Powell knows it happened. Randolph knows it happened. Wilkins knows it happened. King knows it happened. Every one of that Big Six—they know it happened.

Once they formed it, with the white man over it, he promised them and gave them $800,000 to split up among the Big Six; and told them that after the march was over they'd give them $700,000 more. A million and a half dollars—split up between leaders that you have been following, going to jail for, crying crocodile tears for. And they're nothing but Frank James and Jesse James and the what-do-you-call-'em brothers.

As soon as they got the setup organized, the white man made available to them top public-relations experts; opened the news media across the country at their disposal, which then began to project these Big Six as the leaders of the march. Originally they weren't even in the march. You were talking this march talk on Hastings Street, you were talking march talk on Lenox Avenue, and on Fillmore Street, and on Central Avenue, and 32nd Street and 63rd Street. That's where the march talk was being talked. But the white man put the Big Six at the head of it; made them the march. They became the march. They took it over. And the first move they made after they took it over, they invited Walter Reuther, a white man; they invited a priest, a rabbi, and an old white preacher, yes, an old white preacher. The same white element that put Kennedy into power—labor, the Catholics, the Jews, and liberal Protestants; the same clique that put Kennedy in power, joined the march on Washington.

It's just like when you've got some coffee that's too black, which means it's too strong. What do you do? You integrate it with cream, you make it weak. But if you pour too much cream in it, you won't even know you ever had coffee. It used to be hot, it becomes cool. It used to be strong, it becomes weak. It used to wake you up, now it puts you to sleep. This is what they did with the march on Washington. They joined it. They didn't integrate it, they infiltrated it. They joined it, became a part of it, took it over. And as they took it over, it lost its militancy. It ceased to be angry, it ceased to be hot, it ceased to be uncompromising. Why, it even ceased to be a march. It became a picnic, a circus. Nothing but a circus, with clowns and all. You had one right here in Detroit—I saw it on television—with clowns leading it, white clowns and black clowns. I know you don't like what I'm saying, but I'm going to tell you anyway. Because I can prove what I'm saying. If you think I'm telling you wrong, you bring me Martin Luther King and A. Philip Randolph and James Farmer and those other three, and see if they'll deny it over a microphone.

No, it was a sellout. It was a takeover. When James Baldwin came in from Paris, they wouldn't let him talk, because they couldn't make him go by the script. Burt Lancaster read the speech that Baldwin was supposed to make; they wouldn't let Baldwin get up there, because they know Baldwin is liable to say anything. They controlled it so tight, they told those Negroes what time to hit town, how to come, where to stop, what signs to carry, what song to sing, what speech they could make, and what speech they couldn't make; and then told them to get out of town by sundown. And every one of those Toms was out of town by sundown. Now I know you don't like my saying this. But I can back it up. It was a circus, a performance that beat anything Hollywood could ever do, the performance of the year. Reuther and those other three devils should get an Academy Award for the best actors because they acted like they really loved Negroes and fooled a whole lot of Negroes. And the six Negro leaders should get an award too, for the best supporting cast.

"CHICKENS COMING HOME TO ROOST"

In early August 1963, prior to his instructions regarding the March on Washington, Elijah Muhammad wrote to Malcolm X with another warning: "Be careful about mentioning Kennedy in your talks and printed matters by name; use U.S.A. or the American Government."[1] On December 1, 1963, Malcolm spoke in place of Muhammad, who again had taken ill. At the Manhattan Center, he delivered a speech entitled "God's Judgment of White America" before a crowd of seven hundred made up mostly of Mosque No. 7 members but also including a significant minority of non-Muslim blacks and members of the white press. With NOI national secretary John Ali in the audience, Malcolm was sure to address the religious aspects of the organization's program, stressing that followers had been practicing the five pillars of Islam and making pilgrimages since Muhammad first traveled to the Middle East in 1960. The speech was not altogether void of politics, though, and Malcolm argued—as he had in the past several months—that the "Negro revolution" was controlled by the government and white liberals. Again he implicated Martin Luther King Jr.,

1. Elijah Muhammad to Malcolm X, August 1, 1962, box 3, folder 8, Malcolm X Collection, Schomburg Center for Research in Black Culture, New York Public Library.

placing him at the forefront of his critique: "Revolutions are never peaceful, never loving, never nonviolent. Nor are they compromising. Revolutions are destructive and bloody."[2]

However, it was not this tactical political indictment that would earn the ire of Muhammad and the Chicago ruling elite but rather Malcolm's comments during the question-and-answer period. Despite the explicit instructions handed down by Muhammad, he answered a reporter's question regarding the recent assassination of President Kennedy with the analogy of "chickens coming home to roost." "Being an old farm boy myself," he said, "chickens coming home to roost never did make me sad; they've always made me glad." Although many attending the speech thought little of his statement at the time, the New York Times ran a story the following day with the title "Malcolm X Scores U.S. and Kennedy: Likens Slaying to 'Chickens Coming Home to Roost.'"[3] On December 4, Muhammad announced that the minister had been suspended for ninety days and even canceled all his own scheduled appearances for a monthlong "mourning period" out of respect for the late president. Muhammad wrote in the NOI's newspaper that although he did not "classify Minister Malcolm as a hypocrite, for he is no such man, according to his work . . . I do think that all must be reminded that anything that we do must be in accord with our policy."[4] Still described in the press as "the man rumored to be the next leader of the Black Muslims," Malcolm responded to the suspension with his usual humility: "Yes, I'm wrong. I disobeyed Muhammad's order. He was justified 100 per cent. I agree I need to withdraw from public appearance."[5]

The details of Malcolm's suspension were clear. He would

2. "God's Judgment of White America," December 1, 1963, box 5, folders 6–7, Malcolm X Collection, Schomburg Center for Research in Black Culture, New York Public Library.

3. "Malcolm X Scores U.S. and Kennedy: Likens Slaying to 'Chickens Coming Home to Roost,'" New York Times, December 2, 1963.

4. "Nation Still Mourns Death," Muhammad Speaks, December 20, 1963.

5. "Elijah Suspends Malcolm," Amsterdam News, December 7, 1963.

retain his administrative duties at Mosque No. 7 but withdraw from all public activity. However, both Malcolm and many mosque members were unsure of exactly how rigidly these boundaries were drawn. The minister continued to make statements to the press when asked over the telephone about his suspension. Likewise, close associates at the mosque spoke to Malcolm in private but knew that such conversations were a direct violation of Muhammad's edict. Malcolm's "chickens" statement was a public-relations faux pas; however, for Muhammad to declare, as he did, in a public telegram, that "we with the world are very shocked at the assassination of President Kennedy" seemed bizarre for a sect that promoted total separation and political sovereignty.[6] What became painfully clear to many was that Muhammad and Malcolm's enemies in Chicago had seen an opportunity to impose their authority. Such a public suspension restored order, but hostilities quickly escalated to the point where Malcolm's return seemed to all besides Malcolm himself a grave impossibility.

- Raymond Sharrieff FBI file, summary report, Chicago office, February 19, 1964, pages 12–13
- Malcolm X FBI file, memo from FBI director J. Edgar Hoover to Secret Service chief, December 6, 1963

Further reading:

- "Malcolm X Scores U.S. and Kennedy: Likens Slaying to 'Chickens Coming Home to Roost,'" *New York Times*, December 2, 1963
- "Malcolm X Suspended!" *Chicago Defender*, December 5, 1963

6. "Malcolm X Suspended for JFK Remarks," *Amsterdam News*, December 7, 1963.

- R. W. Apple Jr., "Malcolm X Silenced for Remarks on Assassination of Kennedy," *New York Times*, December 5, 1963

- "Malcolm X Hit for Glee over Kennedy Death," *Los Angeles Times*, December 5, 1963

- "Malcolm X Expected to be Replaced," *New York Times*, December 6, 1963

- "Elijah Suspends Malcolm," *Amsterdam News*, December 7, 1963

- "Malcolm X Suspended for JFK Remarks," *Amsterdam News*, December 7, 1963

- Major Robinson, "May Mean Policy Change: Muzzling of Malcolm X for Indefinite Period," *Pittsburgh Courier*, December 14, 1963

- Gertrude Wilson, "I Hate You!" *Amsterdam News*, December 14, 1963

- "Malcolm X Maintains Silence," *Amsterdam News*, December 14, 1963

- "X on the Spot," *Newsweek*, December 16, 1963

- "Nation Still Mourns Death," *Muhammad Speaks*, December 20, 1963

- Malcolm X FBI file, memo, New York office, January 29, 1964

- Malcolm X FBI file, memo, Indianapolis office, December 10, 1963

- Transcript, Herman Ferguson interview, June 24, 2004, and June 27, 2003, Malcolm X Project

"If they don't want us they should send us back to the East. We have friends there. Our friends in the East have for years begged to help us with money and furnish us with a home. I have turned down these offers because I did not want to obligate you to any other nation."

MUHAMMAD continued that what he wants is for the United States to give Islam some land, and stated:

No nation can survive without having its own land. "They owe it to us for using us to develop the country." They should not only give us some land but should also give us money to develop our land. They should give us arms, not to fight them but to protect ourselves from invasions by our "friends." "Do you know that some of our friends are America's enemies?"

The white man does not want to integrate because in reality it would mean he would have to give up or share the good things that are now his alone to enjoy. No Muslim could stand by and see his women and children attacked by dogs, cattle prods and fire hoses. The record is clear that Muslims carry no arms but with the aid of Allah they have always been able to protect themselves.

At one of the NOI meetings, which was held on October 13, 1963, Supreme Captain RAYMOND SHARIEFF spoke and reminded the members of Savior's Day. He stated:

Expenses have increased tremendously and for the first time in years the Messenger has found it necessary to tax his followers a larger amount. Each FOI is being asked to give $150.00 instead of the usual $125.00.

At one of the FOI meetings, which was held on November 17, 1963, Supreme Captain RAYMOND SHARIEFF announced that ELIJAH MUHAMMAD would appear in New

York on December 1, 1963. He said that members of MT No. 2 should not go because of the small space available where the Messenger would speak. He urged those who had planned to go to New York to put their fare on their Savior's Day gift.

Supreme Captain SHARIEFF then criticized the FOI for not coming out regularly to meetings. He said "with almost 400 FOI, there is no reason why we should not have at least one-half of them out each meeting".

At one of the FOI meetings, which was held on November 22, 1963, RAYMOND SHARRIEFF was in a position to have heard ████████████████ speak as follows:

ELIJAH MUHAMMAD was given the power to lead the black people in America to freedom, justice and equality. Islam stands for peace. There will be no war between whites and blacks because Allah, with his power, will see that the black people receive justice. The Messenger's only weapon is the sword of truth. "Don't be surprised at anything that happens and above all don't feel sorry for what may seem like a tragedy to you. Just remember that Allah is a god of retribution and also remember that your forefathers suffered murder, maiming, and rape at the hands of the devil."

At this same meeting Supreme Captain RAYMOND SHARRIEFF, after the visitors had been dismissed, spoke as follows to the members present:

The death of President KENNEDY today was very tragic. You are to show no jubilation about the matter. "No matter how you feel, don't talk to your friends or on your jobs about this assassination." "The Christians have deep feelings about what has happened and if you say the wrong thing, you can find yourselves in serious trouble. You might even be killed."

Malcolm X FBI File, Memo from FBI Director J. Edgar Hoover to Secret Service Chief, December 6, 1963

Date : December 6, 1963
To: Chief, U. S. Secret Service
From: John Edgar Hoover, Director

Subject: NATION OF ISLAM INTERNAL SECURITY—
NOI

███████████████████████████████████████

███████████████████████████████████████

███████████████████████ had confirmed reports that Malcolm X.
Little, Minister of the Nation of Islam (NOI) Temple in New
York City, and leading NOI spokesman had been suspended
from the NOI on December 4, 1963, by Elijah Muhammad for
expressing joy over the death of President Kennedy.

Malcolm X. Little, who spoke at a rally held by the NOI in
New York City on December 1, 1963, stated that the late President Kennedy had been "twiddling his thumbs" at the slaying
of South Vietnamese President Ngo Dinh Diem and his
brother, Ngo Dinh Nhu. Little added that he "never foresaw
that the chickens would come home to roost so soon." He also
stated, "Being an old farm boy myself, chickens coming home
to roost never did make me sad; they always made me glad."
Elijah Muhammad, National Leader of the NOI was scheduled to speak at this New York rally but canceled his appearance out of respect to the death of President Kennedy and
instructed NOI members to make no comments concerning
the assassination of the President.

The NOI is an all-Negro, anti-white, semireligious organization which advocates complete separation of the races and
teaches extreme hatred of all white men.

MIAMI VACATION

Malcolm had entered the second month of his ninety-day silencing in January 1964 when he was invited to be a part of Cassius Clay's boxing camp as an advisor in Miami. Clay was just a few days shy of his twenty-second birthday and was the consummate underdog poised to challenge defending heavyweight champion Sonny Liston. He had first introduced himself to Malcolm at Mosque No. 2 in Chicago in 1961, after he and his brother Rudy drove from their hometown of Louisville to see Elijah Muhammad speak. However, at the time of Malcolm's visit the young fighter had yet to formally join the Nation of Islam. For their part, Muhammad and the NOI were reluctant to make any commitments to Clay. In general the NOI frowned upon sports, especially violent ones, and Clay hardly looked like a horse worth betting upon. However, with Malcolm's suspension still unsettled, he recognized the coup that Clay would represent should he defeat Liston and proclaim himself a follower of Muhammad.

The trip to Miami was Malcolm and Betty's first and only vacation together, and he used the time to recraft his image. In his diaries Malcolm scribbled a series of small blurbs about "Malcolm X, the Family Man" to accompany a portrait of his family with Clay.[1] The photograph was eventually published

1. Miami Vacation Notebook (1964), box 1, folder 5, Malcolm X Collection, Schomburg Center for Research in Black Culture, New York Public Library.

in both the *Amsterdam News* and *Chicago Defender* and was the first time Malcolm publicly presented his family.[2] Although Betty and the children returned after only four days, Clay and Malcolm stayed through January 2 before the boxer unorthodoxly broke camp and flew to New York to tour Harlem and attend an NOI rally. Despite still remaining uncommitted, Clay reportedly stated, "I'm a race man, and every time I go to a Muslim meeting I get inspired."[3] Meanwhile, Malcolm was still appealing to Muhammad for reinstatement and the silencing was not suiting him. An FBI memo from Miami reported Malcolm as saying, "If you think Cassius Clay was loud, wait until I start talking on the first of March."[4]

When Malcolm returned to Miami, the heavyweight bout itself was in jeopardy. Clay's rumored ties to the NOI had turned away white fans, and the general public felt the young pugilist had little chance of winning. Malcolm agreed to keep a lower public profile during the final five days preceding the fight, though he would still be given a ringside seat with his favorite number: seven. Desperate for reinstatement, Malcolm called Chicago headquarters with a final offer. He would bring a victorious Clay to the annual Saviour's Day convention, held only days after the fight, and in return his suspension would be lifted and his old position in Mosque No. 7 and as national minister promptly restored. Unfortunately for Malcolm, at this point the NOI reserved doubts not only about the possibility of Clay's victory but also about the likelihood of the minister's reinstatement. Although Clay became the youngest boxer ever to dethrone the heavyweight champion and soon proclaimed his allegiance to Elijah Muhammad, changing his name to Muhammad Ali, Malcolm X was soon forced to leave the NOI and form his own religious group. His relationship with Clay subsequently diminished to the point that the boxer

2. "Clay Celebrates with Malcolm X," *Chicago Defender*, February 6, 1964; "Malcolm X's Family and Friend," *Amsterdam News*, February 1, 1964.

3. "Cassius Clay Almost Says He's a Muslim," *Amsterdam News*, January 25, 1964.

4. Malcolm X FBI file, memo, Miami office, March 3, 1964.

publicly denounced him later in the same year during a chance meeting in Ghana. Ali clearly understood that allegiances had to be firm, and his were to Elijah Muhammad. Of Malcolm, he concluded, "Man, he's gone. He's gone so far out he's out completely."[5]

- George Plimpton, "Miami Notebook: Cassius Clay and Malcolm X," *Harper's Magazine* 228, 1369 (June 1964): 54–61

Further reading:

- "Cassius Clay Almost Says He's a Muslim," *Amsterdam News*, January 25, 1964

- "Malcolm X in Florida," *Amsterdam News*, January 25, 1964

- "Malcolm X's Family and Friend," *Amsterdam News*, February 1, 1964

- "Clay Celebrates with Malcolm X," *Chicago Defender*, February 6, 1964

- Title unknown, *New York Herald Tribune*, February 20, 1964, page 9

- "Malcolm X 'Comeback' in March," *Amsterdam News*, February 22, 1964

- Robert Lipsyte, "Clay Discusses His Future, Liston and Black Muslims," *New York Times*, February 27, 1964

- Malcolm X FBI file, memo, New York office, January 20, 1964

- Malcolm X FBI file, memo, Miami office, January 21, 1964

- Malcolm X FBI file, memo, New York office, January 29, 1964

- Malcolm X FBI file, memo, New York office, February 20, 1964

- Malcolm X FBI file, memo, Miami office, March 3, 1964

---

5. Lloyd Garrison, "Clay Makes Malcolm Ex-Friend," *New York Times*, May 18, 1964.

George Plimpton, "Miami Notebook: Cassius Clay
and Malcolm X," *Harper's Magazine* 228, 1369
(June 1964): 54–61

"These are the things you are teaching Cassius?" Plimpton
asked. "He will make up his own mind," said the true revolutionary.

I.

The press was incensed at Cassius Clay's behavior before
the Liston fight. You could feel it. They wanted straight answers, and they weren't getting them. Usually, particularly
with fighters, the direct question of extreme simiplicity—
which is of great moment to the sportswriters—will get a reply
in kind. "Champ," asks the sportswriter, "how did you sleep
last night and what did you have for breakfast?" When the
champ considers the matter and says he slept real fine and had
six eggs and four glasses of milk, the sportswriter puts down,
"gd sleep 6 eggs 4 gl milk," on his pad, and a little while later
the statistic goes out over Western Union.

But with Clay, such a question simply served to unleash an act,
an entertainment which included poetry, the brandishing of arms
and canes, a chorus thrown in—not a dull show by any standard,
even if you've seen it a few times before. The press felt that the
act—it was constantly referred to as an "act"—was born of terror or lunacy. What *should* have appealed, Cassius surely being
the most colorful, if bizarre, heavyweight since, well, John L.
Sullivan or Jack Johnson, none of this seemed to work at all.
The press's attitude was largely that of the lip-curling disdain

the Cambridge police have toward the antics of students heeling for the *Harvard Lampoon*.

One of the troubles, I think—it occurred to me as I watched Clay at his last press conference on February 24 before the fight—is that his appearance does not suit his manner. His great good looks are wrong for the excessive things he shouts. Archie Moore used the same sort of routine as Clay to get himself a shot at both the light-heavyweight and heavyweight championships—self-promotion, gags, bizarre suits, a penchant for public speaking—but his character was suited to it, his face with a touch of slyness in it, and always humor. So the press was always very much in his support, and they had much to do with Moore's climb from obscurity. At his training camp outside San Diego—the Salt Mines it is called, where Cassius himself did a tour at the start of his career—Moore has built a staircase in the rocks, sixty or seventy steps, each with a reporter's name painted in red to symbolize the assistance the press gave him. Clay's face, on the other hand, does not show humor. He has a fine grin, but his features are curiously deadpan when the self-esteem begins, which, of course, desperately needs humor as a softening effect. Clay himself bridled at the resentment he caused. It must have puzzled him to be cast as the villain in a fight with Liston, who, on the surface at least, had absolutely no flair or panache except as a symbol of destructiveness.

Clay made a short, final address to the newspapermen. "This is your last chance," he said. "It's your last chance to get on the bandwagon. I'm keeping a list of all you people. After the fight is done, we're going to have a roll call up there in the ring. And when I see so-and-so said this fight was a mismatch, why I'm going to have a little ceremony and some *eating* is going on—eating of words." His manner was that of the admonishing schoolteacher. The press sat in their rows at the Miami Auditorium staring balefully at him. It seemed incredible that a smile or two wouldn't show up on a writer's face. It was so wonderfully preposterous. But I didn't see any.

2.

In the corridors around the press headquarters in the Miami Auditorium, one was almost sure to run into King Levinsky, a second-rate heavyweight in his prime (he was one of Joe Louis' bums of the month) who fought too long, so that it had affected him, and he is now an ambulatory tie-salesman. He would appear carrying his ties, which are labeled with a pair of boxing gloves and his name, in a cardboard box, and he'd get rid of them in jig time. His sales technique was formidable: he would single out a prospect, move down the corridor for him fast, and sweeping an arm around the fellow's neck pull him in close . . . to within range of a hoarse and somewhat wetly delivered whisper to the ear: "From the King? You buy a tie from the King?" The victim, his head in the crook of the fighter's massive arm, would mumble and nod weakly, and fish for his bankroll. Almost everyone had a Levinsky tie, though you didn't see too many people wearing them. When the King appeared around a corner, the press would scatter, some into a row of phone booths set along the corridor. "Levinsky!" they'd say and move off quickly and officiously. Levinsky would peer around and often he'd pick someone *in* a phone booth, set his cardboard box down, and shake the booth gently. You'd see him watching the fellow inside, and then the door would open and the fellow would come out and buy his tie. They only cost a dollar.

Sometimes Levinsky, if he knew he'd already sold you a couple of ties, would get you in the crook of his arm and he'd recount things he thought you ought to know about his career. "Joe Louis finished me," he'd say. "In one round that man turned me from a fighter to a guy selling ties." He said this without rancor, as if Louis had introduced him to a chosen calling. "I got rapport now," he'd say—this odd phrase—and then he'd let you go. Clay came down the corridors after the weigh-in and Levinsky bounded after him. "He's gonna take you, kid," he hollered. "Liston's gonna take you, make you a guy selling ties . . . partners with me, kid, you kin be *partners* with me." Clay and his entourage were moving at a lively clip, canes on high, shouting that they were ready to "rumble," and it was doubtful the chilling offer got through.

At the late afternoon press parties in the bar of the Roney Plaza, the promoters had another fighter at hand—the antithesis of Levinsky—a personable Negro heavyweight, Marty Marshall, the only man to beat Liston. The promoters brought him down from Detroit, his hometown, to impress the writers that Liston wasn't invincible, hoping that this notion would appear in their columns and help promote a gate lagging badly since the fight was universally considered a mismatch. Marshall met Liston three times, winning the first, then losing twice, though decking Liston in the second, always baffling him with an unpredictable attack. Liston blamed his one loss on making the mistake of dropping his jaw to laugh at Marshall's maneuvers, and *bam*, getting it broken with a sudden punch.

Marshall didn't strike one as a comic figure. He is a tall, graceful man, conservatively dressed, a pleasant face with small, round, delicate ears, and a quick smile. Greeting him was a complex matter, because he was attended for a while by someone who introduced him by saying, "Shake the hand that broke Sonny Liston's jaw!" Since Marshall is an honest man and it was a left hook that did the business, his *left* would come out, and one had to consider whether to take it with one's own left or with the right, before getting down to the questions. There was almost always a circle around him in the bar. The press couldn't get enough of what it was to be in the ring with Liston. Marshall didn't belittle the experience (after all, he'd been beaten twice), and indeed some of the things he said made one come away with even more respect for the champion.

"When I knocked him down with that hook in the second fight, he got up angry," said Marshall. "He hit me three shots you shouldn't've thrown at a bull. The first didn't knock me down, but it hurt so much I went down anyway."

"Geezus," said one of the reporters.

"Does he say anything—I mean when he's angry—can you see it?"

"No," said Marshall. "He's silent. He just comes for you."

"Gee*zus*," said the reporter again.

We all stood around, looking admiringly at Marshall, jiggling the ice in our glasses.

One of the writers cleared his throat. "I heard a story about the champion this morning," he said. "He does his roadwork, you know, out at the Normandy Golf Course, and there was this greenskeeper working out there, very early, pruning the grass at the edge of a water hazard, the mist coming off the grass, very quiet, spooky, you know, and he hears this noise behind him and there's Liston there, about ten feet away, looking out of his hood at him, and this guy gives a big scream and pitches forward into the water."

"Yeah," said Marshall. He was smiling. "I can see that."

3.

Each fighter had his spiritual adviser, his *guru* at hand. In Liston's camp was Father Murphy, less a religious adviser than a confidant and friend of the champion. In Clay's camp was Malcolm X, who was then one of the high officials of the Black Muslim sect, indeed its most prominent spokesman, though he has since defected to form his own black nationalist political movement. For months he had been silent. Elijah Muhammad, the supreme leader, the Messenger of Allah, had muzzled him since November for making intemperate remarks after the assassination of President Kennedy. But he had been rumored to be in Miami, and speculation was strong that he was there to bring Cassius Clay into the Muslim fold.

I was riding in a car just after the weigh-in with Archie Robinson, who is Clay's business manager and closest friend—a slightly built young man, not much older than Clay, one would guess, very polite and soft-spoken—and he asked me if I'd like to meet Malcolm X. I said yes, and we drove across Biscayne Bay to the Negro-clientele Hampton House Motel in Miami proper—a small-town hotel compared to the Babylon towers across the Bay, with a small swimming pool, a luncheonette, a pitch-dark bar where you had to grope to find a chair, with a dance floor and a band which came on later, and most of the rooms in balconied barracks-like structures out back. It was crowded and very lively with people in town not only for the fight but also for an invitation golf tournament.

I waited at a side table in the luncheonette. Malcolm X came in after a while, moving by the tables very slowly. Elijah Muhammad's ministers—Malcolm X was one of them—are said to emulate him even to the speed of his walk, which is considerable. But the luncheonette was not set up for a swift entrance. The tables were close together, and Malcolm X came by them carefully—a tall, erect man in his thirties, a lean, intelligent face with a long pronounced jaw, a wide mouth set in it which seems caught in a perpetual smile. He was carrying one of the Cassius Clay camp's souvenir canes, and with his horn-rimmed glasses, his slow stately walk, and with Robinson half a step behind him, guiding him, I thought for a second that he'd gone blind. He sat down, unwrapped a package of white peppermints which he picked at steadily, and began talking. Robinson sat with us for a while, but he had things to attend to.

I took notes from time to time, scratching them down on the paper tablecloth, then in a notebook. Malcolm X did not seem to mind. He said he was going to be unmuzzled in March, which was only five days away. He himself wrote on the tablecloth once in a while—putting down a word he wanted to emphasize. He had an automatic pen-and-pencil set in his shirt pocket—the clasps initialed FOI on one (Fruit of Islam, which is the military organization within the Muslim temple) and ISLAM on the other. He wore a red ring with a small crescent.

Malcolm X's voice is gentle, and he often smiles broadly, but not with humor, so that the caustic nature of what he is saying is not belied. His manner is distant and grave, and he asks, mocking slightly, "Sir?" when a question is not heard or understood, leaning forward and cocking his head. His answers are always skilled, with a lively and effective use of image, and yet as the phrases came I kept thinking of Cassius Clay and *his* litany—the fighter's is more limited, and a different sort of thing, but neither of them ever *stumbles* over words, or ideas, or appears balked by a question, so that one rarely has the sense of the brain actually working but rather that it is engaged in rote, simply a recording apparatus playing back to an impulse. Thus he is truly intractable—Malcolm X—absolutely dedicated, self-assured, self-principled, with that great energy . . . the true revolutionary. He does not doubt.

When give-and-take of argument is possible, when what Malcolm X says can be doubted, his assurance and position as an extremist give him an advantage in debate. He appreciates that this is so, and it amuses him. "The extremist," he said, "will always ruin the liberals in debate—because the liberals have something too nebulous to sell, or too impossible to sell— like the Brooklyn Bridge. That's why a white segregationalist— what's his name, Kilpatrick—will destroy Farmer, and why William Buckley makes a fool of Norman Mailer, and why Martin Luther King would lose a debate with me. Why King? Because integration is ridiculous, a dream. I am not interested in dreams, but in the nightmare. Martin Luther King, the rest of them, they are thinking about dreams. But then really King and I have nothing to debate about. We are both indicting. I would say to him: 'You indict and give them hope. I'll indict and give them no hope.'"

I asked him about the remarks that had caused him his muzzling by Elijah Muhammad. His remarks about the assassination had been taken out of context, he said, though it would be the sheerest hypocrisy to suggest that Kennedy was a friend to the Negro. Kennedy was a politician (he wrote down the word on the paper tablecloth with his FOI pencil and circled it)—a "cold-blooded politician" who transformed last year's civil-rights march on Washington into a "crawl" by endorsing the march, joining it, though it was supposed to be a protest against the country's leaders . . . a politician's trick which tamped out the fuse though the powder keg was there. Friend of the Negro? There never had been a politician who was the Negro's friend. Power corrupts. Lincoln? A crooked, deceitful hypocrite, claiming championship to the cause of the Negro who, one hundred years later, finds himself singing "We Shall Overcome." The Supreme Court? Its decision is nothing but an act of hypocrisy . . . nine Supreme Court justices expert in legal phraseology tangling the words of their decision in such a way that lawyers can dilly-dally over it for years—which of course they will continue to do . . .

I scribbled these phrases, and others, on the paper table-cloth, mildly surprised to see the Muslim maxims in my own handwriting. We talked about practicality, which is the weakest area of the Muslim plans, granted the fires of resentment are justifiably banked. Malcolm X was not particularly concerned. What may be illogical or impractical in the long run is dismissed as not being pertinent to the *moment*—which is what the Negro must concern himself with. He could sense my frustration at this. It is not easy to dismiss what is practical. He had a peppermint and smiled.

I changed the subject and asked him what he did for exercise.

"I take walks," he said. "Long walks. We believe in exercise, physical fitness, but as for commercial sport, that's a racket. Commercial sport is the pleasure of the idle rich. The vice of gambling stems from it." He wrote down the word "Promoter" on the tablecloth with his FOI pencil and circled it. "The Negro never comes out ahead—never *one* in the history of sport."

"Clay perhaps."

"Perhaps." He liked talking about Clay. "I'm interested in him as a human being," he said. He tapped his head. "Not many people know the quality of the mind he's got in there. He fools them. One forgets that though a clown never imitates a wise man, the wise man can imitate the clown. He is sensitive, very humble, yet shrewd—with as much untapped mental energy as he has physical power. He should be a diplomat. He has that instinct of seeing a tricky situation shaping up—my own presence in Miami, for example—and resolving how to sidestep it. He knows how to handle people, to get them functioning. He gains strength from being around people. He can't stand being alone. The more people around, the better—just as it takes water to prime a country well. If the crowds are big in there tonight in the Miami Auditorium, he's likely to beat

Liston. But they won't be. The Jews have heard he's a Muslim and they won't show up."

"Perhaps they'll show up to see him taken," I said.

"Sir?" he said, with that slight cock of the head.

"Perhaps . . ."

"When Cassius said, 'I am a man of race,'" Malcolm X went on, "it pleased the Negroes. He couldn't eliminate the color factor. But the press and the white people saw it another way. They saw him, suddenly, as a threat. Which is why he has become the villain—why he is booed, the outcast." He seemed pleased with this.

Wasn't it possible, I asked, that the braggart, the loudmouth was being booed, not necessarily the Black Muslim? After all, Clay had been heartily booed during the Doug Jones fight in Madison Square Garden, and that was before his affiliation with the Muslims was known.

"You, you can't tell," replied Malcolm X. "But a Negro can feel things in sounds. The booing at the Doug Jones fight was good-natured—I was there—but the booing is now differ-ent . . . defiant . . . inflamed by the columnists, all of them, critical of Cassius for being a Muslim."

"And as a fighter?"

"He has tremendous self-confidence," said Malcolm X. "I've never heard him mention fear. Anything you're afraid of can whip you. Fear magnifies what you're afraid of. One thing about our religion is that it removes fear. Christianity is based on fear."

I remarked that the Muslim religion, since it has its taboos and promises and threats, is also based on fear—one remem-bers that British soldiers extracted secrets from terrified Mus-lim captives by threatening to sew them up for a while in a pig's skin.

Malcolm X acknowledged that the Muslims had to adapt Islam to their purposes. "We are in a cage," he said. "What must be taught to the lion in a cage is quite different from what one teaches the lion in the jungle. The Mohammedan abroad believes in a heaven and a hell, a hereafter. Here we believe that heaven and hell are on this earth, and that we are in the hell and must strive to escape it. If we can adapt Islam to this purpose, we should. For people fighting for their freedom there is no such thing as a bad device."

He snorted about peaceful methods. "The methods of Gandhi!" Another snort. "The Indians are hypocrites. Look at Goa. Besides, they are the most helpless people on earth. They succeeded in removing the Brtish only because they outnumbered them, out*weighed* them—a big dark elephant sitting on a white elephant. In this country the situation is different. The white elephant is huge. But we will catch him. We will catch him when he is asleep. The mice will run up his trunk when he is asleep.

"Where? They will come out of the alley. The revolution always comes from the alley—from the man with nothing to lose. Never the bourgeois. The poor Negro bourgeois, with his golf clubs, his golfing hat"—he waved at the people in the lunchroom—"he's so much more frustrated than the Negro in the alley; he gets the doors slapped shut in his face every day. But the explosion won't come from him. Not from the pickets either, or the nonviolent groups—these masochists . . . they *want* to be beaten—but it will come from the people *watching*—spectators for the moment. They're different. You don't know. It is dangerous to suggest that the Negro is nonviolent.

"There *must* be retribution. It is proclaimed. If retribution came to the Pharoah for his enslavement of six hundred thousand, it will come to the white American who enslaved twenty million and robbed their minds."

"And retribution, that is in the Koran?"

"Sir?"

"The Koran . . . ?"

He said, "Chapter 22, verse 102."

I put the numbers down, thinking to catch him out; I looked later. The verse reads: *"The day when the trumpet is blown. On that day we assemble the guilty white-eyed (with terror)."*

"These are the things you are teaching Cassius?"

"He will make up his own mind."

He popped a peppermint in his mouth. We talked a little longer, somewhat aimlessly. He had an appointment with someone, he finally said, and he stood up. The noise of conversation dropped noticeably in the luncheonette as he stood up and walked out, erect and moving slowly, holding his gaudy souvenir cane out in front of him as he threaded his way between the tables; the people in the golfing hats watched him go.

4.

I went out into the lobby of the hotel, just standing around there feeling low. A phrase from Kafka, or rather the *idea* of some phrases from *The Trial* came to me. I looked them up the other day: "But I'm not guilty, said K. It's a mistake. Besides, how can a man be guilty? We're all men. True, said the priest: but that's how the guilty talk."

The lobby was crowded. I didn't feel comfortable. I went out to the street and stood *there*, watching the traffic. The cars came by going at sixty, none of them taxis. I went back to the lobby. The armchairs, not more than four or five, were occupied. I wouldn't have sat down anyway.

Then a fine thing happened. I was talking into the desk telephone, trying to find Archie Robinson, and a Negro, a big fellow, came up and said softly. "Hello, man, how's it?"—smiling somewhat tentatively, as if he wasn't quite sure of himself. I thought he was talking to someone else, but when I glanced up again, his eyes were still fixed on me. "We looked for you in New York when we came through," he said.

I recognized him, the great defensive back on the Detroit Lions, Night Train Lane, a good friend. "Train!" I shouted. I could sense people turn. It crossed my mind that Malcolm X might be one of them. "Hey!" I said. *"Hey!"* Lane looked a little startled. He hadn't remembered me as someone who indulged in such effusive greetings. But he asked me to come back to his room where he had friends, most of them from the golf tournament, dropping in for drinks and beans. I said that would be fine.

We went on back. Everyone we passed seemed to know him. "Hey man," they'd call, and he'd grin at them—a strong presence, an uncomplicated confidence, absolutely trusting himself. He had the room next to mine at the Detroit Lions' training camp (I was out there, an amateur among the pros, trying to play quarterback and write a book about it) and it was always full of teammates, laughing and carrying on. A record player, set on the floor, was always going in his room—Dinah Washington records. He had married her earlier in the year, her ninth or tenth husband, I think. The volume was always up, and if you came up from the practice field late, her voice would come at you across the school grounds. She had died later that year.

His room was small and full of people. I sat quietly. Train offered me some beans, but I wasn't hungry. He said, "What's wrong with you, man?"

"I'm fine," I said.

"Hey!" someone called across the room. "Was that you in the lunchroom? What you doin' talking to that guy X?"

"Well, I was listening to him," I said.

"They were telling around," this man said, "that X had a vision—he seen Cassius win in a *vision*."

Someone else said that in a fight they'd rather be supported by a Liston left jab than a Malcolm X vision. A big fine hoot of laughter went up, and Night Train said it was the damnedest co-in-cidence but a *horse* named Cassius had won one of the early races at Hialeah that afternoon—perhaps *that* was Malcolm X's vision.

They talked about him this way, easily, matter-of-factly. They could take him or leave him, which for a while I'd forgotten. Malcolm X had said about them: "They all know I'm here in the motel. They come and look at me through the door to see if I got horns . . . and you can see them turning things over in their minds."

5.

The day after he beat Liston, Cassius turned up at a news conference at the Miami Beach Auditorium. The rumor was that he had gone to Chicago for the Muslim celebrations there, and the press was surprised when he appeared—and even more so at his behavior, which was subdued. Since a microphone system had gone out, his voice was almost inaudible. Cries went up which one never expected to hear in Clay's presence: "What's that, Clay? Speak up, Cassius!"

Archie Robinson took me aside and told me that he and Clay had dropped in on the celebrations at the Hampton House Motel after the fight, but it had been too noisy, so they'd gone home. It was quieter there, and they had been up until 4:00 a.m. discussing Cassius' "new image."

I remarked that this was a rare kind of evening to spend after winning the heavyweight championship. I'd met a young singer named Dee Something-or-other who had been waiting for Clay outside his dressing room after the fight. She had some idea she was going to help Cassius celebrate. She was very pretty. She had a singing engagement at a nightclub called the Sir John. Her mother was with her. She was very anxious, and once in a while when someone would squeeze in or out of the dressing room she'd call out: "Tell Cassius that Dee . . ." The girl was calm. "I call him Marcellus," she said. "A beautiful name. I can say it over and over."

The newspapermen waiting to get into the dressing room looked admiringly at her. "Clay's little fox," they called her, using Clay's generic name for girls—"foxes"—which is half affectionate and half suspicious; he feels that girls can be "sly" and "sneaky" and are to be watched warily. When the new champion finally emerged from his dressing room in a heavy press of entourage, photographers, and newspapermen, he seemed subdued and preoccupied. He didn't glance at Dee, who was on her toes, waving shyly in his direction. "Marcellus," she called. The crowd, packed in tight around him, moved down the corridor, the photobulbs flashing. The mother looked quite put out.

6.

The living accommodations for Liston and Clay were as different as their fighting styles. Liston had a big place on the beach, a sixteen-room house next to the Yankees' owner, Dan Topping, reportedly very plush, wall-to-wall carpeting, and each room set up like a golf-club lounge—a television set going interminably, perhaps someone in front of it, perhaps not, and then invariably a card game.

Clay's place was on the mainland, in North Miami, in a low-rent district—a small plain tater-white house with louvered windows, a front door with steps leading up to a little porch with room for one chair, a front yard with more chairs set around and shaded by a big ficus tree with leaves dusty from the traffic on Fifth Street. His entire entourage stayed there, living dormitory-style, two or three to a room. Outside the yard was almost worn bare. There wasn't a neighborhood child on his way home from school who didn't pass by to see if anything was up. Films were shown there in the evening, outside, the children sitting quietly until the film started. Then the questions and the exclamations would come, Clay explaining things, and you could hardly hear the soundtrack. Only one film kept them quiet. That was the favorite film shown two or three times, *The Invasion of the Body Snatchers* ... Watched wide-eyed in the comforting sounds of the projector and the traffic going by occasionally on Fifth Street. When the big moths would show up in the light beam, almost as big as white towels they seemed, a yelp or two would go up, particularly if a body was being snatched at the time, and the children would sway for one another.

The children were waiting for Clay when he drove up from his press conference the day after the fight. So was Malcolm X, a camera slung from his neck; his souvenir cane was propped against the ficus tree. The children came for the car, shouting, and packing in around so that the doors had to be opened gingerly. Clay got out, towering above them as he walked slowly for a chair in the front yard. The litany started almost as soon as he sat down, the children around him twelve deep, Malcolm X at the periphery, grinning as he snapped pictures.

"Who's the king of kings?"

"*Cassius Clay!*"

"Who shook up the world?"

"*Cassius Clay!*"

"Who's the ugly bear?"

"*Sonny Liston!*"

"Who's the prettiest?"

"*Cassius Clay!*"

Sometimes a girl, a bright girl, just for a change would reply "*me*," pointing a finger at herself when everyone else was shouting "*Cassius Clay*," or she might shout "*Ray Charles*," and the giggling would start around her, and others would join in until Clay, with a big grin, would have to hold up a hand to reorganize the claque and get things straightened out. Neither he nor the children tired of the litany. They kept at it for an hour at a time. Malcolm X left after awhile. There were variations, but it was essentially the same, and it never seemed to lack for enthusiasm. The noise carried for blocks.

We went inside while this was going on. The main room, with an alcove for cooking, had sofas along the wall. The artifacts of the psychological campaign against Liston were set around—signs which read "settin' traps for the Big Bear," which had been brandished outside his training headquarters, and a valentine, as tall as a man, complete with cherubs, which had been offered Liston and which he had refused. It stood in a corner, next to an easel. Newspapers were flung around— there had been some celebrating the night before—and someone's shoes were in the middle of the room. Souvenir canes were propped up by the side of the stove in the cooking alcove. It was fraternity-house clutter.

I was standing next to Howard Bingham, Clay's "official" photographer. "It was fun, wasn't it?" I asked.

"Oh my," he said. "We have the *best* time here."

He had joined up with Clay after the George Logan fight in California, about Clay's age, younger perhaps, and shy. He stutters a bit, and he told me that he didn't take their kidding lying down. He said: "I walk around the house and sc . . . sc . . . scare people, jump out at them. Or they d . . . doze off on the c . . . couch, and I sneak around and tickle them on the nose, y'know, with a piece of string. Why I was agitating C . . . C . . . Cassius for half an hour once when he was dozing off. And I give the hot f . . . f . . . feet around here, a lot of that. We had a high time."

I asked what Cassius' winning the championship meant for him.

"Well, of course, that must make me the greatest ph . . . ph . . . photographer in the world." He couldn't keep a straight face. "Oh please," he said. His shoulders shook. "Well, I'll tell you. I'm going to get me a mo . . . mo . . . mohair wardrobe, that's one thing."

At the kitchen table Archie Robinson was sorting telegrams, stacked up in the hundreds. He showed me some of them—as impersonal as an injunction, from the long sycophantic messages from people they had to scratch around to remember, to the tart challenges from fighters looking to take Clay's title away from him. Clay wasn't bothering with them. He was going strong outside—his voice rising above the babble of children's voices: "Who shook up the world?"

"Cassius Clay!"

I wandered back to his room. It was just large enough for a bed, the mattress bare when I looked there, an armchair, with clothes including his Bear Huntin' jacket thrown across it, and a plain teak-colored bureau which had a large-size bottle of Dickinson's witch hazel standing on it. A tiny oil painting of a New England harbor scene was on one wall, with a few newspaper articles taped next to it, illustrated, describing Clay at his most flamboyant. A training schedule was taped to the mirror over the bureau. It called for "all" to rise at 5:00 a.m. The bedclothes were in a corner. One corner of the mattress was covered with Cassius Clay's signature in a light-blue ink, flowery with the Cs tall and graceful, along with such graffiti as: "Cassius Clay Is Next Champ"; "Champion of the

World"; "Liston Is Finished"; "The Next Champ: Cassius Clay" . . .

Outside, it had all come true. His voice and the answers were unceasing. "You," he was calling to the children, "you all are looking . . . at . . . the . . . champion . . . of . . . the . . . whole . . . wide . . . world."

FORMATION OF MUSLIM MOSQUE, INC.

The fact that Malcolm X was barred from the Saviour's Day convention in late February 1964 left little doubt as to his standing within the NOI. Whatever lingering hope he may have had about being reinstated at the conclusion of his ninety-day silencing was quickly extinguished when a letter arrived from NOI officials writing on behalf of Elijah Muhammad. Muhammad dictated the letter from his home in Phoenix and described his formerly prized minister as "drunk over publicity and leadership."[1] Furthermore, in the first move of litigious antagonism between Malcolm and Muhammad, the Messenger inquired with his chief advisors about the payments for Malcolm's home and suggested that the NOI would soon ask him to vacate. On the other hand, Malcolm had been given three months to ponder life outside the NOI and quickly made his move, announcing the formation of a religiously oriented black nationalist organization, Muslim Mosque, Inc. (MMI), which would "cooperate with local civil rights actions in the South and elsewhere."[2]

1. Karl Evanzz, *The Messenger: The Rise and Fall of Elijah Muhammad* (New York: Pantheon Books, 1999), 288.

2. M. S. Handler, "Malcolm X Splits with Muhammad," *New York Times*, March 9, 1964.

A small group of supporters first met at Malcolm's home to incorporate the new organization on March 9, 1964. Malcolm, Earl Grant, and James 67X Shabazz were elected trustees for exactly one year, and the group was designed largely as a spiritual alternative for Malcolm X loyalists who had chosen to leave Mosque No. 7 with the minister. Malcolm encouraged members of the NOI to remain within the organization and stated that he would continue to promote Muhammad's program, but do so externally. For the time being, he also remained publicly loyal to Muhammad, writing in an open telegram: "I've never spoken one word of criticism . . . about your family. I will always be a Muslim, teaching what you have taught me, giving you full credit for what I know and what I am."[3] The principal features of MMI were first announced at a midday press conference held at the posh Tapestry Suite of the Park Sheraton Hotel. MMI's headquarters would be in the Hotel Theresa, and no whites would be allowed to join because "when whites join an organization they usually take control of it."[4]

The challenges of building an organization such as MMI were numerous, but adding to those frustrations was the fact that Malcolm had not yet fully broken ideologically with Muhammad and arrived at what he later called his "psychological divorce from the Nation of Islam."[5] He also struggled to enlist support from other civil rights leaders, whom he had spent years deriding. Responses from activists were lukewarm at best, yet he still managed to organize a meeting of the Reverend Milton Galamison, Gloria Richardson, Dick Gregory, and Stanley Branche in Chester, Pennsylvania, which resulted in the formation of the organization ACT. The major obstacle facing the growth of MMI, though, was that it was primarily a religious group with members devoted to the traditions and

---

3. "Telegram to Muhammad," *Amsterdam News*, March 14, 1964.

4. M. S. Handler, "Malcolm X Sees Rise in Violence," *New York Times*, March 12, 1964.

5. Malcolm X and Haley, *Autobiography*, 313.

ideology of the Nation of Islam; even the daily schedule mirrored the NOI's. Ultimately, Malcolm would be forced to create a second group, the Organization of Afro-American Unity (OAAU), to act as a more secular, political alternative to MMI. The two groups, which had little in common besides a shared space in suite 128 of the Hotel Theresa, embodied the symbolic division of politics and religion that Malcolm struggled to unite during his final year. Perfectly capturing this tension, Melvin Tapley's cartoon in the March 14, 1964, edition of the *Amsterdam News* depicted Malcolm with his legs spread and arms splayed. Hanging from his clenched right fist is politics personified, and clinging to his left arm with index finger pointed upward is a man labeled "Muslims."[6]

- "Rights Groups Give Malcolm X Cool Reception," *Hartford Courant*, March 11, 1964

- James Booker, "Malcolm X: 'Why I Quit and What I Plan Next': His Resignation Stuns Muhammad," *Amsterdam News*, March 14, 1964

- Malcolm X, "Telegram to Muhammad," *Amsterdam News*, March 14, 1964

- Melvin Tapley, "In the Middle," Editorial Cartoon, *Amsterdam News*, March 14, 1964

Further reading:

- "Malcolm X Plans a New Negro Group," *Chicago Tribune*, March 9, 1964

- "Malcolm X Forming Own Muslim Group," *Los Angeles Times*, March 9, 1964

---

6. Melvin Tapley, "In the Middle," editorial cartoon, *Amsterdam News*, March 14, 1964.

- M. S. Handler, "Malcolm X Splits with Muhammad," *New York Times*, March 9, 1964

- "'I'll Just Wait and See'—Muhammad," *Chicago Defender*, March 10, 1964

- "Malcolm X to Form 'Black Nationalists,'" *Pittsburgh Courier*, March 14, 1964

- Fred Powledge, "Negroes Ponder Malcolm's Move," *New York Times*, March 15, 1964

- "Malcolm X Charts," *Jet*, April 2, 1964, pages 54–56

- Malcolm X FBI file, memo, New York office, March 11, 1964

- Malcolm X FBI file, summary report, New York office, June 18, 1964, page 33

- Malcolm X FBI file, memo, New York office, March 9, 1964

- Malcolm X FBI file, memo, Phoenix office, March 12, 1964

- Malcolm X FBI file, memo, New York office, March 13, 1964

- Malcolm X FBI file, memo, New York office, March 26, 1964

"Rights Groups Give Malcolm X Cool Reception," *Hartford Courant*, March 11, 1964

NEW YORK (AP)—Many leaders of the established civil rights groups have laid an "unwelcome" mat at the door where Malcolm X, erstwhile Black Muslim leader, plans to enter the civil rights fight.

In bolting the parent organization to form his own mosque, the fiery Negro, who was No. 2 in the Black Muslim hierarchy, said he will tell civil rights groups what a real revolution means. He said he would accept invitations to join civil rights forces in the South and promote "active self-defense against white sepremacists."

"There can be no revolution without bloodshed, and it is nonsense to describe the civil rights movement in America as a revolution," he said.

James Farmer, national director of the Congress of Racial Equality, said that the answer to whether CORE could cooperate with Malcolm X depended on the nature of the new organization.

Roy Wilkins, executive secretary of the National Association for the Advancement of Colored People, and the Rev. Dr. Martin Luther King, president of the Southern Christian Leadership Conference, would not comment on Malcolm X's new role.

Elijah Muhammad, the leader of the Muslims, predicted that the Negro people will not follow his former chief aide and turn to violence in their quest for equal justice.

"My people are more adapted to peace. They believe in peaceful solutions," he said.

James Booker, "Malcolm X: 'Why I Quit and What I Plan Next': His Resignation Stuns Muhammad," *Amsterdam News*, March 14, 1964

Black Muslim leader Malcolm X has filed papers for an incorporation, and will shortly open his own Muslim Mosque, Inc., here to continue his religious activities, he revealed to the Amsterdam News Wednesday.

The fiery leader, who announced earlier this week that he was pulling out of Elijah Muhammad's Nation of Islam to form his own group, said that he would hold his first public meeting Sunday at the Hotel Theresa, where he is establishing temporary headquarters for his new group.

"FORCED ME"

In an exclusive interview with this newspaper, Malcolm charged that the Muslims Chicago headquarters had been waging a power struggle against him that led to his suspension last Dec. 3 by Mr. Muhammad allegedly for statements he made criticizing the late President Kennedy.

"They forced me to take the stand I am taking because I had to find a way to circumvent the forces in the movement that opposed me and at the same time to expedite Mr. Muhammad's program as I understand it," Malcolm said.

What kicked off Malcolm's announcement was a letter he received from Mr. Muhammad last Thursday informing him that his suspension was remaining "for an indefinite period," even though he had been under suspension for three months.

Accusing officials in the Chicago headquarters of being "narrow minded," Malcolm charged that certain officials there had "misinformed" Muhammad of his activities for years because they feared his rising strength within the group.

LOYAL

While refusing to openly criticize any individual in the Muslim group, Malcolm said that even though his suspension was originally said to be an official silence, he had been relieved of his non-public church duties shortly after the suspension was announced.

Despite his split, however, Malcolm said "I will still pay homage to Mr. Muhammad for teaching me everything I know and making me what I am."

He said he would still teach and preach the 12 basic Muslim principles, but would have no connection with the Chicago headquarters of Muhammad.

ACTION PROGRAM

While Malcolm has advised Muslims to remain in the Muhammad-led group, it was highly likely that many in the New York area would seek to join with him. Malcolm said he doubted Cassius Clay would join his group.

"I have no fear or doubts that I will be successful," Malcolm said.

Malcolm criticized the Muhammad group for failing to have an action program to assist Negroes in achieving social and political gains, and asserted that his group would seek to eliminate the basic causes behind the "social, economic, political, moral, mental, and spiritual ailments of 22 million American Negroes."

"I have reached the conclusion that I can best spread Mr. Muhammad's message by staying out of the Nation of Islam, and continuing to work on my own among America's 22 million non-Muslim Negroes. But, I will always remain a

Muslim, and will always teach what Mr. Muhammad has taught me, as I best understand it," Malcolm declared.

He asserted that his personal philosophy is black nationalism, and he would travel the nation and speak before any group to help to stir Negroes.

IN TEARS

Meanwhile in Phoenix, Ariz., Elijah Muhammad told newsmen that he was "stunned" over Malcom's defection.

"I never dreamed this man would deviate from the Nation of Islam. Every one of the Muslims admired him," the 65-year-old Muhammad said as he was in tears over Malcolm's statements.

African nationalist leader James R. Lawson charged that Malcolm's attempt to unify black nationalist forces was "another attempt to subvert, control and destroy black nationalism."

Malcolm X, "Telegram to Muhammad,"
Amsterdam News, March 14, 1964

"You are still my leader and teacher, even though those around you won't let me be one of your active followers or helpers," Minister Malcolm X said in a telegram to Elijah Muhammad Wednesday attempting to explain why he had left the following.

Asserting that he had been "pressured out" of the nation of Islam, Malcolm said, "the tears you shed in Arizona gave the public the impression that you are also of the opinion that left of my own free will," Malcolm told Muhammad.

"The national officials there at the Chicago headquarters know that I never left the nation of my own free will. It was they who conspired with Captain Joseph here in New York to pressure me out of the nation.

ONLY WAY

"In order to save the national officials and Captain Joseph the disgrace of having to explain their real reason for forcing me out. I announced through the press that it was my own decision to leave.

"I did not take the blame to protect these national officials but to preserve the faith your followers have in you and the nation of Islam.

"I've never spoken one word of criticism to them about your family. I will always be a Muslim, teaching what you have taught me, giving you full credit for what I know and what I am."

"The present course I am taking is the only way I can circumvent their obstacles and still expedite your program," Malcolm's telegram said.

Melvin Tapley, "In the Middle,"
Editorial Cartoon, *Amsterdam News*,
March 14, 1964

"THE BALLOT OR
THE BULLET"

Although he had only left the Nation of Islam in March, things moved quickly for Malcolm X during the following month. In that time he formed his new religious organization, Muslim Mosque, Inc.; delivered speeches at Harvard University and New York's Rockland Palace; visited the Senate to observe a civil rights filibuster; faced eviction from his home in Queens; and prepared to complete one of the five pillars of Islam: the hajj. During this period he also delivered a speech that would, along with "Message to the Grass Roots," come to be his most influential. "The Ballot or the Bullet," as it was called, was ranked in 2008 as the seventh most significant speech of the twentieth century by leading scholars of American public address.[1]

Malcolm delivered a similar speech several times in late March, but it is his address at a debate with Louis Lomax at Cory Methodist Church in Cleveland that is best remembered. The event was sponsored by CORE, and between two thousand and three thousand people attended. As he had done in weeks prior, Malcolm stressed that although he considered himself a Muslim, "unity is the right religion."[2] Many took

1. "Top 100 American Speeches of the 20th Century," http://www.news.wisc.edu/misc/speeches/.

2. "Malcolm X to Organize Mass Voter Registration," *The Militant*, April 6, 1964.

from the speech only the message of violence; he had recently promoted the formation of "rifle clubs" and reiterated that blacks were constitutionally within their rights to defend themselves and their property if the government failed to do so. However, what had changed dramatically from years past and the rhetoric of the Nation of Islam was the possibility for reform through voting. Where he had previously described voting as a bourgeois pastime for the "Uncle Tom" and the "house Negro," he now recognized the potential of such mobilization. As always, he still prescribed caution and skepticism: "A ballot is like a bullet. You don't throw your ballots until you see a target, and if that target is not within your reach, keep your ballot in your pocket." Although he still believed himself to be "carrying into action the teaching of Elijah Muhammad," Malcolm had also taken a bold step toward the possibilities of electoral politics.

Malcolm began to carve out a position of his own in the political landscape, one that opted for neither the subdued public politics of Elijah Muhammad nor the nonviolent resistance of Martin Luther King. He continued to speak to the growing constituency of young activists within the civil rights movement who saw the value and potential in political processes yet the need for self-defense and militant mobilization.

- "It's Ballot or Bullet Answers Malcolm X," *Cleveland Plain Dealer*, April 4, 1964

- "2,000 Hear Malcolm X in Cleveland," *The Militant*, June 13, 1964

- Malcolm X, "The Ballot or the Bullet," in George Breitman, ed., *Malcolm X Speaks: Selected Speeches and Statements* (New York: Grove Weidenfeld, 1990), pages 23–44

Further reading:

- "Organize Rifle Club in Ohio: Malcolm X on the Scene," *Amsterdam News*, April 11, 1964

- Malcolm X FBI file, memo, Cleveland office, April 7, 1964

- "Malcolm X to Organize Mass Voter Registration," *The Militant*, April 6, 1964

"It's Ballot or Bullet Answers Malcolm X," *Cleveland Plain Dealer*, April 4, 1964

Author Louis Lomax last night asked the question, "What Next in the Negro Revolt?" An hour later Malcolm X, leader of his own Black Nationalist group, said he felt that coming next would be either the "ballot" or the "bullet."

Lomax prefaced his speech by stating that there were many areas of disagreement between Malcolm X and himself. He added, however, that Malcolm is "a man who can't be ignored. It is foolish for conservative Negroes to pretend he does not exist."

The two men appeared at a meeting sponsored by the Congress of Racial Equality at Cory Methodist Church, 1117 E. 105th Street.

Actually, there were few areas of disagreement between the two. Both pointed out that the American Negro has been denied his rights for several hundred years because of the duplicity of white politicians and that it was time for the Negro to stand up and claim his rights.

Although the Supreme Court declared in 1954 that school segregation is illegal, Lomax said, there are twice as many predominantly Negro—therefore segregated—schools in Cleveland and three times as many in Washington and five times as many in New York, as there were in 1954.

He said that at the time of the decision, a Southern senator predicted it would take 100 years to integrate the schools. This country is keeping pace with the senator's timetable, he said.

Integration, said Lomax, can be summed up in one phrase: "Leave Louis Lomax alone; let me be what my brain, my hands, my talents and my training say I can become."

He cited economic integration as most important. "Seek ye the kingdom of the dollar bill is the white man's creed," he said. "Once we have economic integration we have nothing to worry about."

Malcolm X, former right hand man to Elijah Muhammed, leader of the Black Muslim movement, said the Negro could find little help from the government in gaining his civil rights.

Washington is controlled by the party which embraces the most anti-Negro element of the political spectrum, he said.

The Negro must look to himself, he told the crowd of more than 2,000,—many of them whites. He must develop his own community to the point where he does not need the white man.

He said that in areas where the government has proven itself unable and unwilling to protect Negroes and their property they must defend themselves.

This might mean investing in a rifle or a shotgun, he said.

CLEVELAND—Reflecting and responding to the growing desire for unity in action, Malcolm X, outstanding spokesman for the new black nationalism, and Louis Lomax, noted lecturer and writer currently working on a TV documentary on the Negro in Cleveland, shared the platform at an April 3 public meeting sponsored by the local chapter of the Congress of Racial Equality.

An audience of almost 2,000, including many whites, heard the two speakers discuss "The Negro Revolt—What Comes Next?"

The discussion was a symposium, not a debate, and the speeches tended to complement each other rather than pose sharp or irreconcilable differences.

Malcolm X's answer to "What Comes Next?" had the directness his audience expected: "The ballot or the bullet."

"1964 threatens to be the most explosive year America has ever witnessed," he said. "It is a political year. All the white politicians will be back in the so-called Negro communities jiving you and me." But the 22 million victims of American democracy are waking up, becoming politically mature.

Malcolm X devoted a major part of his talk to exposing and castigating the Democratic party, the "con game they call the filibuster," and the "white political crooks" who keep the black man from control of his own community.

He appealed to the audience to set aside religious differences, organizational divisions, personal jealousies, and unite for action on their common problems: political oppression, economic exploitation and social degradation at the hands of white men.

"I am not anti-white," he said, "I am anti-exploitation, anti oppression."

"You are not faced with a segregationist conspiracy, we are

faced with a government conspiracy ... to deprive you of your voting rights, housing rights, job rights ... The government itself is responsible for the exploitation."

"Where do we go from here?—We need new friends. We need new allies. We need a new interpretation of the civil rights struggle to include the black nationalists. We have to tell the handkerchief heads and the compromisers we don't intend to let them dilly-dally any longer!"

Malcolm X projected a black nationalist convention by August, with delegates from all over the country, followed by seminars and meetings to decide what course to take. "If it's necessary to form a black nationalist party, we'll form a black nationalist party. If it's necessary to form a black nationalist army, we'll form a black nationalist army."

Lomax took the Supreme Court decision against segregated schools in 1954 as his point of reference for gauging the claims of progress in the Negro struggle, and rejected the claims. After ten years "only 9.8 per cent of the Negro kids in the Deep South are in integrated schools," he said. There are almost twice as many predominantly Negro—segregated—schools in Cleveland now, three times as many in Washington, D.C., five times as many in New York City as in 1954.

The only gains, he said, have been "a few hamburgers, a few restrooms ... That's where we are in 1964."

"Now the objective of the Negro Revolt is to provide for the Negro individual the same rights, the same freedoms and the same opportunities as anyone else in America."

The first emphasis, Lomax stated, must be on jobs, economic equality. Non-violence, he said, can be a "tactical maneuver, an effective one on a mass basis. This can be debated. But for any tactics to get results, we must quit fighting one another and pull together."

Ruth Turner, executive secretary of Cleveland CORE, led a torchlight parade of 300 persons from the enthusiastic audience to a construction site where school segregation was symbolically "buried" in a coffin carried by black pallbearers.

She announced plans to start picketing the building project the following Monday.

"The Ballot or the Bullet," in George Breitman, ed.,
Malcolm X Speaks: Selected Speeches and Statements
(New York: Grove, Weidenfield, 1990), 23-44

I say again, I'm not anti-Democrat, I'm not anti-Republican, I'm not anti-anything. I'm just questioning their sincerity, and some of the strategy that they've been using on our people by promising them promises that they don't intend to keep. When you keep the Democrats in power, you're keeping the Dixiecrats in power. I doubt that my good Brother Lomax will deny that. A vote for a Democrat is a vote for a Dixiecrat. That's why, in 1964, it's time now for you and me to become more politically mature and realize what the ballot is for; what we're supposed to get when we cast a ballot; and that if we don't cast a ballot, it's going to end up in a situation where we're going to have to cast a bullet. It's either a ballot or a bullet.

In the North, they do it a different way. They have a system that's known as gerrymandering, whatever that means. It means when Negroes become too heavily concentrated in a certain area, and begin to gain too much political power, the white man comes along and changes the district lines. You may say, "Why do you keep saying white man?" Because it's the white man who does it. I haven't ever seen any Negro changing any lines. They don't let him get near the line. It's the white man who does this. And usually, it's the white man who grins at you the most, and pats you on the back, and is supposed to be your friend. He may be friendly, but he's not your friend.

So, what I'm trying to impress upon you, in essence, is this: You and I in America are faced not with a segregationist conspiracy, we're faced with a government conspiracy. Everyone who's filibustering is a senator—that's the government. Everyone who's finagling in Washington, D.C., is a congressman—that's the government. You don't have anybody putting blocks in your path but people who are a part of the government. The same government that you go abroad to fight for and die for is the government that is in a conspiracy to deprive you of your voting rights, deprive you of your economic opportunities, deprive you of decent housing, deprive you of decent education. You don't need to go to the employer alone, it is the government itself, the government of America, that is responsible for the oppression and exploitation and degradation of black people in this country. And you should drop it in their lap. This government has failed the Negro. This so-called democracy has failed the Negro. And all these white liberals have definitely failed the Negro.

So, where do we go from here? First, we need some friends. We need some new allies. The entire civil-rights struggle needs a new interpretation, a broader interpretation. We need to look at this civil-rights thing from another angle—from the inside as well as from the outside. To those of us whose philosophy is black nationalism, the only way you can get involved in the civil-rights struggle is give it a new interpretation. That old interpretation excluded us. It kept us out. So, we're giving a new interpretation to the civil-rights struggle, an interpretation that will enable us to come into it, take part in it. And these handkerchief-heads who have been dillydallying and pussyfooting and compromising—we don't intend to let them pussyfoot and dillydally and compromise any longer.

How can you thank a man for giving you what's already yours? How then can you thank him for giving you only part of what's already yours? You haven't even made progress, if what's being given to you, you should have had already. That's not progress. And I love my Brother Lomax, the way he pointed out we're right back where we were in 1954. We're not even as far up as we were in 1954. We're behind where we were in 1954. There's more segregation now than there was in 1954. There's more racial animosity, more racial hatred, more racial violence today in 1964, than there was in 1954. Where is the progress?

And now you're facing a situation where the young Negro's coming up. They don't want to hear that "turn-the-other-cheek" stuff, no. In Jacksonville, those were teenagers, they were throwing Molotov cocktails. Negroes have never done that before. But it shows you there's a new deal coming in. There's new thinking coming in. There's new strategy coming in. It'll be Molotov cocktails this month, hand grenades next month, and something else next month. It'll be ballots, or it'll be bullets. It'll be liberty, or it will be death. The only difference about this kind of death—it'll be reciprocal. You know what is meant by "reciprocal"? That's one of Brother Lomax's words, I stole it from him. I don't usually deal with those big words because I don't usually deal with big people. I deal with small people. I find you can get a whole lot of small people and whip hell out of a whole lot of big people. They haven't got anything to lose, and they've got everything to gain. And they'll let you know in a minute: "It takes two to tango; when I go, you go."

The black nationalists, those whose philosophy is black nationalism, in bringing about this new interpretation of the entire meaning of civil rights, look upon it as meaning, as Brother Lomax has pointed out, equality of opportunity. Well, we're justified in seeking civil rights, if it means equality of opportunity, because all we're doing there is trying to collect for our investment. Our mothers and fathers invested sweat and blood. Three hundred and ten years we worked in this country without a dime in return—I mean without a dime in return. You let the white man walk around here talking about how rich this country is, but you never stop to think how it got rich so quick. It got rich because you made it rich.

You take the people who are in this audience right now. They're poor, we're all poor as individuals. Our weekly salary individually amounts to hardly anything. But if you take the salary of everyone in here collectively it'll fill up a whole lot of baskets. It's a lot of wealth. If you can collect the wages of just these people right here for a year, you'll be rich—richer than rich. When you look at it like that, think how rich Uncle Sam had to become, not with this handful, but millions of black people. Your and my mother and father, who didn't work an eight-hour shift, but worked from "can't see" in the morning until "can't see" at night, and working for nothing, making the white man rich, making Uncle Sam rich.

This is our investment. This is our contribution—our blood. Not only did we give of our free labor, we gave of our blood. Every time he had a call to arms, we were the first ones in uniform. We died on every battlefield the white man had. We have made a greater sacrifice than anybody who's standing up in America today. We have made a greater contribution and have collected less. Civil rights, for those of us whose philosophy is black nationalism, means: "Give it to us now. Don't wait for next year. Give it to us yesterday, and that's not fast enough."

I might stop right here to point out one thing. Whenever you're going after something that belongs to you, anyone who's depriving you of the right to have it is a criminal. Understand that. Whenever you are going after something that is yours, you are within your legal rights to lay claim to it. And anyone who puts forth any effort to deprive you of that which is yours, is breaking the law, is a criminal. And this was pointed out by the Supreme Court decision. It outlawed segregation. Which means segregation is against the law. Which means a segregationist is breaking the law. A segregationist is a criminal. You can't label him as anything other than that. And when you demonstrate against segregation, the law is on your side. The Supreme Court is on your side.

Now, who is it that opposes you in carrying out the law? The police department itself. With police dogs and clubs. Whenever you demonstrate against segregation, whether it is segregated education, segregated housing, or anything else, the law is on your side, and anyone who stands in the way is not the law any longer. They are breaking the law, they are not representatives of the law. Any time you demonstrate against segregation and a man has the audacity to put a police dog on you, kill that dog, kill him, I'm telling you, kill that dog. I say it, if they put me in jail tomorrow, kill—that—dog. Then you'll put a stop to it. Now, if these white people in here don't want to see that kind of action, get down and tell the mayor to tell the police department to pull the dogs in. That's all you have to do. If you don't do it, someone else will.

If you don't take this kind of stand, your little children will grow up and look at you and think "shame." If you don't take an uncompromising stand—I don't mean go out and get violent; but at the same time you should never be nonviolent unless you run into some nonviolence. I'm nonviolent with those who are nonviolent with me. But when you drop that violence on me, then you've made me go insane, and I'm not responsible for what I do. And that's the way every Negro should get. Any time you know you're within the law, within your legal rights, within your moral rights, in accord with justice, then die for what you believe in. But don't die alone. Let your dying be reciprocal. This is what is meant by equality. What's good for the goose is good for the gander.

When we begin to get in this area, we need new friends, we need new allies. We need to expand the civil-rights struggle to a higher level—to the level of human rights. Whenever you are in a civil-rights struggle, whether you know it or not, you are confining yourself to the jurisdiction of Uncle Sam. No one from the outside world can speak out in your behalf as long as your struggle is a civil-rights struggle. Civil rights comes within the domestic affairs of this country. All of our African brothers and our Asian brothers and our Latin-American brothers cannot open their mouths and interfere in the domestic affairs of the United States. And as long as it's civil rights, this comes under the jurisdiction of Uncle Sam.

But the United Nations has what's known as the charter of human rights, it has a committee that deals in human rights. You may wonder why all of the atrocities that have been committed in Africa and in Hungary and in Asia and in Latin America are brought before the UN, and the Negro problem is never brought before the UN. This is part of the conspiracy. This old, tricky, blue-eyed liberal who is supposed to be your and my friend, supposed to be in our corner, supposed to be subsidizing our struggle, and supposed to be acting in the capacity of an adviser, never tells you anything about human rights. They keep you wrapped up in civil rights. And you spend so much time barking up the civil-rights tree, you don't even know there's a human-rights tree on the same floor.

When you expand the civil-rights struggle to the level of human rights, you can then take the case of the black man in this country before the nations in the UN. You can take it before the General Assembly. You can take Uncle Sam before a world court. But the only level you can do it on is the level of human rights. Civil rights keeps you under his restrictions, under his jurisdiction. Civil rights keeps you in his pocket. Civil rights means you're asking Uncle Sam to treat you right. Human rights are something you were born with. Human rights are your God-given rights. Human rights are the rights that are recognized by all nations of this earth. And any time any one violates your human rights, you can take them to the world court. Uncle Sam's hands are dripping with blood, dripping with the blood of the black man in this country. He's the earth's number-one hypocrite. He has the audacity—yes, he has—imagine him posing as the leader of the free world. The free world!—and you over here singing "We Shall Overcome." Expand the civil-rights struggle to the level of human rights, take it into the United Nations, where our African brothers can throw their weight on our side, where our Asian brothers can throw their weight on our side, where our Latin-American brothers can throw their weight on our side, and where 800 million Chinamen are sitting there waiting to throw their weight on our side.

Let the world know how bloody his hands are. Let the world know the hypocrisy that's practiced over here. Let it be the ballot or the bullet. Let him know that it must be the ballot or the bullet.

When you take your case to Washington, D.C., you're taking it to the criminal who's responsible; it's like running from the wolf to the fox. They're all in cahoots together. They all work political chicanery and make you look like a chump before the eyes of the world. Here you are walking around in America, getting ready to be drafted and sent abroad, like a tin soldier, and when you get over there, people ask you what are you fighting for, and you have to stick your tongue in your cheek. No, take Uncle Sam to court, take him before the world.

By ballot I only mean freedom. Don't you know—I disagree

with Lomax on this issue—that the ballot is more important than the dollar? Can I prove it? Yes. Look in the UN. There are poor nations in the UN; yet those poor nations can get together with their voting power and keep the rich nations from making a move. They have one nation—one vote, everyone has an equal vote. And when those brothers from Asia, and Africa and the darker parts of this earth get together, their voting power is sufficient to hold Sam in check. Or Russia in check. Or some other section of the earth in check. So, the ballot is most important.

Right now, in this country, if you and I, 22 million African-Americans—that's what we are—Africans who are in America. You're nothing but Africans. Nothing but Africans. In fact, you'd get farther calling yourself African instead of Negro. Africans don't catch hell. You're the only one catching hell. They don't have to pass civil-rights bills for Africans. An African can go anywhere he wants right now. All you've got to do is tie your head up. That's right, go anywhere you want. Just stop being a Negro. Change your name to Hoogagagooba. That'll show you how silly the white man is. You're dealing with a silly man. A friend of mine who's very dark put a turban on his head and went into a restaurant in Atlanta before they called themselves desegregated. He went into a white restaurant, he sat down, they served him, and he said, "What would happen if a Negro came in here?" And there he's sitting, black as night, but because he had his head wrapped up the waitress looked back at him and says, "Why, there wouldn't no nigger dare come in here."

So, you're dealing with a man whose bias and prejudice are making him lose his mind, his intelligence, every day. He's frightened. He looks around and sees what's taking place on this earth, and he sees that the pendulum of time is swinging in your direction. The dark people are waking up. They're losing their fear of the white man. No place where he's fighting right now is he winning. Everywhere he's fighting, he's fighting someone your and my complexion. And they're beating him. He can't win any more. He's won his last battle. He failed to win the Korean War. He couldn't win it. He had to sign a truce. That's a loss. Any time Uncle Sam, with all his machinery for warfare, is held to a draw by some rice-eaters, he's lost the battle. He had to sign a truce. America's not supposed to sign a truce. She's supposed to be bad. But she's not bad any more. She's bad as long as she can use her hydrogen bomb, but she can't use hers for fear Russia might use hers. Russia can't use hers, for fear that Sam might use his. So, both of them are weaponless. They can't use the weapon because each's weapon nullifies the other's. So the only place where action can take place is on the ground. And the white man can't win another war fighting on the ground. Those days are over. The black man knows it, the brown man knows it, the red man knows it, and the yellow man knows it. So they engage him in guerrilla warfare. That's not his style. You've got to have heart to be a guerrilla warrior, and he hasn't got any heart. I'm telling you now.

I just want to give you a little briefing on guerrilla warfare because, before you know it, before you know it—It takes heart to be a guerrilla warrior because you're on your own. In conventional warfare you have tanks and a whole lot of other people with you to back you up, planes over your head and all that kind of stuff. But a guerrilla is on his own. All you have is a rifle, some sneakers and a bowl of rice, and that's all you need—and a lot of heart. The Japanese on some of those islands in the Pacific, when the American soldiers landed, one Japanese sometimes could hold the whole army off. He'd just wait until the sun went down, and when the sun went down they were all equal. He would take his little blade and slip from bush to bush, and from American to American. The white soldiers couldn't cope with that. Whenever you see a white soldier that fought in the Pacific, he has the shakes, he has a nervous condition, because they scared him to death.

The same thing happened to the French up in French Indochina. People who just a few years previously were rice farmers got together and ran the heavily-mechanized French army out of Indochina. You don't need it—modern warfare today won't work. This is the day of the guerrilla. They did the same thing in Algeria. Algerians, who were nothing but Bedouins, took a rifle and sneaked off to the hills, and de Gaulle and all of his highfalutin' war machinery couldn't defeat those guerrillas. Nowhere on this earth does the white man win in a guerrilla warfare. It's not his speed. Just as guerrilla warfare is prevailing in Asia and in parts of Africa and in parts of Latin America, you've got to be mighty naive, or you've got to play the black man cheap, if you don't think some day he's going to wake up and find that it's got to be the ballot or the bullet.

MALCOLM X IN GHANA

On April 7, 1964, Malcolm used funds furnished by his half sister Ella Collins to purchase a round-trip ticket to Africa, with stops in Cairo, Jeddah, Khartoum, Nairobi, Lagos, Accra, and Algiers. He left the following week, under the name Malik el-Shabazz, to make the hajj at the holy city of Mecca. Amid a pending eviction battle and reported attempts on his life, he told the *Amsterdam News*, "I want to get my spiritual self strengthened."[1] With the exception of the religious experience of the hajj, the highlight of his one-month sojourn was a weeklong stop in Ghana, where he was met by a small group of African American expatriates: writer Julian Mayfield and his wife, Ana Livia Cordero, a Puerto Rican doctor; American intellectual-exile Preston King; social worker and secretary to the Ethiopian ambassador Alice Windom; Leslie Lacy, a black American university student; and young Maya Make (Angelou), then working for the University of Ghana's School of Music and Drama while editing for the *African Review*.

After settling down and dining with many in the expatriate community, Malcolm spent his first few days in a hectic series of meetings with, among others, the Cuban ambassador, Armando Entralgo González, and Ghana's minister of defense, Kofi Boaka. His lecture at the Accra Press Club also coincided

---

1. James Booker, "Seek to Evict Malcolm X from Home in Queens," *Amsterdam News*, April 18, 1964.

with a visit by Michigan politician Gerhard Mennen Williams, who was serving as assistant secretary of state for African affairs. Williams had generated quite a stir in recent years by echoing Marcus Garvey's famous anticolonial refrain "Africa for the Africans." However, Malcolm X was less impressed, remarking during a press conference that his father was lynched in Williams's home state. The *Ghanaian Times* detailed Malcolm's significant move from civil rights to human rights and his call for African support for black Americans: "The Afro-American Muslim leader, who is visiting Africa to acquaint himself with the mounting wave of nationalism in the continent, pointed out that there was a growing tendency in America that the civil rights issue has been mislabelled. The 22 million Afro-Americans now being humiliated he said needed the strong and profound moral support of Africans at home in their struggle for racial equality, he said."[2] Several days later Malcolm remarked that the only difference between apartheid in South Africa and American racism was that "while South Africa preaches and practises segregation the United States preaches integration and practises segregation."[3] Malcolm also lectured before a full hall at the University of Ghana, where he praised Ghanaian premier Kwame Nkrumah as one of Africa's "most progressive leaders."[4] He then managed to meet with members of parliament before attending a private audience with Nkrumah. On May 15 Malcolm addressed two hundred students at the Kwame Nkrumah Ideological Institute, forty miles outside of Accra. He later met Shirley Graham Du Bois, the widow of historian W. E. B. Du Bois. Malcolm's final full day was spent meeting with Nigerian high commissioner Alhaji Isa Wali and attending a party held in his honor by the Cuban ambassador.

On his way out of Accra, Malcolm encountered Muhammad Ali and his new boxing manager, Elijah Muhammad's son,

2. "Civil Rights Issue in U.S. Is Mislabelled," *Ghanaian Times*, May 13, 1964.

3. "African States Must Force U.S. for Racial Equality," *Ghanaian Times*, May 15, 1964.

4. Ed Calvin Smith, ed., *Where to, Black Man?* (Chicago: Quadrangle Books, 1967), 211–20.

Herbert. The meeting was the first since Ali had pledged his allegiance to Muhammad, and the boxer was quick to denounce his former friend, laughing at Malcolm's "funny white robe" and adding that "nobody listens to that Malcolm anymore," before the two men headed their separate ways.[5] Just after his return home, Malcolm was also derided in the *Ghanaian Times* by exiled South African journalist H. M. Basner, who charged that the black nationalist failed to recognize the class aspects of racism and instead was consumed by racialism.

"By ignoring economic motivations and the class function of all racial oppression," Basner wrote, "Malcolm X discussed the Afro-American position as if he hadn't a clue how American society evolved or how it can change in the foreseeable future." Basner lamented that in such a view Karl Marx and John Brown are excluded "by their racial origin from being regarded as human liberators, and must be regarded as white liberators only."[6] Julian Mayfield wasted no time in rebutting Basner, claiming that none of Malcolm's arguments excluded a Marxist approach to race. "Basner's is the classical Marxist interpretation of U.S. racial problems," Mayfield wrote. "Put briefly it is this: the only solution is the overthrow of U.S. capitalism, and this can only be brought about by the unity of black and white workers." However, with regards to Malcolm X and American race relations, Mayfield concluded that Basner was "so far off the point that he could not hit a barn door with a shotgun."[7] What ultimately upset the expatriate community the most was that Basner's criticisms were sanctioned by a government-controlled paper, one that repressed criticisms against Nkrumah's administration. However, despite the uproar after his departure, Malcolm later wrote a laudatory account of his time in Ghana, and the trip greatly influenced his

5. Lloyd Garrison, "Clay Makes Malcolm Ex-Friend," *New York Times*, May 18, 1964.

6. H. M. Basner, "Malcolm X and the Martyrdom of Rev. Clayton Hewett," *Ghanaian Times*, May 18, 1964.

7. Julian Mayfield, "Basner Misses Malcolm X's Point," *Ghanaian Times*, May 19, 1964.

growing devotion to Pan-Africanism. Soon he would call for a return to Africa both "philosophically and culturally" and portray Ghana as the "fountainhead of Pan-Africanism."[8]

Further reading:

- "X Is Here," *Ghanaian Times*, May 12, 1964

- "Black Muslim Leader Arrives in Accra, Ghana," *Chicago Tribune*, May 13, 1964

- "Civil Rights Issue in U.S. Is Mislabelled," *Ghanaian Times*, May 13, 1964

- "African States Must Force U.S. for Racial Equality," *Ghanaian Times*, May 15, 1964

- H. M. Basner, "Malcolm X and the Martyrdom of Rev. Clayton Hewett," *Ghanaian Times*, May 18, 1964

- "Mr. X Really Back Home," *Ghanaian Times*, May 18, 1964

- Lloyd Garrison, "Clay Makes Malcolm Ex-Friend," *New York Times*, May 18, 1964

- Julian Mayfield, "Basner Misses Malcolm X's Point," *Ghanaian Times*, May 19, 1964

- "Malcolm X Gives Africa Twisted Look," *New York Journal-American*, July 25, 1964

- Malcolm X FBI file, summary report, New York office, January 20, 1965, pages 55, 70, 90, 94–95

- Revolutionary Action Movement FBI file, memorandum, October 1, 1964

- Letter from Alice Windom, John Henrik Clarke Papers, box 24, folder 33, Schomburg Center for Research in Black Culture, New York Public Library

8. Malcolm X to Muslim Mosque, Inc., May 11, 1964, box 13, folder 2, Malcolm X Collection, Schomburg Center for Research in Black Culture, New York Public Library.

MALCOLM X DEBATES
LOUIS LOMAX

On May 21, 1964, Malcolm X was greeted at the airport in New York by approximately sixty supporters. Just as they had in the NOI, many in his security detail were dressed in the distinctive Fruit of Islam uniform of dark blue suit, white shirt, and bow tie. The following day, Malcolm set off with MMI secretary James 67X Shabazz for a press conference in Chicago. There he promoted his debate with Louis Lomax at the Civic Opera House on May 23. At the debate, before a crowd of nearly fifteen hundred, Malcolm proclaimed that "separation is not the goal of the Afro-American. Nor is integration his goal. They are merely methods toward his real end—respect as a human being." The debaters had been billed as representing the "two extremes of the Negro community's sentiment on race relations," and surely Malcolm's revised stance on racial separation came as a surprise. As he worked to remake his image and insert himself into the civil rights discourse, he added that he had experienced a "spiritual rebirth" and would no longer "subscribe to a sweeping indictment of any race."[1]

Although those familiar with the nuances of Malcolm's speeches may have recognized that since the late 1950s he had condemned whites according to their actions, to most listeners

1. "Goals Changed by Malcolm X," *Los Angeles Times*, May 24, 1964.

his turn from the "blue-eyed devils" rhetoric of the NOI represented an ideological about-face. He also worked to distance himself from the violent image that had followed him from his time in the NOI. While abroad, Malcolm was erroneously linked to a Harlem gang called the "Blood Brothers," which was charged with killing whites around the neighborhood. And although he was careful to eschew any association with such violence, he still remained a staunch advocate of self-defense. The *Los Angeles Times* reported that Malcolm's greatest applause during the debate came from his statement that "unless the race issue is quickly settled, the 22 million American Negroes could easily adopt the guerrilla tactics of other deprived revolutionaries."[2] So while some newspapers heralded what they saw as Malcolm's dramatic ideological shift, many activists continued to identify with his racial militancy and revolutionary rhetoric.

Later that night Malcolm appeared with Lomax on Irv Kupcinet's television program, *Kup's Show*, where he assured viewers that he had had no trouble proving his legitimacy to the orthodox Muslim world. "The only qualification for entering Mecca," he said, "is if you bear witness . . . I had no trouble. Besides, Prince Faisal had given me his Deputy Chief of Protocol who went with me before the Court and acted as my interpreter. So I had no trouble at all."[3] In truth, there was much skepticism by the hajj court prior to Faisal's interference, and Malcolm's approval took several days. However, after only a few days back in the United States, Malcolm had already begun to establish himself as a liaison to the world community of Islam and remake his image from one of racial essentialism to a historical condemnation of racism. For Louis Lomax, who had followed Malcolm's public trajectory from *The Hate That Hate Produced* to "The Ballot or the Bullet" speech just months prior, Malcolm X's transformations must have seemed endless.

2. Ibid.

3. Malcolm X FBI file, summary report, New York office, January 20, 1965, 100.

- MMI FBI file, summary report, Chicago office, June 19, 1964, pages 3–6, 11–13

Further reading:

- Photo standalone, *Chicago Defender*, May 20, 1964
- "Malcolm Says He Is Backed Abroad," *New York Times*, May 22, 1964
- "Goals Changed by Malcolm X," *Los Angeles Times*, May 24, 1964
- Malcolm X FBI file, summary report, New York office, January 20, 1965, pages 10–11, 15, 98–100
- MMI FBI file, summary report, New York office, November 6, 1964, page 14
- Malcolm X FBI file, memo, Chicago office, May 27, 1964

TO: DIRECTOR, FBI (100-441765)
FROM: SAC, CHICAGO (100-41040) (P)
SUBJECT: MUSLIM MOSQUE, INCORPORATED IS—MMI
(OO: NEW YORK)

MALCOLM X appeared on "Kup's Show," Channel 7, TV, Chicago, Illinois, on 5/23/64. This show is moderated by IRV KUPCINET and is a local TV panel show. KUPCINET is a Chicago TV personality and newspaper columnist.

This telecast was tape recorded by SA █████████████ of the Chicago Office. Enclosed for the Bureau are four (4) copies of the taped transcription. Four (4) copies are enclosed in New York.

This information is not being set forth in LHM form as it contains information which MALCOLM X has previously publicly stated. No new pertinent statements appear in the enclosed recordings.

DR. LOUIS LOMAX: I have blood in its soil, I have tilled its land, I have picked its cotton, I have grown its corn, my taxes are not segregated, my taxes are not separated, when Uncle Sam points his finger and says I want you, he doesn't say black or he doesn't say white. In essence—I'll stretch it one more point—I am an American. The American Negro is a man-made race. I say it not with any degree of pride, just as a matter of biological reality. I'm partly African and partly a great deal else, and I have no more stake to going back to where I didn't come from in Africa than I have in going back to Holland where my great-grandfather on both sides may have come from. I'm one of the results of it and so is MALCOLM X.

America is my Israel, and dammit, I'm going to take it. It is my position whether I go to complete involvement, beyond hamburgers, beyond bathrooms, beyond jobs, beyond housing. I'm going to integrate your money, your politics, everything that there is American belongs to me and the only limitations I will abide are those provided by my own gifts, my own talents and my own mind, and I for one am ready and already have done it and will continue to do it and I have an 11 year-old son who is already starting to take to the streets, to the highways, to the by-ways to wherever I must go to fight for and win that which is mine, and may I tag it all with just this particular thought, and I hope Dr. KIRK had a dialogue on this point. I don't like the notion, and this may be flippant but it approaches the truth, that the Catholic Church and the Communist Party are the only two people in America to come to realize that with out the philosophy, perhaps even a theology, either way you're going. And I personally have a deep-seated philosophical position which roots itself into what I think America is, what America is about, and my notion that democracy is not the freedom to build ghettos, ghettos in the mind and geographic ghettos but rather that democracy is a mandate to build ghettos and if this be true, then I am ready to sustain philosophical notion that there is meaning not only in man but meaning in history and there is meaning in America and that the principal meaning today of America is that at long last this by-pass of tribalism, be it ethnetic or religious, is being drawn as it were from the body politic of man as he grows it becomes something else. Until I get the distinct feeling of being a participant in an exciting, you know, like the old 18th century philosophers who had the capacity at least they said they did, to stand outside of themselves and watch themselves as part of the human drama. I think this is the role of the perceptive American Negro today that around me, America is realizing itself it will not go back to the 13th and 15th and 17th century. And I have a very real feeling about this.

MALCOLM X: Well, first I think I would like to point out to Brother LOMAX, Dr. LOMAX here that he has kind of overlooked . . .

KUPCINET: You kind of emphasized the X I noticed when you said LOMAX.

MALCOLM X: Yes, not accidentially. You're overlooking something when you say that any tendency to advocate a form of separation is an affront to the morality of democracy, especially when this same democracy has allowed or permitted the existence of 22 million Afro-Americans who are nothing but second class citizens that this does not, if this isn't an affront to the democracy, nothing can affront, nothing can cast any shadows on it and when a person is regarded as a separationist, as a reaction to the inability of the so-called democracy to practice what it professes or practice what it preaches, then you can't condemn the person who reacts in the direction of separation unless you're going to also condemn that democracy that produced this reaction. If I may finish. Secondly, it is not a case of our people in this country wanting either separation or integration, the use of these two words actually clouds the real picture. The 22 million Afro-Americans don't seek either separation or integration. They seek recognition and respect as human beings and when you think in terms of segregationist or rather separationist or integrationist, it actually clouds the issue. Integration is only a method that is used by some Negroes to get what they really want—recognition and respect as human beings. And separation is a method that is used by other segments of the Negro community to get what they want—respect and recognition as human beings. But the objective, the goal of all factions among our people in this country is the same. The only differences lie in the methods or in the means whereby these goals, these common goals will be achieved so that if we agree that it is respect and recognition as human beings that our people want, then integration and separation is out of the picture completely and the desire, an effort on our part to get this respect as human beings does not even involve civil rights. It first has to involve human rights and our people have actually clouded the picture themselves or allowed themselves to be side-tracked or made to bark up the wrong tree by placing so much stress on civil rights before they first have their actual human rights so where you and I probably differ and differ greatly is this stress on civil rights and in acceptance into the American society as citizens before the society itself has even permitted itself to recognize us as human beings, and I very much doubt that you can make a citizen out of anyone that you don't regard as a human being. We make a mistake by running around here begging for this and begging for that, and I'll go along with you when you say that we should get what we have coming to us, but many of the Negro leaders are playing a very dangerous game if they're going to encourage our people or constantly remind our people of what we have coming to us and get us involved in a struggle and at the same time expect us to remain the peaceful, non-violent victims of the attackers who themselves don't intend for us to be recognized and accepted as an integral part of this society.

* * *

KUPCINET: Let me stop you right there. Do you recommend separation as the means of achieving this goal?

MALCOLM X: I recommend any means necessary.

KUPCINET: Now you're ducking the point.

MALCOLM X: No, I'm not ducking the point.

KUPCINET: Do you recommend separation? You often have stood for it when you were a member of ELIJAH MUHAMMAD's group.

MALCOLM X: Right. That was when I was a member of the Nation of Islam and was a spokesman for the Honorable ELIJAH MUHAMMAD.

KUPCINET: Someone has said you're ELIJAH MUHAMMAD's first drop-out.

MALCOLM X: And was expressing—Well, DICK GREG-ORY probably dropped out himself.

KUPCINET: Well, go ahead. I'm sorry to interject.

MALCOLM X: I don't think in terms of what's good for any particular organization, whether it be a religious organization, a political organization or political party. But I'm primarily concerned as I believe Dr. LOMAX is, with the plight of the entire 22 million Afro-Americans, some of whom are Muslims, some of whom are Christian, some of whom profess to be Democratic, others of whom profess to be Republican. But representing a certain party or a certain religious group is not going to solve the problem of 22 million Afro-Americans. So this is why I say that.

KUPCINET: Explaining why you have separated from Brother ELIJAH MUHAMMAD.

MALCOLM X: No. This is not why I separated from him.

KUPCINET: Did this narrow the confines of your operation?

MALCOLM X: There were very narrow confines which there are always narrow confines when you're working within a religious group. And also usually when you're working with a religious group or within a religious framework, you're already in a position to be in constant opposition to other people whose religious persuasion happens to be different.

UNKNOWN PARTICIPANT: Hasn't your position changed, Minister MALCOLM, in the sense of accepting, or there seems to me to be an implication every now and then in things that you say that it is possible, bad as things are, bad as the white record may be, the possibility of achieving a solution in the United States is there.

MALCOLM X: Yes.

UNKNOWN PARTICIPANT: My main reason is if the statement you wrote about on my book ends, if the warning contained in this book goes unheeded, then America is indeed beyond hope and all is lost. Well, this implies that there must be some hope present.

MALCOLM X: I think if you read or review any speech that I have ever made, no matter how severe the indictment was, right within it there was always the constant warning that if America could change, which America has not changed nor has America shown any real sincere signs of changing when it comes to the treatment of black people in this country. They might change in their method or they might change in the degree to which they apply these methods, but the overall treatment remains with us.

LOMAX: Again if I may here, we are again back to my point of this static view. You say it's methodology between us. It's more than methodology because you see and this is what you're saying, and I think this is so common but I think it is true of our conservative friends and I want to hear Mr. KIRK on this and what you say here is a goal and then you get into an argument over, like you're going to Milwaukee from Chicago so you get into an argument over which train you're going to take. I think we better back up and take the rather fluid view. The road to Rome is Rome itself.

KUPCINET: Right.

FORMATION OF THE ORGANIZATION OF AFRO-AMERICAN UNITY

Following his return from Africa, Malcolm continued to draw crowds of several hundred to MMI rallies at New York City's Audubon Ballroom. However, there were many interested young activists and older Harlemites who were drawn to Malcolm but skeptical about the religious aspects of Muslim Mosque, Inc. The first informal meetings of what would later become the Organization of Afro-American Unity were held at the apartment of Lynne Shifflett, a young journalist at NBC. There Hunter College professor John Henrik Clarke suggested that the group be named and modeled after the recently formed Organization of African Unity (OAU), a group of African nations dedicated to anticolonialism and continental solidarity. Its American counterpart was not a coalition of nations, however, but a group young activists, such as Shifflett, Peter Bailey, and Sara Mitchell, and seasoned Harlem veterans such as photographer Robert Haggins, journalist Sylvester Leaks, writer John Oliver Killens, and actors Ossie Davis and Ruby Dee.

The OAAU's first public rally was held at the Audubon on June 28 before nearly a thousand spectators. Malcolm read the "Statement of Basic Aims and Objectives," which outlined issues ranging from self-defense and education to cultural nationalism and the need for alliances with other civil rights groups. He further stated that he would send a telegram to Martin Luther King offering his support and had already received encouragement from local organizations as well as nations within the Afro-Asian world. It was hoped that close association with, and recognition by, the OAU would help the OAAU accomplish one of its central goals: to bring the plight of African Americans before the United Nations. However, as much as Ghana and other emerging independent African nations offered enthusiastic support for Malcolm X, they were still reluctant to stand before the UN and indict the United States for violations of human rights. While an international scope was a crucial component of the OAAU, the group also focused on its local base in Harlem, addressing community issues such as police brutality and voter registration.

Despite Malcolm's initial insistence that he would carry on Elijah Muhammad's work and that no Muslims should leave the sect, the two leaders now openly waged a membership war. While Malcolm was drawing high-profile personages such as Juanita Poitier and author Paule Marshall to the unveiling of the OAAU, Elijah Muhammad spoke before a crowd of between six thousand and twelve thousand at the 369th Regiment Armory, only a few miles south. Muhammad's rally was an open challenge to Malcolm X in both its extravagance and location. However, in historical significance the NOI rally would pale in comparison with the formation of the OAAU, which promised to be the most significant secular black nationalist movement since Marcus Garvey's United Negro Improvement Association. Although the OAAU would suffer from Malcolm's long absences abroad and his assassination shortly thereafter, its aims and objectives proved to be foundational to the nascent ideologies of Black Power.

- "OAAU Statement of Basic Aims and Objectives," from OAAU FBI file, June 24, 1964

Further reading:

- "Muhammad Here, Malcolm Where?" *New York Journal-American*, June 29, 1964

- "Elijah Muhammad Rallies His Followers in Harlem," *New York Times*, June 29, 1964

- "Muslims Rally to Muhammad," *Amsterdam News*, July 4, 1964

- Joseph Gravitt FBI file, summary report, New York office, January 25, 1965, pages 3–4

- Raymond Sharrieff FBI file, summary report, Chicago office, August 27, 1964, pages 16–17

- Raymond Sharrieff FBI file, summary report, Chicago office, March 17, 1965, pages 13–14

- Malcolm X FBI file, summary report, New York office, January 20, 1965, pages 5–6, 25, 29, 30–31, 76

OAAU Statement of Basic Aims and Objectives, OAAU FBI File, June 24, 1964

A cross section of the Harlem Community has been working for sometime on the formation of an organization that would transcend all superficial, man made divisions between the Afro-American people of this country who are working for Human Rights, and that would in no way compete with already existing successful organizations.

I have been requested, and indeed it is my pleasure, to announce the existence of the ORGANIZATION OF AFRO-AMERICAN UNITY (OAAU), patterned after the letter and the spirit of the Organization of African Unity (OAU). Its purpose is to unite Afro-Americans and their organizations around a non-religious and non-sectarian constructive program for Human Rights.

The Organization of Afro-American Unity is well aware of your interest, work, and involvement in freedom struggles over the years, and you have proven to be sincere in your area of endeavor.

Therefore, the Organization of Afro-American Unity would like you to be its guest at a rally Sunday, June 25, 1964 at 5:00 p.m. at the Audubon Ballroom, 166th Street and Broadway in New York City, at which time the organization of Afro-American Unity and its aims and objectives will be announced publicly.

So that you might meet the other guests prior to the rally, the Organization of Afro-American Unity would like to extend to you an invitation to be present at 6:30 p.m. for an informal reception in the rear of the main ballroom at the Audubon.

In order to facilitate seating arrangements please respond either by mail or telephone, on or before Friday, June 26, 1964.

Sincerely,

Malcolm X
(El-Hajj Malik El-Shabazz Al-Sabban)

The Organization of Afro-American Unity, organized and structured by a cross section of the Afro-American people living in the United States of America, has been patterned after the letter and spirit of the Organization of African Unity established at Addis Ababa, Ethiopia, May 1963.

We, the members of the Organization of Afro-American Unity gathered together in Harlem, New York;

CONVINCED that it is the inalienable right of all people to control their own destiny;

CONSCIOUS of the fact that freedom, equality, justice and dignity are essential objectives for the achievement of the legitimate aspirations of the people of African descent here in the Western Hemisphere, we will endeavor to build a bridge of understanding and create the basis for Afro-American Unity;

CONSCIOUS of our responsibility to harness the natural and human resources of our people for their total advancement in all spheres of human endeavor;

INSPIRED by a common determination to promote understanding among our people and cooperation in all matters pertaining to their survival and advancement, we will support the aspirations of our people for brotherhood and solidarity in a larger unity transcending all organizational differences;

CONVINCED that, in order to translate this determination into a dynamic force in the cause of human progress, conditions of peace and security must be established and maintained;

DETERMINED to unify the Americans of African descent in their fight for Human Rights and Dignity, and being fully aware that this is not possible in the present atmosphere and condition of oppression, we dedicate ourselves to the building of a political, economic, and social system of justice and peace;

DEDICATED to the unification of all people of African descent in this hemisphere and to the utilization of that unity to bring into being the organizational structure that will project the black people's contributions to the world;

PERSUADED that the Charter of the United Nations, the Universal Declaration of Human Rights, the Constitution of the United States of America and the Bill of Rights are the principles in which we believe and these documents if put into practice represent the essence of mankind's hopes and good intentions;

DESIROUS that all Afro-American people and organizations should henceforth unite so that the welfare and well-being of our people will be assured;

RESOLVED to reinforce the common bond of purpose between our people by submerging all of our differences and establishing a non-religious and non-sectarian constructive program for Human Rights;

DO hereby present this charter.

I. ESTABLISHMENT

The Organization of Afro-American Unity shall include all people of African descent in the Western Hemisphere, as well as our brothers and sisters on the African Continent.

II. SELF-DEFENSE

Since self-preservation is the first law of nature, we assert the Afro-American's right of self-defense.

The Constitution of the United States of America clearly affirms the right of every American citizen to bear arms. And as Americans, we will not give up a single right guaranteed under the Constitution. The history of unpunished violence against our people clearly indicates that we must be prepared to defend ourselves or we will continue to be a defenseless people at the mercy of a ruthless and violent racist mob.

We assert that in those areas where the government is either unable or unwilling to protect the lives and property of our people, that our people are within their rights to protect themselves by whatever means necessary. A man with a rifle or club can only be stopped by a person who defends himself with a rifle or club.

Tactics based solely on morality can only succeed when you are dealing with basically moral people or a moral system. A man or system which oppresses a man because of his color is not moral. It is the duty of every Afro-American and every Afro-American community throughout this country to protect its people against mass murderers, bombers, lynchers, floggers, brutalizers and exploiters.

III. EDUCATION

Education is an important element in the struggle for Human Rights. It is the means to help our children and people rediscover their identity and thereby increase self-respect. Education is our passport to the future, for tomorrow belongs to the people who prepare for it today.

Our children are being criminally short-changed in the public school system of America. The Afro-American schools are the poorest run schools in New York City. Principals and teachers fail to understand the nature of the problems with which they work and as a result they cannot do the job of teaching our children. The textbooks tell our children nothing about the great contributions of Afro-Americans to the growth and development of this country. The Board of Education's integration plan is expensive and unworkable; and the organization of principals and supervisors in the New York City school system has refused to support the Board's plan to integrate the schools, thus dooming it to failure.

The Board of Education has said that even with its plan there are 10% of the schools in the Harlem-Bedford-Stuyesant community they cannot improve. This means that the Organization of Afro-American Unity must make the Afro-American community a more potent force for educational self-improvement.

A first step in the program to end the existing system of racist education is to demand that the 10% of the schools the Board of Education will not include in its plan, be turned over to and run by the Afro-American community. We want Afro-American principals to head these schools. We want Afro-American teachers in these schools. We want textbooks written by Afro-Americans that are acceptable to us to be used in these schools.

The Organization of Afro-American Unity will solicit and recommend people to serve on local school boards where school policy is made and passed on to the Board of Education.

Through these steps we will make the 10% of schools we take over educational showplaces that will attract the attention of people all over the nation.

If these proposals are not met, we will ask Afro-American parents to keep their children out of the present inferior schools they attend. When these schools in our neighborhood are controlled by Afro-Americans, we will return to them.

The Organization of Afro-American Unity recognizes the tremendous importance of the complete involvement of Afro-American parents in every phase of school life. Afro-American parents must be willing and able to go into the schools and see that the job of educating our children is done properly.

We call on all Afro-Americans around the nation to be aware that the conditions that exist in the New York City public school system are as deplorable in their cities as they are here. We must unite our efforts and spread our program of self-improvement through education to every Afro-American community in America.

We must establish all over the country schools of our own to train our children to become scientists and mathematicians. We must realize the need for adult education and for job retraining programs that will emphasize a changing society in which automation plays the key role. We intend to use the tools of education to help raise our people to an unprecedented level of excellence and self-respect through their own efforts.

IV. POLITICS-ECONOMICS

Basically, there are two kinds of power that count in America: economic and political, with social power deriving from the two. In order for the Afro-Americans to control their destiny, they must be able to control and affect the decisions which control their destiny: economic, political and social. This can only be done through organization.

The Organization of Afro-American Unity will organize the Afro-American community block by block to make the community aware of its power and potential; we will start immediately a voter-registration drive to make every unregistered voter in the Afro-American community an Independent voter; we propose to support and/or organize political clubs, to run Independent candidates for office, and to support any Afro-American already in office who answers to and is responsible to the Afro-American community.

Economic exploitation in the Afro-American community is the most vicious form practiced on any people in America; twice as much rent for rat infested, roach-crawling, rotting tenements; the Afro-American pays more for foods, clothing, insurance rates and so forth. The Organization of Afro-American Unity will wage an unrelenting struggle against these evils in our community. There shall be organizers to work with the people to solve these problems, and start a housing self-improvement program. We propose to support rent strikes and other activities designed to better the community.

V. SOCIAL

This organization is responsible only to the Afro-American people and community and will function only with their support, both financially and numerically. We believe that our communities must be the sources of their own strength politically, economically, intellectually and culturally in the struggle for Human Rights and Dignity.

The community must reinforce its moral responsibility to rid itself of the effects of years of exploitation, neglect and apathy, and wage an unrelenting struggle against police brutality.

The Afro-American community must accept the responsibility for regaining our people who have lost their place in society. We must declare an all out war on organized crime in our community; a vice that is controlled by Policemen who accept bribes and graft, and who must be exposed. We must establish a clinic, whereby one can got aid and cure for drug addiction; and create meaningful, creative, useful activities for those who were led astray down the avenues of vice.

The people of the Afro-American community must be prepared to help each other in all ways possible; we must establish a place where unwed mothers can get help and advice, a home for the aged in Harlem and an orphanage in Harlem.

We must set up a guardian system that will help our youth who get into trouble and also provide constructive activities for our children. We must set a good example for our children and must teach them to always be ready to accept the responsibilities that are necessary for building good communities and nations. We must teach them that their greatest responsibilities are to themselves, to their families and to their communities.

The Organization of Afro-American Unity believes that the Afro-American community must endeavor to do the major part of all charity work from within the community. Charity, however, does not mean that to which we are legally entitled in the form of government benefits. The Afro-American veteran must be made aware of all the benefits due him and the procedure for obtaining them. These veterans must be encouraged to go into business together, using G.I. loans, etc.

Afro-Americans must unite and work together. We must take pride in the Afro-American community, for it is home and it is power.

What we do here in regaining our Self-Respect, Manhood, Dignity and Freedom helps all people everywhere who are fighting against oppression.

VI. CULTURE

"A race of people is like an individual man; until it uses its own talent, takes pride in its own history, expresses its own culture, affirms its own selfhood, it can never fulfill itself."

Our history and our culture were completely destroyed when we were forceably brought to America in chains. And now it is important for us to know that our history did not begin with slavery's scars. We come from Africa, great continent and a proud and varied people, a land which is the new world and was the cradle of civilization. Our culture and our history are as old as man himself and yet we know almost nothing of it. We must recapture our heritage and our identity if we are ever to liberate ourselves from the bonds of white supremacy. We must launch a cultural revolution to unbrainwash an entire people.

Our cultural revolution must be the means of bringing us closer to our African brothers and sisters. It must begin in the community and be based on community participation. Afro-Americans will be free to create only when they can depend on the Afro-American community for support and Afro-American artists must realize that they depend on the Afro-American for inspiration. We must work toward the establishment of a cultural center in Harlem which will include people of all ages, and will conduct workshops in all of the arts, such as film, creative writing, painting, theatre, music, Afro-American history, etc.

This cultural revolution will be the journey to our rediscovery of ourselves. History is a people's memory, and without a memory man is demoted to the lower animals.

Armed with the knowledge of our past, we can with confidence charter a course for our future. Culture is an indespensible weapon in the freedom struggle. We must take hold of it and forge the future with the past. . . .

When the battle is won, let history be able to say of each one of us: "He was a dedicated patriot: DIGNITY was his country, MANHOOD was his government, and FREEDOM was his land." (from And Then We Heard The Thunder by John Oliver Killens)

EVICTION TRIAL AND PATERNITY SUITS

Elijah Muhammad's March 1964 inquiry into the title and property rights to Malcolm's home was not mere idle curiosity. Weeks after Malcolm announced the formation of MMI, Mosque No. 7 secretary Maceo X Owens filed papers on behalf of the Nation of Islam to have the former minister and his family evicted from their Queens home. Meanwhile, Malcolm made efforts to publicize Muhammad's extramarital affairs, outing Muhammad on Mike Wallace's CBS news program and sending top aide James 67X Shabazz to Phoenix to gain signatures necessary for a paternity suit by two of his former secretaries. The NOI's grounds for eviction were that the home had been purchased for Malcolm in his ministerial capacities, and that, with the establishment of MMI, he had severed that relationship. Conversely, Malcolm's argument was that he had never been given a proper trial according to established NOI protocol, which included a hearing in front of the local mosque. To be brought before a civil court, rather than a Muslim court, was to him a clear deviation from NOI principles.

The eviction trial itself took place on June 15–16, 1964, and featured NOI witnesses such as Captain Joseph, defectors loyal to Malcolm such as Charles 37X Kenyatta, and a two-hour-long testimony by Malcolm himself. The scene was tense, and Malcolm arrived guarded by ten of his followers and thirty-two policemen, while nearly fifty members of the Fruit of Islam stood intimidatingly by. Although Malcolm's legal representative, Percy Sutton, clearly did not want to broach the issue of Muhammad's affairs at the trial, his client could not resist dangling it before the court. When asked about his public comments on President Kennedy, Malcolm stated that he was "publically suspended" for that reason but really suspended for "something private . . . very private."[1] Finally, despite Sutton's attempts to move away from that line of questioning, Malcolm told the court that Muhammad had taken nine wives (six of whom were impregnated) and that his suspension was a result of spreading this information among top NOI officials and ministers. Due to the presence of top-level Nation of Islam officials at the eviction trial, Malcolm's pronouncement was on one level a declaration of war.

Malcolm's airing of Muhammad's affairs at the trial and on CBS were only the beginning of a larger act of public defamation. Just weeks before the eviction trial, James 67X Shabazz had secured the signatures of Lucille Rosary and Malcolm's teenage sweetheart, Evelyn Williams, and taken the paternity suit to Los Angeles attorney Gladys Towles Root. John Ali and Raymond Sharrieff quickly attempted to refute rumors of Muhammad's affairs in a press conference. Five women—at least three of whom were mistresses of Muhammad—also held a press conference in Los Angeles protesting the paternity suit. The three mistresses also appeared with Delores Jardan, the widow of Ronald Stokes, in support of Muhammad.[2]

Just before his death, Malcolm met with Root, Rosary, and Williams and volunteered information, assuring his testimony in the upcoming case. However, following his death, the next month, the case lost all momentum. Meanwhile, in the eviction trial, the judge ruled in favor of the Nation of Islam in September 1964 but tabled the execution of the

1. Transcript of Queens County Civil Court trial, June 15–16, 1964, box 9, folder 20, New York City Department of Records—Municipal Archives.

2. "5 Muslim Women Rap Suits Against Leader," *Los Angeles Times*, August 9, 1964.

warrant until January 1965. The eviction notice had just been served before Malcolm's death; he and his family moved to the home of a close friend, Thomas Wallace, only three days before his assassination. However, more significant than the outcome of either case is that the eviction trial and paternity suits represented the public souring of a relationship that Malcolm X had once described as like that of a father and son.

- "Ex-Sweetheart of Malcolm X Accuses Elijah: Denies Paternity Charges," *Amsterdam News*, July 11, 1964

- Transcript of Queens County Civil Court trial, June 15–16, 1964, box 9, folder 20, New York City Department of Records—Municipal Archives (excerpt)

Further reading:

- "Muslims Deny Fight Going On Within Ranks," *Chicago Defender*, June 18, 1964

- "Paternity Suits Name Chief of Black Muslims," *Los Angeles Times*, July 3, 1964

- "Deny Paternity Suits Against Elijah Muhammad," *Chicago Defender*, July 6, 1964

- Stanley Robertson, "Paternity Charge Faces Muhammad," *Los Angeles Sentinel*, July 9, 1964

- "5 Muslim Women Rap Suits Against Leader," *Los Angeles Times*, August 9, 1964

- "Order Eviction of Malcolm X," *Amsterdam News*, September 5, 1964

- Malcolm X FBI file, summary report, New York office, January 20, 1965, pages 56–58, 73–74

- MMI FBI file, memo, New York office, June 19, 1964

- MMI FBI file, Teletype, New York office, June 17, 1964

- Malcolm X FBI file, memo, assistant attorney general to FBI director, September 2, 1964

- Malcolm X FBI file, memo, New York office, September 3, 1964, pages 2–3

- Malcolm X FBI file, Teletype, New York office, February 18, 1965

- Malcolm X FBI file, summary report, New York office, January 20, 1965, pages 19–25, 59–68, 72

- Malcolm X FBI file, memo, New York office, July 7, 1964

- Malcolm X FBI file, summary report, New York office, September 8, 1965, pages 19–20, 37

BULLETIN

LOS ANGELES—Lucille Rosary, 30-year-old secretary who has accused Black Muslim Leader Elijah Muhammad of fathering two of her children, gave birth to a baby girl here Tuesday and named Mr. Muhammad as the father.

At the same time Miss Rosary and Evelyn Williams, both of whom have filed paternity suits against the Muslim leader, filed affidavits in Superior Court here alleging that they had been told that some "fanatic followers" might kill them if they tried to prove that Muhammad fathered their children.

The mushrooming power struggle between Black Muslim leader Elijah Muhammad and his former disciple, Malcolm X broke wide open this week as Malcolm charged that he is "marked for assassination by Muhammad, but that it will not be done until Elijah Muhammad gives the word."

As Malcolm made his charges in a radio broadcast and in a statement to the Amsterdam News this week, two former sweethearts of Malcolm X filed suit in Los Angeles accusing Elijah Muhammad of fathering three children, and conceiving a fourth.

DENIED

In Chicago, National Captain Raymond Sharrieff and National Secretary John Ali of the Muslims, issued a bitter and vigorous denial of the charges.

"We have held our peace for some time as we have heard the

evil charges made public by Malcolm because of his evil, jealous and malicious intention to attempt to disgrace Messenger Muhammad," the statement from the two top men in Muhammad's empire declared.

Asserting that Muhammad would not dignify the charges by answering them, the two charged that Malcolm and one of Muhammad's accusers, Evelyn Williams, were once engaged. "As to who is the father of Evelyn's and Lucille's children, Allah is the best Knower," the statement said. They added, however, that the women and their babies have been and are still being cared for by the Chicago headquarters.

Malcolm admitted to this newspaper that he had once been engaged to Miss Williams.

In her suit, Miss Williams charges the 67-year old Muhammad with fathering her daughter Eva Marie, 4, born in Lynbrook, Calif., while Miss Lucille Rosary's suit names Muhammad as the father of her daughter Saudi, 1, and Lisha, 2, both born in Hyannis, Mass.

She said she is expecting a third child by Muhammad. Both young women formerly worked in the secretarial pool in Muhammad's Chicago headquarters.

SON

Meanwhile as activities inside the Muslim empire began to be exposed by former members of the group, one of Muhammad's sons, Wallace Muhammad, sent out announcements indicating that he was joining with Malcolm in the power struggle, and breaking away from the forces around his father.

Sharrieff and Ali, in their prepared statement, said that Muhammad would "state the law as given in the Holy-Quran against hypocrites and disbelievers in the next issue of Muhammad Speaks newspaper," asserting that they would continue to build the "Nation of Islam regardless of what is said or may be attempted against us."

A By misquote, if I may explain. The quote is incomplete. It conveys an idea that is—it's limited or was not designed to project the idea that I had in mind.

Q *Mr. Malcolm, we are quibbling.*

MR. SUTTON: Just a moment. Don't argue with the witness, "we are quibbling." Ask him the question.

THE COURT: If you have any objections, make it to me.

MR. SUTTON: Of course.

THE COURT: You are interrupting him right in the middle.

MR. SUTTON: I sort of have to.

Q *Is it your testimony that you said the words that were quoted here but you said more than this, is that correct?*
　　A That's not correct. I said that's incorrectly quoted. It's incomplete. The words have been rearranged.

Q *Were these words used? Did you say those words that I read to you?*
　　A In that structure?

Q *I mean, did you say these words that I read? Did you say that?*

A Sir, I had given an hour's talk before Presbyterian ministers in Brooklyn—

Q *Excuse me, sir. You said—*
A During that hour's talk I said many things and probably those words in one part or another was in some of the sentences and paragraphs that I used.

Q *Did you ever see this article before?*
A Yes.

Q *Did you ever say or write a letter to the Times that you were misquoted?*
A I'm misquoted in so many papers that it would take all my time to answer their misquotes.

THE COURT: Your answer is no, I take it?

THE WITNESS: That's right.

Q *Now, when you say your own organization—joining your organization, that's another organization you are speaking of?*

MR. SUTTON: Just a moment. I don't believe I heard him testify to that.

MR. WILLIAMS: Withdrawn and move on to something else.

Q *When you were suspended, weren't you told the reason why you were suspended?*
A Yes or no?

Q *Yes or no.*
A Which suspension?

Q *Well—*
A There was—

Q *Suspension of the Honorable Elijah Muhammad?*
  A There were three suspensions. One was made public.

Q *I meant the one when you were suspended by the Honorable Elijah Muhammad?*
  A There were three. One was made public.

Q *Let's go to the first one, the first one in point of time by the Honorable Elijah Muhammad. You are saying now he suspended you three specific times?*
  A He suspended me in part, the suspension.

Q *Everything is part, the hearing is part, now this is part.*

MR. SUTTON: Just a moment, I object to that remark.

THE COURT: Yes. That's more like this. This is like a Perry Mason case.
  A Sir, my suspension involved three stages or three parts. The first one was made public. It was made known internationally by the press out of Chicago. There was another part of that same suspension that was made known only to the Muslims and there was another part of that that was made known only to me and the national officials and this part of this suspension was supposed to come out at the time I was given a hearing. They didn't want it to come out so they wouldn't give me a hearing in front of the Muslims.

Q *Now I am going back to the time when you were suspended whether it was first, second or third. You were told a reason were you not or you were given some reasons.*
  A Yes.

Q *Isn't it a fact that you were suspended because the Honorable Elijah Muhammad said you should not make political statements as a religious group?*
  A Sir?

Q *That you made a political statement and he felt you shouldn't make one as a political group.*
  A No.

Q *Wasn't there a directive that you should not make political statements that went out to all ministers?*

MR. SUTTON: I object. I think we are getting into things not before the court.

THE COURT: This is cross examination.

MR. SUTTON: It opens the avenue to a number of things.

THE COURT: Let him open it.

MR. WILLIAMS: I'm going to open it.

THE COURT: Proceed.

THE WITNESS: What is your question?

MR. WILLIAMS: Please read the last question, Mr. Reporter. (The question was read.)
  A He called me on the telephone. There was no directive. The instruction that I got came from him personally over the telephone in regard to a certain situation.

Q *But didn't all the ministry receive instruction that they not comment on certain events?*
  A Yes.

MR. SUTTON: Objection.

THE COURT: Overruled.

Q *And you commented, is that correct?*
  A Yes.

Q   *That resulted in your suspension?*
A   No, no, it did not.

Q   *You broke the rule?*
A   No.

Q   *You violated the directive, is that correct?*
A   The Honorable Elijah Muhammad told me himself that he would have made the statement that I made, that he had the same feelings that I expressed.

Q   *But yet he suspended you for it?*
A   He did not suspend me for that.

Q   *He publicly said he suspended you for it.*
A   Yes.

Q   *But he suspended you for something private?*
A   Yes, he suspended me for something private.

Q   *Let's move to—*
A   Very private.

MR. SUTTON: Just a moment.
A   (continuing) I am answering your question. The suspension—I think it was on the 3rd of December that the suspension was announced supposedly attached to a statement that I had made on the 1st of December. The reason for my suspension was not the statement that I made concerning that situation.

Q   *Did you receive a letter suspending you?*
A   No.

Q   *You only got it on the telephone, is that correct?*
A   No, I went to Chicago.

Q   *And he told you personally why you were being suspended?*

A He told me that because of the climate of the country and the statement that had been made.

Q *By whom?*
    A By me, it would be better for me to remain silent for ninety days.

Q *That's your suspension?*
    A Yes. He told me that it would be better for me to remain silent for ninety days.

THE COURT: Is this a political statement you made?

THE WITNESS: Yes.

THE COURT: Affecting what?

THE WITNESS: You mean what did it pertain to?

THE COURT: Democrat or Republican or . . .

THE WITNESS: Both.

THE COURT: Go ahead.

Q *You have testified that you spoke all around the country and you received fees for this, is that correct?*
    A No fees. I never received a fee.

Q *For speaking you never received a fee?*
    A No.

Q *They paid it to the mosque?*
    A No. Whenever any group before whom I spoke or before which I spoke had anything that they wanted to give, I told them they would only accept a contribution to the mosque.

Q *That was the local mosque?*

A Sometime it was the local mosque and sometime it was the national mosque.

Q *What happens to these monies that were given to the local mosque?*

A They go to Chicago.

Q *Did you ever have these checks cashed and cash given to you?*

A Only if—

Q *Answer yes or no.*

A I will answer with an explanation.

Q *Answer yes or no first.*

A No.

Q *All right.*

A Sir, every question, can I answer—

THE COURT: If you say no, that's it. That's the end.

THE WITNESS: It's yes or no and I would like to explain.

Q *Yes and no?*

THE COURT: He may answer it.

A If I went to speak at Harvard and it would cost me, say $100 or $90 or something like that, whatever the expense was, if they'd give it to me, it would appear as income wherein actually it would be money that I was receiving for that which I had already taken out of my pocket, so whatever place before whom or before which I spoke or at which I spoke, I asked them always to make a contribution to the mosque. Whatever amount of money that I had spent in the form of expenses after that check was cashed, I asked the secretary to give me back that which I had spent.

Q *Now, the check that these people gave you, was that expense money or fees? What was it?*
A Contribution to the mosque.

Q *Was that for your speaking?*
A In some cases it would be. It was a contribution to the mosque.

Q *Which mosque?*
A Number—whatever it is, number 7 mosque or the Chicago mosque.

Q *Did you make a record of those contributions when you turned them in?*
A How do you mean?

Q *Did you get a receipt for them?*
A I turned them over to the secretary. They never came to me.

Q *The monies never came to you?*
A No.

Q *When you spoke at Harvard for Mosque 14, didn't you get a check?*
A I gave it back to them because—

Q *You gave it to Minister Thomas X?*
A It was made out in my name.

Q *You sent it out and had it made out to the name of the mosque?*
A Yes.

Q *You cashed the check and took the cash?*
A No.

Q *You never got money from the minister?*
A No.

Q *Let me—*

A Just a moment. All you have to find out is the amount of the check that was given and you will see that it cost no more to go to Harvard and back.

Q *Was the check that was made out to the mosque, was that not cashed and the cash given to you?*

A No. Wait a minute, sir.

Q *Didn't you—*

A Wait a minute, I don't want to put—to be put in a position of giving you the wrong answer. When you say the check was made out, which one are you talking about?

Q *You said they sent you two checks. The first one was made out in your name which you sent back, not to them, but to the minister.*

A I gave it back.

Q *Was it made out in the name of Mosque 14?*

A No, Mosque 7, if my memory serves me correct. I'm not sure but I think it was made out to Mosque 7 because it was my policy always to have my contributions that were once for personal appearances that I made to be turned over to the mosque.

Q *Wasn't Thomas J. X the minister of that mosque?*

A Which mosque?

Q *14.*

A Yes.

Q *Didn't you give the check to him to cash?*

A No, sir. If my memory serves me—wait a minute. If I know my procedure—

Q *I'm not talking about your procedure. When you get that second check, did you give it to Minister Thomas J. X to cash it?*

MR SUTTON: I'm objecting. The Witness was about to respond. He was continuing his answer when he was interrupted.

THE COURT: Proceed.

A (continuing) See, sir, with all due respect to the court and everybody else, you are dealing with a time, a year ago at least and this is something that happened with me every single day. For me to remember the intricate details of what took place on a certain day between me and a remote individual, I can't give you the exact date but to my knowledge—

THE COURT: Mr. Witness, nobody is asking you to remember. If you don't remember, say so.

THE WITNESS: I don't remember. Thank you, Judge.

Q *When you spoke to the Ford Hall Forum—you remember that?*
  A Ford? Yes.

Q *You got a check there, did you not?*
  A If I did, it was—if my memory serves me correct, it was made out to the mosque.

Q *Did you cash that check?*
  A I have never cashed a check.

Q *Did you have anybody cash that check?*
  A Not have them cash it for me. All checks I received I turned over to the secretary of the mosque.

Q *You are saying that you received none of these monies yourself?*
  A That's right.

Q *You received no salary? All this money you got, this mini-mum amount of $150, you got each week was used for your travel around, is that correct?*

A Not only that, I had access to unlimited funds.

Q *I'm talking about the $150.*
A I had access to unlimited funds.

Q *You had to put in a requisition to approve it?*
A No, all I had to do was ask the Honorable Elijah Muhammad for any amount I wanted.

Q *I'm talking about locally.*
A Also locally.

Q *Did you ever have to verify what you were going to do with it?*
A Sometimes yes and sometimes no.

Q *If it was over $150 you had to verify what you had to do with it?*
A No. As they testified yesterday, the minister was in complete authority and got the directives from the Honorable Elijah Muhammad.

Q *Yes, sir. So, therefore, if you say the minister was in complete authority and got all of his directives from the Honorable Elijah Muhammad, do you know of any particular case where a local mosque had passed on the removal of a minister?*
A The local—yes.

Q *Where was this?*
A Philadelphia. The minister—

Q *Was this at a meeting?*
A It was a trial. Charges were brought in front of him and whenever a charge is brought against any Muslim that Muslim must be brought before the body, no charges were brought before the minister in Philadelphia just two months ago while all of this stuff was going on about me and he was given a hearing. He was found guilty and still Chicago wouldn't remove

him because he knew too much so they had to give him another hearing and Chicago still wouldn't remove him until the
Muslims themselves demanded his removal.

Q *Isn't it also a fact that every mosque you go to, that the
mosque themself takes care of your expenses?*
    A No. In some cases yes and some cases no.

Q *But usually, isn't that so?*
    A No. I can name the ones that do and the ones that don't
and the ones that don't number more than—

Q *I want to ask—*
    A (continuing)—The number that don't and the number
that didn't and the number that couldn't were far greater than
those that could. This is why I had to travel to those mosques
all the time. They stayed in financial distress. They didn't
know how to organize their finances.

Q *Did you give this money to these mosques? You said they
were financially in distress.*
    A I went to help them organize their business procedures
which were very slack as testimony in this trial has already
pointed out.

Q *Do you think this mosque here that you headed from
1952 had good financial procedures from the testimony you
heard here today?*
    A It was the most economically sound.

Q *That's not the question.*
    A It was only one of the temples that is in the black. The
rest were in the red.

Q *Was it good?*
    A I founded the procedure that the Honorable Elijah Mu-
hammad gave me in everything I did. I followed the procedure,
the instructions, the orders of the Honorable Elijah Muhammad.

Q *All right. Did you ever make any records, sir, of these monies that you received on these speaking engagements that you gave back to the mosque?*

A No, I didn't have to.

Q *Was any record made in the temple of them?*

A You would have to ask the secretary. I don't know.

THE COURT: Will you be much longer with this witness?

MR. WILLIAMS: Not much longer.

Q *Now, when payments are made into the mosque, isn't it a fact that a written record is kept of each payment that is made and all monies that are received? Is that the procedure?*

A I don't quite understand you, sir.

Q *If a believer would come in and bring some money, isn't it a fact that a record was kept of every dime that went in?*

A Yes.

Q *You insisted upon that, didn't you?*

A Yes.

Q *When these other monies that were supposed to come in and you gave them to the secretary, did you insist that he make a record of those monies, too?*

A How do you mean?

Q *You said that you spoke around the country almost daily and received these checks that you brought back to the mosque, is that correct?*

A Yes.

Q *Yet you say that there was no record from 1952 down to the time you were suspended as to any of these monies, is that correct?*

A I didn't say that.

Q *Well, are there records of these monies you received?*
   A The secretary keeps records, I imagine, of everything he receives. I wasn't the secretary.

Q *You said previously that you ran this mosque; you knew everything that was going on, didn't you?*
   A I thought I did. I thought I did.

Q *Did you know anything about the financial—*
   A I now know there was much going on that I didn't know.

Q *Answer me about the financial structures. Did you know the financial structure?*
   A Yes.

Q *You saw the records, too, didn't you?*
   A When you say I saw them—

Q *You made a statement here—*

MR. SUTTON: Just a moment. Objection. He was about to explain.

THE COURT: Did you finish?

THE WITNESS: No, I don't think so. Did I have a minute knowledge of the exact state of every aspect of the economy in the financial transactions of the mosque?

Q *No, I didn't mean that. I mean, that those checks and so forth you didn't keep any track; these were the fruits of your labor?*
   A The entire income of the mosque was the fruit of my labor.

Q *The entire?*
   A Yes.

Q *Were there donations and contributions?*
A Yes.

Q *Are you the entire mosque?*
A No, I am not.

Q *Weren't there other believers who donated to the house? Didn't they donate to that?*
A When I say that I was the entire economy income of the mosque, was due to my labor, I'm going back to the statement where I said it was the only mosque that was in the black, it was the only mosque that had made any progress economically. All of the others were in the red including the headquarters mosque at number 2. That stayed in the red.

Q *Now, sir, when this house was being purchased, you were not even around when they met to buy this house. When they had the first discussion in the mosque about the house you weren't around, were you? You were out of town, is that not a fact?*
A I stayed out of town most of the time but when the purchase of the house was being discussed, naturally it had to be brought to my attention.

Q *After you came back, is that correct?*
A With an explanation.

Q *Answer yes or no. After you came back they told you they had agreed to buy a house, is that correct?*
A I had always—

Q *Is that correct or not?*
A Only with an explanation can I say yes or no.

Q *Say yes or no with an explanation.*
A Yes, with an explanation. I never sought to gain anything personally from the Nation of Islam. This is why I lived in a room and then lived in three rooms.

Q   *And the believers while you were away said that you should have better quarters, isn't that a fact?*

A   They had been saying that few about three years—about two years and I had gotten married and had a child and that it was not good for me to live where I had been living and since I was working so hard they insisted that a house be purchased for me. This idea was presented to the Honorable Elijah Muhammad.

Q   *By whom?*

A   By me and by them. All of us.

Q   *All of you together?*

A   Not all together.

Q   *By letter?*

A   Yes, and in person.

Q   *Who wrote the letter?*

A   I imagine some of the officials.

Q   *You were the head?*

A   I didn't really have to read to him because I saw him periodically.

Q   *But you conveyed this idea, is that correct?*

A   I told the Honorable Elijah Muhammad that the Muslims in New York wanted to buy me a house. He felt they should but dealt—he transacted the business through the then secretary at that time.

Q   *Now, sir, let me get back to the house. You said when the believers agreed to buy the house you came back, is that correct?*

A   They wanted to surprise me with a gift.

Q   *So you didn't know anything about it?*

A   Yes, I did.

Q   *They were not surprising you with a gift?*
 A   Yes.

Q   *You know all that was going on?*
 A   I had an idea of what was going on, yes, because, sir, they had been trying all of the time to get me a house.

Q   *For the minister to live in?*
 A   No, not for the minister to live in. They were trying to get me a house because of the work I was doing.

Q   *You were trustee, were you not?*
 A   Yes.

Q   *They were buying you this house for a gift, is that correct?*
 A   They were buying the house for me.

Q   *As a gift, right?*
 A   I don't know whether you would word it as a gift.

Q   *This was to be yours?*
 A   Yes.

Q   *And they were using the monies from the mosque to do this?*
 A   The group of Muslims got together and raised sufficient funds for a down payment on a house.

Q   *This house from the very inception was known throughout the mosque as being owned by the temple, is that correct?*
 A   The Honorable Elijah Muhammad, not the temple.

Q   *Is that correct? In the temple?*
 A   No, sir. In the Muslim movement, as you probably learned from the testimony of your witnesses, the Honorable Elijah Muhammad gave orders, directives.

Q *Are you saying that the Honorable Elijah Muhammad di-rected this house to be purchased?*

A Honorable Elijah Muhammad gave orders through me. The Honorable Elijah Muhammad consented for the purchase of the house. He o.k.'d the purchase of the house. The Honorable Elijah Muhammad gave orders concerning the house through me. The Honorable Elijah Muhammad himself stated to me that the house was mine, that it was to be for me.

Q *Now, sir, then this was not an official set of the body?*

A The witnesses yesterday said—

Q I'm asking you, sir: Was this an official set of the corporation?

A I don't know.

MR. WILLIAMS: No further questions.

THE COURT: How long will you be? I'm not limiting you.

MR. SUTTON: Not long.

THE COURT: We will take a recess.
(Whereupon, a short recess was taken.)

THE COURT: All right. Proceed.

MALCOLM X LITTLE, resumed the stand.

REDIRECT EXAMINATION

BY MR. SUTTON:

Q *The question was just asked of you was this giving over of the house to you an official act of the corporation. Now, was this an official act of the corporation?*

A No, sir. To my knowledge the corporation never met to perform any official set.

Q *Since the date the corporation was organized, during the entire time you were trustee, did the corporation ever hold a corporate meeting?*

A No, sir, not one time. I had followed the Honorable Elijah Muhammad's instructions to have it incorporated for tax purposes but we never did function as a corporation and never held meetings—corporate meetings.

Q *Did the wages come from corporate funds?*

A It came from the spiritual body from the Muslims.

Q *Were there monies that came in for the purpose of purchasing that house outside of the Muslim movement?*

A I don't know.

Q *All right. Did the corporation ever have a bank account?*

A Not—

Q *At that time?*

A Not at that time.

Q *Did the corporation ever hold a meeting for the purpose of purchasing a house?*

A No, sir, never did.

Q *Did they hold any meetings?*

A No, sir.

Q *Was there money set aside, not even in a bank in the corporate name of Muhammad's Temple of Islam, Inc. and the corporate name?*

A There was never any money set aside for the purchasing of this in the corporate name.

Q *Was there ever any money set aside in the corporate name?*

A No, sir, not at that time.

Q *Since the date of your suspension and to the present, has a hearing been held for removing you as is the practice, custom and procedure of the faith?*

A No, sir. My suspension, as I said, was in three parts and I was to have—the Honorable Elijah Muhammad told me that I would get a hearing at the end of ninety days and the hearing was to be based upon some information that had been reported to him by Captain Joseph. I had told him and the secretary and the minister in Boston that the Honorable Elijah Muhammad had taken on nine wives besides the one that he had.

MR. WILLIAMS: I object and move that be stricken.

MR. SUTTON: I'm not asking that.

THE WITNESS: This is the reason for my suspension.

Q *I'm not asking that. What I want to know is—I'm sorry, I probably phrased it improperly—from the time of your suspension until the present, sir, has there been any termination of your employment by a hearing as is provided in the customs, practices and procedures of the Nation of Islam?*

A This hearing was to have—was supposed to have taken place at the end of February and I wrote to the Honorable Elijah Muhammad and asked him for the hearing but they were afraid to bring me before the Muslim body for fear of what I would tell them.

MR. WILLIAMS: I move it be stricken.

THE COURT: Overruled. I don't see the bearing yet.

Q *From the time of your suspension until this procedure was starting in March, the question was asked of you whether during that time you consulted with any attorney to find out why you were not getting a hearing. Did you hear the question asked of you by Mr. Williams?*

A Yes. At that point, the Honorable Elijah Muhammad

was my attorney. I wrote to him and I asked him for a hearing immediately because I knew he was the one that knew the house was mine. He knew it. It was an agreement between him and me.

THE COURT: Is he a member of the bar?

THE WITNESS: He is in the Muslim bar, in the Nation of Islam.

THE COURT: Is he licensed to practice law?

THE WITNESS: Not in the legal structure of the state.

THE COURT: Proceed, sir.

Q   *Now, sir, so that from the time that you were suspended until the time these procedures were brought, were you still of the belief that you would have your hearing?*
   A   Yes.

Q   *Did you have any doubt until this procedure was brought that you would have a hearing?*
   A   Up to the time that procedure was brought I absolutely felt that the Honorable Elijah Muhammad out of a sense of justice would see that I was brought before the Muslims and given a hearing. I requested that of him.

Q   *Over and apart from ministers, what is the custom, practice and procedure within the Nation of Islam for the removal of a brother or sister from the faith?*

MR. WILLIAMS: Objection. There is only a minister involved.

THE COURT: Yes, I'm not really concerned. If you want to go ahead—

Q   *Even a member, must he have the opportunity of confrontation before he can be removed?*

A   No Muslim can be charged by a lone individual without four witnesses and no Muslim is ever charged with anything without giving—without being given an opportunity to defend himself.

Q   *Not "charged," you mean removed.*

MR. WILLIAMS: Just a second. He made a statement. I object to Mr. Sutton testifying.

THE COURT: It's harmless.

Q   *Did you say he is never charged without an opportunity to defend himself?*
A   That's right. He cannot be removed without charges being placed.

Q   *What is the procedure for that?*
A   Our law is that when charges are leveled against a brother or sister, that brother or sister is brought before the Muslim body and these charges are stated and then that person who is being accused is given an opportunity to defend himself. In any case I was suspended and my mouth was closed so that I couldn't talk. Then they poisoned the Muslim body to keep me from—to keep them from demanding that I get a hearing. That's all. That's what I fought against. I said I would have kept the whole thing secret and private if they would give me a hearing. They would rather take the public court than keep it private among the Muslims simply because I told Joseph that the Honorable Elijah Muhammad had taken on nine wives.

Q   *Mr. Williams asked the question, sir, about your seeking counsel. Now, I ask you, sir, even now, even though you say the house does not belong to them, would you remove from the house if you had your hearing?*
A   All I asked—yes, if I was given a hearing in front of the Muslims as is our law and custom, they would have no trouble out of me whatsoever.

MR. SUTTON: No further questions.

MALCOLM X
DENOUNCED BY NOI

Between several failed attempts on Malcolm X's life and his looming eviction trial, it was clear that Malcolm's falling-out with the NOI was more serious than anyone could have anticipated. And although *Muhammad Speaks* was almost entirely silent about Malcolm's activities during the early 1960s, he became its primary subject in 1964. The newspaper devoted pages of each issue to slandering its former spokesman, even drawing in Malcolm's older brothers Wilfred and Philbert, both of whom remained ministers, in Detroit and Lansing respectively. Philbert publicly denounced Malcolm, calling him "cunning and clever," and warned that his "reckless efforts . . . will cause many of our unsuspecting people who listen and follow him unnecessary loss of blood and life." Philbert added: "I have seen and bear witness as to how Malcolm was raised from a level of nothing to a place of honor and respect through the world as a result of Mr. Muhammad's direction. Now I see my brother pursue a dangerous course which parallels that of the precedents set by Judas, Brutus, Benedict Arnold and others who betrayed the fiduciary relationship between them and their leaders."[1] Most intimately, he drew parallels between Malcolm's condition and the mental illness that had beset

---

1. "Malcolm Exposed by His Brother," *Muhammad Speaks*, April 10, 1964.

their mother, Louise, and brother Reginald.[2] Malcolm accurately suspected that his brother's critique was not in fact his own but written by national secretary John Ali, and he retorted that only Philbert "is dumb enough to let someone put a script in his hand and read it."[3] The condemnation was published in *Muhammad Speaks* alongside the now iconic cartoon of Malcolm's decapitated head, horned and catapulting down toward the skulls of the other notorious traitors.[4]

Other former associates within the Nation of Islam also took turns denouncing Malcolm as a traitor and hypocrite. Ministers Louis X (Farrakhan), John Shabazz, and Jeremiah X Shabazz all contributed articles lambasting their former mentor and colleague. John Shabazz wrote that Malcolm was unworthy of the epithet Uncle Tom as "it would have been an insult to all the Uncle Toms on earth to class you with them. The worst Uncle Toms you yourself ever criticized look ten feet tall beside you now."[5] Louis X offered a more theological explanation: "Malcolm is fulfilling the prophetic role of Korah, the wealthy (popular) one who rebelled against the leadership of Moses because he coveted Moses' position. He is fulfilling the picture of Cain and Abel. Cain also was jealous of Abel and the blessings that Almighty God had showered on Abel. Cain wanted to and did slay his brother. Then, because of the wicked thing he had done, Cain said, 'Everyone that sees me shall slay me.'"[6]

Talk of Malcolm in the private confines of the mosque, as recorded by FBI informants, was even more vitriolic and violent. Supreme Captain Raymond Sharrieff told Mosque

2. Malcolm X FBI file, memo, Chicago office, March 27, 1964.

3. "Malcolm X Tells Attempt on Life; Hits Brother," *Chicago Defender*, March 30, 1964.

4. Eugene Majied, "On My Own," editorial cartoon, *Muhammad Speaks*, April 10, 1964.

5. John Shabazz, "Muslim Minister Writes to Malcolm," *Muhammad Speaks*, July 3, 1964.

6. Minister Louis, "Fall of a Minister," *Muhammad Speaks*, June 5, 1964.

No. 7 members that "Elijah Muhammad used to like former Minister Malcolm X more than he did his own son, but Malcolm X hurt Elijah Muhammad deeply" and predicted that he would "soon die out."[7] In Chicago, Malcolm began to be referred to as Big Red and portrayed as a former "thief, dope addict, and a pimp." Perhaps the most graphic critique was from Edwina X of the Newark mosque, who peppered her "Open Invitation" to the mosque with antagonisms: "Such a deceiver should dig a hole and crawl into it and pray that the parasites in the hole have mercy on him. For one who has heard the truth and still wants to go astray—there is nothing but total destruction for such a defector."[8] Although the order for Malcolm X's assassination has never been directly traced back to Elijah Muhammad or any other high-ranking NOI officials, the rhetoric of the NOI during the months following Malcolm's disaffection created an atmosphere in which no such order was necessary. It was made apparent to all within the sect that Malcolm's death was not only a possibility but an eventuality.

Further reading:

- "Hit Malcolm X as 'Judas,'" *Chicago Defender*, March 28, 1964

- "'My Brother Was Wrong,'" *Chicago Defender*, March 30, 1964

- "Malcolm X Tells Attempt on Life," *Chicago Defender*, March 30, 1964

- James Booker, "Malcolm X Ignores Brother," *Amsterdam News*, April 4, 1964

7. Raymond Sharrieff FBI file, summary report, Chicago office, August 27, 1964, 15–16.

8. Edwina X, "Open Invitation: Come to Muhammad's Mosque," *Muhammad Speaks*, November 26, 1964.

- "Malcolm Exposed by His Brother," *Muhammad Speaks*, April 10, 1964

- Minister Lewis [*sic*], "Rips Malcolm's Treachery, Defection," *Muhammad Speaks*, May 8, 1964

- Minister Louis [X], "Fall of a Minister," *Muhammad Speaks*, June 5, 1964

- John Shabazz, "Muslim Minister Writes to Malcolm," *Muhammad Speaks*, July 3, 1964

- "Mr. Muhammad Speaks: Calls Malcolm X Greatest Hypocrite He's Ever Seen," *Pittsburgh Courier*, September 5, 1964

- Jeremiah X and Joseph X, "Biography of a Hypocrite," *Muhammad Speaks*, September 25, 1964

- Jeremiah X and Joseph X, "Minister Exposed by Those Who Knew Him through Life," *Muhammad Speaks*, October 9, 1964

- "Quotations from the Holy Qur-an, Hypocrites Condemmed [*sic*]," *Muhammad Speaks*, October 23, 1964

- Lucius X, "Why Allah Sent Us His Messenger," *Muhammad Speaks*, November 6, 1964

- Edwina X, "Open Invitation: Come to Muhammad's Mosque," *Muhammad Speaks*, November 26, 1964

- Louis X, "Boston Minister Tells of Malcolm—Muhammad's Biggest Hypocrite," *Muhammad Speaks*, December 4, 1964

- Malcolm X FBI file, summary report, New York office, June 18, 1964, pages 28–30

- Raymond Sharrieff FBI file, summary report, Chicago office, August 27, 1964, pages 15–16

FIREBOMBING

Early on the morning of February 14, 1965, several Molotov cocktails were thrown into the first floor of Malcolm X's home, where his pregnant wife and four daughters slept. Malcolm had fallen asleep in his study while preparing for his address in Detroit later that day, and he rushed to help them escape the flames. The family watched, in the bitter cold, as their house burned, and Malcolm and Betty decided to take the children to stay in hiding with family friend Thomas Wallace, brother of actress Ruby Dee. Much to his wife's dismay, however, Malcolm insisted that he would honor his speaking commitment in Michigan. Less than seven hours after escaping his burning home, Malcolm arrived in Detroit and checked into the Statler-Hilton Hotel. His clothing reeked of smoke, and he had not slept; friends worried and gave him a sedative, but he was woken after a brief nap for an interview that afternoon.

That night Malcolm gave the keynote address at an awards ceremony sponsored by the Afro-American Broadcasting and Recording Company, at the Ford Auditorium. Recognized at the event were Sidney Poitier, Marian Anderson, and Jackie Gleason. Malcolm had been invited by his friend Milton Henry, a leader of the Freedom Now Party, and he gave a speech that mirrored those delivered on his recent visit to Europe. His address again revealed a budding cultural nationalism, and he stressed the need for connections both culturally and politically with postcolonial Africa. Also, despite the likelihood that the NOI had just made an attempt on his life and endangered his family, he cast the organization in a favorable light, saying it had "made the whole civil rights movement become more militant, and more acceptable to the white power structure . . . We forced many of the civil rights leaders to be even more militant than they intended."[1]

While Malcolm spoke in Detroit, however, New York was rife with rumors about the source and intent of the firebombing. The NOI claimed that it would not have bombed a house it was scheduled to repossess, and representatives even boldly showed up at the property to assess the damages. Meanwhile, a bottle of gasoline had been found on one of the children's dressers, and insinuations were made that Malcolm had set the fire himself in a spiteful attempt to destroy the NOI's property. For Malcolm, the entire scenario must have recalled painful memories from his childhood in Lansing; like his father, Malcolm faced accusations of arson to his own home in the midst of an eviction battle. The primary difference, which he was quick to lament, was that unlike the Lansing fire, which had surely been set by local whites, the firebombing seemed to be the work of his former organization. Anticipating the tragedy of the following week, he stated, "The only thing I regret is that two black groups have to fight and kill each other off."[2]

- "Malcolm X's Home Is Bombed: Black Nationalist Leader, Family Flee Unhurt," *Chicago Tribune*, February 15, 1965

- Malcolm X FBI file, memo, February 15, 1965, page 6

---

1. Steve Clark, ed., *Malcolm X: February 1965: The Final Speeches* (New York: Pathfinder, 1992), 98.

2. "Malcolm Accuses Muslims of Blaze: They Point to Him," *New York Times*, February 16, 1965.

Further reading:

- "Three Fire Bombs Hit Home of Malcolm X," *Los Angeles Times*, February 15, 1965

- "Malcolm X's Home Is Firebombed," *Washington Post*, February 15, 1965

- "Malcolm X, Kin Flee Bombing," *New York Daily News*, February 15, 1965

- "Who Bombed Malcolm X's Home?" *New York Post*, February 15, 1965

- "Malcolm Accuses Muslims of Blaze: They Point to Him," *New York Times*, February 16, 1965

- "Bottle of Gasoline Found on Dresser in Malcolm X Home," *New York Times*, February 17, 1965

- "Malcolm X Promises Names of Bombers," *Los Angeles Sentinel*, February 18, 1965

- "Malcolm X Denies He Is Bomber," *Amsterdam News*, February 20, 1965

- Malcolm X FBI file, memo, W. C. Sullivan to J. F. Bland, February 1, 1965

- Malcolm X FBI file, memo, Detroit office, February 17, 1965

- Malcolm X FBI file, Teletype, New York office, February 14, 1965

- Malcolm X FBI file, memo, New York office, February 16, 1965

- Malcolm X FBI file, summary report, New York office, September 8, 1965, pages 36–37

"Malcolm X's Home Is Bombed: Black Nationalist Leader, Family Flee Unhurt," *Chicago Tribune*, February 15, 1965

New York, Feb. 14 (AP)—Three gasoline bombs hurled thru a living room window early today extensively damaged the home of Malcolm X, the black nationalist leader. Malcolm X and his wife and four children fled thru a rear door of the house to escape injury.

"It could have been done by any one of the many," the Negro leader told reporters in discussing who might have thrown the bomb. "I'm not surprised that it was done. It doesn't frighten me. It doesn't quiet me down in any way or shut me up."

WIFE TELLS THREATS

His wife said many threats had been made against his life recently. Malcolm left by plane a few hours after the fire to address an Afro-American rally in Detroit.

Police said the bombs—bottles filled with gasoline with a rag for a wick—probably were thrown from a passing automobile. The blaze turned two of the two-story brick house's nine rooms into charred shells and also damaged three others. The family was asleep at the time.

REFUSES TO LEAVE

The house is located in a mixed Negro and white neighborhood in the Elmhurst section of Queens. It originally was owned by the Black Muslims.

Malcolm X began occupying it while he was a leader in the organization and refused to leave after he broke with the Muslims last year.

A judge ordered him evicted, but the Negro contended the dwelling was given to him. Litigation postponed carrying out of the eviction order.

RETURNING TODAY

Joseph X, who described himself as a business manager in the Black Muslims, went to the house shortly after the fire and told reporters:

"We own this place, man. He was going to be evicted tomorrow. We have money tied up here. We have to hear about it on the radio. He didn't even give us the courtesy of a phone call."

The black nationalist leader, who has advocated a doctrine of Negro "self defense against white supremacists," said he would return to New York tomorrow.

"I intend to point out to the people of New York who I think is behind this and what will develop from it, if something is not done about it," he said.

He came back yesterday from a European trip. Commenting on the refusal of France to allow him entry to make a speech, He said: "Gen. de Gaulle had too much gall in keeping me out of France." French immigration officials said his presence was undesired.

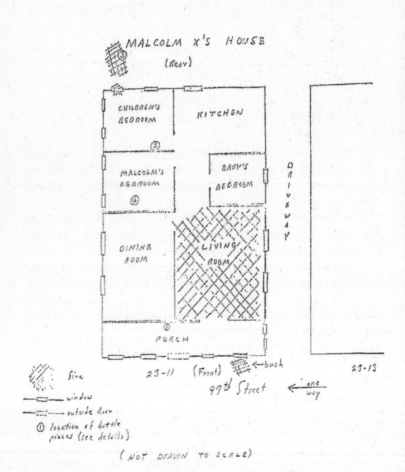

MALCOLM X'S HOUSE (Rear)

CHILDREN'S BEDROOM

KITCHEN

MALCOLM'S BEDROOM

BABY'S BEDROOM

DRIVEWAY

DINING ROOM

LIVING ROOM

PORCH

23-11 (Front) ←bush

97ᵗʰ Street ← one way

23-13

fire

window

outside door

① location of bottle pieces (see details)

(NOT DRAWN TO SCALE)

ASSASSINATION

Malcolm X woke up at the New York Hilton on the morning of February 21, 1965, to a menacing voice over the phone: "Wake up, brother."[1] He was scheduled to speak later that afternoon at an OAAU rally, along with guest speaker Rev. Milton Galamison. There were several oddities at the Audubon Ballroom that day, one of which was Malcolm's request, earlier in the morning, that his wife and children attend the rally. Betty had been discouraged from engaging in either of Malcolm's political groups since his return from Africa, and she was surprised at his late invitation. Malcolm also appeared hurried and agitated, lashing out at several of his staff, as well as Sheikh Hassoun, a religious mentor he had met while abroad and employed as a spiritual teacher for the MMI. Finally, Malcolm ordered that his security not be armed or search people upon entering as they were accustomed to doing. Although most members of the MMI were comfortable with such procedures from their time in the NOI, Malcolm feared that the more middle-class OAAU crowd would be put off.

As was customary, MMI member Benjamin 2X Karim opened the rally. "Few men will risk their lives for somebody else," he said. Most would be "running away from death, even if they're in the right," but Malcolm X is one who "cares noth-

---

1. Peter Goldman, *Death and Life*, 268.

ing about the consequences [and] cares only for the people."[2] At 3:00 p.m. Malcolm approached the stage briskly and sat before the crowd of four hundred, which included at least three undercover police officers. Karim quickly brought his address to a close and introduced Malcolm, who began with the usual Muslim greeting, "As-salaam alaikum." A commotion then started several rows back, with one man yelling, "Get your hands out of my pockets."[3] A smoke bomb then went off toward the back of the room, and a man in the front row stood and walked toward the stage. He then pulled out a sawed-off shotgun and shot Malcolm in the side and chest. Two other men ran forward and fired shots from a Luger and a .45 and then fled up the rows of toppled chairs toward the main entrance. One of Malcolm's guards, Reuben Francis, who had disobeyed orders and carried his weapon, shot a fleeing man in the leg. Outside, that conspirator, Thomas Hagan, was eventually pulled by a policeman away from the crowd that was beating him to death. Meanwhile, a BOSS undercover agent and Malcolm's bodyguard, Gene Roberts, worked to resuscitate Malcolm on the stage, while the crowd waited anxiously for an ambulance to arrive. Eventually his supporters rushed him to nearby Columbia Presbyterian Hospital, where doctors worked for fifteen minutes to revive him. However, by 3:30 p.m. a physician emerged and announced, "The gentleman you knew as Malcolm X is dead."[4]

In the following week, there was a constant fear of retribution. Just nights after Malcolm's assassination, Mosque No. 7 was burned to the ground when a firebomb was thrown through the fourth-floor window. Elijah Muhammad was guarded by twenty-four-hour security in his Chicago home, and many of Malcolm's close friends and followers went into hiding. The police had trouble prying any information from

2. Audiotape transcript of address by Benjamin 2X Karim (Goodman), February 21, 1965, in possession of the author.

3. Ibid.

4. Goldman, *Death and Life*, 268.

Hagan but had arrested two Mosque No. 7 members, Norman
3X Butler and Thomas 15X Johnson, by the first week of
March. Both Butler and Johnson were wanted by New York
law enforcement for their involvement in another murder in
the Bronx, and Hagan was at first unwilling to clear their
names. By the time he admitted that the two men were not involved, the court believed he was sacrificing himself to get his
accomplices acquitted. However, Hagan had not met either
man before, and the conspiracy involved not three but five
NOI members. Hagan signed affidavits in 1977 and 1978 with
new information about his co-conspirators, but the courts refused to retry the case. Butler and Johnson were both paroled
in the mid-1980s, and Hagan in March 2010. As many in Harlem mourned the death of their charismatic leader, Malcolm's
brother Wilfred spoke that Sunday at Mosque No. 1 in Detroit, where the two had first joined the Nation of Islam. "No
sense in getting emotional," he told the assembly. "This is the
kind of times we are living in. Once you are dead your troubles are over. It's those living that're in trouble."[5]

- "Negro Leaders Express Dismay over Slaying," *Los Angeles Times*, February 22, 1965
- Malcolm X FBI file, memo, W. C. Sullivan to J. F. Bland, February 22, 1965

Further reading:

- "Malcolm X Killed at N.Y. Meeting," *Chicago Defender*, February 22, 1965
- Stanley Scott, "'I Saw Malcolm X Die . . .'" *Chicago Defender*, February 22, 1965
- Philip Benjamin, "Malcolm X Lived in 2 Worlds, White and Black, Both Bitter," *New York Times*, February 22, 1965

5. DeCaro, *On the Side of My People*, 274–75.

- Paul Montgomery, "Harlem Is Quiet as News Spreads," *New York Times*, February 22, 1965

- "Malcolm X Gunned Down," *Los Angeles Times*, February 22, 1965

- Theodore Jones, "Malcolm Knew He Was a 'Marked Man,'" *New York Times*, February 22, 1965

- Peter Kihss, "Malcolm X Shot to Death at Rally Here," *New York Times*, February 22, 1965

- "Malcolm X Shot Dead at Rally of 500 in N.Y.," *Washington Post*, February 22, 1965

- Robert Lipsyte, "Other Muslims Fear for Lives," *New York Times*, February 22, 1965

- Gay Talese, "Police Save Suspect from the Crowd," *New York Times*, February 22, 1965

- Will Lissner, "Malcolm Fought for Top Power in Muslim Movement, and Lost," *New York Times*, February 22, 1965

- Leon 4X Ameer FBI file, summary report, Boston office, March 25, 1965, pages 1–2

- Benjamin Karim FBI file, summary report, New York office, February 17, 1966, pages 2–3

"Negro Leaders Express Dismay Over Slaying,"
Los Angeles Times, February 22, 1965

(AP)—Negro leaders Dr. Martin Luther King Jr. and Roy Wilkins reacted to the slaying of Malcolm X Sunday with assertions that violence was not the way to settle disputes.

They headed a host of others in their racial community who expressed shock at the shooting of the black nationalist leader.

There was no immediate comment in Chicago from Elijah Muhammad, whose Black Muslim organization Malcolm had left.

Dr. King, head of the Southern Christian Leadership Conference, said in Atlanta, that the assassination showed "our society is still sick enough to express dissent with murder."

Dr. King, the 1964 Nobel peace prize winner, declared "This evil act should be strongly condemned by all people of good will. This vicious assassination should cause our whole society to see that violence and hatred are evil forces that must be cast into unending limbo."

Dr. King, one of the foremost advocates of non-violence in civil rights struggles, added:

"We have not learned to disagree without being violently disagreeable. I am deeply saddened and appalled . . . "

Wilkins, executive secretary of the NAACP, said in New York it was a "shocking and ghastly demonstration of the futility of resorting to violence as a means of settling differences."

Wilkins added: "Violence is not the answer to disputes either between warring factions within a group or between groups in the large society."

Malcolm X FBI File, Memo, Sullivan to Bland, February 22, 1965

TO: Mr. W. C. Sullivan   DATE: February 22, 1965

FROM: Mr. J. F. Bland

SUBJECT: MALCOLM K. LITTLE
             INTERNAL SECURITY - MMI

At 1:45 a.m., February 22, 1965, ██████████ New York Office, telephonically furnished the following additional information which had been received from the ██████████

The autopsy of subject's body was concluded and there was found: one .45 caliber slug, one nine millimeter slug from an automatic, and several pellets from a shotgun. There were ten holes in the body; seven of which were in the left chest (probably from shotgun blast), two in left thigh and one in left ankle. There were also four creases, three of which were across the chest and one on right knee of Little.

In addition to the above, ██████████ stated that the police found the following items from a search of the Audubon Ballroom where Little was killed:

    1. One "sawed off" two-barrel shotgun with two "expended" shells in the chambers. The shells (which had been discharged) were 12 gauge Remington Express, Single O buckshot. The shotgun was found wrapped in a jacket. A search of the jacket by the New York City Police Department revealed one Yale key, some cigarettes, and an empty case for eyeglasses. On top of the case was the following: M. M. Pine, Optometrist, 3901 Main Street, Flushing, New York.

2. Ten pieces of lead, presumably from shotgun.

3. Two, nine millimeter slugs from the nine millimeter automatic weapon.

4. Three .45 caliber slugs from .45 automatic.

5. Three .32 caliber slugs from revolver.

6. Six, nine millimeter shell casings.

7. Three .45 caliber Western shell casings.

SA ▮▮▮▮▮▮▮▮▮ stated he had learned from the police that Thomas Hagan (later identified as Talmadge Hayer) would be charged with homicide in the death of Malcolm Little.

ACTION:
For information. This is being followed closely, and you will be kept advised.

FUNERAL

In death Malcolm proved to be as controversial as he had been in life. While his body was held at the Unity Funeral Home, churches around Harlem, including Adam Clayton Powell's Abyssinian Baptist Church, refused to hold the funeral ceremony for fear of reprisals by the NOI. Meanwhile, a group known as the Federation for Independent Political Action called for all Harlem stores to close out of respect for the slain leader. Although the Uptown Chamber of Commerce rejected the proposal, the group still offered threats of boycott and retaliation for stores that refused to comply. Although many stores chose not to close, they reported that business had slowed to a halt anyway, due to the pervasive fear of violence in the community. The Unity Funeral Home received bomb threats for the four days that Malcolm's body lay in state. Despite this constant danger, nearly thirty thousand mourners viewed his body and paid their respects.[1]

Once a venue finally agreed to host the funeral, over a thousand people gathered to pay homage at the Faith Temple Church in west Harlem. Some black leaders and former debate partners, such as Bayard Rustin and James Farmer, were in attendance, but many were missing. Most notably absent from the ceremonies was Malcolm's family, with the exception of

1. James Booker, "30,000 Mourn Malcolm X," *Amsterdam News*, March 6, 1965.

his wife, Betty, and half sister Ella. His brothers Wilfred and Philbert had recently denounced him again in prepared statements read at the Saviour's Day convention in Chicago. Wilfred told those gathered: "We must not let our natural enemy, the white man, come between us, get us to kill each other. I was shocked to hear the news of my brother's death but from my heart I ask Allah to strengthen me as a follower of Elijah Muhammad."[2]

Others not attending the ceremony—such as Martin Luther King, Whitney Young, and Kwame Nkrumah—sent condolences that were read by Ruby Dee and Ossie Davis. Davis then delivered a eulogy for Malcolm X that has remained central in understanding Malcolm's legacy. "Malcolm was our manhood," Davis stated, "our living black manhood! And we will know him then for what he was and is—a prince—our own black shining prince—who didn't hesitate to die, because he loved us so."[3] Finally, as several hundred gathered at the gravesite, Malcolm's nephew Rodnell Collins and others in the MMI and OAAU protested that white cemetery workers shouldn't be the ones to shovel dirt upon Malcolm. In a final symbolic moment, Malcolm was buried in the falling rain by his followers, at Ferncliff Cemetery, some twenty miles north of Harlem.

- "Stores Told to Close for Malcolm X Funeral," *Hartford Courant*, February 26, 1965

- "Ossie Davis' Stirring Tribute to Malcolm X," *Amsterdam News*, March 6, 1965

- "A Conversation with Ossie Davis," *Souls* 2, 3 (Summer 2000), pages 14–16

2. Thomas Fitzpatrick, "Muslim Sect Hears Chief Hit Malcolm," *Chicago Tribune*, February 27, 1965.

3. "Ossie Davis' Stirring Tribute to Malcolm X," *Amsterdam News*, March 6, 1965.

Further reading:

- "Stores Prodded to Hail Malcolm X," *New York Times*, February 26, 1965

- "Move Body of Malcolm X in Tight Security," *Chicago Tribune*, February 27, 1965

- "Demand Harlem Shops Closed as Memorial to Malcolm X," *Chicago Defender*, February 27, 1965

- Homer Bigart, "Black Muslim Guard Held in Murder of Malcolm X," *New York Times*, February 27, 1965

- "Malcolm's Funeral Services," *Amsterdam News*, February 27, 1965

- Martin Arnold, "Harlem Is Quiet as Crowds Watch Malcolm X Rites," *New York Times*, February 28, 1965

- David Alpern, "Malcolm's Funeral Is Heavily Guarded," *Washington Post*, February 28, 1965

- "Malcolm X Is Buried: Armed Police Dot Roofs," *Hartford Courant*, February 28, 1965

- Malcolm X FBI file, Teletype, New York office, February 27, 1965

- Malcolm X FBI file, memo, F. J. Baumgardner to W. C. Sullivan, February 27, 1965

"Stores Told to Close for Malcolm X Funeral,"
Hartford Courant,
February 26, 1965

NEW YORK (AP)—White and Negro storekeepers along Harlem's main crosstown thoroughfare, bustling 125th Street, were under pressure Thursday to close their doors for the funeral of Malcolm X, or face a boycott.

"The stores must close from 3 p.m. Friday, all day Saturday" read handbills distributed by the Federation for Independent Political Action, which includes left-wing Negro groups in its ranks. Its spokesman is Jesse Gray, who led a rent strike in Harlem 14 months ago. He has denied Communist affiliations.

One merchant said he was told: "If you don't close down by 3 p.m., you won't be in business by 3:30."

RAINS CLEAR STREETS

Heavy rains cleared Harlem streets and brought at least a momentary lull in the tensions that have gripped the uptown Manhattan area since Malcolm's assassination last Sunday. Mourners continued to file past his bier in a Harlem funeral parlor, where the body has been since Tuesday.

Funeral services for the goateed black nationalist leader, 39, are scheduled for 9:30 a.m. Saturday at the Faith Temple, Church of God in Christ, at 147th Street and Amsterdam Avenue.

The pastor of the church, Bishop Alvin A. Childs, said already has received half a dozen anonymous bomb threats against his church and his home in the Bronx. He shrugged them off.

HARLEM'S 'MAYOR'

A gray-haired, stocky man with a small gray mustache, Bishop Childs is referred to as unofficial "mayor of Harlem."

He said of Malcolm: "He was a militant and vocal person. I did not agree with all of his philosophy, but this did not affect our friendship."

Five men were believed involved in the slaying. Under arrest in the case is Talmadge Hayer, 22, a Negro who was shot in the leg by a Malcolm bodyguard while fleeing the ballroom after the murder. He has refused to say whether he is a Black Muslim.

Police first hinted Wednesday at progress in their murder investigation, including information as to who may be responsible.

HANDBILL QUOTED

The handbills distributed by the Federation for Independent Political Action read in part: "The stores along 125th Street (river to river) have been asked to cooperate with us and close Friday from 3 p.m. and all day Saturday in respect for Malcolm and in observance of what he meant to our community and all oppressed people.

"Some of the stores we feel may cooperate, others may not. Those stores that refuse to cooperate are showing contempt for our community and especially our bereavement over our beloved Malcolm.

"This is very little to ask of the community and the storekeepers. Community give up the shopping along 125th Street. Storekeepers close your doors.

"We must not be led into fratricide. This should not be war

between rivals of a religious sect but open season on the main story, our common enemy that suppresses us all.

"If the stores refuse to close, they identify with our enemy—therefore we must close them—pass them by.

"Those that shop along 125th Street during the hours that the stores are to be closed identify with the murderous stooge that allowed the terror structure to use his hands to kill brother Malcolm."

"Ossie Davis' Stirring Tribute to Malcolm X,"
Amsterdam News, March 6, 1965

(Delivered at Faith Temple Church of God, Feb. 27, 1965)

Here—at this final hour, in this quiet place, Harlem has come to bid farewell to one of its brightest hopes—extinguished now, and gone from us forever.

For Harlem is where he worked and where he struggled and fought—his homes of homes, where his heart was, and where his people are—and it is, therefore, most fitting that we meet once again—in Harlem—to share these last moments with him.

For Harlem has ever been gracious to those who have loved her, have fought for her, and have defended her honor even to the death. It is not in the memory of man that this beleaguered, unfortunate but nonetheless proud community has found a braver, more gallant young champion than this Afro-American who lies before us—unconquered still.

I say the word again, as he would want me to: Afro-American—Afro-American Malcolm, who was a master, was most meticulous in his use of words. Nobody knew better than he the power words have over the minds of men. Malcolm had stopped being a "Negro" years ago.

It had become too small, too puny, too weak a word for him. Malcolm was bigger than that. Malcolm had become an Afro-American and he wanted—so desperately—that we, that his people would become Afro-Americans too.

There are those who will consider it their duty, as friends of the Negro people, to tell us to revile him, to flee, even from the presence of his memory, to save ourselves by writing him out of the history of our turbulent times.

Many will ask what Harlem finds to honor in this stormy, controversial and bold young captain—and we will smile.

Many will say turn away—away from this man, for he is not a man but a demon, a monster, a subverter and an enemy of the black man—and we will smile.

They will say that he is of hate—a fanatic, a racist—who can only bring evil to the cause for which you struggle!

And we will answer and say unto them: Did you ever talk to Brother Malcolm? Did you ever touch him, or have him smile at you? Did you ever really listen to him? Did he ever do a mean thing? Was he ever himself associated with violence or any public disturbance? For if you did you would know him. And if you knew him you would know why we must honor him: Malcolm was our manhood, our living, black manhood! This was his meaning to his people. And, in honoring him, we honor the best in ourselves.

Last year, from Africa, he wrote these words to a friend: "My journey," he says, "is almost ended, and I have a much broader scope than when I started out, which I believe will add new life and dimension to our struggle for freedom and honor, and dignity in the States. I'm writing these things so that you will know for a fact the tremendous sympathy and support we have among the African States for our Human Rights struggle. The main thing is that we keep a United Front wherein our most valuable time and energy will not be wasted fighting each other."

However much we may have differed with him—or with each other about him and his value as a man, let his going from us serve only to bring us together, now. Consigning these mortal remains to earth, the common mother of all, secure in the knowledge that what we place in the ground is no more now a man—but a seed—which, after the winter of our discontent—will come forth again to meet us. And we will know him then for what he was and is—a Prince—our own black shining Prince!—who didn't hesitate to die, because he loved us so.

(Eulogy delivered by Ossie Davis at the funeral of Malcolm X.)

Ossie Davis, "A Conversation with Ossie Davis,"
Souls 2, 3 (Summer 2000): 14–16

MANNING MARABLE: *Now, for people who came up in the '60s, Malcolm X is in so many ways our political and spiritual touchstone. We relate the black struggle fundamentally to the heroic figure of Malcolm X. But you and Ruby knew Malcolm both as a leader and as a human being, as a man. He visited your home for several days in New Rochelle, before he was assassinated. When he was murdered, you actually gave the eulogy at his funeral. Now, I just want to read a few of the sentences from the eulogy, which has been widely quoted and long remembered within the black freedom movement. This is part of what you said: "Malcolm was our manhood, our living, black manhood! This was his meaning to his people. And, in honoring him, we honor the best in ourselves. And we will know him then for what he was and is—a Prince—our own Black, shining prince!—Who didn't hesitate to die, because he loved us so." Ossie, when you think of Malcolm, as a person, not just a leader, what are the most striking things about him? How do you see Malcolm's relevance today?*

OSSIE DAVIS: I see Malcolm as a central figure in any effort to unite, to regroup our forces and to prepare ourself for the onslaught that is sure to be visited upon us in this new century. Much as I loved and admired Dr. King, Malcolm, to me, still reached out to others—particularly people like me. I very rarely like to speak publicly about Malcolm, to talk about Malcolm and to explain about Malcolm. However, I feel I can do it in a situation like this, where I'm among friends, and we're talking about somebody we love. If you talk too much about somebody, you will ultimately destroy their meaning. So I try not to talk about Malcolm too much. Having said that, Malcolm's central position in the class struggle was in his capacity for connecting with people out in the street, drug addicts, criminals, and hustlers—these were folks outside the middle class, people that Dr. King certainly couldn't relate to. His capacity to look into their eyes and into their souls, his ability to speak directly to them and to help turn their lives around—this is perhaps his most valuable contribution.

I remember walking on the street with Malcolm, and people would come up to him and he'd respond to them, and I would respond to them in a different way. While some would be chastising him, Malcolm always had something positive to say. Malcolm was an expert on the damage that slavery and racism had done to the black man's image of himself. He was equally expert in what had to be done to remedy that egregious lack of self-esteem. He knew it would take more than civil rights legislation, jobs, and education to really save the black man. And he knew that none of the traditional organizations that serviced black folk, such as black churches, colleges, sororities and fraternities, the NAACP, the Urban League, were capable of doing what needed to be done. He felt, as did some of us, that to ask a man who had already been beaten up and beaten down to be nonviolent was only to change black pathology into another religion.

The last time we saw Malcolm, he came to our house in New Rochelle, and he came alone. He sat across from Ruby and me in the dining room with his back to the wall and he talked. He didn't come for advice, he didn't come for sympathy or consolation, he didn't come to listen, he came to talk. Quietly, reflectively, in his heart's own way, this talk bonded him to us forever. He spoke to us of Elijah Muhammad but without rancor. Malcolm at the end was a hunted and haunted man, running for his life. Still, he was not deterred from his main objective: to bridge the gap between him and the rest of the civil rights movement with an organization that would give him a broader base from which to operate, the details of which he planned to unveil that Sunday afternoon at the Audubon Ballroom, where he was assassinated.

Malcolm had invited us to the Audubon that day, but we had a previous commitment downtown and had left the three children in Harlem with Mother. When we returned to pick them up, the kids told us that something had happened to Malcolm. We turned on the television as a bulletin interrupted the ballet. Malcolm X was dead—shot down in front of Betty and the children. We were stunned and deeply, deeply saddened. That night, we drove back into Harlem and walked the streets, mingling and talking with the crowds about Malcolm's death and what it meant to black people.

Fear and sorrow were mixed with a desire to give Malcolm a decent funeral. Percy Sutton, Malcolm's friend and lawyer, went from church to church trying to secure a place for Malcolm's funeral, but most of them said no—it was too dangerous. There was a lot of politics involved and the big challenge was figuring out a way to bury Malcolm in the spirit that the community called for and the spirit he warranted. Finally, Bishop Church offered his small church on Amsterdam Avenue. Sylvester Leaks, speaking for Percy Sutton and Malcolm's family, asked me to give the eulogy and I asked him, "Why me?" The answer was that Ruby and I were widely known to have been among his earliest friends and supporters. Also, I was a man with whom nobody in this shooting argument could quarrel. Ruby and I were honored to accept.

Well, that Saturday, we went to the little Faith Memorial Chapel on Amsterdam Avenue. It wasn't much of a day and I remember there was no sunshine at all. The funeral was at ten o'clock. Ruby and I sat in the pulpit and our job was to read the messages that were pouring in. At the proper time, I arose to give the eulogy, trying to be simple, plain, honest, and sincere, saying by way of farewell what, in my heart, I believed Harlem wanted me to say. Afterward, we followed him to the cemetery where the professional grave diggers were waiting. We said no and took their shovels from them. Malcolm was ours, and if he had to be buried, we would do it. He loved us and we loved him.

PART II

ORAL HISTORIES

GERRY FULCHER

Gerry Fulcher, born in 1937 and raised in uptown Manhattan, became a police officer in 1962 after leaving the Congregation of Christian Brothers just before final vows. Fulcher started as a foot patrolman in the South Bronx but was quickly promoted to a position in the NYPD's special unit BOSS. There he illegally wiretapped Malcolm X's office at the Hotel Theresa in Harlem. Fulcher speculates that his college degree and fluency in French and Spanish made him an ideal candidate despite being new to the force. He spent four months in this capacity, generally working the "day tour," from 8:00 a.m. to 4:00 p.m., in a cubbyhole without windows on the fourth floor of the Twenty-eighth Precinct house. Despite knowing little about the surveillance project, Fulcher was expected to listen to conversations through a small bug in the telephone and bring the tapes to a midtown intelligence division every evening. He recalls that many of the conversations were with celebrities such as David Susskind, Ossie Davis, Ruby Dee, Harry Belafonte, and James Baldwin.

Most remarkable in Fulcher's account is not only the unabashed racism of a novice police officer, but that the same officer was prompted, after listening to Malcolm X, to wonder: "What's wrong with that? What am I here for?" Fulcher recounts "making bones" as a young cop by beating a black man arrested for disorderly conduct after a sergeant intimated that he did not want to see the man "walking by the time you get back to the station house."[1] However, after he was assigned to take notes at several of Malcolm X's speeches in Harlem,

1. Gerry Fulcher interview with Manning Marable, October 3, 2007, Malcolm X Project.

Fulcher began voicing his support for Malcolm's views—an unpopular opinion among other white members of the force.

According to Fulcher, the NYPD also had an officer stationed under the stage at the Audubon Ballroom to tape Sunday meetings of the OAAU. A compulsive gambler, Fulcher would often leave his tap to go to the racetrack. On February 21, 1965, the day of Malcolm X's assassination, Fulcher was actually "cheating on the tap," since he knew Sunday would be quiet at the Hotel Theresa. However, when he arrived at his parents' house on Sedgwick Avenue in the Bronx, his mother shouted out the window, "They just killed Malcolm X!"[2] Fulcher raced back to the wiretap just before detectives arrived and asked him if he had heard anything. He noticed that "the brass" seemed largely uninterested in what he knew, and he was excluded from the ensuing meeting at the Thirty-fourth Precinct house, never again to be questioned. Shortly after the assassination, Fulcher was let go from his position at BOSS and reassigned to a less prominent beat in Fort Apache in the Bronx. Although his demotion was ostensibly for his gambling habit, Fulcher speculates that it had to do with a police cover-up and describes the cleanup of the Audubon crime scene within hours of the assassination as highly irregular police procedure. Fulcher's testimony stands as a unique firsthand account of Malcolm X by a police operative who was once an admittedly bigoted member of BOSS but remains deeply skeptical that the NYPD was uninvolved in the assassination.

- Transcript, Gerry Fulcher interview, October 3, 2007, Malcolm X Project

2. Ibid.

GERRY FULCHER: Oh, really. I mean, more than that. It was don't tell no one. That kind of thing. Actually tell nobody what you're doing.

MANNING MARABLE: So the FBI may not have known, or probably didn't know, that Gene Roberts, who was NYPD, is in Malcolm's security entourage. They just thought he was just some normal guy who was in Malcolm's group. Not NYPD.

GF: That day especially. That time. That '60s frame, when people were not telling one another anything. Everybody wanted to get credit for everything. You couldn't get any information. That was the thing we hated about the FBI. They would ask information, and use their power, J. Edgar, what have you, to get it. But we couldn't ask them anything about anything.

MM: All right. Now, the day before the assassination, that evening, there was actually a walk-through of the hit. To the best of our knowledge now, based on my discussions with people who have studied this, there were about six men involved.

GF: That would have been a Saturday night?

MM: Saturday night. There were about six men involved in the murder plot, not three. Two of the three men who were arrested and convicted of murdering Malcolm in all probability were not even physically in the Audubon that time. Okay? Hayer was, but the other two men were not.

GF: Were they the ones who started the commotion?

MM: No, they weren't physically there. Yes, who started the commotion. "Get your hand out of my pocket!" And then there's a smoke bomb that goes off in the rear of the building. People are diverted. But there were a lot of strange things that happened with security. I don't want to divert our discussion, because our primary focus today is really on the NYPD, but my sense of what happened is that Francis was really in the position to direct certain things. And Malcolm was left on the stage alone. That's not the protocol for the Nation of Islam. You never leave the principal unguarded, ever. You always have at least two men on either side of him, flanking.

GF: See, that's the time I was cheating on the tap. I know where is every Sunday. I know no phone calls are going to be there and nothing's going to come in. So I snuck the day off. I drive up to—I live with my parents up on Sedgwick Avenue, across from Hunter College, and I pull up in my unmarked car. My mother shouts out the window, "They just killed Malcolm X!" I jumped in that car and drove 100 miles an hour back to my cubbyhole in the 2-8. And got there just before every high brass person in the world comes into this little cubbyhole. About 12 guys—Chiefs of detectives for the whole department, and blah-blah—"What'd you hear, what'd you hear? What have you got on your tape?" I said, "Shit, I got nothing." I said, "Well, it's not unusual. They don't do anything on Sunday." "Yes, I was here the whole time." I was never there. As soon as he left the office, I left, because there was nothing—it was a half day off, as far as I was concerned. And I knew nothing about that. And then of course once I heard, I was back again, I hung around 3-4 like everyone else did, and everything else. In fact, they expected, I got in trouble, they fell for that coming up with the fact—what was it, two weeks later or a week later, they blew up the mosque.

MM: It was less than that. It was about three days later.

GF: Three days later. I had nothing on that. Nobody discussed that in the office. They were expecting me to have something on that.

MM: But James Shabazz, and others, insist that they had absolutely nothing to do with blowing up the mosque. So that there is this question, who was responsible for blowing up the mosque?

GF: I would say there was that faction that was always afraid of violence? That was my suspicion, that whoever those guys were. That faction that was afraid of violence and kept saying, "Elijah Muhammad's not going to let this go. He's going to be tallying. He doesn't take this kind of defeat." Those were discussions that took place. So my opinion is that those guys might have done it. That faction, I thought that way.

MM: But is it possible that the FBI, or their informants, rather, operatives, people with whom they were working, to continue the tension between the two groups, may have carried out the . . . is that possible?

GF: Oh, yes, I would think so, given the mentality of the time. That was bitter. They were afraid. The good guys on Malcolm's side on this issue were afraid. "You just can't do this, Malcolm!" He's not going to sit back. Of course there was always the rumor that he was going to expose the sexual stuff with Elijah and younger girls and other people.

MM: And in fact that's exactly what he did in early July or late June of 1964, and that, more than anything else, basically convinced the Nation of Islam that Malcolm had to be silenced. That when he did that he crossed the Rubicon. And there was no going back.

GF: That would have fit in, to me with the other philosophy. Forget the Black Panthers. Who do you kill? You kill Martin

Luther King, because he had the answer. He had the answers. If people followed Martin Luther King, black people were going to rise, okay? And get what they deserved in this thing. So you worry about the crazy guys. Well, the same over here. We would probably sided with, given the fact that he hated Malcolm, sided with Elijah Muhammad doing that, because the guy with the real answer to improve the racial situation was Malcolm. I mean, Elijah to this day is written off, and all his followers, as the "nut jobs." The crazy guys. And nobody likes them. So the guy with the real answer, in this case Malcolm, he had to go. The guy with the real answer was not the Black Panthers, it was Martin Luther King. That's my feeling about that. You get rid of the people that can really make the change.

MM: There are a series of questions that I have now that are based on your best experience, that we may or may not have objective answers to, but I value your experience in the NYPD. That I have to make a judgment call. I'm an historian, I'm not a detective. So the nice thing about being historian, I say that, is that we have to make calls based on the best evidence we have. And so there are a series of questions. Here's the first one. The assassination day, February 21, 1965: It's a Sunday. This was the 17th or 18th event that they had rented out the Audubon, up on Broadway and 166th.

GF: I'm working a day tour, which would have been 8 to 4.

MM: All right. The routine of the NYPD is that they had kind a desk commander and a group of police officers, between 12 to 24, who were stationed at the Audubon. When you walked into the Audubon. . . .

GF: Was this every Sunday?

MM: This was almost every Sunday, but every other Sunday, pretty much, especially when he gets back from Africa in November 1964 through his assassination in February 1965. About every other Sunday there's an event. So when you count all of the events from the time he leaves the Nation of Islam in March 1964 to February 1965, there are about 20 events. The police show up at the events. They put a number of police officers in a park directly outside the front door. They put several officers at the front door. Then there is a kind of who-ever the commander of the day is, he is in an office that's glassed in, at the top of the steps on the second floor, that abuts the main ballroom. You got to walk past the office—that's where they collect the tickets. So there are police officers who are all around and visible. On this day, there were only two police officers that are in the smaller Rose Ballroom at the furthest end from the building. Nobody's outside, nobody's the front door. Later the police explain to the press that they had been ordered by one of Malcolm's guys . . . [end of tape 2; begin tape 3]

MM: . . . would the police listen to James Shabazz to do anything because previously their basic protocol had been to have like maybe 20 guys who were there, and because they know, also, that there's a real threat of danger or violence. And the week before, that Sunday, Malcolm's house had been fire-bombed, for God's sake. So why do you pull the police away from the Audubon?

GF: Well, first of all, did you verify that Shabazz did tell them that?

MM: He denies it. He denied it.

GF: Okay. That's a detail. Cops hate details. They're long, they're boring. I can tell you in that neighborhood, on a Sunday, there was no special event. If you said to me, if the end of your question was, the police said that there was a special event they had to pull them away for, they needed the manpower, I would have said that's bullshit. Okay? Because it's Sunday, it's dead. People are doing their Sunday things. The lowest crime elements in the South Bronx, for example, on Sundays in the summer, when they're all at Orchard Beach. You know, all that kind of thing. So they were smart to use that excuse. But it was not for any other reason that they were drawn back.

MM: Right. Because what happens is, they argue that they essentially put their men at the hospital, at Columbia Presbyterian. And they're like about four blocks away from the building.

GF: Actually, it's right across the street, isn't it?

MM: Yeah, actually it is. It's kind of across the street. They're at 168th, And this is at 166th. So—but they're not physically there. And there's a real difference. There is no police presence subsequently. And so historians have been trying to figure out why.

GF: My guess is, I don't think they could have pulled it themselves, only because there was too much potential for too many people talking about it.

MM: Well, actually, that's another question. Did the NYPD, or their elements in BOOSI [Bureau of Special Services and Investigations], or some higher-ups, did they have advance knowledge? Well, clearly, they did have advance knowledge that the assassination may take place, because there's evidence of that, okay? We know that. But the question is, did operatives that were working with the NYPD or BOSSI or informants, did they carry out the plot? That's the question and/or did operatives of the FBI carry out the crime?

GF: My guess would be informants. They would want to keep their hands clean from the actual thing. But I have no doubt that they had the mentality of wanting an assassination.

MM: So you're convinced that the higher-ups in the NYPD clearly would be happy if Malcolm was assassinated.

GF: Oh, yes, I mean, we know what J. Edgar did with the letter to Martin Luther and . . . "Kill yourself," you know?

MM: All right, so I'm just trying to understand this in an objective way. Malcolm's house has been firebombed the previous Sunday, so there's a real danger of violence.

GF: I remember them talking about that.

MM: But they pull the officers away from the building, and I'm trying to understand what's the justification for that.

GF: Well, Shabazz says he didn't ask them. I'm siding with the police on that. I mean, I'm siding with Shabazz on that.

MM: All right. So why did the cops pull back? Did they know that there was going to be violence that day? That's another question.

GF: Certainly not all of them, but they could have got a call from downtown, whether it would be our office or the FBI or whatever, and said, "Listen, we want you to, you know, cancel the Malcolm X assignment, detail, for Sunday." Wouldn't give any reason necessarily. Would not give any reason.

MM: Okay. That may have occurred.

GF: Mm-hmm. It seems logical, given, again, the mentality of the time. You see, you would *think*—and this is what I said to myself, was part of my change, is changing my mind about it—this is a guy we should be supporting. If you're logical, this is the guy you should be supporting. He has the answer. And you know the favorite things, "them niggers on welfare?" He wants them off, too. I mean this should have been a companion, not an enemy. But they always viewed them like the enemy.

MM: So let's go back to this day on the 21st. All right. So the police aren't there. The FBI has a handful of informants within, that are at the Audubon. I have serious questions about the chief of security, Reuben Francis, possibly being either an informant or an operative. I know that Charles Kenyatta was an informant of the NYPD or at least as soon as Malcolm is assassinated, he just opens up. And then you get this tremendous flow of information from him. So Malcolm's group is infiltrated.

GF: By the way, Shabazz would not have been the guy, given what you said about the chief of security. That would have been the guy that told the police.

MM: Reuben Francis. But then that raises an interesting question.

GF: I mean, he didn't tell them, obviously.

MM: There are only two men who had the power to do it. Either Shabazz did, or Francis did. Francis may have done that, but then Francis may have been an operative of the FBI. And if he was, then there is a real question of who were—I mean, what was his role in this. And then he disappears. And he's never found again, literally. So what happened? I mean, based on your experience—and I know that we have no way of proving this—based on what I've said . . .

GF: Given that evidence, I'd say Francis was the guy.

MM: By "the guy" you mean . . .

GF: He organized it. And he wanted to get out Dodge when he knew things were going to get hot. I would come back to him.

MM: So you think that Francis may have been the organizer of the murder.

GF: Yes.

MM: Now if Francis in some way was either an operative of the FBI—

GF: He had to have contacts within the agency, or with our office or whatever.

MM: Right. But because of competition between BOSSI and the FBI, there'd be no way of knowing [from] the record by BOSSI what Francis's role was.

GF: That's right. That's exactly right. The last thing the FBI would ever tell BOSSI is that Francis was an informant, okay?

MM: The other theory that I have about the murder is that the ADA and the District Attorney of New York County were concerned in the prosecution of the three men who had been accused of the murder. They were concerned that their operatives of BOSSI and then, of course, the FBI were not revealed. And that even though there was a kind of evidence against all three men, that they discounted the evidence that was exculpatory and actually convicted men who may have been innocent. In part to protect their operatives who were working within Malcolm on a covert basis.

GF: There's no reason I would not have been allowed inside that 34th Precinct where all the big bosses were meeting, ordinarily.

MM: What do you mean?

GF: Well, because I was on the tap. I should have been an indispensable part of finding out what went on and so on, because they should have been grilling me—I should have been—ordinarily, the guy on the wiretap has the right to walk in when they're discussing the case. I felt that my exclusion—I was flat-out told, you know, "Stay out, you're not involved." Made me think that they could have been getting their stories straight, so to speak, without the interference of this young guy who didn't know any—

MM: Let me back up a bit. So you're driving 100 miles an hour. You get to the 34th Precinct.

GF: Right. All they wanted to know is, "Did you hear anything on the phone?" To me that was just a show. They knew I wouldn't hear anything on the phone, because there'd be nobody there. They knew the schedule. I used to write down when they were there, and when they're not there. They're not there after about 11 in the morning on Sundays, when they're preaching. So I think they were playing their roles. We gotta check with the guy on the wiretap and see if he has any information for us. I think that was all bullshit. And when I went up and tried to join them, you know—"No, no, this is where we get our stories straight. You're out, kid."

MM: So let me get this straight, just so I understand that. On that afternoon when you arrived, they basically, other than a kind of perfunctory check with you if you heard anything—but they knew you probably hadn't heard anything—then you get cut out of everything.

GF: Told to go home. "All right, you can home." I mean, this should have been—if they were really involved in an investigation as to how this happened, they would have been asking me, the only guy who was doing it every day . . .

MM: What that implies to me is that some higher-ups actually knew or had advance knowledge that this thing was going to occur.

GF: Yes. I would say so. It would just be a guess, but I would say so based on all the weird things that happened. The pulling the cops off, so on. Not letting me just have the normal part that I should have had, the main guy. I put in more hours there.

MM: So it wouldn't surprise you that the NYPD's higher ups knew in advance about the murder. And then pulled the cops off, so they would not—there would not be any kind of collateral shootings or whatever. There's one other kind of piece of evidence . . .

GF: And by the way, another thing that only came to me today. I was dumped out of BOSSI shortly thereafter. Now they had a reason, namely I was a compulsive gambler, I had some bad checks out, and I cut out to go to the race track, and so on. I gave them the reason to, but I've seen them cover for cops a lot better than that and let me stay on their detail. They dumped me back to Fort Apache over in the Bronx in uniform. And that's when I resigned after a couple of years there. I'm not going to spend my next 15 years on the job walking in alleyways in Fort Apache with a Master's degree, speaking French and Spanish, you know. So I was dumped out of the unit, and I never made a tie-in there until this conversation today. It was shortly thereafter that I was dumped out. Couple of weeks.

MM: Couple of weeks? So you have been saying to police officers that Malcolm is not the bad guy that we've been told about. He's saying positive things. Then he's killed. The police are pulled on that day. There are no police officers except two that are even in the building. [Patrolman Thomas] Hoy drives by, by accident, and saves Talmadge Hayer's life. And then a couple of weeks later you get kicked out of BOSSI.

GF: Right. I never made the tie-in before today. Because they had so much ammunition, meaning if they wanted to. But now when I compare—I mean, I've seen guys that shoot people by mistake, and they'll cover up for that. So I had a gambling problem. Big deal. You tell me not to do it any more, you know? Or whatever. But, yes, now I'm beginning to see possible reasons.

MM: Right. So two other pieces, two other questions. Herman Ferguson describes this scene. He states in his interviews that he saw two men who were shot. One, Talmadge Hayer. Who gets shot in the leg. He's an assailant of Malcolm. A second guy he describes, he stands out at the corner at 166th and Broadway. A limo drives up and guy who he describes as a senior police officer, NYPD commander . . .

GF: What time is this, now?

MM: This is like roughly 3:30 or 3:15. It's about 15 to 20 minutes after the murder. [OAAU member Herman] Ferguson said he had "scrambled eggs" on his cap—which is like he's a commander of some type. He gets out, he goes into the building. He brings back a person of an olive complexion who is grabbing his stomach. He's doubled over like he's been shot. And he puts this man in the back seat of the car. He gets into the front seat, on the passenger side, and the car takes off. But it doesn't go to the hospital. It goes down the hill like it's going to Riverside, to the George Washington Bridge, right? And this is what Ferguson states in his oral history. Now the question—we know that several people got shot by ricochet bullets in the foot, or whatever, who were in the audience. So that's a possibility. But there is a real question, because it's possible that another assailant was shot and that he was protected by the NYPD. Based on, again, there is no direct evidence on this, but just based on the story I'm relating, what's your impression about this? I mean, is that possible?

GF: Well, the best I could just say, it's not the standard procedure. Highly unlikely, you know. I can't think of another reason of why, first of all, why he wouldn't just tell some cop, "Take him across the street," so on and so forth.

MM: Unless this was a person who was also a police operative.

GF: Yes, or somebody certainly involved in the situation. Because bosses don't do that.

MM: So if Ferguson's eyewitness account is true, if it's true, then what do you think happened? What explains what was going on? What do you think was going on?

GF: Well, it looks like they wanted to get everybody out of the way who could have some information. Okay? They dismissed right away, told me to go home, not come up to the 34th Precinct. And then rushing that guy out. It looks like a cover-up. It looks like there was some sort of plan involved that could have been an actual plot to have him killed. And then get rid of anybody who could—I wonder if anybody did a check of other surrounding hospitals on that day and found out [if] someday came in with a wound. You said he went toward the George Washington Bridge?

MM: Well, the final questions I have are, so there's a trial. Three men get convicted of murdering Malcolm X. The best evidence is that one of the three men was an assailant. In 1977 he admitted to his religious counselor, an imam in prison that the other two men who were convicted were innocent.

GF: They can't get a new trial for this?

MM: William Kunstler tries to get a new trial. The judge hearing the case in New York State rules against it. Says no. There was a valid conviction in 1966; that's it.

GF: See, they don't want anything that's going to open up the whole thing again. That's the problem. That would mean somebody influencing judges, and judges do check back on those things and say, "What's the story with this case?" And if they're told, absolutely, no, the man did it, they're not going to follow that through. Just another bullshit convict trying to get off, that sort of thing.

MM: The last question I have is about forensics and about the crime scene. Malcolm is assassinated at 3:05 in the afternoon. The police are there covering the place within six minutes. The photo unit is there by 4 o'clock and they're taking photographs of the crime scene. There are still people hanging around, but there is the crime scene, not really cordoned off. People are walking through the thing.

GF: That's way out of line.

MM: What's protocol for a murder?

GF: Oh, yes, you just protect the whole area. You get rid of everybody who's not going to be a witness. Anybody who they didn't question. You want everybody out of that thing. You don't want evidence destroyed, you don't want people finding things, like a camera up here or maybe a guy coming out from underneath the stage, whatever. That surprises me. I didn't even know that. At that time I was rushing back to my wife.

MM: It gets worse. That they do find forensic evidence, the bullets, bullet holes, and they dig out the bullets and things like this. It's just before five o'clock. They pretty much shut down and they leave. And several women come out with buckets and bleach, and they wash the blood off the floor, so that the crime scene is really not cordoned off for more than about an hour, hour and a half. And they hold a dance at seven o'clock in the Audubon. Did you know about this?

GF: No.

MM: They held a party. There were hundreds of people there, dancing. No kidding. Now, I'm not an expert on forensics, but this seems kind of cavalier . . .

GF: Yes, absolutely.

MM: How would you describe the forensics?

GF: Totally contrary to what should be standard operating procedure. That thing should have been covered all night long. That thing should have been delved into all night long. Cavalier—

MM: You would think—

GF: Oh, absolutely.

MM: So they spent about an hour and a half—there's a dance there at 7 o'clock that night. So you're saying that that's unusual in the sense of what . . .

GF: Oh, absolutely. I've seen crime scenes stay locked up for days. And this is a high profile thing, with a high profile—I've seen ordinary murders, crime scenes, you know?

MM: So what does it tell you, based on your experience, that the NYPD did that? What does that say?

GF: Alls I'm saying is, extremely unusual procedure that would kind of hint to me that they wanted to get this thing over, out of the news, and out of everything else as quickly as possible.

MM: But it also might say that they either anticipated what was going to occur, or they simply did not want people to investigate deeply.

GF: Oh, yes. I would say that, sure. That's what I meant when I said they just wanted to wind this thing up.

MM: So who do you think really killed Malcolm X?

GF: I don't know. This has certainly got me thinking, since I read your stuff, and first contacted you about this two years ago. But I wouldn't put it past them, and I didn't put all these pieces together until most recently discussed in this conversation. My getting dumped from the unit that never struck me as being connected. My guess is that it very well could have been—and that's as far as I can say—I can't say for sure—but could have been an inside job with cover-up following.

MM: Right. And what's complicated is because you have law enforcement agencies that aren't communicating with each other, that are competitive, both protecting their own operatives. Gene Roberts for the NYPD, perhaps Reuben Francis, maybe by the FBI or others, who have in the latter case, may have had a hand in setting up the murder.

GF: That time frame, that mid-sixties era, was the time where the communications between departments may have been worse than it ever was.

ABDULLAH ABDUR-RAZZAQ
(JAMES 67X SHABAZZ)

James 67X Shabazz, born James Warden in 1931 in New York City, was one of Malcolm X's most trusted associates during the final years of his life. After being granted a full scholarship from Lincoln University, serving a brief stint in the military, and receiving a master's degree from Columbia University, Shabazz joined the Nation of Islam in 1958. He quickly moved up the ranks and by 1960 had become a lieutenant in the Fruit of Islam. When Malcolm left the NOI in 1964 and formed his own group, Muslim Mosque, Inc., Shabazz pledged that he would leave too and offer one year of his services. With Malcolm abroad during much of that year, Shabazz led MMI meetings, corresponded with Malcolm and other civil rights leaders, and was handed responsibility for the newly founded OAAU. Despite sharing an office in the Hotel Theresa, the two organizations feuded in Malcolm's absence over a variety of religious, political, and class differences. Following Malcolm X's assassination, leadership of the OAAU was assumed by his half sister Ella Collins, and the remaining membership of MMI disintegrated with time.

In this interview Shabazz locates the source of tension between Malcolm X and Elijah Muhammad in the 1962 shooting of Ronald Stokes by Los Angeles police. The lack of an aggressive response to the brutality of the LAPD chafed Malcolm, who had to bite his tongue and support Muhammad's stance of nonaggression. After hearing rumors of discord in 1963, Shabazz met Malcolm for a nighttime meeting in the latter's Oldsmobile, by Morningside Park, to discuss the recent fracture. Although Malcolm had difficulty conceiving of himself outside the NOI, Shabazz stressed the severity of the situation, revealing rumblings that called for his death. It was at this meeting that Shabazz pledged Malcolm one year of his service under one condition: "Don't lie to me. Don't tell me something that's not true, or tell me something that is true that's not . . . I gave three years to the United States Army. They treated me like dog droppings. So [I'll do this for a year]."[1] Now known as Abdullah Abdur-Razzaq, Shabazz has been one of the most outspoken firsthand sources on Malcolm X over the last decade. This interview represents one of his most recent recollections of the black nationalist leader and his organizations.

- Transcript, Abdullah Abdur-Razzaq interview, August 1, 2007, Malcolm X Project

Further reading:

- Transcript, Abdullah Abdur-Razzaq interviews, June 18, 2003, and July 24, 2007, Malcolm X Project

---

1. James 67X Shabazz interview with Manning Marable, August 1, 2007, Malcolm X Project.

Transcript, Abdullah Abdur-Razzaq (James 67X Shabazz) Oral History Interview, August 1, 2007, by Dr. Manning Marable, Tape 2, p. 1–Tape 2, p. 9

MANNING MARABLE: . . . MMI, its formation and the OAAU. Because not enough has been written about MMI, and some stuff that has been has simply been wrong, or incorrect.

ABDULLAH ABDUR-RAZZAQ: That's right. A lot of the stuff written about the OAAU didn't apply to the OAAU. It applied to the Muslim Mosque.

MM: So I want you to set the record straight today. All right. Malcolm announces on March the 8th, 1964, he's leaving the Nation of Islam. A number of men who were very close to him, yourself, Benjamin, Reuben Francis, and others, have this decision to make. Do they leave the NOI and they join Malcolm? I'm trying to understand how each of them made this difficult decision. How you made this decision.

AAR: Okay. As I said before, and I'll keep repeating, the real problem that occurred between Malcolm and the Nation of Islam, and the Honorable Elijah Muhammad was the killing of Ronald Stokes in April of 1962 with nothing being done about it, although the rank-and-file believers, some of the hardened brothers, was ready to go down and exact retribution for the killing of Ronald Stokes, who was not just a brother, he was the secretary of the mosque, a college graduate, a Korean vet, and about to become a father. Now, heretofore, every time Mr. Muhammad spoke or Malcolm spoke, we were told to never to be an aggressor. It is forbidden. Well, you have in the front of your thing. Never be an aggressor. But if anyone puts his hands on you, we are not taught to turn the other cheek. That was the difference between Malcolm and the Nation and the Civil Rights movement. This was considered ridiculous in the Nation, to allow someone to strike you, and not strike him back. And I've said this to you, and I'm going to say it again. Mr. Muhammad said it to [illegible copy] and it's also written down in a publication, that if you put your hands on one of these brothers and kill him, you must die. That is the price you must pay for killing one of these FOI. You must die. Even if a brother kills a brother by accident, his life must be forfeited. Okay. So we accepted this. And we thought this put us in the position to say the things the were being said about the church and about the nonviolent movement, and that Martin Luther King was leading our people into this and that and the other. And this is something that has not been brought up by anyone, which really shocks me.

MM: Well, it is being brought up by me. So . . . I understand how crucial this was.

AAR: Okay. So now Malcolm had to go back home to the very churches which he called "ice houses" and with the Bible that he called "the poison book" and these were the people who supported him. And the Nation of Islam, who sent him out on a limb, did not support him. Is that clear? This, more than anything else, caused Malcolm to re-evaluate his evaluation of the Nation of Islam and of Mr. Muhammad. That's my opinion. And subsequently I know I was correct, because although Brother Malcolm never mentioned any of this to me while he was still in the nation, and while there was still a possibility of his getting back into the Nation, once the bridge had been burned behind him, he told me a lot of things that corroborated everything that I had, though.

MM: Right. Malcolm may have thought that Wallace Muhammad would leave with him, and Wallace soon did leave. But he may have also thought that perhaps Farrakhan, Louis X would leave. Perhaps he thought that Muhammad Ali would leave. You might remember that several days before March the

8th, Muhammad Ali came to New York City, and Malcolm went to the United Nations with Cassius X. What was your perspective on this? Go back to the first week of March 1964, just before Malcolm broke. What do you think would happen?

AAR: I knew he wasn't going back in the Nation. Because I had heard the Brothers talking about—this requires a long answer, if you want it. I mentioned this before. I had written Mr. Muhammad and I said, "Dear Honorable Elijah Muhammad . . . I believe that Brother Malcolm needs a rest because he's doing things . . ." Little did I realize that it was April 1962 that was on him, plus other internal things that I don't know anything about. Then there was a minister, as I say, who was taking money in his mosque. And I wrote a letter to Joseph and Joseph said, "Hah-hah-hah," and tried to make a joke out of it. "Oh, you write a letter." I said, "I'll write a letter on you. What's so funny?" I mean, here's a man who supposedly—and you see, in retrospect, I see I was becoming like Malcolm. Because I was associating with him so much. And unbeknownst to me, I was told that Malcolm was trying to get rid of Joseph to make me the captain of the mosque, which would have never worked. But in any event, Joseph—now our relationship became even more tenuous. Because I think he was saying to himself, "I got another damned Malcolm on my hands. So I got to watch him." So when the break came, whatever was going on, Joseph tried to find out which way I would go, with Brother Malcolm or with Mr. Muhammad? But until they started talking about killing Malcolm, I was with Mr. Muhammad, 100 percent. But then when they started talking about killing Malcolm, I said, "Well, if they'd kill Malcolm, they'll kill me." Because the only one I knew was a more faithful and devout follower of Mr. Muhammad than Malcolm was me. And I got it from Malcolm. So when this business came about, talking about "oh, don't call him Malcolm, call him Red; of, let's kill Malcolm," and all that, I was sitting in the restaurant at the time, so I figured that Joseph was doing this to try to find out which way I would bend. So I went on eating like nothing was going on. It was like a poker game, you know? I said, "Who do they think they're dealing with, some fool?" You know, and I just go on, eating my soup.

MM: This was in the mosque restaurant?

AAR: This was in Temple No. 7 Restaurant, where I used to work. Me and Reuben were waiters there. And the guy who was my boss, Charles 24 [x], would start talking about killing Malcolm. I said—Joseph. Joseph is slick. That's another thing, most people don't give Joseph credit for. Joseph was slick as goose grease, man. He was not no fool. Joseph told me once, he said, "Yes," he said, "Generals come and generals go, but J. Edgar Hoover, he been there all the time. He ain't been removed." So he saw himself . . .

MM: As Hoover.

AAR: Yes, as a counterpart of Hoover. So all of these things. I said, oh, they're trying to get to me, they're trying to get to me. This is coming from Joseph. But then when John Ali came and started saying the same thing, from Chicago, I said, well, this is how Chicago was thinking. And then I started getting scared. And then I called Malcolm, and I said, "Man, this thing is getting bad." And then he asked me to meet him, and I did meet him.

MM: Where did you meet Malcolm?

AAR: By Morningside Park, below, down in the black part of Morningside Park, between 114th and 115th Street.

MM: It was at night.

AAR: At night.

MM: You were in a car?

AAR: It was in his car.

MM: His Oldsmobile.

AAR: Yes.

MM: And what was the—what did you talk about?

AAR: Talked about what was going on in the Nation. About the children. Never said nothing to me about Ronald Stokes. But I'm sitting there, and not to be coarse, I said, "So Mr. Muhammad's been getting some nookie." I mean, that's part of power, you know? If men didn't have access to women as a result of powerful positions, why would they want to be in a powerful position, you know? So that kind of puzzled me. And I said Islamic leader, there is a philosophical concept of polygamy.

MM: So you weren't shattered by these revelations that he had more than one wife, or that he had children out of wedlock?

AAR: No, not at all. As a matter of fact, people started talking about adultery, I never saw it as adultery. I saw it as fornication. Adultery is when you lay down with somebody else's wife, like Lemuel. David's son, Lemuel, so that he could lay with Bathsheba, who was Lemuel's wife, or something like that. That's adultery.

MM: All right. So then what did Malcolm then say to you?

AAR: Oh, I didn't argue with him. I just listened. I didn't take my position on it. I just listened to him. He said about corruption in the Nation and a whole bunch of other stuff, and my position was very simple. I said, "They talking about killing you." I said, "Look, Brother Minister. You were seen in favor by Mr. Muhammad. And I hope you will return to his favor." And he said something about going back in the Nation. And I said, "No, you're not going back in the Nation, Brother. I hope you do, but that's not going to happen. People are talking about killing." So he started musing, and I said, "Listen. I don't know what your plans are. But I will help you for a year." I said, "I have one favor to ask of you. Don't chump me off. Don't lie to me. Don't tell me something that's not true, or tell me something that is true that's not." I said, "That's all I ask of you. I'm not asking what you're going to do, how you're going to do it, just don't lie to me. Tell me the truth." I said, "I'll help you for one year." I gave three years to the United States Army. They treated me like dog droppings. So—

MM: "I'll do this for a year."

AAR: For one year.

MM: Whose idea was MMI?

AAR: Malcolm's, not mine.

MM: All right. So he laid out to you his idea of MMI.

AAR: That's right.

MM: Was the effort of MMI to be a place where Muslims from the Mosque No. 7, could, if they were leaving the Mosque, could find a spiritual home? Was that the idea?

AAR: That's a complicated question.

MM: Help me out here.

AAR: You will notice that on March 8th, he encouraged those who were in the Nation of Islam to remain in the Nation Islam.

MM: Yes. And he said repeatedly in March that the best program for the Negro, for African-American people, was that provided by the Honorable Elijah Muhammad.

AAR: So, so true.

MM: All right. So I'm clear about all that. So what I want to understand is, who was MMI formed for? And who joined it?

AAR: Okay. That's a very delicate question that requires a delicate answer. When you say, "who was in the Nation of Islam," who are you speaking of?

MM: No, who was in MMI—who was MMI created for?

AAR: I'm answering that question. You say, "Who was in the Nation of Islam?" When you ask the minister of a Christian church how many parishioners do you have here, what does he go by? The number of people who come to church on Easter and Christmas? He can't do that, because most of them don't ever come back.

MM: No, but people who tithe, people who . . .

AAR: Okay. You take people who tithe. If you take the people who come Christmas and the people who come Easter . . .

MM: No. Those aren't members.

AAR: And the people who tithe, there's a big difference, right? Well, you had according to the FBI files, someone gave them 291 double-sided typed pages, giving the name and address of everyone who went into the Nation of Islam, to Mosque No. 7, from 1954 to 1964. Now how many do you think were there in the end? A whole lot had come in and gone, right? Why did they go? A whole lot did not like the fact that they couldn't smoke cigarettes. A whole lot didn't like the fact that he couldn't lay down with whatever sweet little lady—

MM: Or you couldn't dance, or enjoy jazz music . . .

AAR: Right. You couldn't go to movies. You couldn't eat a Hershey bar with almonds in it. You couldn't eat sweet potatoes.

You couldn't eat black-eyed—so a lot of people who thought of this as a good idea said, "Yeah, but I can't make these moral adjustments in my life." A lot of people were living—as we say down South—common-law. And they were supposed to get married. Or a guy had two or three women. Everything was confused. So there was a very small number of people who could accept the restrictions of the Nation of Islam and remain there. Okay?

MM: All right, let's try to get to MMI.

AAR: Okay. Well, now, a lot of these people came—and then there were brothers who wanted to go and set things right with . . . about Ronald Stokes. So they had lost their verve, based on Captain Joseph's throwing cold water on their aspirations, you see. So these people came into Muslim Mosque, but although they had X's, they were not participants in the Nation of Islam anymore. They weren't going to Chicago, they weren't putting up Saviour's Day, they weren't putting money in for the charity slip.

MM: So there were people who had joined the NOI but who were no longer active because they had felt disillusioned because of the failure to respond to Stokes' murders, as well as other kinds of issues. The fact that the NOI was on the sidelines. Say like with Birmingham. And here they are bombing black churches and fire-hosing little kids and the NOI is doing nothing.

AAR: Nothing. Absolutely nothing.

MM: And there were criticisms by people. There were criticisms.

HERMAN FERGUSON

Herman Ferguson, like many Malcolm X loyalists who left the Nation of Islam with the minister in 1964, believed in the NOI's message of self-determination, cultural pride, and economic independence but did not care for its religious aspect. Ferguson was born in Fayetteville, North Carolina, on New Year's Eve in 1920.[1] His parents both taught, and his family was so tied to education that an elementary school in his hometown shared the family name. After graduating from Wilberforce University and earning a master's degree from New York University, Ferguson became a public school assistant principal, the position he held when first introduced to the Nation of Islam. Although the NOI could not technically participate in the local demonstrations Ferguson was organizing, NOI members cooperated by passing out flyers for the protests while selling copies of *Muhammad Speaks*. Ferguson and other activists attended services at Mosque No. 7 and were impressed enough with Malcolm X to invite him to speak at a Rochdale Movement demonstration in South Jamaica, Queens, on Thanksgiving Day 1963. The movement was a community effort to halt construction of a housing development on the grounds of the old Jamaica Racetrack because it excluded blacks from construction employment and from its roughly five thousand planned apartments.

Although members such as James 67X Shabazz were willing to convert to the NOI's particularist brand of Islam, Ferguson was hopeful that he could participate in its political aspects alone. However, after asking Mosque No. 7 assistant minister

1. Iyaluua Ferguson with Herman Ferguson, *An Unlikely Warrior: Evolution of a Black Nationalist Revolutionary* (North Carolina: Ferguson-Swan Publications, 2011), 25.

Larry 4X Prescott about the possibility of joining the group without becoming Muslim and receiving no reply, Ferguson remembered: "I had made up my mind if [Malcolm] left the Nation of Islam—and I always assumed that he would continue his political work and expand on it—that I would join up with anything that he did."[2] Shortly after Malcolm's speech at the demonstration in Queens, Ferguson would get his chance, first joining MMI and later becoming chair of the OAAU's educational committee. Ferguson was present at the rally on February 21, 1965, when Malcolm was assassinated and became convinced that the federal government was responsible. He then joined the militant Revolutionary Action Movement and eventually became a political exile in Guyana, after an all-white jury found him guilty of plotting to kill moderate black leaders Roy Wilkins and Whitney Young. Ferguson finally returned to the United States in 1989, after eighteen years in exile during which he lived under the alias Paul Adams. He now lives in North Carolina and published his memoir, *An Unlikely Warrior: Evolution of a Black Nationalist Revolutionary*, in 2011.

- Transcript, Herman Ferguson interview, June 24, 2004, Malcolm X Project

2. Herman Ferguson interview with Manning Marable and Russell Rickford, June 24, 2004, Malcolm X Project.

Q: You know, he walked down to the front, and before he spoke he said, "You know, this person is going with that white woman over here."

FERGUSON: Right. Right.

Q: And you said, "Well, how did you know?" And because he was so observant, he was just like picking up cues.

FERGUSON: Right. All the time. I can remember the scene clearly. He was—

Q: Talk about that.

FERGUSON: He had a yellow legal pad, type pad, like the pad you have there, lawyers use that sort of thing, and I had leaned over and peeked to see what he was writing, and he was just jotting down, I suppose, things that he wanted to touch on in his speech. That amazed me, that Malcolm always spoke, and I just thought that, you know, he must have some notes or something to speak to somebody. He was just like writing headings, you know, and things that he wanted to speak about. Those headings would keep him on track.

So between making jottings occasionally on the pad, he was looking around in the audience, and then he said to me, "That fellow there is going with that white girl there." Now, there was quite a difference, a lot of space in between them. I think the girl was sitting in the front row or somewhere, and then the guy he was talking about was about maybe a dozen rows or so behind her. There was no indication, nobody would have known or suspected that there was anything between them. Only those of us in the inner circle knew what was going on, that there was anything going on. And when Malcolm said that, that blew my mind that he just picked up on that, and I knew there was no way that he could have known those two people. Could not have known anything about them, but he just picked up on it.

I asked him, if I recall correctly, as I recall, "How do you know that?" And he just passed it off in some way that, well— he said something or other, and to the—that, well, you know, you can't just, you know, know. And so there was nothing that I could say, because he was right on target.

I found that oftentimes Malcolm would make little observations, because he was very—he observed things. He observed people and things that were going on around him, and from time to time he would make little comments to let you know that he had picked up on something that was happening around him or something that was going.

But that was the one instance that always stuck with me. It was like he was reading people's minds, although I know that you can't do that. But something had just clicked. Something caused him to pick up on the fact that there was something between those two people.

Q: Do you recall if the substance of what Malcolm talked about in that talk—and I think it's important because he was still a member of NOI [Nation of Islam] at that time—what was the occasion that prompted you to invite him to speak?

FERGUSON: Well, we had, our organization, the Rochdale Movement, had been picketing and demonstrating down on Jamaica Avenue, a commercial area there in Queens, that area, and the target was the Jamaica Savings Bank, because they had an offensive mural on the wall. We called it the "Banjo Billy" mural, because it showed the history of the development of Long Island and Queens, and this big mural depicted key happenings in the development of Long Island and Queens. They had the big factories and all of the other things that were characteristic of that area.

And then as a bone, they threw a bone to the black people, they had a picture of a slave, obviously a slave. He was standing in front of a big plantation building, big white house, that was the master's house, and in the background you could see the slave quarters. He had one leg up on a stump of a tree and he was playing a banjo and there was some white children around him. He was in rags, and the children were well dressed, and obviously, the family of the plantation owner, and it was called "Banjo Billy."

Nobody had mentioned—said anything about—it was accepted by everyone. Our so-called leaders, the politicians, the influential people, and so on, they all just like had accepted it. When we looked at it, we said, "Well, let's focus on this and let's bring that down."

At the time there was a small newspaper, little neighborhood newspaper in South Jamaica; the editor of it was Ella Ferguson. We're not related. But she was an activist in the real sense of the word. She got out in the community, found things that were wrong and used her newspaper to talk about it, to take positions against and so on. So largely through her interest in removal of "Banjo Billy" and that kind of space that we got from her paper, that [unclear].

At the same time we were in touch with the Nation of Islam, the fruit—what do they call it?

Q: The Fruit of Islam?

FERGUSON: The Fruit of Islam, yes. And the brother who was in charge of that area of Queens, Brother Larry, who is now known as Akbar Muhammad, I think, and he's the representative in Ghana, or in Africa, for [Louis] Farrakhan. He was just Brother Larry then. Good brother, loyal, committed to Elijah Muhammad, and very close to Malcolm. It was through him that we met Malcolm and he introduced

Malcolm and brought us over to the mosque, and we asked him to ask Malcolm to come out and see what we were doing.

Q: Do you remember where the mosque in Queens was?

FERGUSON: No.

Q: Okay. But you met at Larry's mosque, as opposed—

FERGUSON: No, they had no mosque.

Q: They didn't have one?

FERGUSON: No, because Larry was like—when I say he was the leader, he was—I don't know what the title he had or anything, but he was—

Q: He was in [unclear].

FERGUSON: He was a leader in terms of those brothers on the street.

Q: The FOI [Fruit of Islam]?

FERGUSON: The FOI. And they seemed to follow Larry's lead. Quite influential.
    So he had told Malcolm what we were doing, and they were helping us out, and Malcolm had given us his blessing and encouraging us to keep on doing what we were doing. It was Larry who brought Malcolm out to look at what we were doing. Well, you have all of this anyway.

Q: And this led to the invitation from Malcolm to speak.

FERGUSON: Yes, right. Okay. We had started going to the mosque on 116th Street on Sundays, and after the ceremony and the things, the program would be over, Malcolm customarily stood on the stage and people came up on the stage and talked with him. And we would always come up and speak with him, let him know we were there, say things to him.

It was largely through Brother Larry that we reached out to Malcolm and asked him if he would be willing to come out to Queens, because we felt that Queens needed a shot of Black Nationalism from Malcolm, and he said yes. He looked through his schedule and the only time that he could give us was Thanksgiving. So of course we took it. This was Malcolm. [Laughs] We didn't care what day it was; Christmas. These are European holidays anyway.

So anyway, we set it up, and Larry was the liaison person between Malcolm and us. All the arrangements, the pulling of the FOI into the event, and they did a lot of work themselves, advertising, helping us get flyers and posters together and all that sort of thing.

On the day we had quite a crowd. Quite a crowd. We had a heavy detachment of police officers. It was like half the police force in Queens was assigned to that place that day.

Interestingly enough, a lot of people—and as I said we had a good crowd, it even surprised us. We didn't realize the drawing power of Malcolm, but, again, a traditional holiday when people stay at home and their family is there for the meal and whatnot.

Q: So this was on Thanksgiving?

FERGUSON: As I recall, it was Thanksgiving Day. Because we said to feed folks—instead of—I'm trying to think of the slogan we used. It was something like—I can't get all of the exact wording, but it was something to this effect, "Instead of a traditional Thanksgiving dinner, come out and spend Thanksgiving with Malcolm," something like that.

Q: Now, [John F.] Kennedy's assassination had just taken place about two days before.

FERGUSON: Yes.

Q: Was there any discussion about this, any discussion about calling it off because of the assassination?

FERGUSON: No. No, and in terms of trying to recall the specifics of the speech that he gave, I really can't do that. All I know is that it was a traditional Malcolm-type speech, laying out the problems that we have, our inability, our unwillingness to recognize the problem that we have, to accept the fact that the white man is our enemy and deal with that, and, of course, dealing with the Uncle Tom element. I mean, he was in his element there, because he knew Queens and he knew that this was a middle-class bourgeois-type audience that he was speaking to, and so he had a lot of good things for them. He was well received, no question about that. We really were proud of what we had done. We'd brought Malcolm and had given Malcolm to the middle-class Negroes of Queens.

Q: Now, a week later, on December 1st, Malcolm gives a talk. Elijah Muhammad is supposed to arrive and speak in New York City, and because of ill health he's not able to do it. There's a discussion inside of the NOI, do we cancel, do we not. We put a deposit on the facility; let's go ahead and do it. Malcolm is authorized to give an address, and it's not in the address, but after the talk he makes the comment about the so-called—

FERGUSON: In response to a question that someone asked him.

Q: You were there?

FERGUSON: Yes.

Q: Talk about that a bit more.

FERGUSON: Okay. I don't remember which day of the week

it was, but we knew that Malcolm was going to speak instead of Elijah Muhammad, and what I don't understand was the way it developed that way, but they couldn't their money back. The deposit they had put down on the place, the owners refused to give that deposit back to them.

So then Malcolm was told to speak for, in place of Elijah Muhammad, and Malcolm spoke and then he called for questions. As I recall it, some male, I don't know where he came from, but anyway, stood up and said, "Malcolm, President Kennedy has just been assassinated. What do you have to say about that?"

And I do remember Malcolm saying, "Well, we have been instructed by Elijah Muhammad to not make any comments on that." He said, "So I can't make any comments." And then he paused and then he said, "But I will say that it was just the chickens coming home to roost, and me being an old country boy, chickens coming home to roost never bothered me."

It was an innocuous comment, we all thought, and nobody paid any particular attention to it. The audience didn't go [gasps]. There wasn't any kind of outburst or any coming from the audience. It was taken in stride. Then we found out later that someone had called Chicago and reported this to—

Q: John Ali. John Ali was in attendance.

FERGUSON: Yes, I understand that he was there. And that it was then that, when this was put to Elijah, that he had to take some action and that's when the suspension took place.

Q: Go back in your mind. When did you first hear about the suspension and what did you think about it? Were you surprised, not surprised? Did you think, given what you'd heard of Malcolm up to that point, that he might ultimately break from the NOI?

FERGUSON: I had always felt, long before I'd met Malcolm, that he needed to break with the Nation of Islam, because I felt the Nation of Islam held him back, his development.

I thought that he was the leader, type of leader that we needed. His message needed to be heard [unclear] that the straitjacket that the Nation of Islam put him in was holding back his development as a leader with a particular point of view that needed to be heard, the voice that was offering another alternative to integration. Those of us who weren't particularly interested in integration and certainly not interested in what [Martin Luther] King [Jr.] was offering.

I always felt that for his own development, he needed to get away from the Nation of Islam. I didn't know what would happen when he left, but I had made up my mind if he left the Nation of Islam—and I always assumed that he would continue his political work and expand on it—that I would join up with anything that Malcolm did, because I had come to the conclusion by that time that his particular message and his philosophy were certainly in keeping with what I thought was the correct road that he should travel.

So when the break took place, I don't remember how or when we were told that it happened, but I took it in stride. I thought it was too long in coming, you know. "Where have you been all this time? We've been waiting for you, brother. Now you're here." And as soon as I learned that he had started Muslim Mosque, Inc., I joined. I know we talked about it.

Q: That's right.

FERGUSON: In the discussion we were—I don't know how it came up, that should my membership be advertised publicly. Malcolm was interested in the fact that I had a high position, because I was an assistant principal at that time in an elementary school in Queens, and he was the one—as far as I was concerned, that was what I was committed to. I didn't make any—there was no problem and I made no bones about the fact that I was an admirer of Malcolm. I felt that he had the correct solution to our problems as black people here in the United States and that was my leader.

Some of the people in the school I was in, some of the other assistant principals, they were pro Adam Clayton Powell. "Why don't you follow Adam Clayton Powell?"

I said, "Malcolm is the man. I mean, that is the man," you know. So I was not hiding my politics, so it didn't really make that much difference to me whether it was announced publicly or whatever, but Malcolm felt that I should keep it quiet. He mentioned at the first speech that there are many different types of people, people who were in the organization, we even had an assistant principal, and I was a little surprised because he had suggested to me that we not really make that public. Then when he said that, I said, "Well, we might as well [unclear]." But that was it. I was not surprised, because I felt Malcolm belonged to the people in a secular sense rather than in a religious sense.

Q: Talk about that a little bit more. What do you mean by a secular sense?

FERGUSON: Well, that there were many black people who were not pro Nation of Islam for many reasons. Many of them were afraid of the Nation of Islam. The emphasis on the Fruit of Islam, the apparent military nature of the organization, the searching of people when they came into the meetings, separation of the men and women, and all of those kinds of things that would tend to make black people, many of them, a little leery, a little nervous about that. So I felt that if Malcolm could strip his religion, put it on the side, and present his politics minus the religious side of it, that that would remove a lot of the concerns that many black people had about the Nation of Islam.

I felt that he had a lot to offer from his own perspective, rather than always paying homage to Elijah Muhammad. "Elijah Muhammad tells us," and always that sort of thing. It sort of got to be a little—what do I want to say? Like the bell on the ice cream trucks. Icy or salty? Mr. Salty. Why do you have to—you. That's your mind, that's you, that's not Elijah Muhammad. Elijah Muhammad doesn't have that kind of insight. He may have the insight, but I understand he was a very—in terms of a man who had very little education, he had a good mind, a keen mind, he just wasn't a public speaker, because I heard him try to speak, and very unimpressed. Very unimpressed. Because Malcolm was there, Malcolm introduced him and he just wasn't—he just didn't cut the mustard.

So I felt that Malcolm, once he became his own man, and I saw him—in leaving the Nation of Islam Malcolm became his own man then. So basically what I'm saying is that I wasn't shocked, as I recall, I wasn't taken aback. I didn't feel that this would be a terrible loss. I knew that Malcolm would need to build a base of support. I assumed that he had it, you know. But then I discovered that by working with the Organization of Afro-American Unity, that our people, while they would come out to the rallies when they knew Malcolm was going to be speaking, they didn't join up, sign up and join up in the large numbers that we had anticipated and hoped that would have come forward and then get involved.

One of the reasons that we had taken the decision to form these different committees in various areas, that people could join a specific committee, the education committee, the cultural committee, the communications. Wherever their interest lay, or their expertise, you know, they could join that particular committee and work in that area. But all of the committees were—they all had the same problem of the lack of large numbers of people coming forward to join those committees. We would have people come to some of our meetings, which are open meetings, and yet some of these people were not even members.

Malcolm was aware of the fact that we were having problems, and from time to time he would make a—he would, as part of his speaking, would make mention of the fact that the organization was open for membership and what the requirements were, and we always had a table there where people could sign up and get a membership card. As I recall, it was one or two dollars to join, very, very small amount of money. So that was no object to that.

Q: So now as you think back on it, why do you think—well, when Malcolm—

FERGUSON: Could you hold on a minute? I'd like to go to the bathroom.

Q: Sure.
[Tape recorder turned off.]

Q: James Shabazz, we interviewed James, and he told us that from MMI's [Muslim Mosque, Incorporated] point of view, within MMI there were a lot of criticisms of the OAAU [Organization of Afro-American Unity], and it really falls under two kind of things. One, that the brothers in MMI and the sisters in MMI were basically people in [Mosque No.] Seven who left with Malcolm.

FERGUSON: Right.

Q: They felt they owned him.

FERGUSON: Right.

Q: They owned him.

FERGUSON: Right.

Q: And you guys were interlopers, Johnny-come-latelys, you were not part of the Nation, you didn't have the discipline, you couldn't be trusted, and Shabazz was very frank about this. He also said that a number of the brothers got heavily into the gun club thing, they were carrying rifles through Harlem, and that there were real tensions between the MMI's claim on Malcolm versus the tension with the need to build a broad pluralistic like nationalist movement that would largely be secular. You would have middle-class folk, working-class folk, and they didn't really feel that this was—Shabazz never said it's not in Malcolm's interest, but they didn't really trust it.

The second thing that he said that surprised us was about the women issue.

FERGUSON: I expected you to say that, yes.

Q: He said that James [67X Shabazz] and Lynne Shifflett banged heads constantly.

FERGUSON: Right.

Q: Now, in much of the literature about OAAU nobody talks about this. We would like you to talk about both of these issues from your point of view.

FERGUSON: Yes. What you've said is accurate. James was leveling with you and there was resentment against the members of the OAAU because they didn't go through the struggle in the Nation of Islam. Those brothers and sisters who left, who were in the Nation of Islam with Malcolm and came out and joined him in the Muslim Mosque, Incorporated, they did that with the knowledge that the Nation of Islam would not be friendly toward them. So they felt, to a great extent, responsible for Malcolm and his safety and protecting him against the Nation of Islam.

When you speak of their rifles and so on, their arms, and the gun club; and all of that sort of thing, yes. At the beginning of our rallies that we had in the Audubon Ballroom, Malcolm's security was made up of those brothers who protected him with their weapons in the open. Their rifles, shotguns, were carried openly. Their pistols, they did not carry them openly, but their rifles and shotguns, yes.

I remember clearly the first instance when they provided security for Malcolm, and when he finished speaking, everyone had to remain seated while Malcolm left. I can recall clearly, because I'm right here [gestures], when Malcolm would come off the stage, they brought him off here, and right here is the little aisle, walkway, behind those booths.

Q: The booths, yes. There's a walkway.

FERGUSON: Booths, yes. Okay. Malcolm came that way.

And these brothers—he came off and he walked out here and then he—where's the exit?

Q: It's right up here.

FERGUSON: And then came to, yes, right here and out. I must have been over here in the center, but I can see these brothers. Some of them, I don't remember how many, were walking in front of Malcolm leading, and then another group behind him, and Malcolm in the center. You know, I mean, to me that was the way it should have been. I felt very proud that these were black men, you know, escorting our leader out of the building, that he was safe, he had these weapons. And this is, as far as I was concerned, is the way that the movement would have to go anyway. So I appreciated and like that.

But it was shortly after that, that the order came down that weapons would be no longer—the security would no longer carry weapons. And there was a meeting. I've always thought of that meeting as being on a Tuesday night.

Q: Yes, when Malcolm got back from Detroit.

FERGUSON: I don't remember where he—

Q: Well, on Sunday you had the firebombing. Monday morning he got up early and flew to Detroit. He gets back.

FERGUSON: Wait a minute.

Q: Are you talking—

FERGUSON: This is long before that.

Q: This is long before?

FERGUSON: Yes.

Q: Okay.

FERGUSON: They were ordered to—

Q: Not carry weapons.

FERGUSON: Yes, not to carry weapons. Because all those brothers had left. There was a terrible—didn't Shabazz say about—didn't he talk about that?

Q: Tell me what—

Q: This was late '64, wasn't it?

FERGUSON: It would have been shortly after the OAAU began to have the Sunday rallies in the Audubon.

Q: This is like June of '64. This is summer of '64. Malcolm is back from the hajj and he's back for about seven weeks or so. In fact, in June, Lynne Shifflett made the reservations, made a reservation for the use of the facility. And so there are already tensions between MMI and OAAU about where is this thing going. But that's the question I'm asking you.

I mean, I know that Malcolm, in August, writes a letter back on his second trip, really talking, substantively talking about the problems within OAAU and MMI, and about brothers threatening to quit, resign and leave. That's already been published in *By Any Means Necessary*. So we're not talking out of school; I mean, we know about that. We're trying to figure out, from your point of view, your perspective, what was occurring during those early months when you were trying to build this thing, and how did people interact with each other when Malcolm wasn't around?

FERGUSON: I know that during the time that Malcolm was out of the country for the first trip, we knew that there were problems between the MMI and some of the non-religious people, and when I say non-religious, I mean those who had not come through the Nation of Islam. They were not part of the old guard. There was tension and resentment.

And it was after the OAAU came into existence that I think that the problems began to arise around the role of the females. Some of the brothers were very concerned about Malcolm's relationship with the females, certain specific females, not in the sense that Malcolm was having any affairs or anything of that sort, but their training and their beliefs were women played a secondary role to the men. The men were out front; the protectors, the warriors, etc. And Malcolm felt that the women had equal position with the men. As a matter of fact, there were women that Malcolm, I believe, felt deserved appointments to higher positions that he would not have put any of the men in.

Q: Who in particular?

FERGUSON: Muriel Grey [phonetic]. Lynne Shifflett. A sister named Ethel [Minor]; she was from Chicago. She was a schoolteacher. And later on a sister named—she was a writer. Sara. Sara Mitchell.

As a matter of fact, a couple of brothers came to me and said that because the minister had a lot of respect for me, they wanted me to approach him about their concerns about the role of the women and how it was not sitting well with many of the brothers. So I said, "Well, why don't you all—why me?"

They said, "No, he won't listen to us. He'll listen to you, though."

Q: Do you remember who came to you?

FERGUSON: Sure. Specifically one brother, Earl. Earl Grant. I don't know if he would admit that, and that's why I was asking you if you had talked with him.

Anyway, he came to me and was speaking on behalf of some of the brothers who had observed that Malcolm was placing too much confidence and responsibility in the women, and they felt that it was harming the organization. But I knew the position of the Nation of Islam and those people who were from it. You know, I didn't find that particularly alarming or disturbing. But I did say to him, "Well, why don't you all go and tell him?" They knew Malcolm would eat their heads off. He didn't take any nonsense from those guys.

So I guess they figured that Malcolm might listen to me because Malcolm might think that—but anyway, whatever. But I didn't do it. I didn't have any problem with that. I felt it was what should be done, and as a matter of fact, the women that Malcolm seemed to place a lot of confidence in, they were responsible, they were well educated, and I felt that his respect for them and his responsibility that he placed in them was the correct thing to do. But it was there.

So after a time, the Muslim Mosque, Incorporated and the OAAU sort of like drifted apart. Some people came in and were not part of the MMI, and all of the MMI people were not part of OAAU. So there was that gap there. And I think that Malcolm, he saw the MMI as, what should I say, his mosque. Maybe I should say it that way. This is where the religious part of the program and his activities would be centered there. But the OAAU would be a more secular-type organization. It was not based on religion and it was based on politics and economics and so on.

As a matter of fact, at one of our meetings, I remember him speaking very forcefully and directly to this whole concept of religion, of the separation of religion from politics, and the example he used, as he stood there in front of us, was, "If you have your politics in your hands and your religion, you have them there in your hand now. When you're dealing with things that are religious in nature and you put the politics in your pocket," and he closed his hand and put his hand in his jacket pocket, like this, and he said, "When you're dealing with things that are religious, you put the politics in your pocket and you deal with your religion."

In other words, he was making the point there should be a separation and you should be able to separate the two, and that religion, you did your prayers, you spoke with your god in the closet or somewhere else, but you separated the two. You didn't try to mix them. I think the point he was trying to make was—he was trying to resolve that problem that he knew we were having between those two forces.

Q: How effective do you think he was in putting that philosophy into practice in his administration of the OAAU and MMI? I guess this is a question that gets back to Malcolm's demeanor and Malcolm's manner. Was he, in your mind, with OAAU, exclusively a political leader, a political figure, or were there times when the roles overlapped and he did do the kind of ministering, almost pastoring, that one would expect of a religious figure?

FERGUSON: I saw Malcolm as a political figure who had a deep-seated belief in Allah, his god, and his religion, totally committed, but had the ability to separate one out from the other. He could be political without being like a Baptist preacher, let's say, you know. And I could appreciate that in him, because I had no particular commitment to any kind of religion. I felt that religion was—even the Muslim religion, operated as a kind of break from the things that we as black people knew to really—to liberate ourselves. And I felt that Malcolm had this uncanny ability to remove from his political activities his religion, you know, and that he could accept people if they were of the Muslim faith, if they were Baptists or Methodists. He was serious and sincere when he talked about those things, about we were not punished or treated the way we were treated in America because we are Muslim, because we are Baptists, or Methodists, or Catholic, or whatever; we're treated that way because we are black and we're in America.

And that's why I respected the man so, because he was sincere. I never ever observed him say or do anything that caused me to question his beliefs. I felt that here was a man who was ready to go to the end of the line, to walk that last mile in support of the things that he believed in. There would be nothing that would cause him to change his thinking. And this is where I have had my problems with those people who have tried to rewrite or change history in terms of his thinking about who our enemy was.

Malcolm didn't change his ideas one iota, not one bit about who the enemy was. He knew it was the white man. He knew the white man had all the power and he was using it against us, so it was only natural. So he didn't equivocate that, "Well, there are a handful of whites that are [unclear]." Malcolm used to say, when you'd mention to him that some white person or some white dude had done something on the behalf of black people, he would say, "Well, it's just a case of the devil doing some good." He said, "Sometimes the devil does good." That's what he used to say to us.

Q: All right. Now, let me raise this question, because this always comes up on Malcolm and especially in part because of Alex Haley. Malcolm is meeting with Haley all throughout '63. Nobody hardly knows about this. Haley rarely shows up at the mosque; only occasionally. Then he moves to Rome, New York, in November—October, actually, of 1963, and he's up there writing and he stays in telephone contact, occasionally meets with Malcolm at Idlewild, than name change JFK Airport Hotel. He's writing his book.

Haley would lead us to believe that when Malcolm went to Mecca in April of '64 and came back, that he had seen this vision of multiracial humankind, that with power of Allah and through faith, white people would overcome their racism. And so if you could bring that kind of power of faith to the U.S., it was possible for white people to be transformed. Part of what Haley implies is, is that Haley doesn't say Malcolm became an integrationist—I'm not putting words in Haley's mouth, but others who had read Haley they argue exactly that. And in fact, when they had the postage stamp of Malcolm back in '98, the description of Malcolm that was released by the U.S. Postal Service says exactly that; it says he moved after Mecca into an integrationist frame of mind. What's your view about this, since you knew the man when he came back from the hajj?

Now, there's another thing to think about. When Malcolm sent these letters back from Mecca, from Saudi Arabia, James Shabazz put the letter in his pocket for a couple of days. He was very upset about it, he didn't want people to see it, he didn't know what to do, and it was only after several days that he released it. So clearly Shabazz, James is saying to us that what Malcolm is saying seems a departure to him; otherwise, why did he hold the letter? So we're looking to you to help us straighten this out. What was your [unclear]?

FERGUSON: Okay. As I recall, when Malcolm came back, he told us his experiences in great detail. When I say *we*, I'm talking about the members of the OAAU. And after he described his experience with meeting a Muslim who was also a revolutionary, and the man saying to him, "I'm white, so therefore you don't include me in your struggle," and then Malcolm had to think about that sort of thing. He realized—he accepted that, yes, he had been excluding some people based on the fact that he had said that all white people are the devil.

He said also that maybe if the white man in America could embrace Islam, that he could change his feelings and actions toward black people, and this is where I think that Alex Haley stops, at that point, but Malcolm went on and said to us, "But we know the white man cannot accept Islam or any religion that will cause him to see us in a favorable light." He said, "That's impossible."

Because if I had for a moment even suspected that Malcolm was changing his thinking, I would have walked away. And he never, other than for the fact that he liked to examine ideas, he was a true intellectual and he liked to think aloud and work through problems, intellectual problems, and then come up with his conclusion. So sometimes he might be doing that and people might think that he is going through a period of uncertainties, the fact that he's verbalizing a kind of a contradictory thought that he may be having, and he's trying to take a position on it.

But finally, when Malcolm had resolved the matter and come up with his own interpretation and his thinking on the matter, that was it. After he went through that intellectual process and weighed the pros against the cons and finally decided this is way we want, this is the solution to the problem, and I've seen him do that on many occasions when he would think through, "Well, we can do it this way or we could do it that way, but then if we do it this way, we're run into this problem down the road," and that thinking. He works his way through the problem and comes up with what he thinks is the right solution.

So he, in my opinion, had offered to white people the possibility of Islam correcting their sense of values and their opinions and their actions towards white people, but he was of the opinion that they could never accept the teachings of Islam. The white man, the European, could never accept those teachings.

Q: So you don't think it was a political stretch?

FERGUSON: No.

Q: You don't think Malcolm was trying to signal, for instance, to a larger black audience that he had made a clear intellectual break from the dogma of the Nation; it wasn't a bid to—

Q: Right. Or say a break from Yacub, that literally the white man is literally a devil, that perhaps one argument that people make is that if one reads—and in fact, the Socialist Workers Party, they make this argument. They argued that if you look at the text, the context of what Malcolm's speeches were in November and December of '64, and then in the first months of 1965, he actually stops using the words, the phrase "Black Nationalist," or "Black Nationalism," and that he says at one point that he was searching for another word, a phrase, some of us would say Pan-Africanism, some of us would say something else, but he was trying to figure out a terminology that more closely or accurately spoke to the kind of revolutions that were occurring in the black world and a kind of way of speaking about that in a way that was a new kind of category, and that Black Nationalism didn't quite fit that category. And you yourself said, how do you then deal with the Algerian revolution, or, say, the Vietnamese revolution, people of color fighting against French and then U.S. imperialism. And we know Malcolm was dead set against Vietnam. It comes out through all those speeches. So how does the Black Nationalist actually speak to those kinds of things?

FERGUSON: Well, I can only speak for myself, that my feeling was that Malcolm, in searching for a position that would replace the term "Black Nationalism," revolutionary Black Nationalism, Pan-Africanism, my feeling was that he would have eventually wound up embracing socialism. Because of the kind of mind that he had, the way he worked out these contradictions in his own mind, I believe that he would have been led to that particular position, embracing socialism as an economic vehicle for Black Nationalism. I think he recognized—there's no question about it, he recognized the shortcomings of the term "Black Nationalism," which really, so many I found to be Nationalists don't have a clear understanding of what that means. Some of them are quite happy to be absorbed into the capitalist system, and there are some that are not even—that are not that way out, some who are, consider them totally black, they wanted to have black businesses and blacks run the schools and whatever.

But if you're a Nationalist, you have to be committed to and a patron of some land mass that you control. And that's why I am a citizen of the Republic of New Africa, and I don't consider myself an American. I don't consider myself an Afro American, or an African American. I am a new African, even the limitations that that implies.

I still think that Malcolm would have embraced some version of, well, scientific socialism. I think he would have gone there. I think that's where he would have gone.

Q: I wanted to return real briefly, maybe, to a few questions about OAAU, MMI and a few of the conflicts that you broached. Well, maybe I should back up even before that and talk a little bit about the numbers, numbers of OAAU and numbers of MMI, because we've had a tough time actually nailing down numbers.

Q: Only one person has given us hard numbers.

Q: Right. So I guess to the extent that you can—

FERGUSON: I imagine that was James Shabazz. No?

Q: I mean, you mentioned that there was this ongoing recruiting problem and that the OAAU was just not drawing the numbers that you all had expected and that Malcolm wanted. So I guess my first question would be, what were the numbers? And then what I asked you in the second question is to speculate some more as to what was the problem, why weren't people joining up?

FERGUSON: Well, in terms of the numbers, I'm trying to think of who would have that information, other than Malcolm himself. And then if Malcolm had those numbers, who would he have depended on to pass that information on to them? I don't know. All I know is that all of the committees that were active had very low membership.

Malcolm wrote to some of us that the only committee that was really functioning in a lot of the countries was the education committee. He was satisfied with where we were functioning. That was Jim Campbell and me working together, and we had the Liberation School, and Malcolm was impressed by that. As a matter of fact, when we had our first graduation, he signed off on the certificates that we gave out. I think it was for like ten of the first class. Yuri [Kochiyama] was a member of that graduating class. We had started a second class that never graduated, because Malcolm was assassinated and the whole thing fell apart.

So if you take that as an indicator, the education committee, I can tell you that the education committee, I don't think we ever had at any one time more than a dozen people, if that many. The people who did most of the work was Jim Campbell and myself, although at the Liberation School we would sign up a class of people. You know, we might have ten, twelve, fourteen people, but they were not actually all members.

Q: Wasn't there an executive committee, especially during that seventeen-week period when Malcolm was out of the country in the second half of '64? That you have different committees doing work, your committee functioned best, the other committees less so, according to Malcolm.

FERGUSON: And some of them were inactive.

Q: Okay. So that—
    [Begin Tape 1, Side B]

Q: Maybe instead of an executive, thinking about not executive, but a nucleus. The nucleus is really about, what, about twenty people, maybe fifteen? I mean, a real nucleus of the people who actually were there, dependable, Peter Bailey, the newsletter, people who actually did stuff.

FERGUSON: Right. I think that that nucleus would have been the chairs of the various committees, and particularly those committees that were active. You mentioned Peter Bailey, Muriel.

Q: Sara Mitchell.

FERGUSON: Sara Mitchell came on towards the end.

Q: Later.

FERGUSON: Much later.

Q: Lynne Shifflett.

FERGUSON: Lynne, of course, is the secretary, general secretary role. So of course, she would have been part of that group.

Q: But she also would have had the numbers.

FERGUSON: Yes, she would have the numbers.

Q: So Muriel Grey was the cultural committee. So that was active, correct?

FERGUSON: Yes.

Q: So education was active.

FERGUSON: The communication—I don't remember whether Peter's committee was the communication committee, but anyway, his committee was responsible for getting out the newsletter, the newspaper.

Q: Right. And it got out.

FERGUSON: Yes. Right. Right. But a lot of it was basically because of the hustle and the hard work that Peter himself put into it. In terms of a group of people around him, I don't know about that.

Q: Were there people that were kind of coming in and out of the organization that were not consistent or not really dependable, but that were on the fringes?

FERGUSON: Yes.

Q: So to some extent there was maybe, to some degree, a fluctuation in terms of the size of the membership. What you're describing, really, is a very small concentrated core of basically the committee heads that were doing the work.

Q: Dedicated people.

FERGUSON: That's right.

Q: What was the problem with recruiting? Why weren't more people coming?

FERGUSON: That's a good question. It has many facets to it. We have to look at the time that all of this was going on. There was a lot of turmoil and uncertainty and suspicion. The counterintelligence program, which we, at that time, although we were victims of it and targets, targets of it, because they hadn't begun yet to really to victimize anybody, we didn't understand this. We were very naïve about that. So their work was going on. We had infiltrators whose job was to create dissention, to start rumors, so there were a lot of rumors going on, a lot of rumor monitoring going on.

Q: What kinds of rumors?

FERGUSON: This person is an agent, or that person doesn't like the minister, certain people are having affairs with each other. All of these things were going on, and that was one thing.

I don't think there was even an outreach, organized outreach approach to the general population to bring in members. We talked about it. We tended to rely mainly on Malcolm's popularity and the fact that people knew Malcolm and respected him. We sort of hoped he would be like the magnet that would draw the people in. It didn't really work.

As I said, people would come out in large numbers to the rallies that we had, but when it came to the actual joining of the organization, that was a commitment that you had to think about, because immediately when you became a known member of Malcolm's organization, I mean, you stood out like a sore thumb. You could be a Panther, you know. It was easier to be a Black Panther than to be a Malcolmite.

Q: So in your mind it was the fear of being associated with the militancy of Malcolm, less so perhaps the aura of, for instance, the fear of the Nation of Islam and the concern over the animosity between Malcolm's people and the Nation of Islam. It would be like that was secondary to the outright fear?

FERGUSON: I think that's all part of the mix. I was going to come to that, because Malcolm addressed that when he said that early on there would be no searching of people. He said that was too much of a reminder of what it was like in the Nation of Islam. So we were copying from the Nation of Islam, and he didn't want—and it showed that we didn't feel safe around the general public. We wanted the public to feel that this is a different type of organization. It's not a carbon copy of the Nation of Islam, so, no searching.

Then when he ruled that there would be no weapons displayed at the meetings, because that was also playing into the hands of the media and those people who stamped him as being a militant, weapons and guns and violence, you know, and he felt that that might ease our problem in terms of bringing other people, ordinary people, in to join the organization.

So I think that was all part of the things that we had against us, you know, and try as we might, you know, we did not resolve that problem. Now, had Malcolm lived long enough, there were a lot of problems that Malcolm would have eventually resolved, he would have worked out of that, around that, but he didn't get the chance to do it.

So when I say that there are a mix of things—but if you look at the environment at that time, and plus there were many of the Negro organizations that were still opposed to Malcolm and what he stood for, you know, NAACP, the Urban League, SLCLC, or whatever that is, and King and his organization, they're always, like, saying, "You better deal with us or you got that guy over there." You know, they were saying, not only to black people, they were saying it to white people as well, particularly to the white power structure, "Deal with us. Send us the money. We know what to do it and we'll keep everybody quiet. That guy, you know, you can't trust him."

So I think it was all a part of the forces that were in resistance to what we were trying to do at that time, and to give black people power to take a decision, to do what they wanted to do, which we hoped would be to form our own nation.

KHALIL ISLAM
(THOMAS 15X JOHNSON)

Khalil Islam, formerly known as Thomas 15X Johnson, is widely recognized as one of the three men convicted in 1966 for the assassination of Malcolm X. However, prior to the infamous trial, Johnson was close to Malcolm as a member of his security detail. Johnson joined the Nation of Islam in early 1960; like other new members of the mosque, he had converted to Islam while incarcerated. After one year, Johnson received a quick promotion to lieutenant of Mosque No. 7, under the auspices of Captain Joseph. In this capacity, he came to know Malcolm X, buying groceries for Betty Shabazz at the NOI's supermarket in Brooklyn and ensuring that the minister had a parking space before speaking on Sundays. Johnson, who had been working as a house painter, was laid up with rheumatic arthritis for much of 1964. That same year, he was charged in the killing of Benjamin Brown, who defected from the NOI and opened an independent mosque in the Bronx. With a fellow suspect in the Brown shooting, Norman 3X Butler, already charged in the Malcolm X murder, Johnson was brought to the Bronx County Courthouse as the third and final suspect on March 3, 1965.

Johnson was paroled in 1987, and his interview five years before his death in August 2009 looks at his relationship to Malcolm prior to his conviction. His proximity to the Shabazz family lends credence to his claim that he was not in attendance at the Audubon Ballroom on February 21, 1965. As many of Malcolm's close associates later noted, Johnson and Butler would both have been easily recognized as hostile loyalists to Elijah Muhammad. In the following excerpt from his interviews, Johnson describes his duties as a lieutenant and the hierarchy of command that existed within the NOI's system of enforcement. He is frank about the culture of violence that existed and the way discipline was enacted. As a minister, Malcolm was insulated from specific crimes and any disciplining of a minister had to come through Chicago's supreme captain, Raymond Sharrieff. Finally, Johnson claims that Malcolm had an illegitimate child while married to Betty Shabazz, a fact he claims was concealed within the mosque from all but a few in leadership. The following is one of Johnson's final interviews on Malcolm X and offers a compelling case for his exoneration as well as a detailed account of the violence that plagued the Nation of Islam during the 1960s.

- Transcript, Khalil Islam interview, September 29, 2004, Malcolm X Project

Transcript, Khalil Islam Oral History Interview, September 29, 2004, by Dr. Manning Marable

MANNING MARABLE: There were about five lieutenants. This was around 1961, '62?

KHALIL ISLAM: Yeah. '61, '62.

MM: Okay. Now, there was a brother who provided security for Malcolm, who we believe was in the Nation in '62, named Reuben Francis.

KI: Yeah, and Reuben Francis was just another lieutenant. Matter of fact, Reuben Francis—that's who was missing, yeah, Reuben Francis.

MM: He was also a lieutenant.

KI: He was a lieutenant, too, but see—

MM: But wasn't he also providing security for Malcolm?

KI: No. No, no. We were providing the security for Malcolm. He was just a lieutenant. He had nothing to do with Malcolm. He got involved later on, when he shot Thomas Hagan.

MM: We have photos of him selling copies of Muhammad Speaks in late '60, so he was already affiliated with the NOI by then.

KI: Oh, we all were. We were [unclear].

MM: So you did know him back then.

KI: Oh, yeah. I knew him. I know him very well. I'd have to know him, because he was a lieutenant. Yeah, I'd have to know him.

MM: So what was your response? When you became a lieutenant, you were charged by Joseph to provide security for Brother Malcolm.

KI: Right. I was assigned to him.

MM: You were assigned to him.

KI: Yeah, and that means any minister that comes in to visit, we would pick him up and bring him in; make sure he's comfortable and that he has something to eat, you know. A regular ambassador thing.

MM: When you said *we*, it was you and who else? Which other lieutenants?

KI: Well, at that time it was me and a brother named Richard, Richard [unclear]. We were in charge at that time. There wasn't a whole lot of lieutenants around; there was only two of us. Like I said, the other two prior to myself, when they left, we took over. There was always just two, unless the first lieutenant decided to ride with us that day. Sometimes Malcolm would say—he was frustrated and he didn't want to go home. I think Malcolm was very disturbed by the fact that he couldn't have a male child. He couldn't produce a male child, and it seemed to me—

MM: Did he ever talk about that?

KI: Yeah, he used to say, "Man," he says, "if I go there, all them women, no telling what I might [unclear], how I'm going to respond." And he's say, "Let's go down to Foley Square." So we would get in the car and go down to Foley Square.

MM: He would avoid going home.

KI: Yeah, if he could. That time, man, he was like—like I said, I see now that it was a big problem with him, because although he had his daughters, he definitely wanted to have a male; his image, you know. So that's something I never heard him talk about.

So let's get back to us two being with him. Anytime we went up, we'd say, "All right, Malcolm X is coming to teach this Sunday," and we'd have to be out there and make sure he's got a parking space. We would supply his family with enough food to last for a month from this Shabazz Supermarket in Brooklyn.

MM: So you would shop for the family?

KI: Well, what happened is, she always made a list for what they need, and we'd go to the supermarket.

MM: Sister Betty would.

KI: Yes. And we would go down the list, whatever. It would be enough to last for a month or better. Everything was very well taken care of. So that was my function also. From there, things just escalated.

MM: Before we get that far, can you tell me a little bit about the chain of command in Temple Seven? You have the minister and you have the captain and you have the secretary, and the lieutenants answer to the captain, correct?

KI: Right.

MM: Are all the lieutenants on the same level?

KI: No. You had a first lieutenant. He was in charge of all the other lieutenants, and anytime the captain would want something or convey something to them, he would call the first lieutenant in and give it to him, and he would bring it to us. So we had a first lieutenant, then we had the other four lieutenants under him. That's how that was.

MM: But the lieutenants are all above the rank-and-file brothers in the FOI?

KI: Right. The lieutenants are responsible to teach the martial arts to the foot soldier, where everybody on that chain was subordinate to the lieutenants, and to answer to the first and then to the captain, and that was that chain.

MM: Could you tell us—one of the things that we're trying to understand is how—and all this is all before the silencing of Malcolm—what life was like inside Mosque Seven in the early sixties when Minister Malcolm and Captain Joseph were there. We already know that back in the mid-fifties, even though Brother Joseph and Brother Malcolm had had their common experience from Detroit and had been very close friends, that there had been tension and there had been real tenseness in their relationship. We know all of this. We know about some of the conflicts over a woman before Malcolm was married to Sister Betty.

KI: And while he was married to Sister Betty.

MM: Why don't you tell us about this.

KI: There's something there, too, you see, and I was always in opposition to this, because there was this family. The father was Commissioner of Sanitation. His name was Brother Hubert, and he had a very distinguished family. He had a lot of daughters, very beautiful, tall, nice-looking girls. I was bidding for one, and I know another brother, he was bidding for one, and I'm going to tell you why I'm saying this, because we found out that Malcolm charged Elijah with having these illegitimate children.

What outside people don't know is Malcolm had an illegitimate child, also, when he was married to Betty. He said that this sister was—[unclear] this was his second theory. He didn't need no second theory. We didn't have that kind of thing there. So, the relationship—there was a child. I don't know if it was a male or a female. Only the real in-crowd knew about this. I mean, the only ones that know about this was lieutenants; maybe Secretary Maceo, maybe.

MM: How did you find out?

KI: By my affiliation, the position that I was in. See, we were [unclear]. I was looking for a wife at that time, and I wanted to marry one of those sisters. So my involvement in that respect brought this information to me. If I wasn't a lieutenant, I would have never known about that.

MM: Since you provided security for Malcolm, you had an opportunity to study the man, to observe his actions. To your knowledge, did he have relationships outside of marriage, sexual relationships with other women outside the relationship?

KI: Not women; I know this took place. Because, like I said, if I wasn't a lieutenant, I would have never been in a position to know that. Plus, like I said, I was involved. I wanted to get involved with one of the sisters, also.

MM: What kind of man was Malcolm? And again, I want you to think about how you felt about it at the time, not today, but then, when you were a member of the NOI working as a loyal lieutenant in the NOI. What was your perception of his behavior? How did you get along after you began to really provide security?

KI: I got along very well with him. Like I said, he was very [unclear]. I couldn't see anything above him. I mean, he was very qualified; there's no doubt about it, at that particular time.

MM: So you believed at that time that he was a loyal follower of Elijah Muhammad?

KI: Oh yeah. Sure. He always was. You see, jealousy played a big part in what we're trying to discuss here. I suffered from it, and I was just a little nobody. He suffered because the other ministers couldn't speak as good as he spoke, and Malcolm was getting so much attention, you see, everywhere he went. People would stand on their head to listen to him. The other ministers was jealous, so what they did was they told Elijah that "This man is trying to take over, take your position." And that's when it started, see?

That jealousy played a major part all throughout the history that I was involved in, because I suffered from the same thing, and that's why, if I can skip a little bit, that's why I became a scapegoat. They set me up because of that, because of the jealousy.

MM: We're definitely going to get there. But you touched Malcolm's family life, so because you were in a very intimate position in terms of working so closely with Malcolm—well, first of all, how many hours of the day on a given day would you spend in Malcolm's presence or near and/or around Malcolm?

KI: Only when he was in New York. Only on the days that we functioned normally, which is on a Monday and a Wednesday and at that time on Sunday.

MM: How much exposure did you have to Malcolm's family life, his personal life, his relationship with Sister Betty, his relationship with his children?

KI: Oh, like I said, we delivered their food. We provided anything they needed. Like I said, I don't care if it was raining or whatever, we had to stand out there and make sure he had a parking space in front of that temple. So anything to accommodate him and the family, we would provide that.

MM: As far as you could see, what was his relationship with his wife like?

KI: As far as I know, it was good. As far as I know, they were truly in love. How that transpired between him and that sister, I—you know, I can't say.

MM: But you didn't see any evidence at that time?

KI: No.

MM: You had just heard this because you were inside of the leadership?

KI: Yeah, well, like I said, it was a pretty big event, because the father got—you know, they didn't bring him up on charges, but there were interviews with the father about this particular incident. They were a very prominent family, they were like a showcase.

MM: Now, let me get this straight. The leadership of Temple Seven was interviewing the father of the woman that—

KI: No, no. In other words, it was like a scandal. It was a hush-hush—

MM: This daughter had become pregnant. Malcolm had impregnated her.

KI: Right.

MM: And who was it, Captain Joseph, initiated an interview? We're trying to understand what you're saying.

KI: Yeah. Well, it would have to be Captain Joseph, because he's the only one next in line. All I can remember is, is that this was a big discussion, because, like I say, it was a scandal. We didn't believe in fornication or adultery.

MM: This is prior to Malcolm being silenced.

KI: Yes.

MM: Do you remember what year this was? Was it '62, '63?

KI: Well, let me see. I had to be '62. '62 going into '63, because '64, I was hospitalized.

That's why I'm putting the [unclear portion]. I'm hospitalized with rheumatic arthritis, and when I was well enough to leave the hospital, that's at the time of the assassination. I was incarcerated in '65. Maybe it was in '63.

MM: Malcolm had a very well known moral reputation, had a reputations for being very strict morally. So, I guess, two questions. How did you learn about this alleged outside child or outside relationship; and, two, how many people knew about it? How did this come to be contained?

KI: Not many, and really, it was contained. Again, if I wasn't a lieutenant, I would have never known about this. I'm trying to get down to the lowest common denominator on this. I don't remember exactly who brought it to me, but it happened. It took place, and like I said, my closeness is what gave me the information.

MM: What came out of interviews with the father of the—

KI: Oh, I wouldn't know that. We didn't take part in that. That was above the lieutenants.

MM: So that's, again, Captain Joseph.

KI: That was Captain Joseph.

MM: What kind of man was Joseph? Could you talk about Joseph?

KI: Yeah. Well, Joseph and Malcolm, in my eyesight, was the greatest things moving at that time. I didn't see anything about them that would give me a negative reaction.

MM: We're not trying to fish; we're just trying to get a sense of what he was like. What was his personality like? How was he similar to Malcolm? How is he different from Malcolm? Just talk about him as a person.

KI: He was different only in the sense of position. The minister was the boss. The minister was the man. The captain was under him. The captain was under the minister.

MM: In a way, no, because as you recall, just before you joined, Malcolm tried to remove Joseph as captain. In fact, he removed him, and Elijah Muhammad overruled him and reinstated Joseph to that position. This was in 1959. So inside of all the temples, all the mosques, there's inherent tension between the captain and the minister, because the two functions were very different.

KI: I can tell you now. Say something would take place. I remember an incident. Malcolm gave us a certain order, instruction. There was so much going down. I'm trying to remember exactly what was it he was instructing us to do. Maybe it will come to me.

Anyway, Captain Joseph called us in the back. He said, "Listen, don't pay it no mind. I'm the one. Do what I tell you to do. Don't worry about Minister Malcolm." See, that part I remember. See, so there was a difference.

MM: Yes, they had different roles, but they were also different people. We're trying to get a sense of what kind of man he was.

KI: Well, one is spiritual, and one is military.

MM: All right. Talk about that. What does that mean to be military?

KI: Paramilitary procedures, that's what we was using at that time, which was a very poor structure. Paramilitary procedure gives the D.A. the opportunity to pinpoint anything he wants to pinpoint, because at that time no soldier would make a move without an instruction from a lieutenant. Let me give you an example.

MM: Give us an example.

KI: A brother got killed in the Bronx, okay? He was worthy of death. I mean, there was no question about that, but he got killed. The D.A. knows we use chain of command, and that works against you, because they know, like I said, nobody would make a move—if I was a lieutenant in the Bronx, and somebody got killed, it was automatic the D.A. thought I pushed the button. It wouldn't happen. It never would happen. I don't know if that's easy for you to understand or not.

MM: Yes, we understand.

KI: Nobody would even think about making a move if there wasn't a direct order from a lieutenant which comes down from the top. So that was a very bad procedure, very bad. It worked against us, see, because they know. So there's a lot of things that was going on at that time that wasn't too healthy for us, but that's what we was using, paramilitary procedure.

MM: Tell me about the role of the enforcer. This is a term that's been used to describe members of the Fruit of Islam, whether they be lieutenants or whether they be foot soldiers. Who would do the dirty work that had to be done? Who would do the disciplining, either within the ranks or perhaps outside? Tell me a little bit about that process. How did that happen? How would the order come down, and how would it get carried out?

KI: Well, it would have to come from Captain Joseph. The lieutenants is the ones who would carry it out; they would execute it.

MM: What would that mean? Tell me about the different means of disciplining.

KI: Whatever. If a brother was totally—he was so extreme—I look back on it now and I say, my god, I had a part in that? Say a brother got caught smoking a cigarette. The would throw him down a flight of stairs.

MM: What do you mean? Who is *they*?

KI: The lieutenants. Or they don't even have to be the lieutenants; it could be any foot soldier. If I'm disturbed about something, I mean, I have to tell the people under me what to do.

MM: Let's say somebody who was a member of Seven violates tenets of the faith, and Captain Joseph decides that the person should be punished. We're trying to understand the exact procedure of how that person ends up being thrown down a flight of steps. Joseph would call in the first lieutenant or perhaps the group lieutenants and give a direct order. Is that what you're saying?

KI: Captain Joseph never talked to us directly. He would talk to the first lieutenant. Then anybody brought up on charges, when we have our big meeting, the would have that mother and they would march him up in front of the whole body, everybody in the temple.

MM: All the [unclear]?

KI: Everybody in the temple.

MM: Including women?

KI: Everybody in the temple. Then we read off the charges. If it was fornication or adultery, he was put in Class F. Class F means defier. Anything outside the temple was deifier, because it was the chaos of this society.

MM: He was excommunicated.

KI: Yes, exiled. He couldn't come to the mosque. He couldn't come to none of the businesses. We couldn't affiliate ourselves with him.

MM: Wasn't this silence; in effect, being silenced?

KI: What do you mean?

MM: In the sense that he could not—what, he was exiled. He was sent out.

KI: He was persona non grata, and the membership couldn't with him.

MM: You couldn't talk to the person. You couldn't—right.

KI: If you was caught in any kind of way affiliating yourself with this particular person, you might get some time out, and nobody wanted to get time out of the temple. That's the worst thing that could happen to you, see, so that's how it was done. Bring them up on charges, whatever it was.

These incidents I'm telling you about sometimes when a brother may have wound up flying down a flight of stairs, you know, that was a—I don't know if you know the staircase in [unclear] temple. It's still there. I don't know if you know how long that thing—it's pretty long, about two flights of stairs, marble, you know, and brothers that sometimes they got sassy out of their mouth or they disrespected the captain, on their way out he would have an accident, and he would just fall down the stairs. So it wasn't nothing direct from up top.

MM: So what you're saying is Captain Joseph wouldn't necessarily have to give a specific order.

KI: No.

MM: But if he felt that some member needed to be disciplined, if he didn't give a direct order to the first lieutenant or to one of the lieutenants, how would that message get communicated?

KI: Just by my understanding, my love for the religion. This guy is in violation, and I don't like that.

MM: That's what captain would say, "This man is in violation"?

KI: No. No, he wouldn't have said that. I'm saying that. See, like I say, it don't have to always come from an order from the top.

MM: I see. So you had some autonomy. You had some autonomy to discipline the membership.

KI: Yeah, see, because anybody that was really loyal and dedicated, anybody that violated in any sense was so—hey, something's got to happen to this guy.

MM: Did Malcolm ever give a specific order for a brother or sister to be disciplined?

KI: No.

MM: That was the captain's role?

KI: Yeah.

MM: But Malcolm was aware of it.

KI: He was aware of it, yeah.

MM: Did Malcolm ever witness people being disciplined?

KI: Not that I know of. Not that I know of. No, nothing ever happened. He would never be on the scene when something like that would take place. We made sure of that, see, because it's just like—in one sense, it may sound a lot like an ambiguous statement, because I remember one time I did something and the brother reported me to the captain, and the captain was infuriated. He called me in, and he berated me something terrible, you know, in front of these particular people. After they left, he said, "Keep up the good work, now. [Unclear] next time." You see, so—you know.

MM: It was just for show.

KI: Yeah.

MM: But you knew the real deal, which was that violators were to be punished harshly.

KI: Well, it depends on—I'll give you another incident. He was a minister. This was unheard of at that time. He had a suite, what you call—we used to call it a kitchenette. Now they call them studio apartments. He had one, and he was smoking a lot of reefer, and he had sisters there. They were fornicating and whatever, you know. So when it was reported, I wasn't on this particular event, but when it was reported, the rest of the lieutenants, from what I found, they went up there, and they damn near kicked his spleen out. They hurt him bad. They kicked him out, because, like I say, that's unheard of, man, violating like that. We didn't even believe in smoking a cigarette. You know what happened to a guy who committed fornication . . .

MM: This was an assistant minister.

KI: No, this was a minister.

MM: Was this in Washington, D.C.?

KI: No, this was here. Minister Adam.

MM: Minister—

KI: Minister Adam.

MM: Adam.

KI: That's right.

MM: So he was put out for good.

KI: I think he felt blessed at not having any more time with us, see, so he just disappeared.

MM: So, in a sense, then, any member, if they violate, no member is above the captain, because the captain can call for the disciplining of anybody, and the lieutenants carry it out. So even though a minister technically is higher than a lieutenant, if that minister is in transgression, and the captain okays it, then the lieutenant could discipline that minister.

KI: No, a lieutenant cannot discipline a minister. The only one can do that is the captain, and that had to be done through the supreme captain in Chicago. They would have a big council, and that's how that came down. They would call in all the captains from all over the United States.

MM: Right. Raymond Sharrieff.

KI: Right. Raymond Sharrieff, and he would decide, because the lieutenant cannot reach that high.

MM: Did Malcolm ever object to the violence that was going on?

KI: Not that I know of, because it wasn't his position. In other words, whatever took place, we had a policy; don't let the minister know. Don't involve him in this. Don't even let him hear about it, see, because that puts him in a bad position. See, so be particular.

Let me show you another instance. A guy made a statement one day. He says, "One day Captain Joseph is going to turn around looking down the barrel of a muzzle." That's a threat. Didn't nobody have to tell me to retaliate for that.

Out of respect for Joseph, I kept my cool. I said, "Who's this guy? He's [unclear]. Come on, [unclear]. You can't make a statement about my captain like that." The captain didn't tell me to do that. See, and that's how I became—I became [unclear], because he took his business. They used to call me Dirty Red, because anytime they see me coming, they know there's going to be some action.

PART III

ARTICLES

James Baldwin, "Malcolm and Martin," *Esquire*, vol. 77, no. 4 (April 1972): 94–97, 195–196, 198, 201–202

"By the time each met his death, there was practically no difference between them"

Since Martin's death, in Memphis, and that tremendous day in Atlanta, something has altered in me, something has gone away. Perhaps even more than the death itself, the manner of his death has forced me into a judgment concerning human life and human beings which I have always been reluctant to make—indeed, I can see that a great deal of what the knowledgeable would call my life-style is dictated by this reluctance. Incontestably, alas, most people are not, in action, worth very much; and yet every human being is an unprecedented miracle. One tries to treat them as the miracles they are, while trying to protect oneself against the disasters they've become. This is not very different from the act of faith demanded by all those marches and petitions while Martin was still alive. One could scarcely be deluded by Americans anymore, one scarcely dared expect anything from the great, vast, blank generality; and yet one was compelled to demand of Americans—and for their sakes, after all—a generosity, a clarity, and a nobility which they did not dream of demanding of themselves. Part of the error was irreducible, in that the marchers and petitioners were forced to suppose the existence of an entity which, when the chips were down, could not be located—i.e., there *are* no American people yet. Perhaps, however, the moral of the story (and the hope of the world) lies in what one demands, not of others, but of oneself. However that may be, the failure and the betrayal are in the record book forever, and sum up and condemn, forever, those descendants of a barbarous Europe who arbitrarily and arrogantly reserve the right to call themselves Americans.

The mind is a strange and terrible vehicle, moving according to rigorous rules of its own; and my own mind, after I had left

Atlanta, began to move backward in time, to places, people, and events I thought I had forgotten. Sorrow drove it there, I think, sorrow, and a certain kind of bewilderment, triggered, perhaps, by something which happened to me in connection with Martin's funeral.

When Martin was murdered, I was based in Hollywood, working—working, in fact, on the screen version of *The Autobiography of Malcolm X*. This was a difficult assignment, since I had known Malcolm, after all, crossed swords with him, worked with him, and held him in that great esteem which is not easily distinguishable, if it is distinguishable at all, from love. (The Hollywood gig did not work out because I did not wish to be a party to a second assassination: but we will return to Hollywood, presently.)

Very shortly before his death, I had to appear with Martin at Carnegie Hall, in New York. Having been on the Coast for so long, I had nothing suitable to wear for my Carnegie Hall gig, and so I rushed out, got a dark suit, got it fitted, and made my appearance. Something like two weeks later, I wore this same suit to Martin's funeral; returned to Hollywood; presently, had to come East again, on business. I ran into Leonard Lyons one night, and I told him that I would never be able to wear that suit again. Leonard put this in his column. I went back to Hollywood.

Weeks later, either because of a Civil Rights obligation, or because of Columbia Pictures, I was back in New York. On my desk in New York were various messages—and it must be said that my sister, Gloria, who worked for me then, is extremely selective, not to say brutal, about the messages she leaves on my desk. I don't see, simply, most of the messages I get. I couldn't conceivably live with them. No one could—as Gloria knows. However, my best friend, black, when I had been in junior high school, when I was twelve or thirteen, had been calling and calling and calling. The guilt of the survivor is a real guilt—as I was now to discover. In a way that I may never be able to make real for my countrymen, or myself, the fact that I had "made it"; that is, had been seen on television, and at Sardi's, could (presumably!) sign a check anywhere in

the world, could, in short, for the length of an entrance, a dinner, or a drink, intimidate headwaiters by the use of a name
which had not been mine when I was born and which love had
compelled me to make my own, meant that I had betrayed the
people who had produced me. Nothing could be more unutter-
ably paradoxical: to have thrown in your lap what you never
dreamed of getting, and, in sober, bitter truth, could never
have dreamed of having, and that at the price of an assumed
betrayal of your brothers and your sisters! One is always dis-
proving the accusation in action as futile as it is inevitable.

I had not seen this friend—who could scarcely, any longer,
be called a friend—in many years. I was brighter, or more
driven than he—not my fault!—and, though neither of us knew
it then, our friendship really ended during my ministry and was
deader than my hope of heaven by the time I left the pulpit, the
church, and home. Hindsight indicates, obviously, that this
particular rupture, which was, of necessity, exceedingly brutal
and which involved, after all, the deliberate repudiation of everything and everyone that had given me an identity until that
moment, must have left some scars. The current of my life
meant that I did not see this person very often, but I was always
terribly guilty when I did. I was guilty because I had nothing to
say to him, and at one time I had told him everything, or nearly
everything. I was guilty because he was just another post-office
worker, and we had dreamed such tremendous futures for ourselves. I was guilty because he and his family had been very
nice to me during an awful time in my life and now none of
that meant anything to me. I was guilty because I knew, at the
bottom of my heart, that I judged this unremarkable colored
man very harshly, far more harshly than I would have done if
he were white, and I knew this to be unjust as well as sinister. I
was furious because he thought my life was easy and I thought
my life was hard, and I yet had to see that by his lights, certainly, and by any ordinary yardstick, my life was enviable
compared to his. And if, as I kept saying, it was not my fault, it
was not *his* fault, either.

You can certainly see why I tended to avoid my old school
chum. But I called him, of course. I thought that he probably

needed money, because that was the only thing, by now, that I could possibly hope to give him. But, no. He, or his wife, or a relative, had read the Leonard Lyons column and knew that I had a suit I wasn't wearing, and—as he remembered in one way and I in quite another—he was just my size.

Now, for me, that suit was drenched in the blood of all the crimes of my country. If I had said to Leonard, somewhat melodramatically, no doubt, that I could never wear it again, I was, just the same, being honest. I simply could not put it on, or look at it, without thinking of Martin, and Martin's end, of what he had meant to me, and to so many. I could not put it on without a bleak, pale, cold wonder about the future. I could not, in short, live with it, it was too heavy a garment. Yet—it was only a suit, worn, at most, three times. It was not a very expensive suit, but it was still more expensive than any my friend could buy. He could not afford to have suits in his closet which he didn't wear, he couldn't afford to throw suits away— he couldn't, in short, afford my elegant despair. Martin was dead, but *he* was living, he needed a suit, and—I was just his size. He invited me for dinner that evening, and I said that I would bring him the suit.

The American situation being what it is, and American taxi drivers being what they mostly are, I have, in effect, been forbidden to expose myself to the quite tremendous hazards of getting a cab to stop for me in New York, and have been forced to hire cars. Naturally, the car which picked me up on that particular guilty evening was a Cadillac limousine about seventy-three blocks long, and, naturally, the chauffeur was white. Neither did he want to drive a black man through Harlem to the Bronx, but American democracy has always been at the mercy of the dollar: the chauffeur may not have liked the gig, but he certainly wasn't about to lose the bread. Here we were, then, this terrified white man and myself, trapped in this leviathan, eyed bitterly, as it passed, by a totally hostile population. But it was not the chauffeur which the population looked on with such wry contempt: I held the suit over my arm, and was tempted to wave it: *I'm only taking a suit to a friend!*

I knew how they felt about black men in limousines—unless they were popular idols—and I couldn't blame them, and I knew that I could never explain. We found the house, and, with the suit over my arm, I mounted the familiar stairs.

I was no longer the person my friend and his family had known and loved—I was a stranger now, and keenly aware of it, and trying hard to act, as it were, normally. But nothing *can* be normal in such a situation. They *had* known me, and they *had* loved me; but now they couldn't be blamed for feeling, *He thinks he's too good for us now.* I certainly didn't feel that, but I had no conceivable relationship to them anymore—that shy, popeyed thirteen-year-old my friend's mother had scolded and loved was no more. *I* was not the same, but *they* were, as though they had been trapped, preserved, in that moment in time. They seemed scarcely to have grown any older, my friend and his mother, and they greeted me as they had greeted me years ago, though I was now well past forty and felt every hour of it. My friend and I remained alike only in that neither of us had gained any weight. His face was as boyish as ever, and his voice; only a touch of grey in his hair proved that we were no longer at P.S. 139. And my life came with me into their small, dark, unspeakably respectable, incredibly hard-won rooms like the roar of champagne and the odor of brimstone. They still believed in the Lord, but I had quarreled with Him, and offended Him, and walked out of His house. They didn't smoke, but they knew (from seeing me on television) that I did, and they had placed about the room, in deference to me, those hideous little ashtrays which can hold exactly one cigarette butt. And there was a bottle of whiskey, too, and they asked me if I wanted steak or chicken; for, in my travels, I might have learned not to like fried chicken anymore. I said, much relieved to be able to tell the truth, that I preferred chicken. I gave my friend the suit.

My friend's stepdaughter is young, considers herself a militant, and we had a brief argument concerning Bill Styron's *Nat Turner*, which I suggested that she read before condemning. This rather shocked the child, whose militancy, like that of many, tends to be a matter of indigestible fury and slogans and quotations. It rather checked the company, which had not imagined that I and a black militant could possibly disagree about anything. But what was most striking about our brief exchange was that it obliquely revealed how little the girl respected her stepfather. She appeared not to respect him at all. This was not revealed by anything she said to him, but by the fact that she said nothing to him. She barely looked at him. He didn't count.

I always think that this is a terrible thing to happen to a man, especially in his own house, and I am always terribly humiliated for the man to whom it happens. Then, of course, you get angry at the man for allowing it to happen.

And *how* had it happened? He had never been the brightest boy in the world, nobody is, but he had been energetic, active, funny; wrestling, playing handball, cheerfully submitting to being tyrannized by me, even to the extent of kneeling before the altar and having his soul saved—my insistence had accomplished that. I looked at him and remembered his sweating and beautiful face that night as he wrestled on the church floor and we prayed him through. I remembered his older brother, who had died in Sicily, in battle for the free world—he had barely had time to see Sicily before he died and had assuredly never seen the free world. I remembered the day he came to see me to tell me that his sister, who had been very ill, had died. We sat on the steps of the tenement, he was looking down as he told me, one finger making a circle on the step, and his tears splashed on the wood. We were children then, his sister had not been much older, and he was the youngest and now the only boy. But this was not *how* it had happened, although I thought I could see, watching his widowed mother's still very handsome face watching him, how her human need might have held and trapped and frozen him. She had been sewing in the garment center all the years I knew them, rushing home to get supper on the table before her husband got home from *his* job; at night, and on Sundays, he was a deacon; and God knows, or should, where his energy came from. When I began working for the garment center, I used to see her, from time to time, rushing to catch the bus, in a crowd of black and Puerto Rican ladies.

And, yes, we had all loved each other then, and I had had great respect for my friend, who was handsomer than I, and more athletic, and more popular, and who beat me in every game I was foolish enough to play with him. I had gone my way and life had accomplished its inexorable mathematic—and what in the world was I by now but an aging, lonely, sexually dubious, politically outrageous, unspeakably erratic freak? His old friend. And what was *he* now? He worked for the Post Office and was building a house next door to his mother, in, I think, Long Island. They too, then, had made it. But what I could not understand was how nothing seemed to have touched this man. We are living through what our church described as "these last and evil days," through wars and rumors of wars, to say the least. He could, for example, have known something about the anti-poverty program if only because his wife was more or less involved in it. He should have known something about the then raging school battle, if only because his step-daughter was a student; and she, whether or not she had thought her position through, was certainly involved. She may have hoped, at one time anyway, for his clarity and his help. But, no. He seemed as little touched by the cataclysm in his house and all around him as he was by the mail he handled every day. I found this unbelievable, and, given my temperament and our old connection, maddening. We got into a battle about the war in Vietnam. I probably really should not have allowed this to happen, but it was partly the stepdaughter's prodding. And I was astounded that my friend would defend this particular racist folly. What for? For his job at the Post Office? And the answer came back at once, alas—yes. For his job at the Post Office. I told him that Americans had no business at all in Vietnam, and that black people certainly had no business there, aiding the slave master to enslave yet more millions of dark people, and also identifying themselves with the white American crimes: we, the blacks, are going to need our allies, for the Americans, odd as it may sound at the moment, will presently have none. It wasn't, I said, hard to understand why a black boy, standing, futureless, on the corner, would decide to join the Army, nor was it hard to decipher the slave master's reasons for hoping that he wouldn't live to come home, with a gun; but it wasn't necessary, after all, to defend it: to defend, that is, one's murder and one's murderers. "Wait a minute," he said, "let me stand up and tell you what I think we're trying to do there." "*We?*" I cried. "What motherf——ing *we*? You stand up, motherf——er, and I'll kick you in the ass!"

He looked at me. His mother conveyed—but the good Lord knows I had hurt her—that she didn't want that language in her house, and that I had never talked that way before. And I love the lady. I had meant no disrespect. I stared at my friend, my old friend, and felt millions of people staring at us both. I tried to make a kind of joke out of it all. But it was too late. The way they looked at me proved that I had tipped my hand. And *this* hurt *me*. They should have known me better, or at least enough to have known that I meant what I said. But the general reaction to famous people who hold difficult opinions is that they can't really mean it. It's considered, generally, to be merely an astute way of attracting public attention, a way of making oneself interesting: one marches in Montgomery, for example, merely (in my own case) to sell one's books. Well. There is nothing, then, to be said. There went the friendly fried chicken dinner. There went the loving past. I watched the mother watching me, wondering what had happened to her beloved Jimmy, and giving me up: her sourest suspicions confirmed. In great weariness I poured myself yet another stiff drink, by now definitively condemned, and lit another cigarette, they watching me all the while for symptoms of cancer, and with a precipice at my feet.

For that bloody suit was *their* suit, after all, it had been bought *for* them, it had even been bought *by* them: *they* had created Martin, he had not created them, and the blood in which the fabric of that suit was stiffening was theirs. The distance between us, and I had never thought of this before, was that they didn't know this, and I now dared to realize that I loved them more than they loved me. And I do not mean that my love was greater: Who dares judge the inexpressible expense another pays for his life? Who knows how much one is loved, by whom, or what that love may be called on to do? No, the way the cards had fallen meant that I had to face more about them than they could know about me, knew their rent, whereas they did not know mine, and was condemned to make them uncomfortable. For, on the other hand, they certainly wanted that freedom which they thought was mine—that frightening limousine, for example, or the power to give away a suit, or my increasingly terrifying transatlantic journeys. How can one say that freedom is taken, not given, and that no one is free until all are free? and that the price is high.

My friend tried on the suit, a perfect fit, and they all admired him in it, and I went home.

Alex Haley edited *The Autobiography of Malcolm X*. Months before the foregoing, in New York, he and Elia Kazan and I had agreed to do it as a play—and I still wish we had. We were vaguely aware that Hollywood was nibbling for the book, but, as Hollywood is always nibbling, it occurred to no one, certainly not to me, to take these nibbles seriously. It simply was not a subject which Hollywood could manage, and I didn't see any point in talking to them about it. But the book was sold to an independent producer, who would produce it for Columbia Pictures. By this time, I was in London; and I was also on the spot. For, while I didn't believe Hollywood could do it, I didn't quite see, since they declared themselves sincerely and seriously willing to attempt it, how I could duck the challenge. What it came to, in fact, was an enormous question: to what extent was I prepared again to gamble on the good faith of my countrymen?

In that time, now so incredibly far behind us, when the Black Muslims meant to the American people exactly what the Black Panthers mean today, and when they were described in exactly the same terms by that High Priest, J. Edgar Hoover, and when many of us believed or made ourselves believe that the American state still contained within itself the power of self-confrontation, the power to change itself in the direction of honor and knowledge and freedom, or, as Malcolm put it, "to atone," I first met Malcolm X. Perhaps it says a great deal about the black American experience, both negatively and positively, that so many should have believed so hard, so long, and paid such a price for believing: but what this betrayed belief says about white Americans is very accurately and abjectly summed up by the present, so-called "Nixon Administration."

I had heard a great deal about Malcolm, as had everyone else, and I was a little afraid of him, as was everyone else, and I was further handicapped by having been out of the country for so long. When I returned to America, I went South, and thus, imperceptibly, found myself mainly on the road. I saw Malcolm before I met him. I had just returned from someplace like Savannah, I was giving a lecture somewhere in New York, and Malcolm was sitting in the first or second row of the hall, bending forward at such an angle that his long arms nearly caressed the ankles of his long legs, staring up at me. I very nearly panicked. I knew Malcolm only by legend, and this legend, since I was a Harlem street boy, I was sufficiently astute to distrust. I distrusted the legend because we, in Harlem, have been betrayed so often. Malcolm might be the torch white people claimed he was—though, in general, white America's evaluations of these matters would be laughable and even pathetic did not these evaluations have such wicked results—or he might be the hustler I remembered from my pavements. On the other hand, Malcolm had no reason to trust me, either— and so I stumbled through my lecture, with Malcolm never taking his eyes from my face.

It must be remembered that in those great days I was considered to be an "integrationist"—this was never quite my own idea of myself—and Malcolm was considered to be a "racist in reverse." This formulation, in terms of power—and power is the arena in which racism is acted out—means absolutely nothing: it may even be described as a cowardly formulation. The powerless, by definition, can never be "racists," for they can never make the world pay for what they feel or fear except by the suicidal endeavor which makes of them fanatics or revolutionaries, or both; whereas, those in power can be urbane and charming and invite you to those houses which they know you will never own. The powerless must do their own dirty work. The powerful have it done for them.

Anyway: somewhat later, I was the host, or moderator, for a radio program starring Malcolm X and a sit-in student from the Deep South. I was the moderator because both the radio station and I were afraid that Malcolm would simply eat the boy alive. I didn't want to be there, but there was no way out of it. I had come prepared to throw various campstools under the child, should he seem wobbly; to throw out the lifeline whenever Malcolm should seem to be carrying the child beyond his depth. Never has a moderator been less needed. Malcolm understood that child, and talked to him as though he were talking to a younger brother, and with that same watchful attention. What most struck me was that he was not at all trying to proselytize the child: he was trying to make him think. He was trying to do for the child what he supposed, for too long a time, that the Honorable Elijah had done for him. But I did not think of that until much later. I will never forget Malcolm and that child facing each other, and Malcolm's extraordinary gentleness. And that's the truth about Malcolm: he was one of the gentlest people I have ever met. And I am sure that the child remembers him that way. That boy, by the way, battling so valiantly for civil rights, might have been, for all I can swear to, Stokely Carmichael or Huey Newton or Bobby Seale or Rap Brown or one of my nephews. That's how long or how short—*oh, pioneers!*—the apprehension of betrayal takes: "If you are an American citizen," Malcolm asked the boy, "why have you got to fight for your rights as a citizen? To be a citizen means that you have the rights of a citizen. If you haven't got the rights of a citizen, then you're not a citizen." "It's not as simple as that," the boy said. "Why not?" asked Malcolm.

I was in some way in those years, without entirely realizing it, the Great Black Hope of the Great White Father. I was *not* a racist—so I thought; Malcolm was a racist, so *he* thought. In fact, we were simply trapped in the same situation, as poor

Martin was later to discover (who, in those days, did not talk to Malcolm and was a little nervous with me). As the G.B.H. of the G.W.F., anyway, I appeared on a television program, along with Malcolm and several other hopes, including Mr. George S. Schuyler. It was pretty awful. If I had ever hoped to become a racist, Mr. Schuyler dashed my hopes forever, then and there. I can scarcely discuss this program except to say that Malcolm and I very quickly dismissed Mr. Schuyler and virtually everyone else and, as old street rats and the heirs of Baptists ministers, played the program off each other.

Nothing could have been more familiar to me than Malcolm's style in debate. I had heard it all my life. It was vehemently nonstop and Malcolm was young and looked younger; this caused his opponents to suppose that Malcolm was reckless. Nothing could have been less reckless, more calculated, even to those loopholes he so often left dangling. These were not loopholes at all, but hangman's knots, as whoever rushed for the loophole immediately discovered. Whenever this happened, the strangling interlocutor invariably looked to me, as being the more "reasonable," to say something which would loosen the knot. Mr. Schuyler often *did* say something, but it was always the wrong thing, giving Malcolm yet another opportunity. All I could do was elaborate on some of Malcolm's points, or modify, or emphasize, or seem to try to clarify, but there was no way I could disagree with him. The others were discussing the past or the future, or a country which may once have existed, or one which may yet be brought into existence—Malcolm was speaking of the bitter and unanswerable present. And it was too important that this be heard for anyone to attempt to soften it. It was important, of course, for white people to hear it, if they were still able to hear; but it was of the utmost importance for black people to hear it, for the sake of their morale. It was important for them to know that there was someone like them in public life, telling the truth about their condition. Malcolm considered himself to be the spiritual property of the people who produced him. He did not consider himself to be their savior, he was far too modest for that, and gave that role to another; but he considered himself to be their servant and, in order not to betray that trust, he was willing to die, and died. Malcolm was not a racist, not even when he thought he was. His intelligence was more complex than that; furthermore, if he had been a racist, not many in this racist country would have considered him dangerous. He would have sounded familiar and even comforting, his familiar rage confirming the reality of white power, and sensuously inflaming a bizarre species of guilty eroticism without which, I am beginning to believe, most white Americans of the more or less liberal persuasion cannot draw a single breath. What made him unfamiliar and dangerous was not his hatred for white people but his love for blacks, his apprehension of the horror of the black condition and the reasons for it, and his determination so to work on their hearts and minds that they would be enabled to see their condition and change it themselves.

For this, after all, not only were no white people needed; they posed, *en bloc*, the very greatest obstacle to black self-knowledge and had to be considered a menace. But white people have played so dominant a role in the world's history for so long that such an attitude toward them constitutes the most disagreeable of novelties; and it may be added that, though they have never learned how to live with the darker brother, they do not look forward to having to learn how to live without him. Malcolm, finally, was a genuine revolutionary, a virile impulse long since fled from the American way of life—in himself, indeed, he was a kind of revolution, both in the sense of a return to a former principle and in the sense of an upheaval. It is pointless to speculate on his probable fate had he been legally white. Given the white man's options, it is probably just as well for all of us that he was legally black. In some church someday, so far unimagined and unimaginable, he will be hailed as a saint. Of course this day waits on the workings of the temporal power which Malcolm understood, at last, so well. Rome, for example, has desanctified some saints and invented, if one dares to use so utilitarian a word in relation to so divine an activity, others, and the Pope has been to Africa, driven there no doubt, however belatedly, by his concern for the souls of black folk: who dares imagine the future of such a litany as *black like me*! Malcolm, anyway, had this much in common with all real saints and prophets, he had the power, if not to drive the money changers from the temple, to tell the world what they were doing there.

For reasons I will never understand, on the day I realized that a play based on *The Autobiography* was not going to be done, that sooner or later I would have to say yes or no to the idea of doing a movie, I flew to Geneva. I will never know why I flew to Geneva, which is far from being my favorite town. I will never know how it is that I arrived there with no toilet articles whatever, no toothbrush, no toothpaste, no razor, no hairbrush, no comb, and virtually no clothes. Furthermore, I have a brother-in-law and a sister-in-law living in Geneva of whom I'm very fond and it didn't even occur to me that they were there. All that I seem to have brought with me is *The Autobiography*. And I sat in the hotel bedroom all the weekend long, with the blinds drawn, reading and rereading—or, rather, endlessly traversing—the great jungle of Malcolm's book.

The problems involved in a cinematic translation were clearly going to be formidable, and wisdom very strongly urged that I have nothing to do with it. It could not possibly bring me anything but grief. I still would have much preferred to have done it as a play, but that possibility was gone. I had grave doubts and fears about Hollywood. I had been there before, and I had not liked it. The idea of Hollywood doing a truthful job on Malcolm could not but seem preposterous. And yet—I didn't want to spend the rest of my life thinking: *It could have been done if you hadn't been chicken*. I felt that Malcolm would never have forgiven me for that. He had trusted me in life and I believed he trusted me in death, and that trust, as far as I was concerned, was my obligation.

From Geneva I eventually went to London, to join my brother and sister. It was from London that I wired Kazan to say that the play was off, and I was doing the movie. This was only to take K. off the hook, for I wired no one else, had made

no agreement to do the movie, and was very troubled and uncertain in my own mind.

Every new environment, particularly if one knows that one
must make the effort to accustom oneself to working in it,
risks being more than a little traumatic. One finds oneself ner-
vously examining one's new surroundings, searching for the
terms of the adjustment; therefore, in the beginning, I made a
somewhat too conscious effort to be pleased by Hollywood.
There was the sky, after all, which New Yorkers seldom see,
and there was space, which New Yorkers have forgotten, there
was the mighty and dramatic Pacific, there were the hills.
Some very valuable and attractive people had lived and functioned here for years, I reminded myself, and there was really
no reason why I could not—so I insisted to myself. I had a few
friends and acquaintances here already, scattered from Watts
to Baldwin Hills to Mulholland Drive, and I was sure they'd
be happy if I decided to stay. If I were going to be in Hollywood for months, there was no point in raising the odds
against me by hating it, or despising it; besides, such an attitude seemed too obvious a defense against my fear of it. As
hotels go, the Beverly Hills is more congenial than most and
certainly everyone there was very nice to me. And so I tried—
too hard—to look about me with wonder, and be pleased. But
I was already in trouble, and the odds against the venture were
very long odds indeed.

I was actually in the Beverly Hills until more permanent
lodging could be found. This was not easy, since it involved
finding someone to take care of me—to keep house, cook, and
drive. I was no help, since I was still, at the beginning of 1968,
committed to various fund-raising functions in the East. Part
of the irreducible conflict which was to drive both Columbia
Pictures and myself up the wall was already implicit during
those early days at The Beverly Hills Hotel. The conflict was
simply between my life as a writer and my life as—not spokesman exactly, but public witness to the situation of black people.
I had to play both roles: there was nothing anyone, including
myself, could do about it. This was an unprecedented situation

for Columbia, which, after all, had me under exclusive contract and didn't really like my dashing off, making public
appearances. It was an unprecedented situation for me, too,
since I had never before been under exclusive contract, and I
had always juggled my conflicting schedules as best I could. I
had lived with my two roles for a long time, and had even, insofar as this is ever true, begun to get used to them—I accepted, anyway, that the dichotomy wasn't likely to end soon.
But it didn't make the Hollywood scene any easier. It wasn't a
matter of wiping the slate clean of existing commitments and
then vanishing behind the typewriter, nor was it even a matter
of keeping outside commitments to a minimum, though I
tried: events were moving much faster than that, creating perpetual crises and making ever new demands. Columbia
couldn't but be concerned about the time and energy I ex-
pended on matters remote from the scenario. On the other
hand, I couldn't really regret it, since it seemed to me that in
this perpetual and bitter ferment I was learning something
which kept me in touch with reality and would deepen the
truth of the scenario.

But I anticipate. People have their environments: The Beverly
Hills Hotel was not mine. For no reason that I could easily
name, its space, its opulence, its shapelessness depressed and
frightened me. The people in the bar, the lounge, the halls, the
walks, the swimming pool, the shops, seemed as rootless as I,
seemed unreal. In spite—perhaps because of—all my efforts to
feel relaxed and free and at home (for America *is* my home!), I
began to feel unreal—almost as though I were playing an unworthy part in a cheap, unworthy drama. I, who have spent
half my life in hotels, sometimes woke up in the middle of the
night, terrified, wondering where I was. But, though I scarcely
realized it and might even have been ashamed to admit it to
myself, I think that this had partly to do with the fact that I
was the only dark person in the hotel. I must stress that in no
way whatever did anyone in the hotel ever make me feel this,
nor, indeed, did I ever consciously feel it—it's only now, in
looking back, that I suspect that it had to be partly that. My

presence in the hotel was absolutely unquestioned, even by people who did not know who I was, or who thought I was Sammy
Davis. It was simply taken for granted that I would not have
been in the hotel if I had not belonged there. This, irrationally
enough, got to me—*did* I belong there? In any case, thousands
of black people, miles away, did *not* belong there, though some
of them sometimes came to visit me there. (People had to come
and get me or come to visit me, because I do not drive.) The
drive from Beverly Hills to Watts and back again is a long and
loaded drive—I sometimes felt as though my body were being
stretched across those miles. I don't think I felt anything so
trivial as guilt, guilt at what appeared to be my comparative
good fortune, I knew more about comparative fortunes than
that, but I felt a stunning helplessness. These two worlds would
never meet, and that fact prefigured disaster for my countrymen and me. It caused me to look about me with an intensity of
wonder which had no pleasure in it.

It began to be very clear that I was never really going to get
any work done in the Beverly Hills—my suite was one of the
busiest in that busy hotel—and so the producer found a cook-
chauffeur, and bundled me south to Palm Springs. There, in
that millionaire's graveyard, I actually began to work. Truman
Capote was there one weekend, thank heaven, and we had a
few drinks together, but he then, very sensibly, left. I took it as
long as I could, the sunshine as bland as milk and honey, the
eerie streets paved with gold, the thunderous silence of wealth,
and then I went north again, to a house in Benedict Canyon.

There is a day in Palm Springs, shortly before I left there, that
I will remember forever, a bright day. Billy Dee Williams had
come to town, and he was staying at the house; and a lot of the
day had been spent with a very bright, young lady reporter,
who was interviewing me about the film version of Malcolm. I
felt very confident that day—I was never to feel so confident
again—and I talked very freely to the reporter. (Too freely, the
producer was to tell me later.) I had decided to lay my cards on
the table and to state, as clearly as I could, what I felt the movie

was about, and how I intended to handle it. I thought that this might make things simpler later on, but I was wrong about that. The studio and I were at loggerheads, really, from the moment I stepped off the plane. Anyway, I had opted for candor, or a reasonable facsimile of same, and sounded as though I were in charge of the film, as, indeed, by my lights, for that moment, certainly, I had to be. I was really in a difficult position because both by temperament and experience I tend to work alone, and I dread making announcements concerning my work. But I was in a very public position, and I thought that I had better make my own announcements, rather than have them made for me. The studio, on the other hand, did not want me making announcements of any kind at all. So there we were, and this particular tension, since it got to the bloody heart of the matter—the question of by whose vision, precisely, this film was to be controlled—was not to be resolved until I finally threw up my hands and walked away.

I very much wanted Billy Dee for Malcolm, and since no one else had any other ideas, I didn't see why this couldn't work out. In brutal Hollywood terms, Poitier is the only really big, black, box-office star, and this fact gave me, as I considered it, a free hand. To tell the bitter truth, from the very first days we discussed it, I had never had any intention of allowing the Columbia brass to cast this part: I was determined to take my name off the production if I were overruled. Call this boneheaded stupidity, or insufferable arrogance or what you will—I had made my decision, and once I had made it nothing could make me waver, and nothing could make me alter it. If there were errors in my concept of the film, and if I made errors on the way to and in the execution, well, then, I would have to pay for my errors. But one can learn from one's errors. What one cannot survive is allowing other people to make your errors for you, discarding your own vision, in which at least you believe, for someone else's vision, in which you do *not* believe.

Anyway, all that shit had yet to hit the fan. This day, the girl and Billy and I had a few drinks by the swimming pool. The man, Walter, was about to begin preparing supper. The girl got up to leave and we walked her to her car and came back to the swimming pool, jubilant.

The phone had been brought out to the pool, and now it rang. Billy was on the other side of the pool, doing what I took to be African improvisations to the sound of Aretha Franklin. And I picked up the phone.

It was David Moses. It took a while before the sound of his voice—I don't mean the *sound* of his voice, something *in* his voice—got through to me.

He said, "Jimmy? Martin's just been shot," and I don't think I said anything, or felt anything. I'm not sure I knew who *Martin* was. Yet, though I know—or I think—the record player was still playing, silence fell. David said, "He's not dead yet"—*then* I knew who Martin was—"but it's a head wound—so—"

I don't remember what I said; obviously I must have said something. Billy and Walter were watching me. I told them what David had said.

I hardly remember the rest of that evening at all, it's retired into some deep cavern in my mind. We must have turned on the television set if we had one, I don't remember. But we must have had one. I remember weeping, briefly, more in helpless rage than in sorrow, and Billy trying to comfort me. But I really don't remember that evening at all. Later, Walter told me that a car had prowled around the house all night.

I went to Atlanta alone, I do not remember why. I wore the suit I had bought for my Carnegie Hall appearance with Martin. I seem to have had the foresight to have reserved a hotel room, for I vaguely remember stopping in the hotel and talking to two or three preacher-type-looking men, and we started off in the direction of the church. We had not got far before it became very clear that we would never get anywhere near it. We went in this direction and then in that direction, but the press of people choked us off. I began to wish that I had not come incognito and alone, for now that I was in Atlanta I wanted to get inside the church. I lost my companions, and sort of squeezed my way, inch by inch, closer to the church.

But directly between me and the church there was an impassable wall of people. Squeezing my way up to this point, I had considered myself lucky to be small; but now my size worked against me for, though there were people on the church steps who knew me, whom I knew, they could not possibly see me, and I could not shout. I squeezed a few more inches, and asked a very big man ahead of me please to let me through. He moved and said, "Yeah. Let me see you get through this big Cadillac." It was true—there it was, smack in front of me, big as a house. I saw Jim Brown in the distance, but he didn't see me. I leaned up on the car, making frantic signals, and finally someone on the church steps did see me and came to the car and sort of lifted me over. I talked to Jim Brown for a minute, and then somebody led me into the church and I sat down.

The church was packed, of course, incredibly so. Far in the front, I saw Harry Belafonte sitting next to Coretta King. Ralph David Abernathy sat in the pulpit. I remembered him from years ago, sitting in his shirt-sleeves in the house in Montgomery, big, black, and cheerful, pouring some cool, soft drink, and, later, getting me settled in a nearby hotel. In the pew directly before me sat Marlon Brando, Sammy Davis, Eartha Kitt—covered in black, looking like a lost, ten-year-old girl—and Sidney Poitier, in the same pew, or nearby. Marlon saw me, and nodded. The atmosphere was black, with a tension indescribable—as though something, perhaps the heavens, perhaps the earth, might crack. Everyone sat very still.

The actual service sort of washed over me, in waves. It wasn't that it seemed unreal; it was the most real church service I've ever sat through in my life, or ever hope to sit through; but I have a childhood hangover thing about not weeping in public, and I was concentrating on holding myself together. I did not want to weep for Martin, tears seemed futile. But I may also have been afraid, and I could not have been the only one, that if I began to weep I would not be able to stop. There was more than enough to weep for, if one was to weep—so many of us, cut down, so soon. Medgar, Malcolm, Martin: and their widows, and their children. Revered Ralph David

Abernathy asked a certain sister to sing a song which Martin had loved—"Once more," said Ralph David, "for Martin and for me," and he sat down.

The long, dark sister, whose name I do not remember, rose, very beautiful in her robes, and in her covered grief, and began to sing. It was a song I knew: *My Father Watches Over Me.* The song rang out as it might have over dark fields, long ago, she was singing of a covenant a people had made, long ago, with life, and with that larger life which ends in revelation and which moves in love.

He guides the eagle through the pathless air.

She stood there, and she sang it. How she bore it, I do not know, I think I have never seen a face quite like that face that afternoon. She was singing it for Martin, and for us.

And surely He
Remembers me,
My heav'nly Father watches over me.

At last, we were standing, and filing out, to walk behind Martin home. I found myself between Marlon and Sammy.

I had not been aware of the people when I had been pressing past them to get to the church. But, now, as we came out, and I looked up the road, I saw them. They were all along the road, on either side, they were on all the roofs, on either side. Every inch of ground, as far as the eye could see, was black with black people, and they stood in silence. It was the silence that undid me. I started to cry, and I stumbled, and Sammy grabbed my arm. We started to walk.

I don't think that any black person can speak of Malcolm and Martin without wishing that they were here. It is not possible for me to speak of them without a sense of grief and rage; and with the sense, furthermore, of having been forced to undergo an unforgivable indignity, both personal and vast. Our children need them, which is, indeed, the reason that they are not here: and now we, the blacks, must make certain that our children never forget them. For the American republic has always done everything in its power to destroy our children's heroes, with the clear (and sometimes clearly stated) intention of destroying our children's hope. This endeavor has doomed the American nation: mark my words.

Malcolm and Martin, beginning at what seemed to be very different points—for brevity's sake, we can say North and South, though, for Malcolm, South was south of the Canadian border—and espousing, or representing, very different philosophies, found that their common situation (south of the border!) so thoroughly devastated what had seemed to be mutually exclusive points of view that, by the time each met his death there was practically no difference between them. Before either had had time to think their new positions through, or, indeed, to do more than articulate them, they were murdered. Of the two, Malcolm moved swiftest (and was dead soonest), but the fates of both men were radically altered (I would say, frankly, sealed) the moment they attempted to release the black American struggle from the domestic context and relate it to the struggles of the poor and the nonwhite all over the world.

To hold this view, it is not necessary to see C.I.A. infiltrators in, or under, every black or dissenting bed: one need merely consider what the successful promulgation of this point of view would mean for American authority in the world. Slaveholders do not allow their slaves to compare notes: American slavery, until this hour, prevents any meaningful dialogue between the poor white and the black, in order to prevent the poor white from recognizing that he, too, is a slave. The contempt with which American leaders treat American blacks is very obvious; what is not so obvious is that they treat the bulk of the American people with the very same contempt. But it will be sub-zero weather in a very distant August when the American people find the guts to recognize this fact. They will recognize it only when they have exhausted every conceivable means of avoiding it.

In the meantime, in brutal fact, all of the institutions of this nation, from the schools to the courts to the unions to the prisons, and not forgetting the police, are in the hands of that white majority which has been promising for generations to ameliorate the black condition. And many white Americans would *like* to change the black condition, if they could see their way clear to do so, through the unutterable accumulation of neglect, sorrow, rage, despair, and continuing, overriding, totally unjustifiable death: the smoke over Attica recalls the bombs of Birmingham and the liberal Mr. Rockefeller reveals himself as being even more despicable than his openly illiberal confreres further down.

But it is not important, however irresistible, to accuse Mr. Rockefeller of anything. He is just another good American; one of the best. It is unlikely that *any* Western people, and certainly not the Americans, have the moral resources needed to accomplish the deep and mighty transformation which is all that can save them. Such a transformation involves unimaginable damage to the American ego; would reduce all the American religious ceremonies, including the Fourth of July and Thanksgiving, to the hypocritically bloody observances many of us have always known them to be; and would shed too unsparing a light on the actual dimensions and objectives of the American character. White Americans do not want to know what many nonwhites know too well, e.g., that "foreign aid" in the "under-developed" countries and "anti-poverty" programs in the ghetto are simply a slightly more sophisticated version of the British policy of Divide and Rule, are, in short, simply another means of keeping a people in subjection.

Since the American people cannot, even if they wished to, bring about black liberation, and since black people want their children to live, it is very clear that we must take our children out of the hands of this so-called majority and find some way to expose this majority as the minority which it actually is in the world. For this we will need, and we will get, the help of the suffering world which is prevented only by the labyrinthine stratagems of power from adding its testimony to ours.

No one pretends that this will be easy, and I myself do not expect to live to see this day accomplished. What both Martin and Malcolm began to see was that the nature of the American hoax had to be revealed—not only to save black people but in order to change the world in which everyone, after all, has a right to live. One may say that the articulation of this necessity was the Word's first necessary step on its journey toward being made flesh.

And no doubt my proposition, at this hour, sounds exactly that mystical. If I were a white American, I would bear in mind that mysteries are called mysteries because we recognize in them a truth which we can barely face, or articulate. I would bear in mind that an army is no match for a ferment, and that power, however great that power may consider itself to be, gives way, and has always been forced to give way, before the onslaught of human necessity: human necessity being the fuel of history.

If my proposition sounds mystical, white people have only to consider the black people, my ancestors, whose strength and love have brought black people to this present, crucial place. If I still thought, as I did when Martin and Malcolm were still alive, that the generality of white Americans were able to hear and to learn and begin to change, I would counsel them, as vividly as I could, to attempt, now, to minimize the bill which is absolutely certain to be presented to their children. I would say: if those blacks, your slaves, my ancestors, could bring us out of nothing, from such a long way off, then, if I were you, I would pause a long while before deciding to use what you think of as your power. For we, the blacks, have not found possible what you found necessary: we have not denied our ancestors who trust us, now, to redeem their pain.

Well. Baby, that's it. I *could* say, and they would both understand me: Don't you think Bessie is proud of Aretha?

Or: Do you think that Americans can translate this sentence both out of and into the original? *My soul is a witness for my Lord.*

Eldridge Cleaver, "Initial Reactions on the Assassination of Malcolm X," *Soul on Ice* (New York: McGraw Hill, 1968), 50–61

Folsom Prison
June 19, 1965

Sunday is Movie Day at Folsom Prison and I was sitting in the darkened hulk of Mess Hall No. I—which convicts call "The Folsom Theatre"—watching Victor Buono in a movie called *The Strangler*, when a convict known as Silly Willie came over to where I was sitting and whispered into my ear:

"Brother J sent me in to tell you it just came over the TV that Malcolm X was shot as he addressed a rally in New York."

For a moment the earth seemed to reel in orbit. The skin all over my body tightened up. "How bad?" I asked.

"The TV didn't say," answered Silly Willie. The distress was obvious in his voice. "We was around back in Pipe Alley checking TV when a special bulletin came on. All they said was Malcolm X was shot and they were rushing him to the hospital."

"Thanks," I said to Silly Willie. I felt his reassuring hand on my shoulder as he faded away in the darkness. For a moment I pondered whether to go outside and get more information, but something made me hang back. I remember distinctly thinking that I would know soon enough. On the screen before me, Victor Buono had a woman by the throat and was frantically choking the last gasping twitches of life out of her slumping body. I was thinking that if Malcolm's wounds were not too serious, that if he recovered, the shooting might prove to be a blessing in disguise: it would focus more intensified attention on him and create a windfall of sympathy and support for him throughout America's black ghettos, and so put more power into his hands. The possibility that the wounds may have been

509

fatal, that as I sat there Malcolm was lying already dead, was excluded from my mind.

After the movie ended, as I filed outside in the long line of convicts and saw the shocked, wild expression on Brother J's face, I still could not believe that Malcolm X was dead. We mingled in the crowd of convicts milling around in the yard and were immediately surrounded by a group of Muslims, all of whom, like myself, were firm supporters of Malcolm X. He's dead, their faces said, although not one of them spoke a word. As we stood there in silence, two Negro inmates walked by and one of them said to us, "That's a goddamn shame how they killed that man! Of all people, why'd they kill Malcolm? Why'n't they kill some of them Uncle-Tomming m.f.'s? I wish I could get my hands on whoever did it." And he walked away, talking and cursing to his buddy.

What does one say to his comrades at the moment when The Leader falls? All comment seems irrelevant. If the source of death is so-called natural causes, or an accident, the reaction is predictable, a feeling of impotence, humbleness, helplessness before the forces of the universe. But when the cause of death is an assassin's bullet, the overpowering desire is for vengeance. One wants to strike out, to kill, crush, destroy, to deliver a telling counterblow, to inflict upon the enemy a reciprocal, equivalent loss. But whom does one strike down at such a time if one happens to be in an anonymous, amorphous crowd of convicts in Folsom Prison and The Leader lies dead thousands of miles away across the continent?

"I'm going to my cell," I told the tight little knot of Muslims. "Allah is the Best Knower. Everything will be made manifest in time. Give it a little time. *As-Salaam Aliakum.*"

"*Wa-Aliakum Salaam,*" the Brothers returned the salutation and we shook hands all around, the double handshake which is very popular among Muslims in California prisons. (It is so popular that one sometimes grows weary of shaking hands. If a Muslim leaves a group for a minute to go get a drink of water, he is not unlikely to shake hands all around before he leaves and again when he returns. But no one complains and the convention is respected as a gesture of unity, brotherly love, and solidarity—so meaningful in a situation where Muslims are persecuted and denied recognition and the right to function as a legitimate religion.) I headed for my cell. I lived in No. 5 Building, which is Folsom's Honor Unit, reserved for those who have maintained a clean record for at least six months. Advantages: a larger cell, TV every Wednesday, Saturday, and Sunday night, less custodial supervision, easier ingress and egress. If while living in the Honor Unit you get into a "beef" which results in action against you by the disciplinary committee, one of the certain penalties is that you are immediately kicked out of No. 5 Building.

As I walked along the first tier toward my cell, I ran into Red, who lived near me on the tier.

"I guess you heard about Malcolm?"

"Yeah," I said. "They say he got wasted."

Red, who is white, knew from our many discussions that I was extremely partial to Malcolm, and he himself, being thoroughly alienated from the *status quo,* recognized the assassination for what it was: a negative blow against a positive force. Red's questions were the obvious ones: Who? Why? The questions were advanced tentatively, cautiously, because of the treacherous ground he was on: a red-headed, blue-eyed white man concerned by an event which so many others greeted with smiles and sighs. I went into my cell.

Although I heard it blared over the radio constantly and read about it in all the newspapers, days passed during which my mind continued to reject the fact of Malcolm's death. I existed in a dazed state, wandering in a trance around Folsom, drifting through the working hours in the prison bakery; and yet I was keen to observe the effect of the assassination on my fellow inmates. From most of the whites there was a leer and a hint of a smile in the eyes. They seemed anxious to see a war break out between the followers of Elijah and the followers of Malcolm.

There are only a few whites in Folsom with whom I would ever discuss the death of Malcolm or anything else besides baseball or the weather. Many of the Mexican-Americans were sympathetic, although some of them made a point, when being observed by whites, of letting drop sly remarks indicating they were glad Malcolm was gone. Among the Negroes there was mass mourning for Malcolm X. Nobody talked much for a few days. The only Negroes who were not indignant were a few of the Muslims who remained loyal to Elijah Muhammad. They interpreted Malcolm's assassination as the will of Allah descending upon his head for having gone astray. To them, it was Divine chastisement and a warning to those whom Malcolm had tempted. It was not so much Malcolm's death that made them glad; but in their eyes it now seemed possible to heal the schism in the movement and restore the monolithic unity of the Nation of Islam, a unity they looked back on with some nostalgia.

Many Negro convicts saw Malcolm's assassination as a historic turning point in black America. Whereas Negroes often talk heatedly about wiping out all the so-called Negro leaders whom they do not happen to like or agree with, this was the fist significant case of Negro leader-killing that anyone could remember. What struck me is that the Negro convicts welcomed the new era. If a man as valuable to us as Malcolm could go down, then as far as I was concerned so could any other man—myself included. Coming a week after the alleged exposé of the alleged plot to dynamite the Statue of Liberty, Washington Monument, and the Liberty Bell, a plot supposedly hatched by discontented blacks, the assassination of Malcolm X had put new ideas in the wind with implications for the future of black struggle in America.

I suppose that like many of the brothers and sisters in the Nation of Islam movement, I also had clung to the hope that, somehow, the rift between Malcolm X and Elijah Muhammad would be mended. As long as Brother Malcolm was alive, many Muslims could maintain this hope, neatly overlooking the increasing bitterness of their rivalry. But death made the split final and sealed it for history. These events caused a profound personal crisis in my life and beliefs, as it did for other Muslims. During the bitter time of his suspension and prior to his break with Elijah Muhammad, we had watched Malcolm X as he sought frantically to reorient himself and establish a new platform. It was like watching a master do a dance with death on a highstrung tightrope. He pirouetted, twirled, turned somersaults in the air—but he landed firmly on his feet and was off and running. We watched it all, seeking a cause to condemn Malcolm X and cast him out of our hearts. We read all the charges and countercharges. I found Malcolm X blameless.

It had been my experience that the quickest way to become hated by the Muslims was to criticize Elijah Muhammad or disagree with something he wrote or said. If Elijah wrote, as he has done, that the swine is a poison creature composed of 1/3 rat, 1/3 cat, and 1/3 dog and you attempted to cite scientific facts to challenge this, you had sinned against the light, that was all there was to it. How much more unlikely was it, therefore, that Muslims would stand up and denounce Elijah himself, repudiate his authority and his theology, deny his revelation, and take sides against him, the Messenger of Almighty God Allah? I never dreamed that someday I would be cast in that hapless role.

After Malcolm made his pilgrimage to Mecca, completing a triumphal tour of Africa and the Near East, during which he received the high honors of a visiting dignitary, he returned to the U.S.A. and set about building his newly founded Organization of Afro-American Unity. He also established the Muslim Mosque, Inc., to receive the Muslims he thought would pull away from Elijah. The Muslim Mosque would teach Orthodox Islam, under the direction of Sheikh Ahmed Hassoun from the Holy City of Mecca. Grand Sheik Muhammad Sarur Al-Sabban, secretary-general of the Muslim World League, had offered the services of Sheikh Ahmed, according to the Los Angeles *Herald-Dispatch,* to "help Malcolm X in his efforts to correct the distorted image that the religion of Islam has been given by hate groups in this country."

I began defending Malcolm X. At a secret meeting of the Muslims in Folsom, I announced that I was no longer a follower of Elijah Muhammad, that I was throwing my support behind Brother Malcolm. I urged everyone there to think the matter over and make a choice, because it was no longer possible to ride two horses at the same time. On the wall of my cell I had a large, framed picture of Elijah Muhammad which I had had for years. I took it down, destroyed it, and in its place put up, in the same frame, a beautiful picture of Malcolm X kneeling down in the Mohammed Ali Mosque in Cairo, which I clipped from the *Saturday Evening Post*. At first the other Muslims in Folsom denounced me; some I'd known intimately for years stopped speaking to me or even looking at me. When we met, they averted their eyes. To them the choice was simple: Elijah Muhammad is the hand-picked Messenger of Allah, the instrument of Allah's Will. All who oppose him are aiding Allah's enemies, the White Devils. Whom do you choose, God or the Devil? Malcolm X, in the eyes of Elijah's followers, had committed the unforgivable heresy when, changing his views and abandoning the racist position, he admitted the possibility of brotherhood between blacks and whites. In a letter sent back to the U.S. from the Holy Land, Malcolm X had stated:

> You may be shocked by these words coming from me, but I have always been a man who tries to face facts and to accept the reality of life as new experiences and knowledge unfold it. The experiences of this pilgrimage have taught me much and each hour in the Holy Land opens my eyes even more. . . . I have eaten from the same plate with people whose eyes were the bluest of blue, whose hair was the blondest of blond and whose skin was the whitest of white . . . and I felt the sincerity in the words and deeds of these "white" Muslims that I felt among the African Muslims of Nigeria, Sudan and Ghana.

Many of us were shocked and outraged by these words from Malcolm X, who had been a major influence upon us all and the main factor in many of our conversions to the Black Muslims. But there were those of us who were glad to be liberated from a doctrine of hate and racial supremacy. The onus of teaching racial supremacy and hate, which is the white man's burden, is pretty hard to bear. Asked if he would accept whites as members of his Organization of Afro-American Unity, Malcolm said he would accept John Brown if he were around today—which certainly is setting the standard high.

At the moment I declared myself for Malcolm X, I had some prestige among the Muslims in the prisons of California, because of my active role in proselytizing new converts and campaigning for religious freedom for Muslim convicts. We sent a barrage of letters and petitions to the courts, governmental officials, even the United Nations.

After the death of Brother Booker T. X, who was shot dead by a San Quentin prison guard, and who at the time had been my cell partner and the inmate Minister of the Muslims of San Quentin, my leadership of the Muslims of San Quentin had been publicly endorsed by Elijah Muhammad's west coast representative, Minister John Shabazz of Muhammad's Los Angeles Mosque. This was done because of the explosive conditions in San Quentin at the time. Muslim officials wanted to avert any Muslim-initiated violence, which had become a distinct possibility in the aftermath of Brother Booker's death. I was instructed to impose an iron discipline upon the San Quentin Mosque, which had continued to exist despite unending efforts of prison authorities to stamp it out. Most of the Muslims who were in prison during those days have since been released. I was one of the few remaining, and I was therefore looked upon by the other Muslims as one who had sacrificed and invested much in the struggle to advance the teachings of Elijah Muhammad. For that reason, my defection to Malcolm X caused a great deal of consternation among the Muslims of Folsom. But slowly, Malcolm was getting his machine together and it was obvious to me that his influence was growing. Negro inmates who had reservations about Malcolm while he was under Elijah's authority now embraced him, and it was clear that they accepted Malcolm's leadership. Negroes whom we had tried in vain for years to convert to Elijah's fold now lined up with enthusiasm behind Malcolm.

I ran a regular public relations campaign for Malcolm in Folsom. I saw to it that copies of his speeches were made and circulated among Negro inmates. I never missed a chance to speak favorably about Malcolm, to quote him, to explain and justify what he was trying to do. Soon I had the ear of the Muslims, and it was not long before Malcolm had other ardent defenders in Folsom. In a very short time Malcolm became the hero of the vast majority of Negro inmates. Elijah Muhammad was quickly becoming irrelevant, passé.

Malcolm X had a special meaning for black convicts. A former prisoner himself, he had risen from the lowest depths to great heights. For this reason he was a symbol of hope, a model for thousands of black convicts who found themselves trapped in the vicious PPP cycle: prison-parole-prison. One thing that the judges, policemen, and administrators of prisons seem never to have understood, and for which they certainly do not make any allowances, is that Negro convicts, basically, rather than see themselves as criminals and perpetrators of misdeeds, look upon themselves as prisoners of war, the victims of a vicious, dog-eat-dog social system that is so heinous as to cancel out their own malefactions: in the jungle there is no right or wrong.

Rather than owing and paying a debt to society, Negro prisoners feel that they are being abused, that their imprisonment is simply another form of the oppression which they have known all their lives. Negro inmates feel that they are being robbed, that it is "society" that owes them, that should be paying them, a debt.

America's penology does not take this into account. Malcolm X did, and black convicts know that the ascension to power of Malcolm X or a man like him would eventually have revolutionized penology in America. Malcolm delivered a merciless and damning indictment of prevailing penology. It is only a matter of time until the question of the prisoner's debt to society versus society's debt to the prisoner is injected forcefully into national and state politics, into the civil and human rights struggle, and into the consciousness of the body politic. It is an explosive issue which goes to the very root of America's system of justice, the structure of criminal law, the prevailing beliefs and attitudes toward the convicted felon. While it is easier to make out a case for black convicts, the same principles apply to white and Mexican-American convicts as well. They too are victimized, albeit a little more subtly, by "society." When black convicts start demanding a new dispensation and definition of justice, naturally the white and Mexican-American convicts will demand equality of treatment. Malcolm X was a focus for these aspirations.

The Black Muslim movement was destroyed the moment Elijah cracked the whip over Malcolm's head, because it was not the Black Muslim movement itself that was so irresistibly appealing to the true believers. It was the awakening into self-consciousness of twenty million Negroes which was so compelling. Malcolm X articulated their aspirations better than any other man of our time. When he spoke under the banner of Elijah Muhammad he was irresistible. When he spoke under his own banner he was still irresistible. If he had become a Quaker, a Catholic, or a Seventh-Day Adventist, or a Sammy Davis-style Jew, and if he had continued to give voice to the mute ambitions in the black man's soul, his message would still have been triumphant: because what was great was not Malcolm X but the truth he uttered.

The truth which Malcolm uttered had vanquished the whole passel of so-called Negro leaders and spokesmen who trifle and compromise with the truth in order to curry favor with the white power structure. He was stopped in the only way such a man can be stopped, in the same way that the enemies of the Congolese people had to stop Lumumba, by the same method that exploiters, tyrants, and parasitical oppressors have always crushed the legitimate strivings of people for freedom, justice, and equality—by murder, assassination, and mad-dog butchery.

What provoked the assassins to murder? Did it bother them that Malcolm was elevating our struggle into the international arena through his campaign to carry it before the United Nations? Well, by murdering him they only hastened the process, because we certainly are going to take our cause before a sympathetic world. Did it bother the assassins that Malcolm denounced the racist strait-jacket demonology of Elijah Muhammad? Well, we certainly do denounce it and will continue to do so. Did it bother the assassins that Malcolm taught us to defend ourselves? We shall not remain a defenseless prey to the murderer, to the sniper and the bomber. Insofar as Malcolm spoke the truth, the truth will triumph and prevail and his name shall live; and insofar as those who oppose him lied, to that extent will their names become curses. Because "truth crushed to earth shall rise again."

So now Malcolm is no more. The bootlickers, Uncle Toms, lackeys, and stooges of the white power structure have done their best to denigrate Malcolm, to root him out of his people's heart, to tarnish his memory. But their million-worded lies fall on deaf ears. As Ossie Davis so eloquently expressed it in his immortal eulogy of Malcolm:

> If you knew him you would know why we must honor him: Malcolm was our manhood, our living, black manhood! This was his meaning to his people. And, in honoring him, we honor the best in ourselves. . . . However much we may have differed with him—or with each other about him and his value as a man, let his going from us serve only to bring us together, now. Consigning these mortal remains to earth, the common mother of all, secure in the knowledge that what we place in the ground is no more now a man—but a seed—which, after the winter of our discontent will come forth again to meet us. And we will know him then for what he was and is—a Prince—our own black shining Prince!—who didn't hesitate to die, because he loved us so.

We shall have our manhood. We shall have it or the earth will be leveled by our attempts to gain it.

Ted Vincent, "The Garveyite
Parents of Malcolm X," *The Black Scholar*,
vol. 2, no. 2 (March/April 1989): 10–13

Recently uncovered articles from 1926 and 1927 issues of Marcus Garvey's *Negro World* newspaper provide documented evidence of the political activity of the parents of Malcolm X.

Malcolm states in his *Autobiography* that his father, the Reverend Earl Little, was a Baptist minister, and "a dedicated organizer for Marcus Aurelius Garvey's UNIA (Universal Negro Improvement Association)." *The Negro World* articles show that Malcolm's mother, Louise Little, also worked in the movement, a factor not noted in the *Autobiography*.[1]

The articles found in *The Negro World* provide some specifics on Little's organizing activities and allow us to view him as a committed revolutionary, not just the powerful mythic hero and literary figure depicted in Malcolm's autobiography.

Malcolm tells how his father took him to meetings of Garvey followers who lived in the area near the Littles' home in Lansing, Michigan.

> I remember how the meeting always closed with my father saying, several times, and the people chanting after him, "Up, you mighty race, you can accomplish what you will."[2]

1. See "Omaha" in UNIA reports on Divisions sections in *The Negro World*, May 22, June 19 and July 3, 1926; and "Milwaukee" in January 29, February 5 and February 19, 1927.

2. Malcolm X, Alex Haley, compiler, *The Autobiography of Malcolm X*. (New York: Grove Press, 1966), pp. 6–7.

ACTIVITIES PROVOKE RACISM

The Autobiography of Malcolm X notes that the political activities of Earl Little were dangerous. His family believed that his mysterious death in 1931 was a murder perpetrated by racists in the Lansing area who had been harassing the Littles since their arrival in the late 1920s. Two white men burned the Littles' home in 1929.[3]

The Littles also had trouble with white racists when they lived in Omaha, Nebraska, where they lived before moving to Michigan. Malcolm begins his autobiography with a description of the night in 1925 when Ku Klux Klan riders came to the family home in Omaha looking for Malcolm's father. The Klansmen came to demand that Little get out of town, declaring, as Malcolm relates it:

"'The good Christian white people' were not going to stand for my father's 'spreading trouble' among the 'good' Negroes of Omaha with the 'back to Africa' preachings of Marcus Garvey." Louise Little was pregnant at the time with Malcolm. She came to the door and explained that her husband was not home. She convinced the Klan to leave, but not before they had broken the windows of the house.[4]

The Littles appear to have come to Omaha from Philadelphia sometime between 1922 and 1923 (using the cities of birth of Malcolm's older siblings as a guide).[5] Just when Little became president of the Omaha branch of the UNIA is still unknown. However, by May 1925, when Malcolm X was born, Rev. and Mrs. Little's work in the black community had become effective enough to attract the attention of the KKK.

From *The Negro World* we learn that Little led a far larger group of the UNIA in Omaha than he later did in rural Mich-

---

3. Ibid, pp. 3 and 10.

4. Ibid, p. 1.

5. Ibid, p. 2.

igan. It was more than Garveyite talk that led the Omaha Ku Klux Klan to think that Rev. Little was "spreading trouble."

Malcolm's father was president of the Omaha UNIA branch. Wherever Garvey branches were located, there was a great effort to raise money for the local group to have its own meeting hall. Under Little's leadership, the Omaha branch became strong enough to obtain its own "Liberty Hall." The organization was often denied hall rental or the permits that were readily given to white and "acceptable" black groups.[6]

MALCOLM'S MOTHER AS REPORTER

Louise Little assisted her husband with his UNIA work in Omaha. Malcolm's mother served as the branch reporter, sending in accounts to *The Negro World* of Omaha UNIA meetings. During 1926, the internationally distributed newspaper published four articles about Omaha UNIA activities on the "News Of Divisions" page.

During the mid-1920s, the newspaper published weekly reports from a dozen or more of the nearly 2,000 UNIA branches spread throughout the world. It was something of an achievement for a branch in a town like Omaha to make the "News Of Divisions" page, which was more likely to carry reports from the major metropolitan centers, such as Chicago, Detroit, Los Angeles, Havana, London, Capetown, Kingston, Jamaica, and Panama City, Panama.

Undaunted by the Klan confrontation at their home, the Littles not only continued their work, but signed their names to articles in *The Negro World*, as can be noted in three of the four 1926 reports about the local branch. The second report, published May 22, 1926, read as follows:

"Omaha, Nebraska. Omaha Division held its regular mass meeting on Sunday, May 8. Mr. E. Little delivered the principal address. This division is small but much alive to its part in

6. Ted Vincent, *Black Power and the Garvey Movement*. (Oakland, California: Nzinga, 1988), pp. 109–110 and 163–64.

carrying on the great work." (It was common for reports from UNIA branches in areas of KKK activity to use phrases like "carrying on the great work" rather than put anything more radical in print.)

MASS MEETINGS MAKE NEWS

A month later, June 19, 1926, Omaha again made the coveted "News Of Divisions" page, this time adding a mention of who sent in the report:

> The Omaha Division held its regular mass meeting on Sunday, May 23, at 3:30 pm. A short program was rendered as follows. Opening services conducted by the president, Mr. Little, assisted by the secretary, M.L. Holden. A splendid address was delivered by Reverend Moseley.—Louise Little, reporter.

The July 3, 1926, "News Of Divisions" page again included Omaha:

> The Omaha Division met on Sunday, June 13, in Liberty Hall, 2528 Lake Street. The president, Mr. E. Little, presiding. Opening song from Greenland's Icy Mountains. Prayer and preamble by the president. Musical selection. Prof. A Vance was introduced and held his hearer's attention about matters of the organization. A membership drive was launched for the coming week, in which Mr. Vance will participate.—Louise Little, reporter.

Malcolm X relates in his *Autobiography* that after Omaha, the family resided briefly in Milwaukee, Wisconsin, where their next child was born. They appear to have moved to Milwaukee sometime around the end of 1926. Without the Littles, the Omaha UNIA went until mid-1928 before receiving another mention in Garvey's weekly.[7]

7. Malcolm X, op.cit., pp. 2–3; report on "Omaha," *The Negro World*, September 15, 1928.

Little received mentions in *Negro World* for his UNIA work in Milwaukee. As reported in the January 29, 1927, issue of the newspaper, the January 2, 1927, "mass meeting" of the Milwaukee branch included an "address by the ex-president of the Omaha, Neb., Division, Mr. Little."

Little's speech must have been inspiring, since he was followed to the podium by the president of the Milwaukee branch who took the occasion to ask for "the whole-hearted support of each and every member to help put this program over, for there is work for all to do." The president went on to mention some projects of the Milwaukee UNIA, concluding, "We are also holding our religious services every Sunday morning at Liberty Hall. Elder E. Little is our spiritual adviser."

The next issue of *The Negro World*, February 5, 1927, carried a report from Milwaukee noting that: "Sunday mornings are making wonderful progress under the leadership of Elder E. Little and are quite an asset to the division." Two weeks later, February 19, 1927, a "News Of Divisions" listing for Milwaukee began: "Mr. E. Little, ex-president of the Omaha Division, was the honored guest and principal speaker at the mass meeting of the Milwaukee division on Sunday, January 23."

There were no further mentions in *The Negro World* of the Littles in Milwaukee.

SUSPICIOUS DEATH OF EARL LITTLE

According to the *Autobiography of Malcolm X*, the Littles' next residence was Lansing, Michigan.[8] However, an article in *The Negro World* indicates that the family may have lived for a brief period in Indiana Harbor (East Chicago), Indiana, before moving to Lansing.

The May 27, 1927, edition of *The Negro World* reported on a meeting of the Gary, Indiana, UNIA that was attended by "the president of the Indiana Harbor Division, Mr. Little."

8. Ibid, p. 3.

Six months earlier, the Indiana Harbor Division had another person as president. However, Little could have arrived from Milwaukee and assumed leadership. By the end of 1927, the Indiana Harbor division had another leader.

Earl Little's activity in the small black community around Lansing was not mentioned in any of the available *Negro World* issues through 1931—the year of his suspicious death involving a street car that he either fell from or was thrown in front of by the racists who had been threatening him.

Malcolm X was about six years old when his father died and was not able to give details about his father's UNIA work in Omaha or Milwaukee. However, Malcolm did explain that his father believed strongly in the anti-imperialist "Africa for the Africans" message of Marcus Garvey.

Negro World reports give added strength to Malcolm's statement that it was "with the help of such disciples as my father" that Garvey "was raising the banner of black race purity and exhorting the Negro masses to return to their ancestral African homeland—a cause which had made Garvey the most controversial black man on earth."[9]

Understandably, Alex Haley, who compiled *The Autobiography of Malcolm X,* wanted to emphasize the tensions caused by working for a controversial figure like Garvey. However, in writing about Malcolm's account of the KKK raid on the Little home in Omaha, Haley may not have been entirely accurate.

He gives the impression that the family left Omaha in late spring 1925, more than a year before their actual departure.[10] Consequently, historians who have been eager to document the Littles' activities would not have looked for reports from Omaha in mid-1926 or Milwaukee in early 1927—the actual dates for the reports.

9. Ibid, p. 1.

10. Ibid, pp. 1–2.

KLAN RAID

As described in the *Autobiography,* the raid on the Little home in Omaha climaxed with Little's return to the house after the Klan had left. Allegedly, he declared that the family would leave town as soon as the baby was born. Malcolm was born May 19, 1925. We know from *The Negro World* that the Littles remained in Omaha another year and a half, until near the end of 1926.

As for Little's alleged decision to move as soon as Malcolm was born, Malcolm states, "I am not sure why he made this decision, for he was not a frightened Negro, as most then were; and many still are today . . ."[11] Perhaps Little never seriously thought of leaving Omaha after Malcolm's birth. As suggested later in the *Autobiography,* it appears that Little may have decided to stay in Omaha long enough so that the KKK could not think it had driven him out of town.[12]

Garveyite leaders throughout the country were driven from their towns. Trying to decide if and when it was time to leave was something many UNIA officials had to deal with. In 1921 there were two incidents in Florida where UNIA presidents felt the situation was so dangerous that they left by boat rather than risk trips north by land. One UNIA leader went to Cuba, and the other went to the Bahamas.[13]

The June 3, 1922, issue of *The Negro World* reported a shocking incident near Dallas, Texas, in which the UNIA commissioner for the state, R.B. Moseley, was horsewhipped and in other ways humiliated by a group of white racists. Moseley appears to have toughed it out until late 1925, when

11. Ibid, p. 1.

12. Ibid, pp. 2–8.

13. The UNIA leaders were Rev. T.C. Glashen of Key West and Rev. R.H. Higgs of Miami. See *The Negro World*, July 6, 1921, and Robert A. Hill, editor, *The Marcus Garvey and Universal Negro Improvement Association Papers.* (Berkeley, California: University of California Press, 1984), Vol. III. pp. 512–515.

The Negro World reported he had taken up residence in Chicago. He may have been the "Rev. Moseley" who addressed the Omaha UNIA in 1926, as noted in one of the reports sent in by Louise Little.[14]

MALCOLM X'S FAMILY IN CONTEXT

The Negro World articles show Malcolm X's family in the context of the many hundreds of hard-pressed local leaders in the Garvey movement at the time. The arguments between Malcolm's father and mother, for example, are described in the *Autobiography* mostly in terms of domestic problems and personal differences.[15] Largely overlooked are the tremendous outside pressures of impinging upon the domestic tranquility of the families of activists of that time.

The omission from *The Autobiography of Malcolm X* of Louise Little's role in the Garvey movement has left us with an image of a rather frail, partially educated woman with a husband whose flamboyance overshadowed her. Given this picture, her mental breakdown in 1934 suggests general weakness, rather than what Malcolm tried to explain—that her breakdown was principally brought on by the dehumanizing treatment of the Michigan Welfare Department.

Malcolm supported his explanation by stating that his mother had a strong sense of personal pride in earlier years[16]— pride nurtured and expressed through her contributions to *The Negro World*.

14. *The Negro World*, January 16, 1926.

15. Malcolm X, op.cit., pp. 4–5.

16. Ibid, pp. 12–17.

Robin D. G. Kelley, "House Negroes on the Loose: Malcolm X and the Black Bourgeoisie," *Callaloo*, vol. 21, no. 2 (1998): 419–435

There are two types of Negroes in this country. There's the bourgeois type who blinds himself to the condition of his people, and who is satisfied with token solutions. He's in the minority. He's a handful. He's usually the handpicked Negro who benefits from token integration. But the masses of Black people who really suffer the brunt of brutality and the conditions that exist in this country are represented by the leadership of the Honorable Elijah Muhammad.

—Malcolm X "Twenty Million Black People in a Political, Economic, and Mental Prison" (1963)[1]

I gotta represent the real nigga
The field niggas. . . .

—Black Moon, "I Got Cha Opin," *Enta Da Stage* (Wreck Records, 1993)

The Hip Hop generation and their most revered icon have at least one thing in common besides their distrust of white people: they don't have much love for the black bourgeoisie. Most identify with "field niggas," and the current generation of self-styled nationalists and teen gangstas draw much of

---

1. From *Malcolm X: The Last Speeches*, ed. Bruce Perry (New York: Pathfinder Press, 1989), 27. Malcolm frequently gave the house slave/field slave speech, especially in the early 1960s. For different versions, see also *Malcolm X: The Last Speeches* (28–30); "Message to the Grassroots," *Malcolm X Speaks*, ed. George Breitman (New York: Grove Weidenfeld, 1990, new ed.), 10–12; Speech in Selma, Alabama, February 4, 1965, *By Any Means Necessary* (New York: Pathfinder, 1970), 183–84.

their anti-bourgeois rhetoric from Malcolm himself.[2] Indeed, if we could resurrect Malcolm X (circa 1963, let us say) and have him listen to "Black Moon's" lyrics quoted in the epigraph above, he would probably give us one of those flashing wide grins, perhaps even a giggle, and second their emotion that the "field niggas" are indeed the "real niggas."

But that wouldn't be the end of it. Without losing a beat or his smile, the Minister would also give the members of "Black Moon" a gentle tongue-lashing. "My young brothers," he might begin, "if you all want to be *real* revolutionaries rather than just 'real niggas,' if you want to live up to your name 'Black Moon'— which I understand to mean the power unleashed during a solar eclipse, the power to block the Sun and turn the day into night— you all need to clean up your act. Change your clothes, clean up your language, show some respect to the sisters [how that is defined is another essay!], stop glorifying drugs and liquor. The devil sleeps well at night knowing we're caricatures of ourselves. If we want our freedom, we need to be ready to take it. We need to be united. We need our minds and bodies clean and prepared to fight. We're 22 million . . ."

"Excuse me, brother Malcolm; make that 30 million."

"Well, brother, I've been dead a long time." [*Laughter*]

Knowing these Brooklyn-raised rappers are just kids in bad need of direction, his good-natured rebuke would cease as quickly as it began. He most likely would see their potential and hope they could receive the proper spiritual, cultural, and political guidance in order to realize it.

As often as Malcolm invoked the "house slave/field slave" dichotomy in numerous speeches and debates, his relationship to the black middle class was a complicated matter. He hated and emulated them; he ridiculed and admired them; he was part of a movement that tried to turn the most lumpen Ne-

2. For an extended discussion of Hip Hop's critique of the black bourgeoisie, see my book *Race Rebels: Culture, Politics, and the Black Working Class* (New York: Free Press, 1994), chapter 8; and Tricia Rose's *Black Noise: Rap Music and Black Culture in Contemporary America* (Hanover: Wesleyan University Press, 1994).

groes into respectable (by bourgeois standards, at least), well-mannered, "civilized" black men and women. And through it all, Malcolm's critique of the black bourgeoisie floated somewhere between an intuitive hatred born of his past to an insightful analysis of the race/class matrix.[3] However imperfect and contradictory, he did offer a critique of the black bourgeoisie at a time when such a critique was unpopular. His rants against "Uncle Toms" and "house slaves" coincided with the rise of a fairly successful, and by some measures militant, Civil Rights movement led by middle-class blacks. But he was not entirely off the mark, for he struck a deep chord among his working-class and lumpen followers who were sick and tired of being shut out and looked down upon by the "better class Negroes." In some respects, his criticisms found a voice in the urban uprisings and the militant rhetoric of Black Power soon after his death.

THE DIE IS CASTE

Unlike most black leaders prior to the early 1960s, including black working-class heroes such as A. Philip Randolph or Paul Robeson, Malcolm consistently identified with ordinary black working people and those displaced by the economy. He spoke their language and told their jokes. His was not simply another

---

3. Patricia Hill Collins takes Malcolm X to task for failing to develop an "analysis of social class that addresses those features of capitalist political economies." There is no doubt that Malcolm's conception of class is highly problematic and, as Collins demonstrates, simply wrong on several counts. [See Patricia Hill Collins, "Learning to Think For Ourselves: Malcolm X's Black Nationalism Reconsidered," *Malcolm X: In Our Own Image*, ed. Joe Wood (New York: St. Martin's Press 1992), 67–74.] But I'm not interested in whether Malcolm was right or wrong, or whether we could apply his "analysis" (which consists of portions of speeches delivered before a variety of different audiences and thus never intended to be a manifesto) to contemporary realities. Rather, I am trying to understand how Malcolm understands class distinctions and the roots of his hostility to the black bourgeoisie. Moreover, I want to determine why his critique of the black bourgeoisie is so compelling to young African Americans today.

Horatio Alger story of how he rose out of poverty to become a hero. (And despite dozens of opportunities, he never sought wealth, leaving his family virtually penniless.) Rather, he invoked his experiences as an urban kid, former criminal, man of the streets, to show his audience that he knows where they are coming from and never forgot where he came from. In fact, he so depended on this identification with poor black folk—particularly the young—that he exaggerated his criminal exploits, his poverty, and his urban upbringing.[4]

At the same time, Malcolm always had a love/hate relationship with the black bourgeoisie, though like most unconsummated relationships hate eventually became the dominant emotion. Even as a child in Lansing, Michigan, the sons and daughters of the black elite turned their noses up at the skinny red-head from that awful Little family. He was not only poor, but he was practically an orphan; his father was dead, and his mother had been committed to a mental institution. But he soon learned that these Negroes were nothing. He got his first real taste of black bourgeois pretentiousness when he moved to Boston with his half-sister Ella Little in 1941.[5]

In the crazy mixed-up world of interracial class relations, World War II marked a critical moment. Of course, class conflict within African-American communities was hardly new. For some middle-class blacks, for example, the black poor had long been regarded as lazy, self-destructive, and prone to criminal behavior. On the other side of the class spectrum, as black sociologist Allison Davis found in his study of a small Mississippi town during the 1930s, "lower class" blacks often "accused upper-class persons (the 'big shots,' the 'Big Negroes') of snobbishness, color preference, extreme selfishness, disloyalty in caste leadership, ('sellin' out to white folks'), and economic exploitation of

4. Bruce Perry, *Malcolm: The Life of a Man Who Changed Black America* (Barrytown, NY: Station Hill Press, 1991), 182.

5. Malcolm X, with Alex Haley. *The Autobiography of Malcolm X* (New York: Grove Press, 1964), 17–42; Perry, *Malcolm*, 40.

their patients and customers."[6] But during the 1940s, massive Southern black migration to Northern cities exacerbated cultural tensions between longtime urban residents and the newly arrived rural folk. African Americans born and raised in the North, particularly those who owned property and maintained a steady income, looked down on these newcomers and blamed them for neighborhood deterioration.[7]

6. Allison Davis, Burleigh B. Gardner, and Mary R. Gardner, *Deep South: A Social Anthropological Study of Caste and Class* (Chicago: University of Chicago Press, 1941), 230. In addition to classic sociological texts such as E. Franklin Frazier, *Black Bourgeoisie* (Glencoe, IL: Free Press, 1957), and St. Clair Drake and Horace Cayton, *Black Metropolis: A Study of Negro Life in a Northern City* (New York: Harper and Row, 1962, 2nd ed.), several historians have recently explored the issue of class conflict within African-American communities. See especially Kelley, *Race Rebels*; Robin D.G. Kelley, *Hammer and Hoe: Alabama Communists During the Great Depression* (Chapel Hill: University of North Carolina Press, 1990); Earl Lewis, *In Their Own Interests: Race, Class, and Power in Twentieth Century Norfolk, Virginia* (Los Angeles and Berkeley: University of California Press, 1991); Joe William Trotter, *Coal, Class, and Color: Blacks in Southern West Virginia, 1915–1932* (Urbana: University of Illinois Press, 1990); Peter J. Rachleff, *Black Labor in the South: Richmond, Virginia, 1865–1890* (Philadelphia: Temple University Press, 1984); Evelyn Brooks Higginbotham, *Righteous Discontent: The Women's Movement in the Black Baptist Church, 1880–1920* (Cambridge, MA: Harvard University Press, 1993); Kenneth Marvin Hamilton, *Black Towns and Profit: Promotion and Development in the Trans-Appalachian West, 1877–1915* (Urbana: University of Illinois Press, 1991).

7. See Manning Marable, *Race, Reform, and Rebellion: The Second Reconstruction in Black America, 1945–1990* (Jackson and London: University Press of Mississippi, 1991, 2nd ed.), 14–17; Daniel R. Fusfeld and Timothy Bates, *The Political Economy of the Urban Ghetto* (Carbondale, IL: Southern Illinois University Press, 1984), 48–50; Douglas Henry Daniels, *Pioneer Urbanites: A Social and Cultural History of Black San Francisco* (Los Angeles and Berkeley: University of California Press, 1980), 171–75; and Cheryl Lynn Greenberg, who writes about this phenomenon in Harlem during the 1920s and 1930s in *"Or Does it Explode?": Black Harlem in the Great Depression* (New York: Oxford University Press, 1991), 16–17. Eugene Victor Wolfenstein makes a similar observation about the intensification of interracial class divisions, although we disagree significantly as to the meaning of these divisions for the emergence of black working-class opposition. Besides, I am insisting on the simultaneity of heightened intraracial class struggle and racist oppression. *The Victims of Democracy: Malcolm X and the Black Revolution* (London: Free Association Books, 1989, orig. 1981), 175–76.

Ella owned a house on "the Hill," an elite section of the pre-dominantly black Boston neighborhood of Roxbury. Her neighbors consisted of middle-brow black folks with high-brow pretensions, the most prominent of whom belonged to the so-called "Four Hundred." Massachusetts-born and -raised, the "Hills" society Negroes fashioned themselves as colored equivalents of Boston Brahmins. They ridiculed Southern migrants and looked down on most working-class blacks despite the fact that some members of the "Four Hundred" were themselves service workers. Those who qualified for membership in the elite represented a wide range of occupations, from teachers, preachers, and nurses to Pullman porters, dining car waiters, and postal workers. From what Malcolm remembers, none were truly "bourgeois" in the classical sense; they did not own estates, factories, multi-million dollar firms, or exercise real power. What little power they enjoyed, as well as their self-proclaimed status, was dependent on white people. Malcolm often heard neighbors announcing, "'He's in banking,' or 'He's in securities.' It sounded as though they were discussing a Rockefeller or a Mellon—and not some gray-headed, dignity posturing bank janitor, or bond-house messenger."[8]

Malcolm's peers were no better. When he first settled into Roxbury, they made fun of his clothes, which were a tad too small for him and obviously of bargain-basement quality. "To the teenage female sophisticates of the Hill," writes biographer Bruce Perry, "he looked as if he had just come from some farm." If that wasn't bad enough, Ella secured a job for him as a soda jerk at a neighborhood drugstore where his main clientele were the Hill kids. Serving them, he discovered, was even worse than dealing with them in various social settings. Although his employers were Jewish, in reality his immediate bosses were the black bourgeois patrons who came in by the droves and made incessant demands on him. It was steady work, but with it came all the ridicule and snobbery one could imagine. He vividly re-

8. Perry, *Malcolm*, 49; quote from Malcolm X, *Autobiography*, 40.

members having to endure these "penny-ante squares who came in there putting on their millionaires' airs."[9]

As he grew less and less tolerant of the Hill crowd, Malcolm began hanging out in the poorer sections of Roxbury where he "felt more relaxed among Negroes who were being their natural selves and not putting on airs."[10] His newfound friend, Shorty, introduced him to the cool world of the zoot suit, the conk (straightened) hairstyle, and the lindy hoppers who spent their weekend nights at Boston's Roseland State Ballroom. When Malcolm donned his very first zoot suit, he realized immediately that the wild sky-blue outfit, the baggy punjab pants tapered to the ankles, the matching hat, gold watch chain, and monogrammed belt was more than a suit of clothes. It was a ticket into the "in crowd," a new identity that symbolized an increasingly militant and ultramasculine black street culture. The language and culture of the zoot suiters enabled Malcolm to reject white racism and patriotism, the rural folkways (for many, the "parent culture") that still survived in most black urban households, and the petit bourgeois attitudes of his "snooty" middle-class neighbors on the Hill. He found in the Roseland State Ballroom, and later in Harlem's Savoy, spaces of leisure and pleasure free of the bourgeois pretensions of "better class Negroes." For young Malcolm, his new world embodied the "true" black experience: "I couldn't wait for eight o'clock to get home to eat out of those soul-food pots of Ella's, then get dressed in my zoot and head for some of my friends' places in town, to lindy-hop and get high, or something, for relief from those Hill clowns."[11]

Malcolm and his partners did not seem very "political" at the time, but they dodged the draft so as not to lose their lives over a "white man's war," and they avoided wage work when-

9. Perry, *Malcolm*, 49, 54; Malcolm X, *Autobiography*, 59.

10. Malcolm X, *Autobiography*, 43.

11. Malcolm X, *Autobiography*, 59–60. I discuss Malcolm's relationship to the zoot suit culture extensively in "The Riddle of the Zoot: Malcolm Little and Black Cultural Politics During World War II," *Malcolm X: In Our Own Image*, ed. Joe Wood (New York: St. Martin's Press, 1992), 155–67.

ever possible. His search for leisure and pleasure took him to Harlem where petty hustling, drug dealing, pimping, gambling, and exploiting women became his primary source of income. In 1946 his luck ran out; he was arrested for burglary and sentenced to ten years in prison.

His downward descent took a U-turn in prison when he began studying the teachings of the Lost-Found Nation of Islam (NOI), the black Muslim group founded by Wallace Fard and led by Elijah Muhammad (Elijah Poole). While he was no Horatio Alger, as I pointed out above, his rise from petty criminal to the NOI's leading spokesman contains all the classic elements of Horatio's story: he worked very hard, transformed himself, cleaned himself up, educated himself, began conducting himself in a respectable and dignified manner. Submitting to the discipline and guidance of the NOI, he became a voracious reader of the Koran and the Bible, and immersed himself in works of literature and history at the prison library. Behind prison walls he quickly emerged as a powerful orator and brilliant rhetorician. Upon his release in 1952, he was renamed Malcolm "X," symbolically repudiating the "white man's name."[12]

As a devoted follower of Elijah Muhammad, Malcolm X rose quickly within the NOI ranks, serving as minister of Harlem's Temple No. 7 in 1954, and building up temples in Detroit and Philadelphia. Through national speaking engagements, television appearances, and by establishing *Muhammad Speaks*—the NOI's first nationally distributed newspaper—Malcolm X put the Nation of Islam on the map. But what impressed Malcolm more than high profile speaking engagements was grassroots organizing; he enjoyed "fishing" for converts in the bars and poolrooms where poor and displaced working-class men spent too much of their time.[13]

Given Malcolm's experiences thus far, there could not have

12. On this period in Malcolm's life, see Malcolm X, *Autobiography*, 126–235; Perry, *Malcolm*, 104–66; Wolfenstein, *Victims of Democracy*, 184–269; Ferruccio Gambino, "The Transgression of a Laborer: Malcolm X in the Wilderness of America," *Radical History Review* 55 (Winter 1993): 7–31.

13. Perry, *Malcolm*, 145; Benjamin Karim, with Peter Skutches and David

been a more appropriate movement than the Nation of Islam. Its leaders deliberately reached out to wayward youth and the "down and out," and they sustained a fairly antagonistic stance toward the rising black middle class. Indeed, as historian C. Eric Lincoln points out, most of NOI recruits "do not typically identify with the strivers of the black middle class. They tend to live comfortably, but frugally. The Movement continues to emphasize its affiliation with the working class." Although many converts discovered the Nation as prisoners, ex-hustlers, or jobless wanderers, the NOI's highly structured and disciplined environment instilled a strong work ethic into its congregation. Muhammad's followers worked, and worked very hard, but the majority lived in the ghettoes of North America and made barely enough to tithe.[14]

Similarly, another scholarly observer of the NOI, E.U. Essien-Udom, suggested that the Nation came into being when class distinctions within the black community were sharper than they had ever been. He even suggested that the future struggles in the black community "may shift from one between whites and Negroes to a class struggle within the caste, i.e., between a semisatisfied Negro middle class and the Negro masses." Of course, this has not yet happened, but some of his experiences with the NOI gave him good cause for believing it. In one instance, after the NOI in Chicago purchased land in the Chatham-Avalon Community, a recently integrated upper-middle-class neighborhood, whites and middle-class blacks formed a united front to block the Nation's plans to build an Islamic Center. (Ironically, the same black middle-class residents faced opposition from whites when they moved in a few years earlier.) According to Essien-Udom, who attended the meetings, the "Negroes in this community opposed the Muslims' project strictly along class lines.

Gallen, *Remembering Malcolm* (New York: Carol & Graf Publishers, 1992), 70–75.

14. C. Eric Lincoln, *The Black Muslims in America* (Boston: Beacon Press, 1973, 2nd ed.), 26.

They did not want 'those elements'—lower class persons—in their community."[15]

VARIETIES OF HOUSE NEGROES

When it came to attacking and ridiculing the black bourgeoisie, Malcolm was perhaps the least charitable of the NOI leadership. He called them "house slaves," "Uncle Toms," "Nincompoops with Ph.D.s," "Quislings," "sell-outs," and, of course, "bourgeois Negroes." And all of these terms did not necessarily mean the same thing. Malcolm essentially spoke of the black middle class in several different contexts and placed them in different categories. First, there was the elite he knew as a teenager: working-class black folk with upper-class pretensions. By trying to adopt the mannerisms of the authentic bourgeoisie these nouveau riche (without the wealth!) carved out for themselves a whole black elite culture. Second, there were the truly wealthy blacks whose social and cultural lives were inseparable from that of the white elite. He excoriated this class for having little interest or tolerance for the masses of black people. And, finally, there were the self-proclaimed black leaders, the "handkerchief heads" who ran integrationist organizations and begged for Civil Rights.

In Malcolm's view, all three categories of the black bourgeoisie shared a common disdain for the culture of the black masses. Indeed, Malcolm usually identified the black bourgeoisie by its culture rather than its income or occupation. His experience with the "Hill Negroes" demonstrated that wealth wasn't the main factor distinguishing the black bourgeoisie from the rest; it was their attitude, their adoration of European culture, and their distance from anything identified with ghetto blacks that rendered them elites. "They prided themselves on being incomparably more 'cultured,' 'cultivated,' 'dignified,' and better off than their black brethren down in

15. E.U. Essien-Udom, *Black Nationalism: A Search for Identity in America* (New York: Dell Publishing, 1964) 329–35.

the ghetto, which was no further away than you could throw a rock. Under the pitiful misapprehension that it would make them 'better,' these Hill Negroes were breaking their backs trying to imitate white people."[16] In a speech before a predominantly white college audience, he characterized the black bourgeoisie by its dress and mannerisms. "Uncle Tom wears a top hat. He's sharp. He dresses just like you do. He speaks the same phraseology, the same language. He tries to speak better than you do." More than anything, the black bourgeoisie are "ashamed of black, and don't want to be identified with black or as being black." Integration and intermarrying enables them to escape their black identity, which is why well-off black men are so anxious to marry white women and move into white neighborhoods.[17]

Worse yet, the black bourgeoisie would not—or could not—express their true "African" selves. Malcolm was convinced that being black meant being uninhibited: "the real bourgeois Black Americans . . . never want to show any sign of emotion. He won't even tap his feet. You can have some of that real soul music, and he'll sit there, you know, like it doesn't move him. . . . And it doesn't move them because they can't feel it, they've got no soul." Integration was the culprit. He even blamed his experiences at a predominantly white school in Mason, Michigan, for his inability to dance—i.e., the "natural" way Negroes dance—when he first arrived in Boston. But once he was pulled onto the dance floor, his ancient heritage took over: "It was as though somebody had clicked on a light. My long-suppressed African instincts broke through, and loose."[18] The racist

---

16. Malcolm X, *Autobiography*, 40.

17. "Twenty Million Black People . . ." in *Malcolm X: Last Speeches*, 30; Louis Lomax, *When the Word is Given . . . A Report on Elijah Muhammad, Malcolm X, and the Black Muslim World* (Cleveland and New York: The World Publishing Co., 1963), 191.

18. Malcolm X, *Malcolm X on Afro-American History* (New York: Pathfinder Press, 1990, new ed.), 21; Malcolm X, *Autobiography*, 57. According to Bruce Perry, this story was apocryphal. He had distinguished himself as an outstanding dancer in Mason. [Perry, *Malcolm*, 38.]

implications of such claims apparently never occurred to Malcolm, which is surprising given his criticisms of "Tarzan" movies for their portrayal of Africans as uncontrollable savages.

But letting "loose" was hardly what the Nation preached. On the contrary, the ascetic lifestyle NOI members had to live by differed little from the bourgeois values promoted by the very black middle-class uplift organizations Malcolm and his colleagues attacked. Alcohol, drugs, tobacco, gambling, dancing, adultery, premarital sex, profanity, or taking in movies with sex or "coarse speech" was simply not allowed. Even the music was monitored. One of Malcolm's colleagues, Benjamin Karim, recalls that "the jukebox in the temple restaurant played only African or Middle Eastern music, and some jazz, but no blues and no rock-and-roll with its uninspiring music and often downright dirty lyrics." The Nation even impressed black conservative George Schuyler, New York editor of the Pittsburgh *Courier*, who praised them for their values and moral vision. "Mr. Muhammad may be a rogue and a charlatan," wrote Schuyler in 1959, "but when anybody can get tens of thousands of Negroes to practice economic solidarity, respect their women, alter their atrocious diet, give up liquor, stop crime, juvenile delinquency and adultery, he is doing more for the Negro's welfare than any current Negro leader I know."[19]

Malcolm delivered regular speeches emphasizing cleanliness and morality, not so much to condemn wayward sinners but to demand self-transformation. And he remained a staunch devotee of the Nation's strict moral codes and gender conventions: men must lead, women must follow; the man's domain is the world, the woman's is the home.[20] Personally, Malcolm was the epitome of bourgeois respectability when he wasn't standing before a lectern or podium. Always exquisitely dressed, polite, and well-mannered, he could have written a book on

19. Karim, *Remembering Malcolm*, 75; Lincoln, *The Black Muslims*, 142.

20. Lomax, *When the Word is Given*, 27; Perry, *Malcolm*, 148, 171–73; Collins, "Learning to Think for Ourselves," 77–78; Kibbi V. Mack-Williams, "Malcolm X and the Woman Question: A Metamorphosis of Ideas and Attitudes," *Abafazi* 1.1 (Spring 1991): 9–13.

etiquette. He never sucked on chicken bones or licked his fingers at the table, and no matter how much of a hurry he was in he never spoke with his mouth full. "The man had style, grace," recalls Ben Karim. "Amy Vanderbilt would have had to sweat to match him."[21]

It would seem, then, that the Nation shared more in common culturally with the black bourgeoisie than their leaders realized. But we have to be careful before making such a judgment. Historically, notions of respectability, morality, and community responsibility did not originate solely with the black middle class. On the contrary, working-class and mixed-class institutions, such as the Christian church, played a crucial role in determining and instilling modes of behavior, beliefs, expectations, and moral vision. When we begin to look at, say, black churches as places where cultural values were enacted, taught, and policed, we discover that the so-called "lower class" was not always on the receiving end.[22] Working-class women demonstrated as much vigilance as their middle-class counterparts in enforcing

---

21. Karim, *Remembering Malcolm,* 65.

22. Although my general remarks apply to most black denominations, we must remain cognizant of the fact that the "black church" is not a monolithic institution. Not only are there different rituals, modes of worship, and biblical interpretations, but they often differ in terms of class membership. The African Methodist Episcopal Church, for example, has had a much larger middle-class congregation than the Baptist and Pentecostal churches. The Pentecostal churches have had a strong working-class following, especially in the urban North. For more on black churches, see C. Eric Lincoln and Lawrence H. Mimiya, *The Black Church in the African American Experience* (Durham, NC: Duke University Press, 1990); Hans Baer, *The Black Spiritual Movement: A Religious Response to Racism* (Knoxville, TN: University of Tennessee Press, 1984); Hans A. Baer and Merrill Singer, eds., *African-American Religion in the Twentieth Century: Varieties of Protest and Accommodation* (Knoxville, TN: University of Tennessee Press, 1992); Arthur Huff Fauset, *Black Gods of the Metropolis: Negro Religious Cults of the Urban North* (Philadelphia: University of Pennsylvania Press, 1944); William E. Montgomery, *Under Their Own Vine and Fig Tree: The African-American Church in the South, 1865–1900* (Baton Rouge, LA: Louisiana State University Press, 1993); Gayraud Wilmore, *Black Religion and Black Radicalism: An Interpretation of the Religious History of Afro-American People* (Maryknoll, NY: Orbis Books, 1983, 2nd ed.).

the general principle that cleanliness is next to Godliness. Baptist women of all classes distributed small pamphlets published by the National Baptist Convention bearing titles such as "How to Dress," "Anti-Hanging Out Committee," and "Take a Bath First."[23]

And yet, despite the close similarity between the Nation's teachings and Christian tenets of morality, Malcolm's attacks on Christianity struck a powerful chord among his congregations. He constantly argued that Christianity was a white man's religion imposed on black people during slavery. And he pointed to numerous instances in which self-proclaimed Christians— like white Southerners defending segregation and terrorizing black communities—did not practice what they preached. What is perhaps even more striking about the Nation was its willingness to embrace jazz—an aspect of black culture that the African-American church had historically opposed.[24] According to Louis Lomax, it wasn't unusual to hear live jazz combos opening up at Muslim Temples before lectures. And what these musicians played was undeniably "modern": "I have been in temple meetings where a group of brothers set the stage for the service by playing a protracted jazz riff. The music was as complex and as far out as anything you would hear at New York's Five Spot Café or any other den of progressive jazz."[25]

This fact reveals even more about the Nation's ambivalence toward black middle-class culture when we consider the period we are talking about. Unlike the 1920s and 1930s, when jazz was associated with "wild dancing" and seedy dance halls, after World War II jazz carved out a niche for itself in

23. Higginbotham, *Righteous Discontent*, 195; Gloria Wade-Gayles, *Pushed Back to Strength: A Black Woman's Journey Home* (Boston: Beacon Press, 1993), 13.

24. Through newspaper columns and leaflets, male and female activists in the church railed against a range of improprieties, such as "gum chewing, loud talking, gaudy colors, the nickelodeon, jazz," to name but a few. A leader of the Baptist church warned that "The sure way to ruin is by way of the public dance hall." Higginbotham, *Righteous Discontent*, 199, 201; Trotter, *Coal, Class, and Color*, 184.

25. Lomax, *When the Word is Given*, 22, 28.

the haughty world of American high culture. Although black jazz musicians insisted on incorporating black vernacular traditions and continued to be underpaid, overworked, and victims of blatant racist discrimination, more and more white critics viewed jazz as "art"—America's classical music. With the opening up of Carnegie Hall and Lincoln Center, the music became "bourgeoisified." As Karim put it, the Muslims refused to play "uninspiring music" and "downright dirty lyrics" to the sistern and brethren. It was black culture, no doubt, but it was no longer identified with the uncouth masses.[26]

Depending on when you caught him, Malcolm characterized middle-class African Americans as either ignorant of their true selves and thus potentially transformable, or ineluctably exploitative and hopeless. Although self-transformation was crucial to Malcolm's life and ideology, he frequently implied that the black bourgeoisie was incapable of siding with the masses and giving up their class interests—what African revolutionary Amilcar Cabral described as "committing class suicide."[27] After his English teacher, the infamous Mr. Ostrowski, told Malcolm that his aspiration to become a lawyer was "no real-

26. On the shift from "low" to "high" art during the postwar period, see Scott DeVeaux's "Constructing the Jazz Tradition: Jazz Historiography," *Black American Literature Forum* 25 (Fall 1991): 525–60, and "The Emergence of the Jazz Concert, 1935–1945," *American Music* 7 (Spring 1989): 6–29; on the perpetuation of racist structures in the jazz industry, see Frank Kofsky, *Black Nationalism and the Revolution in Music* (New York: Pathfinder, 1970); Paul Chevigny, *Gigs: Jazz and the Cabaret Laws in New York City* (New York and London: Routledge, 1991); quote from Karim, *Remembering Malcolm*, 75. It should also be pointed out that the NOI attracted a fairly substantial number of jazz musicians during this period, including alto saxophonist Sahib Shihab, trumpeter Idris Sulieman, pianist Sadik Hakim, and drummer Kenny Clarke (Liaquat Ali Salaam).

27. For a brilliant discussion of the importance of self-transformation, see Cornel West, "Malcolm X and Black Rage," *Malcolm X: In Our Own Image*, ed. Joe Wood (New York: St. Martin's Press, 1992), 48–58; and on Cabral, see Amilcar Cabral's *Revolution in Guinea* (New York: Monthly Review Press, 1969), 110, and *National Liberation and Culture*, trans. Maureen Webster (Syracuse: Syracuse University Press, 1970); Jack McCulloch, *In the Twilight of Revolution: The Political Theory of Amilcar Cabral* (London: Zed Books, 1983), 72–74.

istic goal for a nigger," he pondered what his future might have been like if he had been encouraged to pursue a career in law. He was convinced that if he had joined the black elite he would have been destined to become a turncoat: "I would today probably be among some city's professional black bour-geoisie, sipping cocktails and palming myself off as a commu-nity spokesman for and leader of the suffering black masses, while my primary concern would be to grab a few more crumbs from the groaning board of the two-faced whites with whom they're begging to 'integrate.'"[28] By making this state-ment, however, Malcolm was not only arguing that the bour-geoisie was hopelessly bankrupt; he was making a case for the primacy of experience. "All praise due to Allah that I went to Boston when I did. If I hadn't, I'd probably still be a brain-washed black Christian." While his gratitude to Allah offers a hint of fatalism, he is nonetheless suggesting that his experi-ence with "ordinary Negroes" shaped his outlook and direc-tion. He took a trip to Hell, no doubt, and even looked the devil in the face. But if he hadn't taken that horrible trip, he implies, he might have ended up with a fate worse than death—Malcolm Little, Esq.

I seriously doubt Malcolm believed that a formal education and a career in law would have corrupted him, however. On the contrary, he probably spent most of his adult life regretful for not pursuing his educational goals. Every time he looked into the eyes of his own attorney, black radical Conrad Lynn, perhaps he saw himself. He fashioned himself as an intellec-tual and spent many mornings at a Harlem coffee shop called 22 West on 135th St. engaged in lively debates with the same "Uncle Toms" he talked about so badly on stage and in the press. In speech after speech, despite his ravings against "nin-compoops with Ph.D.s," he strongly suggested that as black folks became more educated, they would inevitably undermine the status quo. In a speech delivered at Harvard Law School in 1960, he argued: "Once the slave has his master's education, the slave wants to be like his master, wants to share his mas-

28. Malcolm X, *Autobiography*, 36, 38.

ter's property, and even wants to exercise the same privileges as his master even while he is yet in his master's house." He warned Harvard's faculty and administration that "the same Negro students you are turning out today will soon be demanding the same things you now hear being demanded by Mr. Muhammad and the Black Muslims." Thus education, even in the white Ivy League institutions, was seen as potentially emancipatory—that is, as long as it is not limited to the sons and daughters of the elite. Real freedom depends on the poor, downtrodden masses gaining access to the master's knowledge.[29]

It was an incredible speech, for it reveals Malcolm's own envy and appreciation for formal education. Indeed, Malcolm not only showed an enormous amount of respect and admiration for institutions of higher learning, but he suggested that black intellectuals—if properly united—have the capacity to lead African Americans "out of this maze of misery and want." "They possess the academic know-how," he asserted, "great amounts of technical skills . . . but they can't use it for the benefit of their own kind simply because they themselves are also disunited. If these intellectuals and professional so-called Negroes would unite, not only Harlem would benefit, but it will benefit our people all over the world."[30]

Thus Malcolm offered the black elite a ray of hope, a road to redemption if they made the right choices. What choice did he have? As a black nationalist with hopes of building a black nation, all African Americans had to share a common historical bond. What kind of nationalist would argue that the black bourgeoisie could never be allies of the black masses because their political and economic interests are diametrically opposed? And what kind of self-respecting nationalist promoting black enterprise as an emancipatory strategy could completely shut out successful black business people? Most importantly,

29. Karim, *Remembering Malcolm*, 68; Lomax, *When the Word is Given*, 146–47.

30 Lomax, *When the Word is Given*, 155.

how did Malcolm explain these modern class divisions in light of the historical experiences of Africans in the U.S.?

Simple: the Devil made us do it. The black bourgeoisie in America was a creation of the white man and thus has always been dependent on whites for their very existence. He demonstrates this by evoking a romantic image of precolonial Africa in which communalism and collectivism were the natural state of being for black people. Before the white man came, our societies were free of oppression and domination. We lived in the land of milk and honey where there were no slaves and everyone was treated with dignity and respect. Interestingly, Malcolm's ancient Africa was not a classless society. On the contrary, by implication the upper class were the "cream of the crop" whereas the lower class were less desirable. "You and I were produced by kings and queens from the African continent, scientists, the best. They took the best of the African society and sold them as slaves. We brought the highest price. We didn't come here as chumps; we were the cream of the crop on the African continent." On the other hand, the European slave traders and invaders of the so-called New World "were the dregs of society."[31]

In all fairness, by constructing African Americans as the descendants of elites and white Americans as descendants of crooks and vagabonds, Malcolm was consciously creating a counter myth in order to instill ordinary black folks with a sense of pride while enhancing his condemnation of white people. He is essentially saying that the difference between today's black bourgeoisie and the African elite of ancient times was that the latter did not have to depend on white people. They were proud and wealthy, not because they exploited their subordinates but because they had knowledge of self and community. Sure, Malcolm's narrative wrote indigenous slavery out of African history and obscured the kind of class exploita-

31. Malcolm X, *Malcolm X on Afro-American History* (New York: Pathfinder Press, 1990, new ed.), 27–31, 49; also see "Twenty Million Black People in a Political, Economic, and Mental Prison," delivered at Michigan State University, January 23, 1963, *Malcolm X: The Last Speeches*, 37.

tion that made pyramids and cities and higher learning possible, but imagine how it made black people feel—people who spent their lives as second-class citizens, as the butt of racist jokes, as the presumed descendants of savages?

We need to also keep in mind that in the early 1960s, the "nationalist" school of historiography had emerged as the dominant trend in Africanist scholarship. With the coming of independence, African historians challenged colonialist interpretations and re-wrote their pasts in very celebratory and romantic terms.[32] More significantly, African-American historians—particularly those oriented toward black nationalism—had been writing this sort of history for some time. Thus Malcolm's oppression-free Africa was not of his own invention but the product of an insurgent scholarship that emphasized cultural unity, resistance, and the recovery of a glorious precolonial past. Ironically, these historians, which included people such as Senegalese historian Cheikh Anta Diop and African-American scholars J.A. Rogers, William Ferris, Willis N. Huggins, and John Jackson, were still constrained by Western bourgeois notions of civilization and progress. Like Malcolm, they relied on the dominant notions of "civilization," "Progress," even "technology," to prove the antiquity and superiority of Africa.[33]

32. See Arnold Temu and Bonaventure Swai, *Historians and Africanist History: A Critique* (London: Zed Press, 1983); Henry Slater, "The Dar es Salaam Contribution to the Post-Nationalist Historiography of Africa: Towards Methodology and Practice of Proletarian Socialist Historiography," paper presented to the 13th Annual Conference of the Canadian Association of African Studies, Laval University, 1983.

33. Cheikh Anta Diop, *Nations Negres et Culture* (Paris: Editions Africaines, 1955), later published in English as *African Origins of Civilization* (Brooklyn: Lawrence Hill, 1974); Willis Huggins and John Jackson's *A Guide to Studies in African History* (New York: Federation of History Clubs, 1934) and *Introduction to African Civilization* (New York: University Books, 1970, orig. 1937); Carter G. Woodson, *African Heroes and Heroines* (Washington D.C., Association for the Study of Negro Life and History, 1939); J.A. Rogers, *World's Great Men of Color*, 2 vols. (New York, 1947); Valerie Sandoval, "The Brand of History: A Historiographic Account of the Work of J.A. Rogers," *Schomburg Center for Research in Black Culture Journal* (Spring 1978): 11–17; George E.M. James, *Stolen Legacy* (New York: Philosophical Library,

So it is not wealth, per se, that renders the black bourgeoisie useless. It is their station in the Big House and their unwillingness to walk out. Unlike their ancestors, they have failed to live up to their responsibility to assist the downtrodden, to (as one middle-class black women's organization put it) lift as they climb. "The wealthy, educated Black bourgeoisie," Malcolm told a University of California audience in 1963, "those uppity Negroes who do escape, never reach back and pull the rest of our people out with them. The Black masses remain trapped in the slums."[34]

In fact, one of the less talked about reasons why Malcolm left the Nation has to do with the fact that NOI leaders began to look more and more like the greedy, wealthy Negroes he criticized. With disdain and sadness, he watched efforts at self-reliance and economic self-help through the establishment of businesses tragically turn into a private empire for the Messenger and his cronies. By the eve of Malcolm's break, the NOI had become a cross between a black mafia and a legitimate bourgeois enterprise. At one point, the NOI boasted of one of the most successful black-run financial empires in the country, with assets reportedly reaching 45 million dollars. With Elijah and his family riding around in chauffeur-driven cadillacs and living in mansions, the Messenger began to resemble the very black bourgeoisie whom Malcolm hated. And Malcolm was well aware of the unscrupulous ways the NOI took its members' money, which included the outright misap-

---

1976, orig. 1954). Later proponents of this approach to the African past include Ivan Van Sertima, *They Came Before Columbus* (New York: Random House, 1976); Yosef ben-Jochannon, *Africa: Mother of Civilization* (New York: Alkeb-Ian, 1971); John Henrik Clarke, "African-American Historians and the Reclaiming of African History," *African Culture: The Rhythms of Unity,* ed. Molefi Kete Asante and Kariamu Welsh Asante (Westport: Greenwood Press, 1985); Chancellor Williams, *The Destruction of African Civilization: Great Issues of Race From 4500 B.C. to 2000 A.D.* (Chicago: Third World Press, 1974); Molefi Asante, *The Afrocentric Idea* (Philadelphia: Temple University Press, 1987).

34. "America's Gravest Crisis Since the Civil War," *Malcolm X: The Last Speeches,* 64.

propriation of funds. Benjamin Karim remembers one run-in between Malcolm and John Ali over thirty or forty thousand dollars New York's Temple No. 7 had raised to build a new mosque. When Malcolm asked about the money, Ali couldn't exactly account for it; he derisively said it had been invested in some other venture but couldn't say which one. Karim, who had never seen Malcolm so angry, heard him grumble something like, "They probably needed some loose change to dress Ethel [Elijah's daughter who was married to Supreme Captain Raymond Sharrief] up in diamonds and mink for a fancy night on the town."[35]

Ironically, the "house niggas" for whom Malcolm reserved most of his venom turned out to be some of the same people with whom he sought to build an alliance: traditional black political leaders and the Civil Rights establishment. His relationship to other black leaders, in Harlem and elsewhere, was never cut and dried. On the one hand, the Nation of Islam maintained rules against political participation—a policy Malcolm clearly disagreed with. He not only believed that political mobilization was indispensable but occasionally defied the rule by supporting boycotts and other forms of protest. On the other hand, Elijah Muhammad was always open to alliances with traditional black leaders and maintained cordial relations whenever possible. In July 1958, for example, African-American politicians hosted a two-day "Unity Feast" for Elijah Muhammad in Harlem where he was greeted by Manhattan borough president Hulan Jack, City Councilman Earl Brown, and columnist J.A. Rogers, to name a few. And at a Muslim-sponsored Leadership Conference in Harlem less than two years later, several prominent black leaders showed up, including Adam Clayton Powell, Jr. Malcolm even offered his guests bittersweet praise when he thanked black leaders in attendance for "at last catching up with the progressive thinking of the enlightened Negro masses."[36]

35. Perry, *Malcolm*, 221; Lomax, *When the Word is Given*, 79; Karim, *Remembering Malcolm*, 151.

36. Lincoln, *The Black Muslims*, 138–39.

Malcolm, therefore, found himself in the unenviable position of monitoring both his political activities as well as his criticisms of black leaders. Muhammad's posture of trying to keep out of politics while making friends with politicians put an enormous strain on Malcolm, who had gained a reputation in Harlem as one of the most militant, outspoken voices in the community. For example, in the summer and fall of 1959, the NAACP stepped up its denunciations of the Nation of Islam, their tenor and tone equaling Malcolm's most unkind remarks. Roy Wilkins called them a "menace" who do nothing for black people but preach "hatred," and Thurgood Marshall dismissed the NOI as an organization "run by a bunch of thugs organized from prisons and jails, and financed, I am sure, by Nasser or some Arab group." Malcolm shot back immediately, calling Marshall a "twentieth century Uncle Tom." It seemed like war had been declared between the NAACP and the NOI, but the Nation's top leaders—those over Malcolm—were not interested in participating. A few months later, Wallace D. Muhammad, Elijah's son and minister of the Philadelphia Temple, announced a fundraising drive on behalf of Daisy Bates, the NAACP regional executive who had led the school integration struggle in Little Rock, Arkansas. He praised Bates for her courage and stated that the Nation "is striving for the same goal as the NAACP in their fight for our people's rights in this country."[37]

Malcolm, who was probably caught off guard by the gesture of unity, was less charitable than Wallace D. While unwilling to make amends, he did show signs of respect for certain local NAACP leaders. After New York branch president L. Joseph Overton was booed at a reception for Guinean President Sekou Toure, allegedly by Muslims in attendance, Malcolm apologized for the incident and praised Overton—though he took the opportunity to fire a few shots at the NAACP's national leader. "Overton is out there in the street with the rest of us. He's got some idea of what the Black Man wants—what he's

37. Lincoln, *The Black Muslims*, 147–48, 150.

thinking. It's not so with the others. Every time I've seen Roy Wilkins he's been at the Waldorf, or in the vicinity of the Waldorf. I have never seen him with black people unless they were looking for white people!"[38]

In August of 1960, Malcolm held a "Unity Rally" in Harlem (without the approval of Elijah Muhammad) to debate the key issues affecting black people and invited, among others, Dr. Martin Luther King, Jr., Jackie Robinson, Adam Clayton Powell, Jr., Thurgood Marshall, and Roy Wilkins. To Malcolm's disappointment, only Hulan Jack showed up. He delivered a scathing attack on black leaders for shunning the event, calling them every name in the book. Yet, despite his invective, it seemed as if Malcolm's real intention was to throw down the gauntlet and see if these leaders accepted the challenge. He told the audience that they did not show up because they were afraid "of irking their white bosses [or] embarrassing their white liberal friends." At the same time, he called on black leaders to follow the lead of the Non-Aligned nations, who had decided to overlook their differences and come together at an historic unity conference in Bandung, Indonesia, five years earlier. Because black people in the U.S. share a common history of oppression—irrespective of political outlook, religious affiliation, or class differences—we had to find a way to unite. As he put it, "the HOUR is too short today for black people to afford the luxury of 'differences.'"[39]

How much of this was Malcolm and how much was Elijah Muhammad (or Wallace D. Muhammad) is hard to say. After all, Malcolm's strategy for unity was still based on the Honorable Elijah Muhammad's ideas of a separate state for black people. Nevertheless, Malcolm continued to cite the Bandung conference as a model for building unity among different constituents until the eve of the assassination, and eventually the separate state argument gave way to a more nuanced, situa-

38. Lincoln, *The Black Muslims*, 150–51.

39. Lincoln, *The Black Muslims*, 138–39; Perry, *Malcolm*, 212; Lomax, *When the Word is Given*, 151.

tional approach to black liberation after he broke with the Nation. And yet, the greater his independence from the NOI and the closer he moved toward backing the Civil Rights movement, the harsher his denunciations of mainstream black leadership. During a stormy debate with NAACP Youth Secretary Herbert Wright sponsored by Yale University Law School in 1962, Malcolm dismissed the entire Civil Rights establishment as a bunch of sell-outs and "Uncle Toms." He went even further, suggesting that the next President bypass traditional black leaders and talk directly to ordinary folks, or to the Nation of Islam. "The black masses," he argued, "are tired of following these hand-picked Negro 'leaders' who sound like professional beggars, as they cry year after year for white America to accept us as first-class citizens."[40]

Likewise, in his speech before the Northern Negro Grass Roots Leadership Conference in Detroit in 1963, he insisted that the masses had no authentic spokespersons among the "legitimate" black leaders. These men were "handpicked" by white men in power and thus did not represent the wants and needs of ordinary black people. Self-proclaimed Negro leaders were not just misled; their job was to mislead, to keep black folks in check. They were the direct descendants of the "house slave":

The slavemaster took Tom and dressed him well, fed him and even gave him a little education—a *little* education; gave him a long coat and a top hat and made all the other slaves look up to him. Then he used Tom to control them. The same strategy that was used in those days is used today, by the same white man. He takes a Negro, a so-called Negro, and makes him prominent, builds him up, publicizes him, makes him a celebrity. And then he becomes a spokesman for Negroes—and a Negro leader.

40. Lomax, *When the Word is Given,* 180, 191. The claim that black leaders were "handpicked" was not entirely new. In a speech delivered at Harvard Law School in 1960, he called them "Negro puppets whom you yourself have appointed as our 'leaders' and 'spokesmen'" (Lomax 144).

These Civil Rights leaders, he said, were leading a non-violent *Negro* revolution when what was needed was a *Black* revolution. Whereas the former wants to desegregate, the latter demands land, power, and freedom. Whereas the former adopts a Christian philosophy of "love thy enemy," the latter has no love or respect for the oppressor. Malcolm still advocated unity and pointed to Bandung as the grand example, but the only unity he was interested in was under a revolutionary black nationalist banner.[41]

LEFT TURN?

Malcolm's critique of the black bourgeoisie and traditional black leaders, and his strong identification with the poorest of black folks, propelled him to Left wing organizations. The attraction was mutual. Just as the Communist Party had been drawn to Garveyism in the 1920s because they saw so many black working people in the movement and believed it could be transformed into a revolutionary organization,[42] Trotskyites and other Leftists noticed the large numbers of black proletarians flocking to the NOI. As early as 1961, Malcolm established working relationships with several left-wing organizations, and in 1962 spoke at an 1199 rally and shared the podium with A. Philip Randolph and several Puerto Rican labor activists. He eventually gained a small following of radical Marxists, mostly Trotskyites in the Socialist Workers Party. Malcolm convinced some SWP members of the revolutionary potential or ordinary

41. "Message to the Grassroots," *Malcolm X Speaks,* 5–10 (quote from p. 13).

42. On the CP and Garveyism, see *The Marcus Garvey and Universal Negro Improvement Association Papers,* ed. Robert Hill (Berkeley and Los Angeles: University of California Press, 1984), vol. III, 675–81; James Jackson [Lovett Fort-Whiteman], "The Negro in America," *Communist International* (February 1925): 52; Robert Minor, "After Garvey-What?" *Workers Monthly* 5 (June 1926): 362–65.

black slum dwellers, and he began to speak more critically of capitalism.[43]

He also began developing an independent "Third World" political perspective, although he showed signs of such a perspective at least a decade earlier, when anti-colonial wars and decolonization were pressing public issues. As early as 1954, Malcolm gave a speech comparing the situation in Vietnam with that of the Mau Mau rebellion in colonial Kenya, framing both of these movements as uprisings of the "Darker races" creating a "Tidal Wave" against U.S. and European imperialism. Indeed, Africa remained his primary political interest outside of black America.[44]

Yet, despite his internationalism and flirtation with Marxism, his critique of the black bourgeoisie remained ambivalent, at best. At the very same moment black intellectuals such as Frantz Fanon, C.L.R. James, and Amilcar Cabral were grappling with the role of the national bourgeoisie in African independence struggles, Malcolm's pronouncements on the subject were analytically dull by comparison. And yet, in the States he was way ahead of the game, for unlike his detractors in the "Negro revolution," he at least recognized the importance of class differences among African Americans.

In some respects, Malcolm's dilemma was—and still is—inescapable. To escape it requires a remarkable analytical leap that would undermine the fragile basis upon which his conception of black nationalism was built. Like today's young nationalists weighed down by X caps and red, black and green medallions, Malcolm saw the black bourgeoisie as both enemies and misguided souls, sellouts and brainwashed Negroes who simply need a wake-up call from the Motherland. Few are willing to say, in no uncertain terms, that the black poor and

---

43. Perry, *Malcolm*, 212; Wolfenstein, *Victims of Democracy*, 300–28; George Breitman's *The Last Year of Malcolm X: The Evolution of a Revolutionary* (New York: Merit Publishers, 1967) and *Malcolm X: The Man and His Ideas* (New York: Merit Publishers, 1965).

44. Gambino, "The Transgression of a Laborer," 23.

the bourgeoisie have mutually exclusive interests.[45] For to do so would be to call into question the whole basis of nationalism, particularly a nationalism based on racial and cultural affinity. Even more damaging, however, is that it would close off any possibility of achieving individual success. After all, what are these young Soul Rebels striving for anyway? How can anyone expect young people coming up today to completely repudiate the black bourgeoisie, or any bourgeoisie, if contemporary Malcolmites are giving graduation speeches about the importance of getting paid or obtaining that degree "by any means necessary"?

Yet, Malcolm's reputation as a militant is partly built on his denunciation of the "house nigga." His current resurrection has a lot to do with growing class tensions between a successful, suburban, and increasingly disinterested black middle class and the so-called "underclass" left to rot in the slums. The word "bourgeois" has even become common lingo among Hip Hop artists and their fans to refer to black-owned radio stations and, more generally, middle-class African Americans who exhibit disgust or indifference toward young, working-class blacks. For Ice T, living in the lap of luxury is not what renders the black bourgeoisie bankrupt, but rather their inability to understand the world of the ghetto. In an interview a few years back he explained, "I don't think the negative propaganda about rap comes from the true black community—it comes from the bourgeois black community, which I hate. Those are the blacks who have an attitude that because I wear a hat and a gold chain, I'm a nigger and they're better than me." Similarly, the former rap group W.C. and the MAAD Circle levelled an even more sustained attack on those they call "bourgeois Negroes." Proclaiming that the Circle's sympathies lie with "poor folks in the slums," lead rapper W.C. derisively wrote off

45. One scholar, at least, believes Malcolm was on the verge of seeing the black bourgeoisie's interests as diametrically opposed to that of the black working class. I'm still skeptical, however. See Kevin Ovenden, *Malcolm X: Socialism and Black Nationalism* (London: Bookmarks, 1992), 44.

suburban middle-class African Americans as turncoats and cowards.[46]

Even if we are unwilling to call this "class struggle," there is no denying that these young voices are well aware that not all black folks are equally powerless and oppressed. Now that so many urban African Americans are growing up under black mayors and black police officers, they are slowly coming to the conclusion that black politicians and authority figures are as much to blame for the state of the ghetto as their white counterparts. Unlike the "house niggers" of Malcolm's generation, today's black political elite don't need to beg or plead; some of them run the big house. And as long as the status of the "field niggas" remain unchanged, Malcolm's metaphor will continue to articulate the latent class anger that lies muffled beneath a racial blanket.

46. Ice T quoted in Michael Eric Dyson, "The Culture of Hip Hop," *Zeta* (June 1989): 46; Ice T, *The Iceberg/Freedom of Speech . . . Just Watch What You Say* (Sire Records, 1989); see also Ice T, "Radio Suckers," *Power* (Sire Records, 1988) and "This One's For Me," *The Iceberg/Freedom of Speech . . . Just Watch What You Say*; Ice Cube, "Turn off the Radio," *AmeriKKKa's Most Wanted* (Priority Records, 1991); W.C. and the MAAD Circle, *Ain't A Damn Thang Changed* (Priority Records, 1991).

Farah Jasmine Griffin, "'Ironies of the Saint':
Malcolm X, Black Women, and the Price of Protection,"
in Collier-Thomas and Franklin, eds., *Sisters in the
Struggle: African American Women in the Civil
Rights–Black Power Movement* (New York: New York
University Press, 2001), 214–229

This essay grows out of two concerns: First, the re-rise of what I want to call a "promise of protection" as a more progressive counter discourse to elements of misogyny in black popular culture; second, my feeling that the emergence of Malcolm X as an icon of younger African Americans requires a serious and sustained examination and engagement of all aspects of his legacy. Malcolm X has not been the subject of a black feminist critique in the way that Richard Wright or Miles Davis have been. When I looked to black feminists thinkers who have written on Malcolm, few of them were as critical of his views on women as I had expected. Patricia Hill Collins, Barbara Ransby, and Tracye Matthews are among the few to call attention to Malcolm's gender politics.[1]

Black women are reluctant of being critical of Malcolm X: theirs is a reluctance born from the desire not to have such a critique co-opted by those who already hold him in contempt and disdain and a reluctance grounded in the genuine love, respect, and reverence that many black women have for

1. See Barbara Ransby and Tracye Matthews, "Black Popular Culture and the Transcendence of Patriarchal Illusions," in Beverly Guy-Sheftall, ed., *Words on Fire: An Anthology of African American Feminist Thought* (New York: The New Press, 1995), 526–35; and Patricia Hill Collins, "Learning to Think for Ourselves: Malcolm X's Black Nationalism Reconsidered," in Joe Wood, ed,. *Malcolm X: In Our Own Image* (New York: Anchor Books, 1992), 59–85.

Malcolm. I must admit that even as I write this essay, I share this reluctance, for there are few black male leaders whom I hold in as much esteem as I do Malcolm. Nonetheless, while I recognize Malcolm to be a man of his times and a man with tremendous capacity for growth, I am disturbed by any tendency to uncritically adopt his political and rhetorical stance, particularly around gender.

In this essay I will articulate some of the reasons why so many black women, even black feminists, appreciate and revere Malcolm and his legacy. Then I hope to offer a reading of his position on women, not as a means of discrediting the esteem in which we hold him, but as a means to move us beyond the oppressive gender politics embedded in his rhetoric. Malcolm X offered black women a promise of protection, an acknowledgment of the significance of white racist assaults on black beauty and an affirmation of black features, particularly hair and color. In the remainder of this essay, I will examine these two important aspects of his legacy.

THE PROMISE OF PROTECTION

Her head is more regularly beaten than any woman's and by her own man; she is the scapegoat for Mr. Charlie; she is forced to stark realism and chided if caught dreaming; her aspirations for her and hers are, for sanity's sake, stunted; her physical image has been criminally maligned, assaulted, and negated; she's the first to be called ugly, yet never beautiful, and as a consequence is forced to see her man . . . brainwashed and wallowing in self-loathing, pick for his own the physical antithesis of her. . . . Then to add insult to injury, she . . . stands accused as emasculator of the only thing she has ever cared for, her black man . . . Who will revere the black woman? Who will keep our neighborhood safe for black innocent womanhood? . . . black womanhood cries for dignity and restitution and salvation. black womanhood wants and needs protection and keeping and holding. . . . Who will keep her precious and pure?

> Who will glorify and proclaim her beautiful image? To whom
> will she cry rape?
>
> —Abbey Lincoln[2]

Malcolm X's appeal to a broad range of black women lay first
in his courage and commitment to black liberation and second
in his attempt to address the call sent out by Abbey Lincoln
and cited above; a call that had been voiced many times prior
to Lincoln's articulation of it: "Who will revere the black
woman? Who will keep her precious and pure? Who will keep
our neighborhoods safe for innocent black womanhood?
Who will glorify and proclaim her beautiful image?" The terms
"precious," "pure," "innocent," "beautiful," and "revere" were
(and in many instances, continue to be) particularly important
to African American women. Each of these terms has been
equated with white womanhood and thereby with feminin-
ity—both privileged spheres in our society; spheres where
black women have historically been denied access. Poor and
working black women, and dark-skinned black women especially, have been excluded from the discourse of the precious,
pure, and protected.

However, as appealing as the promise of protection and the
guarantee of purity are, they are also intensely problematic:
These are the very same terms used by white American men,
particularly white Southern men, to repress white women and
to systematically brutalize black men—all in the name of protection and (race) purity.

My term "promise of protection" is influenced by Jacquelyn
Dowd Hall's term, "rhetoric of protection." Hall uses the
phrase to describe the discourses of a pure and protected white
womanhood in the American South. According to Hall, "the
rhetoric of protection [was] reflective of a power struggle between men." She continues, "the right of the southern lady to

2. Abbey Lincoln, "Who Will Revere the Black Woman?" *Negro Digest*
(September 1966), reprinted in Toni Cade, ed., *The Black Woman* (New York:
Signet, 1970), 82–84.

protection presupposed her obligation to obey."[3] I have chosen
not to use the word "rhetoric" because I want to avoid the implications of the word that suggest a discourse lacking in conviction or earnest feeling. Malcolm's desire to "protect" black
women grew out of a sincere concern for their emotional, psy-
chic, and physical safety; it was also reflective of the power
struggle between black and white men and black men and
women. Furthermore, the pure and protected black woman of
his vision was also obligated to obey her protector—the black
man. The exchange is as follows: The woman gets protection;
the man acquires a possession.

Nonetheless, many black women were willing to accept the
terms of this contract. Barbara Omolade explains, "The extremes of American patriarchy, particularly under slavery,
pushed black women outside traditional patriarchal protection." Consequently, the promise of patriarchal protection
was certainly much better than the methodical abuse suffered
by black women throughout much of their history in the
New World. As had been the case a century earlier with their
recently freed foremothers, the assurance of their safety was
a very appealing vision for many black women: It stood in direct opposition to the degrading images that bombarded them
on a daily basis and the harsh reality of many of their lives.
Omolade notes, "Most black women accepted traditional notions of patriarchy from black men because they viewed the
Afro-Christian tradition of woman as mother and wife as personally desirable and politically necessary for black people's
survival."[4]

Malcolm X's promise of protection comes from a long tradition in African American writing and organizing. The National Association of Colored Women was formed in 1896 in
part to protect the name and image of black women. Leaders

3. Jacquelyn Dowd Hall, "The Mind That Burns in Each Body: Women,
Rape, and Racial Violence," in Ann Snitow, Christine Stansell, and Sharon
Tompson, eds., *Powers of Desire* (New York: Monthly Review Press, 1983),
335.

4. Barbara Omolade, Hearts of Darkness," in Snitnow, *Powers of Desire*, 352.

like W.E.B. Du Bois and Alexander Crummell both called for the protection of black women from rape, physical abuse, and economic poverty.[5] Large numbers of the urban women to whom Malcolm X spoke were the daughters of or were themselves women who fled the South in an attempt to escape the threat of rape from white males. Black women also found themselves the victims of economic exploitation, unfair employment practices, medical experimentation, and domestic violence. Who was deemed better to play the role of protector than black men? This, of course, is a role that had been denied black men throughout history.

Malcolm's promise of protection assumes a stance of victimization on the part of those who need to be protected without allowing much room for their agency in other spheres. It places the woman in the hands of her protector—who may protect her, but who also may decide to further victimize her. In either case her well-being is entirely dependent on his will and authority. Note Malcolm's words upon hearing the dynamic Fannie Lou Hamer speak of her experiences in Mississippi:

> When I listen to Mrs. Hamer, a black woman—could be my mother, my sister, my daughter—describe what they have done to her in Mississippi, I ask myself how in the world can we expect to be respected as *men* when we will allow something like that to be done to our women, and we do nothing about it? How can you and I be looked upon as men with black women being beaten and nothing being done about it? No, we don't deserve to be recognized and respected as men as long as our women can be brutalized in the manner that this woman described, and nothing being done about it, but we sit around singing "We shall overcome."[6]

5. See Alexander Crummell, *Destiny and Race: Selected Writing, 1840–1898*, edited by Wilson Jeremiah Wilson (Amherst: University of Massachusetts Press, 1992); and W. E. B. Du Bois, "The Damnation of Women," in *Darkwater: Voices from Within the Veil* (New York: Harcourt, Brace, 1920), 164–85.

6. George Breitman, ed., *Malcolm X Speaks: Selected Speeches and Statements* (New York: Grove Weidenfeld, 1965), 107.

Later, when introducing her at the Audubon, Malcolm would refer to her as "the country's number one freedom-fighting woman." However, the predominant tone of this passage refers to Hamer only as a victim in need of protection—not the protection afforded to citizens by their governments (which the South and the nation at large did not provide) but the protection of a black man. Hamer's victimization makes black men the subject of Malcolm's comment. When read closely, the above statement is not a paragraph about Fannie Lou Hamer but about the questionable masculinity of black men, particularly those black men of the southern Civil Rights Movement such as Martin Luther King. If black men protected "their" women, then Ms. Hamer would not be a victim of such abuse. Nor would she be a freedom fighter—that would be a position monopolized by black male protectors.

According to Malcolm in his *Autobiography,* "All women by their nature are fragile and weak: they are attracted to the male in whom they see strength."[7] This assertion of the nature of black women leaves little room for women like Fannie Lou Hamer, Ella Baker, Septima Clark, Harriet Tubman, Mary McLeod Bethune, Ida B. Wells, or Angela Davis.

Malcolm's general understanding about the nature of women was acquired in childhood through witnessing the abusive actions of his father as well as from his days on the streets of Boston and New York. While the discourse of protection emerges from the Nation of Islam, it does not challenge Malcolm's earlier notions of women's nature. Instead, the Nation provides him with a framework that still accepts women's nature as fragile and weak, that also sees women as manipulative, but that encourages men to protect and respect instead of abuse them. Malcolm's mentor Elijah Muhammed shared his sense that the protection of the black woman guaranteed black men their manhood: "Until we learn to love and protect our woman, we will never be a fit and recognized people on earth. The

---

7. Malcolm X and Alex Haley, *The Autobiography of Malcolm X* (New York: Ballentine Books, 1990).

white people here among you will never recognize you until
you protect your woman."[8]

In all of the instances cited above, women are subordinate
to men whether as the objects of abuse or protection. In the
Autobiography, Malcolm notes:

> Islam has very strict laws and teachings about women, the core
> of them being that the true nature of man is to be strong, and a
> woman's true nature is to be weak, and while a man must at all
> times respect his woman, at the same time he needs to under-
> stand that he must control her if he expects to get her respect.[9]

Protection is not in and of itself a bad thing. Patriarchal societies such as ours foster misogyny from which all women need
protection. A racist patriarchal society is particularly dangerous for black women. However, protection need not be equated
with possession. Of course, until the day arrives when we no
longer live in a patriarchal society, women need to be protected
from misogyny and paternalism; however, instead of fighting
simply to protect women from misogyny, we must all engage in
the fight to eradicate patriarchy as well as racism. This dedication is nowhere apparent in Malcolm's writing. Finally, it is one
thing to protect an individual so that she may actually live with
a greater degree of freedom, that is, make our streets safe so
that women may walk alone at night. It is another thing entirely to "protect" someone and in so doing to limit their freedom and mobility. We must be careful to distinguish offers of
protection that are made in a context that places limitations on
women's freedom.

In a brilliant Afro-centric feminist critique of African American nationalism, "Africa on My Mind: Gender, Counter Discourse and African-American Nationalism," E. Frances White

8. Again, here as with Malcolm, protection is really about manhood. It is
quite significant that the editorial from which this statement is taken was recently republished in an edition of *The Final Call* devoted to black women. Reprinted in *The Final Call,* July 20, 1994, 18.

9. Malcolm X, *The Autobiography,* 226.

argues that "black nationalism is an oppositional strategy that both counters racism and constructs utopian and repressive gender relations."[10] Herein lies the paradox of Malcolm's promise of protection. When considered only in contrast to the external discourse of white supremacy, Malcolm's proposal of protection seems to offer a radical stance on black womanhood. However, if we consider what his discourse shares with white sexist discourse, we see something altogether different. Again White warns:

> In making appeals to conservative notions of appropriate gender behavior, African-American nationalists reveal their ideological ties to other nationalist movements, including European and Euro-American bourgeois nationalists over the past 200 years . . . European and Euro-American nationalists turned to their ideology of respectability to help them impose the bourgeoisie manners and morals that attempted to control sexual behavior and gender relations.[11]

Malcolm X's promise of protection falls under the rubric of the "ideology of respectability." The protected woman is the "respectable" woman. The man who protects her is the respected man.

THE AFFIRMATION OF BLACK BEAUTY

> I knew he loved me for my clear brown skin—it was very smooth. He liked my clear eyes. He liked my gleaming dark hair. I was very thin then and he liked my black beauty, my mind. He just liked me.
>
> —Betty Shabazz[12]

10. E. Frances White, "Africa On My Mind: Gender, Counter Discourse and African-American Nationalism," *Journal of Women's History*, 2, no. 1 (Spring 1990), 76.

11. Ibid.

12. Betty Shabazz, "Loving and Losing Malcolm," *Essence* (February 1992): 107.

In addition to the promise of protection, Malcolm X also offered all black people, and black women in particular, an affirmation of black features and physical characteristics. In so doing, he followed the lead of Marcus Garvey and Elijah Muhammad. To many this may seem unimportant or shallow, but when considered in light of constant white supremacist assaults on notions of black beauty, it is of profound significance. From the minstrel caricatures to "serious scientific" studies, black difference has always been predicated on black bodies. Big black lips, nappy black hair, large black thighs and derrieres, black black skin, "oversized" black genitals.

Though African Americans always fought such assaults by establishing and maintaining their own sense of their humanity, dignity, capability, and beauty, perhaps in no realm have our oppressors been more successful than in convincing us of our own ugliness. Throughout our history on this continent, black Americans have accepted and revised white standards of beauty. Yet for large numbers of black women these standards continue to be oppressive, particularly when they are upheld by other African Americans. In 1925, Walter White observed: "Even among intelligent Negroes there has come into being the fallacious belief that black Negroes are less able to achieve success."[13] The color tension between Marcus Garvey and W. E. B. Du Bois is legendary. Garvey questioned Du Bois' credibility as a leader by accusing him of wanting to be "everything but black" and Du Bois referred to Garvey as "fat, black, and ugly."[14] Du Bois' comment is something of a floating trinity in black America. Like the floating blues lyric that appears in diverse songs and contexts, so too does the phrase, "fat, black and ugly"—readily available as an all too familiar taunt. Or,

13. Walter White, "Color Lines" *Survey Graphic* VI (March 1925): 682.

14. For an exploration of the color debate between Garvey and Du Bois, see V. P. Franklin, *Living Our Stories, Telling Our Truths: Autobiography and the Making of the African American Intellectual Tradition* (New York: Oxford University Press, 1996), 122–25.

witness Colin Powell's statement in an interview with Henry
Louis Gates—"I ain't that black."[15]

If black men have used color and features as weapons
against each other, the impact of a color hierarchy on black
women has been especially devastating. In a heterosexist society, standards of beauty always impact upon women more
harshly than upon men. Because black women were always
compared to "the white woman"—the standard bearer—in
the eyes of mainstream society and in the eyes of far too many
black men, they fell short of this ideal.[16]

By the time Malcolm X began speaking to black audiences,
black women had suffered centuries of "humiliating and de-
tested images of [them]selves imposed by other people."[17] Pages
of black magazines were filled with advertisements for hair-
straightening and skin-lightening products; most black sex
symbols were café au lait at best: Lena Horne, Dorothy Dan-
dridge, Eartha Kitt. As Malcolm gained notoriety, black audiences would see the emergence of darker beauties like Abbey
Lincoln, Cicely Tyson, and Nina Simone, but these would still
be rare. It is in this context that we must be aware of the appeal
of Malcolm's affirmation of black features and color. Also, we
must remain cognizant of the class connotations of a color hierarchy in black communities.

When Malcolm X spoke out against racist hierarchies of
beauty, black women heard an admired and respected leader
who finally took seriously an issue that had affected them pro-

15. See Henry Louis Gates, "The Powell Perplex," in *Thirteen Ways of Looking at a Black Man* (New York: Random House, 1997), 84.

16. Even today, more than twenty years after the "black is beautiful" sixties
and the Afro-centric nineties, colorism continues to thrive among African
Americans. As recently as 1994, psychologist Midge Wilson of DePaul University asserted, "Studies show that successful Black men are particularly likely to
marry light-skinned women." Karen Grisby Bates, "The Color Thing," *Essence* (September 1994): 132. See also Kathy Russell, Midge Wilson, and Ronald Hall, *The Color Complex: The Politics of Skin Color Among African
Americans* (New York: Anchor Books, 1992).

17. Editor's Statement from the first issue of *Essence*, April 1970.

foundly—an issue that is often not given serious attention by black leaders and thinkers because it is not considered "political" and because it calls for a self-critique that few leaders have been willing to endure. This was not the case with Malcolm X: "Out in the world, later on, in Boston and New York, I was among the millions of Negroes who were insane enough to feel that it was some kind of status symbol to be light-complexioned—that one was actually fortunate to be born thus."[18]

Many black people, particularly women, welcomed Malcolm's willingness to break the silence around "the color thing." The issue of colorism, of distinctions based on grade of hair and keenness of features, tears at the very fabric of who we are as a people. In the way that certain feminist critiques of the nuclear family uncovered the sexist aspects of that institution, so too do critiques of white standards of beauty and desirability reveal hidden dimensions in black family life. Malcolm exposed this when he said, "I actually believe that as anti-white as my father was, he was subconsciously so afflicted with the white man's brainwashing of Negroes that he inclined to favor the light ones. . . . Most Negro parents . . . would almost instinctively treat any lighter children better than they did the darker ones."[19] With humor and pathos Malcolm taught black people to see the way they came to hate their color, their hair, their features. He also connected this understanding with their political awakening.

> You know yourself that we have been a people who hated our African characteristics. We hated our heads, we hated the shape of our nose, we wanted one of those long dog-like noses, you know; we hated the color of our skin, hated the blood of Africa that was in our veins. And in hating our features and our skin and our blood, why we had to end up hating ourselves.[20]

18. Malcolm X, *The Autobiography*, 4.

19. Ibid.

20. *Malcolm X on Afro-American History* (New York: Pathfinder, 1967), 86.

While contemporary black critics like Lisa Jones and Kobena Mercer[21] challenge the adequacy of the notion of self-hatred for understanding the personal aesthetics of African Americans, Malcolm still has much to teach us about the way we have often uncritically adopted white supremacist standards. Although the black church has also been a sight of affirming black beauty, Malcolm went a step further and suggested that we rid ourselves of all remnants of the white supremacist legacy, including straightened hair. It is quite ironic that other members of the Nation would later charge the organization with its own brand of colorism. In a CBS documentary on Malcolm X, one member even claimed that Malcolm's ascendancy to a position of leadership was aided by his fair coloring.[22] In fact, Malcolm X is even somewhat oppositional from the official Nation of Islam stance on issues like hair and color in his celebration of unstraightened black hair.[23]

For black women in Malcolm's audience, greetings like "My beautiful black brothers and sisters" with which he opened some of his talks, must have come as rare and welcome salutations.[24] In February 1992, *Essence* magazine ran a special issue on "Honoring Our Heroes." Malcolm was on the cover and one of the featured articles was an as-told-to narrative by his widow, Betty Shabazz. Audrey Edwards and Susan Taylor opened the narrative with the following: "He has come to embody the best in black men: strong and uncompromising, clear—committed to securing power 'by any means necessary.'"[25] In that quotation, Malcolm's wife Betty Shabazz recalls her own

21. See Kobena Mercer, *Welcome to the Jungle: New Positions on Black Cultural Studies* (New York: Routledge, 1994); Lisa Jones, *Bulletproof Diva: Tales of Race, Sex and Hair* (New York: Doubleday, 1994).

22. See "The Real Malcolm X: An Intimate Portrait of the Man," CBS News Video, 1992. Executive Producer Andrew Lack, Producer, Brett Alexander.

23. See E. Frances White, "Listening to the Voices of Black Feminism" *Radical America*, 7–25.

24. Malcolm X, *The Autobiography*, 201.

25. Betty Shabazz as told to Audrey Edwards and Susan Taylor, "Loving and Losing Malcolm," *Essence* 22, no. 10 (February 1992): 50.

feeling of affirmation in Malcolm's aesthetic appreciation of her blackness.

Black women cherished Malcolm's willingness to affirm them as worthy of respect, love, and admiration. All hierarchies of beauty are ultimately oppressive. And yet in a context where black women have been constructed as ugly just because they are black, it has been necessary to affirm them by acknowledging the beauty of blackness in all of its various guises. Still, our challenge isn't to reverse their hierarchy but to redefine beauty while questioning it as the most important characteristic for a woman to possess. Finally, our goal ought to be to dismantle all such oppressive hierarchies altogether.

The appreciation of the variety and diversity of black beauty is nowhere more evident than in black nationalist movements. However, this affirmation of black beauty rarely leads to a progressive gender politics. In fact, nationalist movements of all sorts also have been characterized by their patriarchal ambitions. At best black women can expect to be called black queens and we all know that where there are queens there are kings: a pairing that is rarely an equal one (not to mention the class and antidemocratic implications of such titles).

During his time, Malcolm's promise of protection and affirmation of black beauty were welcome and needed. However, even then they held evidence of a very problematic gender politics. Our task is to scrutinize this aspect of his legacy with a critical eye. Of course we must hold on to and value that which sought to affirm black women, but we must rid ourselves of and revise all elements of his philosophy that might be detrimental to them.

WOMANIST MALCOLM?!

do not speak to me of martyrdom
of men who die to be remembered
on some parish day.
i don't believe in dying
though i too shall die

> and violets like castanets
> will echo me.
>
> —FROM "MALCOLM" BY SONIA SANCHEZ

It is quite significant that in spite of the profound sexism of some of his writing, Malcolm X continues to be a hero for many black women, even many black womanist critics, theorists, and artists, myself included. Most black women who had the opportunity to hear Malcolm never flocked to cover their bodies and hair, walk two steps behind their men, and join the Nation of Islam. Nevertheless, many of them appeared to have voiced their admiration and respect for his vision and for his commitment to black women and families. In my classes, it is most often white women who are the first to raise concerns about the sexist moments in the *Autobiography*, while many of my black women students immediately jump to Malcolm's defense, claiming him as a hero.

Black women thinkers like Angela Davis, bell hooks, and Alice Walker have all acknowledged his impact on their intellectual development and politicization. Davis and Walker have sought to rescue his legacy from the misogyny of those black leaders who followed him. hooks applauds his affirmation of blackness in the midst of a society that despises all that is black. Patricia Hill Collins is one of the few contemporary black feminist thinkers to provide a sustained critique of Malcolm's gender politics in an effort to make black nationalism more accountable to black women.[26] Perhaps Collins is able to launch such a critique because she shares Malcolm's black nationalist politics.

If black women critical thinkers have been reluctant to forward a critique of the sexism inherent in much of Malcolm's legacy, black women creative writers, particularly our poets,

---

26. See bell hooks, "Sitting at the Feet of the Messenger: Remembering Malcolm X," in *Yearning: Race, Gender, and Cultural Politics* (Boston: South End Press, 1990), 87; Angela Y. Davis, "Meditations on the Legacy of Malcolm X" and Patricia Hill Collins, "Learning to Think for Ourselves: Malcolm X's Black Nationalism Reconsidered," in Joe Wood, ed., *Malcolm X: In Our Own Image* (New York: Anchor Books, 1992), 36–47, and 59–85.

have praised him in terms that celebrate the very patriarchy of his masculinity and held that up as his value to us as a people. Sonia Sanchez, Lucille Clifton, Margaret Walker Alexander, Gwendolyn Brooks, and Alice Walker are all among the women who have written poems in honor of Malcolm X. In 1968, Brooks published "Malcolm X":

> Original.
> Ragged-round.
> Rich-robust.

> He had the hawk-man's eyes.
> We gasped. We saw the maleness.
> The maleness raking out and making guttural the air
> and pushing us to walls.

> and in a soft and fundamental hour
> a sorcery devout and vertical
> beguiled the world.

> He opened us—
> who was a key,

> who was a man.

Brooks's Malcolm is the one who is loved and revered by many black women: A BLACK MAN, MALE, MALCOLM who could protect us and "open" us as he was a key. The "us" of this poem is a feminized black people who are in need of a very masculinized black leader.

Some black women have pinned their hopes on "What might have been the direction of Malcolm's thinking on questions of gender had he not been so cruelly assassinated?" For some sense of this, we all turn to one statement in particular that has come to represent a kind of beacon light for us:

One thing that I became aware of in my traveling recently through Africa and the Middle East in every country you go to, usually the degree of progress can never be separated from the woman. If you're in a country that is progressive, then woman is progressive. If you're in a country that reflects the consciousness toward the importance of education, it's because the woman is aware of the importance of education. But in every backward country you'll find the women are backward, and in every country where education is not stressed it's because the women don't have education. So one of the things I became thoroughly convinced of in my recent travels is the importance of giving freedom to the woman, giving her education, and giving her the incentive to get out there and put that same spirit and understanding in her children. And frankly I am proud of the contributions women have made in the struggle for freedom and I'm one person who's for giving them all the leeway possible because they've made a greater contribution than many of us men.[27]

This is the comment that leads some black women to say that Malcolm began to reconsider his stance on women, their nature, and their role in the black freedom struggle. It is seen as part of the overall growth and change he experienced following his travels through Africa and the Middle East. Patricia Hill Collins has pointed out that even here, women are not agents. They are given freedom and education so that they may better act upon their roles as mother.[28]

By the end of his life, it appears Malcolm not only changed his opinion about women's position in society, but he also began a much needed self-critique. In the important essay "Black Popular Culture and the Transcendence of Patriarchal Illusions," Barbara Ransby and Tracye Matthews cite the following excerpt from a letter Malcolm wrote to his cousin-in-law in 1965:

> I taught brothers not only to deal unintelligently with the devil or the white woman, but I also taught many brothers to spit acid

27. Paris interview, November 1964.

28. Collins, "Learning to Think for Ourselves," 79.

at the sisters. They were kept in their places—you probably didn't notice this in action, but it is a fact. I taught these brothers to spit acid at the sisters. If the sisters decided a thing was wrong, they had to suffer it out. If the sister wanted to have her husband home with her in the evening, I taught the brothers that the sisters were standing in their way; in the way of the Messenger, in the way of progress, in the way of God himself. I did these things brother. I must undo them.[29]

If Malcolm himself came to be aware of the need to "undo" the work of his teachings about women, certainly we must recognize this need as well. Beyond wondering how Malcolm's view of women might have changed, we are left with the task of critiquing and revising what he left us. The re-emergence of his popularity with young black people, the use of his discourse by present-day nationalist leaders requires us to provide a systematic critique of those elements of his thought that place limits on black women. Angela Davis suggests we concern ourselves with "the continuing influence on both those who see themselves as the political descendants of Malcolm and our historical memory of this man as shaped by social and technological forces that have frozen his memory, transforming it into a backward imprisoning memory rather than a forward looking impetus for creative political thinking and organizing."[30]

Just as there are some who want only to preserve the racial politics of the pre-Mecca Malcolm, so too are there those persons who want to freeze his pre-Mecca statements on women. We must move from Abbey Lincoln's call for a Malcolm-like black man who will revere and protect us in the traditional sense of these words. And we must imagine the possibility that

29. I am grateful to Tracye Matthews for calling my attention to this letter. Letter cited in Guy-Sheftall, ed., *Words of Fire*, 530. It originally appeared in an unpublished manuscript by Paul Lee, "Malcolm X's Evolved Views on the Role in Women in Society."

30. Davis, "Meditations on the Legacy of Malcolm X," 44–45.

Malcolm's legacy might lead to a celebration of the Malcolm X of Alice Walker's poem, "Malcolm":

> Those who say they knew you
> offer as proof
> an image stunted
> by perfection.
> Alert for signs of the man
> to claim, one must believe
> they did not know you at all
> nor can remember the small, less popular
> ironies of the Saint:
> that you learned to prefer
> all women free
> and enjoyed a joke
> and loved to laugh.
>
> —ALICE WALKER[31]

Walker's Malcolm is a man who "learned to love all women free." A mythical Malcolm, yes (for perhaps the real ironies of the Saint are that he loved black women—yet could not imagine them as equal partners and in this way he is no different than most men of his time), but no less mythical than the one who fuels contemporary images of him in popular culture and nationalist discourses.

Malcolm's tremendous capacity for self-reflection, growth, and revision can serve as an example for us. A serious and critical engagement with his words and thought leads us to the understanding that we must respect and acknowledge his continuing importance and significance while moving beyond the limitations of his vision.

31. Alice Walker, "Malcolm," in *Her Blue Body Everything We Know: Earthling Poems 1965–1990 Complete* (New York: Harcourt Brace Jovanovich, 1991), 291.

Manning Marable, "Rediscovering Malcolm's Life:
A Historian's Adventure in Living History," *Souls,*
vol. 7, no. 1 (2005): 20–35

To the majority of older white Americans, the noted African-American leaders Malcolm X and Dr. Martin Luther King, Jr. seem as different from each other as night vs. day. Mainstream culture and many history textbooks still suggest that the moderate Dr. King preached nonviolence and interracial harmony, whereas the militant Malcolm X advocated racial hatred and armed confrontation. Even Malcolm's infamous slogan, "By Any Means Necessary!," still evokes among whites disturbing images of Molotov cocktails, armed shoot-outs, and violent urban insurrection. But to the great majority of Black Americans and to millions of whites under thirty, these two Black figures are now largely perceived as being fully complimentary with each other. Both leaders had favored the building of strong Black institutions and healthy communities; both had strongly denounced Black-on-Black violence and drugs within the urban ghetto; both had vigorously opposed America's war in Vietnam and had embraced the global cause of human rights. In a 1989 "dialogue" between the eldest daughters of these two assassinated Black heroes, Yolanda King and Attallah Shabazz, both women emphasized the fundamental common ground and great admiration the two men shared for each other. Shabazz complained that "playwrights always make Martin so passive and Malcolm so aggressive that those men wouldn't have lasted a minute in the same room." King concurred, noting that in one play "my father was this wimp who carried a Bible everywhere he went, including to someone's house for dinner." King argued, "That's not the kind of minister Daddy was! All these ridiculous clichés. . . ." Both agreed that the two giants were united in the pursuit of Black freedom and equality.

As a child of the radical sixties, I was well ahead of the national learning curve on the King vs. Malcolm dialectic. At age seventeen, as a high school senior, I had attended Dr. King's massive funeral at Ebenezer Baptist Church in Atlanta, on April 9, 1968. I had walked behind the mule-driven wagon carrying Dr. King's body, along with tens of thousands of other mourners. The chaotic events of 1968—the Vietnamese Tet offensive in February, President Johnson's surprise decision not to seek reelection, the assassinations of both Dr. King and Bobby Kennedy, the Paris student and worker uprising that summer, the "police riot" in Chicago at the Democratic National Convention—all were contributing factors in spinning the world upside down.

By the end of that turbulent year, for the generation of African-American students at overwhelmingly white college campuses, it was Malcolm X, not Dr. King, who overnight became the symbol for the times we were living through. As leader of my campus Black student union, I re-read *The Autobiography of Malcolm X* during the winter of 1969. The full relevance and revolutionary meaning of the man suddenly became crystal clear to me. In short, the former "King Man" became almost overnight a confirmed, dedicated "X Man."

Malcolm X was the Black Power generation's greatest prophet, who spoke the uncomfortable truths that no one else had the courage or integrity to broach. Especially for young Black males, he personified for us *everything* we wanted to become: the embodiment of Black masculinist authority and power, uncompromising bravery in the face of racial oppression, the ebony standard for what the African-American liberation movement should be about. With Talmudic-like authority, we quoted him in our debates, citing chapter and verse, the precise passages from the *Autobiography*, and books like *Malcolm X Speaks*, *By Any Means Necessary*, and other edited volumes. These collected works represented almost sacred texts of Black identity to us. "Saint Malcolm X-the-Martyr" was the ecumenical ebony standard for collective "Blackness." We even made feeble attempts to imitate

Malcolm's speaking style. Everyone quoted him to justify their own narrow political, cultural, and even religious formulations and activities. His birthday, May 19, was widely celebrated as a national Black holiday. Any criticisms, no matter how minor or mild, of Malcolm's stated beliefs or evolving political career, were generally perceived as being not merely heretical, but almost treasonous to the entire Black race.

Working class Black people widely loved Brother Malcolm for what they perceived as his clear and uncomplicated style of language, and his peerless ability in making every complex issue "plain." Indeed, one of Malcolm's favorite expressions from the podium was his admonition to other speakers to "Make it Plain," a phrase embodying his unshakable conviction that the Black masses themselves, "from the grassroots," would ultimately become the makers of their own revolutionary Black history. Here again, inside impoverished Black urban neighborhoods and especially in the bowels of America's prisons and jails, Malcolm's powerful message had an evocative appeal to young Black males. In actor Ossie Davis's memorable words, "Malcolm was our manhood! . . . And, in honoring him, we honor the best in ourselves. And we will know him then for what he was and is—a Prince—our own Black shining Prince!— who didn't hesitate to die, because he loved us so."

The Autobiography of Malcolm X, released into print in November 1965, sold millions of copies within several years. By the late sixties, the *Autobiography* had been adopted in hundreds of college courses across the country. Malcolm X's life story, as outlined by the *Autobiography*, became our quintessential story about the ordeal of being Black in America. Nearly every African American at the time was familiar with the story's basic outline. Born in the Midwest, young Malcolm Little became an orphan: his father was brutally murdered by the Ku Klux Klan and his disturbed mother, overwhelmed by caring for seven little children, suffered a mental breakdown and had been institutionalized. Malcolm then relocated east to Roxbury and Harlem. He then became an urban outlaw, the notorious "Detroit Red," a pimp, hustler, burglar, and drug dealer. Pinched by police, "Detroit Red" was sentenced to ten years' hard labor in prison, where he then joined the Black Muslims. Once released, given the new name Malcolm X, he rapidly built the Black Muslims from an inconsequential sect to over one hundred thousand strong. But then Malcolm X grew intellectually and politically well beyond the Muslim. He decided to launch his own Black nationalist group, the Organization of Afro-American Unity. He started preaching about human rights and "the ballot or the bullet." Malcolm made a pilgrimage to the holy city of Mecca, converted to orthodox Islam, and became "El-Hajj Malik El-Shabazz." He was then acclaimed by Islamic, African, and Arab leaders as a leading voice for racial justice. Then, at the pinnacle of his world-wide influence and power, Malcolm was brutally struck down by assassins' bullets at Harlem's Audubon Ballroom. This was the basic story nearly every activist in my generation knew by heart.

A number of Malcolm X's associates and other who had known him personally published articles and books in the late sixties, which firmly established the late leader as the true foun-tainhead of Black Power.[1] Far more influential, however, for popularizing the Malcolm Legend was the Black Arts Move-

---

1. Immediately following Malcolm X's assassination, several individuals who had worked closely with the fallen leader sought to document his meaning to the larger Black freedom struggle. These early texts include: Leslie Alexander Lacy, "Malcolm X in Ghana," in John Henrik Clarke, ed., *Malcolm X: The Man and His Times* (New York: Macmillan, 1969), pp. 217–255; Ossie Davis, "Why I Eulogized Malcolm X," *Negro Digest*, Vol. 15, no. 4 (February 1966): 64–66; Wyatt Tee Walker, "On Malcolm X: Nothing But a Man," *Negro Digest*, Vol. 14, no. 10 (August 1965): 29–32; and Albert B. Cleage, Jr., "Brother Malcolm," in Cleage, *The Black Messiah* (New York: Sheed and Ward, 1968), 186–200.

The advocates of Black Power subsequently placed Malcolm X firmly within the Black nationalist tradition of Martin R. Delany and Marcus Garvey, emphasizing his dedication to the use of armed self defense by Blacks. Amiri Baraka's essay, "The Legacy of Malcolm X, and the Coming of the Black Nation," in LeRoi Jones, *Home: Social Essays* (New York: William Morrow, 1966), pp. 238–250, became the template for this line of interpretation. Following Baraka's Black nationalist thesis were: Eldridge Cleaver, "Initial Reactions on the Assassination of Malcolm X," in Cleaver, *Soul On Ice* (New York: Ramparts, 1968), pp. 50–61; James Boggs, "King, Malcolm, and the Future of the Black Revolution," in Boggs, *Racism and the Class Struggle: Further Pages from a Black Worker's Notebook* (New York: Monthly Review Press, 1970), pp. 104–129; Cedrick Robinson, "Malcolm Little as a Charismatic Leader," *Afro-American Studies*, Vol. 2, no. 1 (September 1972): 81–96; and Robert

ment. Poets were particularly fascinated with the magnetic physical figure of Malcolm, as a kind of revolutionary Black Adonis. In life, towering at six feet, three inches tall and weighing a trim 175 to 180 pounds, broad-shouldered Malcolm X was mesmerizingly handsome, always displaying a broad, boyish smile, and always spotlessly well-groomed; in death, he would remain forever young. In photographs, he seemed both strong and sensitive. Poet Joyce Whitshitt captured this image of the fearless yet vulnerable model for a new Black manhood in "For Malcolm."

> . . . You were the brilliant embodiment
> Of elusive manhood. Those who are less
> Negate your death and fail to acknowledge
> Righteousness felt of your logic.

Celebrated African-American poet Gwendolyn Brooks echoed similar themes and images in her ode to Malcolm:

> He had the hawk-man's eyes.
> We gasped. We saw the maleness.
> The maleness raking out and making guttural the air.
> And pushing us to walls.

One of the most popular and widely-read Black nationalist poets of the period was Sonia Sanchez, who for several years was a Nation of Islam member. Sanchez's Malcolm was less overtly the paragon of Black masculinity, than the tragic symbol of loss for what might have been, an unhealed wound that "floods the womb until I drown":

> Do not speak to me of martyrdom
> of men who die to be remembered
> on some parish day.
> I don't believe in dying
> though I too shall die

Allen, *Black Awakening in Capitalist America* (Garden City, N.Y.: Anchor/Doubleday, 1970), especially pages 30–40.

and violets like castanets
will echo me.

Yet this man
this dreamer,
thick-lipped with words
will never speak again
and in each winter
when the cold air cracks
with frost, I'll breathe
his breath and mourn
my gun-filled nights.

He was the sun that tagged
the western sky and
melted tiger-scholars
while they searched for stripes.
He said, 'Fuck you white
man. We have been
curled too long. Nothing
is sacred now. Not your
white face nor any
land that separates
until some voices
squat with spasms.'

Do not speak to me of living.
life is obscene with crowds
of white on black.
death is my pulse.
what might have been
is not for him or me
but what could have been
floods the womb until I drown.

   Malcolm's powerfully masculinist image was most unam-
biguously on full display in Amiri Baraka's (LeRoi Jones)
famous and frequently-recited "A Poem for Black Hearts." De-

spite its blatantly homophobic final passage, Baraka powerfully projected Malcolm X as the ideal model for the perfect
fulfillment of an ideal Black masculinity:

> For Malcolm's eyes, when they broke
> the face of some dumb white man. For
> Malcolm's hands raised to bless us
> all black and strong in his image
> of ourselves, for Malcolm's words
> fire darts, the victor's tireless
> thrusts, words hung above the world
> change as it may, he said it, and
> for this he was killed, for saying,
> and feeling, and being/change, all
> collected hot in his heart, For Malcolm's
> heart, raising us above our filthy cities,
> for his stride, and his beat, and his address
> to the grey monsters of the world, For Malcolm's
> pleas for your dignity, black men, for your life,
> black men, for the filling of your minds
> with righteousness, For all of him dead and
> gone and vanished from us, and all of him which
> clings to our speech black god of our time.
> For all of him, and all of yourself, look up,
> black man, quit stuttering and shuffling, look up,
> black man, quit whining and stooping, for all of him,
> for Great Malcolm a prince of the earth, let nothing
> in us rest
> until we avenge ourselves for his death, stupid animals
> that killed him, let us never breathe a pure breath if
> we fail, and white men call us faggots till the end of
> the earth.

After receding somewhat during much of the late 1970s and
early 1980s, Malcolm X's cultural reputation among artists,
playwrights, and musicians exploded again with the flowering
of the hip-hop generation. Malcolm's cultural renaissance
began with the 1983 release of Keith LeBlanc's "No Sell-Out,"

a 12-inch dance single featuring a Malcolm X speech set to hip-hop beat. Old School group Afrika Bambaata and the Soul Sonic Force followed in 1986 with "Renegades of Funk," declaring that both King and Malcolm X had been bold and bad "renegades of the atomic age." On its classic 1988 hip-hop album, "It Takes a Nation of Millions to Hold Us Back," Public Enemy (PE) generously sampled from Malcolm's speeches. On the song "Bring The Noise," PE took two different excerpts form a Malcolm X speech, constructing the provocative phrase, "Too Black, Too Strong." On "Party for Your Right to Fight," Public Enemy told the hip-hop nation that "J. Edgar Hoover . . . had King and X set up." PE's massive popularity and its strong identification with Malcolm's image led other hip-hop artists to also incorporate Malcolm X into their own music. In 1989, the Stop the Violence Movement's "Self Destruction" album featured a Malcolm X lecture, and its companion video included beautiful murals of the Black leader as the hip-hop background for rappers. The less commercially popular but enormously talented artist Paris released "Break the Grip of Shame" in 1990, which prominently featured Malcolm's ringing indictment: "We declare our right on this Earth to be a man, to be a human being, to be respected as a human being to be given the rights of a human being in this society on this Earth in this day, which we intend to bring into existence, by any means necessary!"

As "Thug Life" and "Gangsta Rap" emerged from the West Coast and soon acquired a national commercial appeal, these artists painted Malcolm X in their own cultural contexts of misogynistic and homophobic violence. Ice Cube's 1992 "Predator," for example, sampled a Malcolm address over a beat on one cut; on another, "Wicked," Ice Cube rapped: "People wanna know how come I gotta gat and I'm looking out the window like Malcolm ready to bring that noise. Kinda trigger-happy like the Ghetto Boys." Less provocatively, KRS-One's 1995 "Ah-Yeah" spoke of Black reincarnation: "They tried to harm me, I used to be Malcolm X. Now I'm on the planet as the one called KRS." Perhaps the greatest individual artist hip-hop culture has yet produced, Tupac Shakur, fiercely identified himself with Malcolm X. On Tupac's classic 1996 "Makaveli" album, on the song "Blasphemy," he posed a provocative query:

> Why you got these kids minds, thinking that they evil while the preacher being richer. You say honor God's people, should we cry when the Pope die, my request, we should cry if they cried when we buried Malcolm X. Mama tells me am I wrong, is God just another cop waiting to beat my ass if I don't go pop?

The widespread release and commercial success of Spike Lee's 1992 biofilm "X," combined with hip-hop's celebration of Malcolm as a "homeboy," created the context for what historian Russell Rickford has termed "Malcolmology." Hundreds of thousands of African-American households owned and displayed portraits of Malcolm X, either in their homes, places of business, or at Black schools. Malcolm X by the 1990s had become one of the few historical figures to emerge from the Black nationalist tradition to be fully accepted and integrated into the pantheon of civil rights legends, an elite of Black forefathers, who included Frederick Douglass, W.E.B. Du Bois, and Dr. Martin Luther King, Jr.

As with every mythic figure, the icon of Saint Malcolm accommodated a variety of parochial interpretations. To the bulk of the African-American middle class, the Malcolm legend was generally presented in terms of his inextricable trajectory of intellectual and political maturation, culminating with his dramatic break from the NOI and embrace of interracial harmony. For much of the hip-hop nation, in sharp contrast, the most attractive characteristics of Saint Malcolm emphasized the incendiary and militant elements of his career. Many hip-hop artists made scant distinctions between Malcolm X and his former protégé and later bitter rival, Louis X (Farrakhan). Some even insisted that Malcolm X had never supported any coalitions with whites, despite his numerous 1964–1965 public statements to the contrary. The hip-hop Malcolmologists seized Malcolm as the ultimate Black cultural rebel, unblemished and uncomplicated by the pragmatic politics of partisan compromise, which was fully reflected in the public careers of other post-Malcolm Black leaders, such as Jesse Jackson and Harold Washington. Despite their Black cultural nationalist rhetoric, however, hip-hop Malcolmologists also uncritically accepted the main parameters of the Black leader's tragic life story, as presented in *The Autobiography of Malcolm X*. They also glorified Malcolm's early gangster career, as the notorious, streetwise "Detroit Red," and tended to use selective quotations by the fallen leader that gave justification for their use of weapons in challenging police brutality.

The widespread sampling of Malcolm's speeches on hip-hop videos and albums, plus the popular acclaim for Lee's biopic, culminated into "Malcolmania" in 1992–1993. There were "X" posters, coffee mugs, potato chips, T-shirts and "X-caps," which newly elected President Bill Clinton wore occasionally when jogging outside the White House in the morning. CBS News at the time estimated the commercial market for X-related products at $100 million annually. The Malcolmania hype had the effect of transporting the X-man from being merely a Black superhero into the exalted status of mainstream American idol.

This new privileged status for Malcolm X was even confirmed officially by the U.S. Government. On January 20, 1999, about 1,500 officials, celebrities, and guests crowded into Harlem's Apollo Theatre to mark the issuance by the U.S. Postal Service of the Malcolm X postage stamp. Prominently in attendance were actors Ruby Dee, Ossie Davis, and Harry Belafonte. Also on hand was Harlem millionaire entrepreneur, media-mogul (and Malcolm's former attorney) Percy Sutton. The Malcolm X stamp was the Postal Service's latest release in its "Black Heritage Stamp Series." Pennsylvania Congressman Chaka Fattah, the ranking Democrat on the House of Representatives Postal Subcommittee, remarked at the festive occasion, "There is no more appropriate honor than this stamp because Malcolm X sent all of us a message through his life and his life's work." To Congressman Fattah, Malcolm X's "thoughts, his ideas, his conviction, and his courage provide an inspiration even now to new generations to come." Few in the audience could ignore the rich irony of this event. One of America's sharpest and most unrelenting critics was now being praised and honored by the same government that had once carried out illegal harassment and surveillance against him. Ossie Davis, who understood the significance of this bittersweet moment better than anyone else, jokingly quipped: "We in this community look upon this commemorative stamp finally as America's stamp of approval . . ."

The Malcolm X postage stamp was the twenty-second release in the "Black Heritage Series," which had previously featured other Black heroes such as Frederick Douglass, Harriet Tubman, Martin Luther King, Jr., Mary McLeod Bethune, and W.E.B. Du Bois. The U.S. Postal Service also released a short biographical statement accompanying the stamp's issuance, noting that the retouched photographic image of Malcolm X had been taken by an Associated Press photographer at a press conference held in New York City on May 21, 1964. The statement explains that soon after this photograph was taken, that Malcolm X "later broke away from the organization," referring to the NOI, and "disavowed his earlier separatist preaching. . . ." The most generous thing one could say about this curious statement was that it was the product of poor scholarship. The photograph actually had been taken during an interview in Cairo, Egypt, on July 14, 1964. Malcolm X had publicly broken from the NOI on March 8, 1964, two months earlier than the official statement had suggested. More problematic was the U.S. Postal Service's assertion that Malcolm X had become, before his death, a proponent of "a more integrationist solution to racial problems." But none of these errors of fact and slight distortions disturbed most who had gathered to celebrate. The Malcolm X postage stamp was a final and fitting triumph of his legacy. The full "Americanization of Malcolm X" appeared to be complete.

When in 1987 I decided to write what was to have been a modest "political biography" of Malcolm X, there was already a substantial body of literature about him. By 2002, those published works had grown to roughly 930 books, 360 films and internet educational resources, and 350 sound recordings. As I plowed through dozens, then hundreds of books and articles, I was dismayed to discover that almost none of the scholarly literature or books about him had relied on serious research which would include a complete archival investigation of Malcolm's letters, personal documents, wills, diaries, transcripts of speeches and sermons, his actual criminal record, FBI files, and legal court proceedings. Some informative articles had appeared written by individuals who had either worked closely with Malcolm X or who described a specific event in which they had been brought into direct contact with the Black leader. But these reminiscences lacked analytical rigor and critical insight. What staggered the mind, however, was the literal mountain of badly written articles, the turgid prose, and various academic-styled ruminations about Malcolm X's life and thought, nearly all based on the same, limited collection of secondary sources.

There was remarkably little Malcolm X literature that employed the traditional tools of historical investigation. Few writers had conducted fresh interviews with Malcolm X's widow, Dr. Betty Shabazz, any of his closest co-workers, or the extended Little family. Writers made a few efforts to investigate the actual criminal record of Malcolm X at the time of his 1946 incarceration. Not even the best previous scholarly studies of Malcolm X—a small group of books including Peter Goldman's *The Death and Life of Malcolm X* (1973), Karl Evanzz's *The Judas Factor: The Plot to Kill Malcolm X* (1992), and Louis DeCaro's *On the Side of My People: A Religious Life of Malcolm X* (1996)—had amassed a genuine "archival" or substantive database of documentation in order to form a true picture of Malcolm-X-the-man rather than the pristine icon.[2] One problem in this was Malcolm X's inescapable iden-

---

2. The best available studies of Malcolm X merit some consideration here. Although originally written more than three decades ago, *Newsweek* editor/journalist Peter Goldman's *The Death and Life of Malcolm X* (New York: Harper and Row, 1973), still remains an excellent introduction to the man and his times. Well-written and researched, Goldman based the text on his own interviews with the subject. Karl Evanzz's *The Judas Factor: The Plot to Kill Malcolm X* (New York: Thunder's Mouth Press, 1992), presents a persuasive argument explaining the FBI's near-blanket surveillance of the subject. Evanzz was the first author to suggest that NOI National Secretary John Ali may have

tification as the quintessential model of Black masculinity—which served as a kind of gendered barricade to any really objective appraisal of him. Cultural critic Philip Brian Harper has observed that Malcolm X and the Black Powerites who later imitated him constructed themselves as virile, potent, and hypermasculinist, giving weight to the false impression that racial integrationists like King were weak and impotent.[3]

Nearly everyone writing about Malcolm X largely, with remarkably few exceptions, accepted *as fact* most if not all of the chronology of events and personal experiences depicted in the *Autobiography*'s narrative. Few authors checked the edited, published "transcripts" of Malcolm X's speeches as presented in *Malcolm X Speaks* and *By Any Means Necessary* against the actual tape recordings of those speeches, or the transcribed excerpts of the same talks recorded by the FBI. Every historian worth her or his salt knows that "memoirs" like the *Autobiography* are inherently biased. They present a representation of the subject that privileges certain facts, while self-censuring

---

been an FBI informant. Louis A. DeCaro has written two thoughtful studies on Malcolm X's spiritual growth and religious orientation: *On the Side of My People: A Religious Life of Malcolm X* (New York: New York University Press, 1996); and *Malcolm and the Cross: The Nation of Islam, Malcolm X and Christianity* (New York: New York University Press, 1998). De Caro graciously agreed to be interviewed in 2001 for the Malcolm X Project at Columbia.

The field of religious studies has also produced other informative interpretations of Malcolm X. These works include: Lewis V. Baldwin, *Between Cross and Crescent: Christian and Muslim Perspectives on Malcolm and Martin* (Gainesville: University of Florida, 2002); a sound recording by Hamam Cross, Donna Scott, and Eugene Seals, "What's up with Malcolm? The real failure of Islam" (Southfield, Michigan: Readings for the Blind, 2001); Peter J. Paris, *Black Religious Leaders: Conflict in Unity* (Westminster: John Knox Press 1991).

3. Philip Brian Harper, in his book *Are We Not Men? Masculine Anxiety and the Problem of African-American Identity* (New York: Oxford University Press, 1996), argues that the simplistic stereotypes of King and his courageous followers as being "non-masculine" and "effeminate" and leaders such as Malcolm X and Stokely Carmichael as "super-masculine, Black males" became widely promulgated. "The Black power movement," Harper observes, was "conceived in terms of accession to a masculine identity, the problematic quality of those terms notwithstanding" (p. 68).

others. There are deliberate omissions, the chronological re-ordering of events, and name-changes. Consequently, there existed no comprehensive biography of this man who arguably had come to personify modern, urban Black America in the past half century.

There continued to be, for me, so many unanswered basic questions about this dynamic yet ultimately elusive man that neither the *Autobiography*, nor the other nine hundred-plus books written about him had answered satisfactorily. The most obvious queries concerned his murder. Substantial evidence had been compiled both by Goldman and attorney William Kunstler that indicated that two of the men convicted in 1966 for gunning down Malcolm at the Audubon Ballroom, Thomas 15X Johnson and Norman 3X Butler, were completely innocent. In 1977, the only assassin who had been wounded and captured at the crime scene, Talmadge Hayer, had confessed to his prison clergyman that both Johnson and Butler had played absolutely no roles in the murder, confirming that in fact, they had not even been present at the Audubon that afternoon.

There had always been whispers for years that Louis Farrakhan had been responsible for the assassination; he had been Malcolm X's closest protégé, and then following his vitriolic renunciation of Malcolm, inherited the leadership of Harlem's Mosque Number Seven following the murder. Then I had to explain the inexplicable behavior of the New York Police Department (NYPD) on the day of the assassination. Usually one to two dozen cops blanketed any event where Malcolm X was speaking. Normally at the Audubon rallies, a police captain or lieutenant was stationed in a command center above the Audubon's main entrance, on the second floor. Fifteen to twenty uniformed officers, at least, would be milling at the periphery of the crowd, a few always located at a small park directly across the street from the building. On February 21, 1965, however, the cops almost disappeared. There were no uniformed officers in the ballroom, at the main entrance, or even in the park, at the time of the shooting. Only two NYPD patrolmen were inside the Audubon, but at the opposite end of the building. When the NYPD investigation team arrived, forensic evidence wasn't properly collected, and significant eyewitnesses still at the scene weren't interviewed for days, and in several instances weeks, later. The crime scene itself was preserved for only a couple of hours. By 6 p.m. only three hours after Malcolm X's killing, a housekeeper with detergent and a bucket of water mopped up the floor, eliminating the bloody evidence. A dance was held in the same ballroom at 7 p.m. that night, as originally scheduled.

Perhaps I could never answer completely the greatest question about Malcolm X: if he *had* lived, or somehow had survived the assassination attempt, what could he have become? How would have another three or four decades of life altered how we imagine him, and the ways we interpret his legacy? The legion of books that he inspired presented widely different, and even diametrically opposing, theories on the subject. Virtually every group—the orthodox, Sunni Islamic community, Black cultural nationalists, Trotskyists, prisoners and former prisoners, mainstream integrationists, and hip-hop artists— had manipulated the "Black shining prince" to promote their own agendas, or to justify their causes. The enormous elasticity of Malcolm's visual image could be universally appropriated, stretching from Ice Cube's 1992 apocalyptic "predator" to being used as the template for the film character "Magneto" in the 1999 block buster hit, "The X-Men," illustrated the great difficulty I now confronted. Malcolm X was being constantly *reinvented* within American society and popular culture.

But the first, most original, and most talented revisionist of Malcolm X was Malcolm X himself. I slowly began to realize that Malcolm X continuously and astutely refashioned his outward image, artfully redesigning his public style and even language, to facilitate overtures to different people in varied contexts. And yet, beneath the multiple layers of reinvention, *who was he?* Was the powerful impact of his short, thirty-nine years of existence actually grounded in what he had really accomplished, or based on the unfulfilled promise of what he might have become? Malcolm X is memorialized by millions of Americans largely because of the *Autobiography*, which is today a standard text of American literature. But was Malcolm's *hajj* to Mecca in April 1964, the dramatic turning point of the *Autobiography*, the glorious epiphany Malcolm claimed it was at the time, and that virtually all other interpreters of him have uncritically accepted? Was this spiritual metamorphosis, the embracing of color blindness, and the public denouncing of Elijah Muhammad's sexual misconduct, all just part of the political price he was now prepared to pay to gain entry into the Civil Rights Movement's national leadership? Wasn't this final "reincarnation" the necessary role change for El-Hajj Malik El-Shabazz to reach inside the court of the Saudi royal family, and to gain access to the corridors of governmental power throughout the newly independent nations of Africa and Asia?

With so many unanswered questions to explore, there seemed to me to exist paradoxically a *collective conspiracy of silence surrounding Malcolm X*, an unwitting or perhaps witting attempt not to examine things too closely, to stick to the accepted narrative offered by the *Autobiography* and Lee's biopic. By not peering below the surface, there would be no need to adjust the crafted image we have learned to adore, frozen in time. We could simply all find enduring comfort in the safe, masculinist gaze of our "Black shining prince."

Historians are trained in graduate school to state only what we can actually *prove*, based primarily on archival or secondary source evidence. Information we collect from oral interviews can only be used from informed subjects, who have an opportunity to review what they've said for the record. Thus the discipline itself provides certain safeguards to interviewees and informants. Most historians, in other words, do not see themselves as investigative reporters, or would-be "cold case" investigators. Yet the skills of both seemed to me necessary in order to crack open the Malcolm X collective conspiracy of silence. Malcolm's actual legacy was dogmatically preserved and fiercely guarded by nearly everyone privy to important information pertaining to him. This was a highly unusual situation for a researcher to confront, especially considering that Malcolm X lived a very "public" existence, appearing on numerous television shows, and speaking literally at thousands of venues across the country.

When I started my biography of Malcolm X in 1987 I was then Chair of Black Studies at Ohio State University. Working with several graduate students, we began compiling photocopies of articles about Malcolm X that appeared in academic journals. We began a newspaper clipping file of more recent media coverage related to our subject (remember, these were the days before the internet and world-wide web). I knew that I would need to penetrate four principal, core areas of investigation, in order to present a really balanced and fair portrait of the man. These four broad areas were: (1) the Black organizations in which Malcolm X played a significant leadership role—the Nation of Islam, the Muslim Mosque, Inc., and the Organization of Afro-American Unity; (2) the surveillance of Malcolm X by the FBI and other governmental agencies; (3) the materials of Alex Haley, co-author of the *Autobiography*, used in preparing the book; and, of course (4) the family of Malcolm X, especially his widow, Dr. Betty Shabazz, and their access to any manuscripts, correspondence, texts or transcripts of speeches and sermons, legal documents, and odd paraphernalia. All four of these areas, for different reasons, proved to be intractable. In 1989, I accepted a professorship in ethnic studies at the University of Colorado in Boulder, and in the following academic year I organized a research team of six to ten graduate students and work-study assistants, who were dedicated to reconstructing Malcolm's life. After three hard years, we had made at best marginal headway. I then accepted my current appointment at Columbia. I had no idea at that time that another decade would elapse before I could really successfully infiltrate these four core areas of Malcolm-related investigation.

The first nearly overwhelming difficulty was the lack of a comprehensive, well-organized archive on Malcolm X. Primary source materials, such as correspondence and personal manuscripts, were literally scattered and fragmented. For some inexplicable reason, the Shabazz family had never authorized a group of historians or archivists to compile these rare documents into a central, publicly accessible repository. By my own count, as of 2003 chunks of Malcolm's core memorabilia were located at seventy-three different U.S. archives and libraries, including the Library of Congress, New York University's Tamiment Library, the Schomburg Center of the New York Public Library, Cornell University Library, Wayne State University Library, the State Historical Society of Wisconsin, Emory University Library, Howard University Library and Columbia University's Oral History Research Center. I contrasted this chaotic situation to the professionally archived life records of Dr. Martin Luther King, Jr., then at Atlanta's King Center, that would serve as the core database for historian Clayborne Carson's magnificent, 30-year-long effort, the King Papers Project. Booker T. Washington's papers, carefully archived and preserved, fill exactly 1,077 linear feet of archival boxes at the Library of Congress. Most dedicated Malcolmologists also knew that Dr. Shabazz still retained hundreds of documents and manuscripts by her late husband in her Mount Vernon, New York home. But no one really had a clue how much primary source material there was, and whether any efforts had been made to preserve it.

I had more than a nostalgic desire to preserve memorabilia. As a historian, I also knew that all artifacts made by human beings inevitably disintegrate. Paper, left unprotected, without a climate-controlled environment and acid-free folders, "lives" only about seventy-five years. Audiotape recordings based on magnetic recording technology survive about forty years. People who had worked closely with Malcolm X and who had known him intimately would nearly all be dead in another two decades. Only the Shabazz family had the moral authority to initiate such an undertaking, to secure Malcolm X's place in history. It simply didn't make sense. Much later, in 2002, when the near-public auction by Butterfield's of a major cache of Malcolm memorabilia fetching offers of $600,000 and more came to light, I discovered the Shabazz family had squirreled away several hundred pounds of Malcolm X–related documents and material. Malikah Shabazz, the youngest daughter, had, without the rest of the family's knowledge, managed to pack and transport her father's materials to a Florida storage

facility. Her failure to pay the storage facility's monthly fee led
to the seizure and disposition of the bin's priceless contents.
The new purchaser, in turn, had contacted E-Bay and Butterfield's to sell what he believed to be his property. Only a legal
technicality voided the sale, returning the memorabilia to the
Shabazzes.

After the international publicity and outcry surrounding the
Butterfield's abortive auction, however, the Shabazzes decided
to deposit their materials at the Schomburg Center in Harlem.
In January 2003, the Schomburg publicly announced to the
media its acquisition on the basis of a 75-year loan. I have previously written in detail about the Butterfield's abortive auction fiasco, and I had been extensively involved in the financial
negotiations with the auction house and the Shabazzes on behalf of Columbia University. But what *none* of the principals,
including myself, could bear to ask ourselves and the Shabazz
Estate in public, is *why* had hundreds of pounds of documents,
speeches, manuscripts, Malcolm's Holy Qu'ran, etc. been left
deteriorating in storage in their basement *for thirty-five years?*

The intransigence of the Shabazzes forced me to contem-
plate negotiations with the Nation of Islam. I had written extensively, and quite critically, about Louis Farrakhan and his
philosophy over a number of years. Yet during my research, I
had learned that Muslim ministers like Malcolm X, under the
strict authoritarian supervision of Elijah Muhammad, had
been required to submit weekly reports about their mosques'
activities. All sermons they delivered were audiotaped, with
the tapes mailed to the national headquarters in Chicago.
When I broached the possibility of examining their archives
through third parties, the NOI curtly refused, explaining that
they wished to "protect Dr. Betty Shabazz and her family."

Another potential avenue of biographical inquiry existed
among Malcolm X's friends and associates in Muslim Mosque,
Inc., and the Organization of Afro-American Unity, two groups
formed in 1964, and that had disintegrated in the months after
Malcolm's assassination. Here I had better luck. Prior friend-
ships with several prominent individuals, such as actor Ossie
Davis, provided valuable oral histories of their relationships

with Malcolm X. Most key individuals I wanted to interview, however, were either reclusive or elusive. Some were literally "underground," and living in exile in either South America, the Caribbean, or in Africa. A few, such as writer Sylvester Leaks, cordially agreed to converse off the record, then angrily refused to be formally interviewed. Some pivotal figures such as Malcolm X's personal bodyguard, Reuben Francis, had literally disappeared months following the murder. I subsequently learned that Francis had somehow been relocated to Mexico sometime in 1966, and from then fell into complete obscurity. Lynn[e] Shif[f]lett, OAAU secretary and a trusted personal assistant to Malcolm X, had refused all interviews and even written contacts since 1966.

The FBI avenue of inquiry proved to be even more daunting. Despite the passage of the Freedom of Information Act, which required the Bureau to declassify its internal memoranda that required secrecy for the sake of national security, by 1994 only about 2,300 pages of an estimated *50,000 pages* of surveillance on Malcolm X was made public. Much of this information was heavily redacted or blacked out by FBI censors, supposedly to protect its informants, or to preserve "national security." For several years, a group of my student research assistants helped me to make sense of this maze of FBI bureaucratic mumbo jumbo. I learned eventually that whatever the FBI's original motives, they fairly accurately tracked Malcolm X's precise movements, public addresses and dozens of telephone calls, all without legal warrants, of course. In 1995, Farrakhan had proposed announcing a national campaign to pressure the Bureau to open up its archives about Malcolm X, and especially to release any relevant information concerning his assassination. According to Farrakhan, the Shabazz family insisted that there be no effort to force the Bureau to divulge what it knew. Friends close to the family subsequently explained to me that the memories were still too painful, even after thirty long years. A public inquiry would be too traumatic for all concerned.

Without my knowledge, historian Clayborne Carson at Stanford University was, in the early 1990s, working independently along parallel lines. He successfully annotated the FBI memoranda at that time available, publishing an invaluable reference work, *Malcolm X: The FBI File* (New York: Ballantine Books, 1995). Prior to the book's publication, however, attorneys for Dr. Shabazz expressed concerns that Carson should severely *limit* the amount of original material lifted by the FBI from Malcolm X's orations, writings, and wiretapped conversations. Thus the book that was comprised of letters and transcribed tape recordings already heavily censored by the FBI was, in effect, *censored a second time* for the purpose of not violating copyright infringement. When Black Studies scholar Abdul Alkalimat prepared a primer text, *Malcolm X for Beginners*, Dr. Shabazz threatened a lawsuit, based on the unusual legal claim that *anything* ever uttered by her late husband was her "intellectual property." Alkalimat finally consented to surrender any and all claims to royalties from the book to the Shabazz estate.

I then confronted the enigma of Alex Haley. Haley was the highest-selling author of Black nonfiction in U.S. history. His greatest achievement had been the 1976 book *Roots*, which like the co-authored *Autobiography* had become a celebrated, iconic text of Black identity and culture. Yet statements about Malcolm X made by Haley shortly before his death seemed to me strangely negative. Haley had even asserted that both Malcolm X and Dr. King were going "downhill" before their deaths.[4] Haley had placed his papers at the University of Tennessee's archives, in January 1991. Yet there remained unusual restrictions on scholarly access to his personal records. I personally visited his archives in Knoxville twice. No photocopying of any docu-

---

4. In an extraordinary interview with writer Thomas Hauser, Alex Haley stated that he had "worked closely with Malcolm X, and I also did a *Playboy* interview with Martin Luther King during the same period, so I knew one very closely and the other a little." Based on his knowledge of both men, he had concluded that they had "both died tragically at about the right time in terms of posterity. Both men were . . . beginning to decline. They were under attack." In Haley's opinion, Malcolm, in particular, "was having a rough time trying to keep things going. Both of them were killed just before it went really downhill for them, and as of their death, they were practically sainted." See Thomas Hauser, *Muhammad Ali: His Life and Times* (New York: Touchstone/Simon and Schuster, 1991), p. 508.

ment in the Haley file is permitted, without the prior written approval of his attorney, Paul Coleman of Knoxville, Tennessee. My letters to Coleman were unanswered. When in Knoxville during my second visit, I persuaded the archive's curator to phone Coleman directly on my behalf. Attorney Coleman then explained to me over the telephone that he needed to know the *precise pages* or documents to be photocopied, *in advance*! In practical terms, scholars are forced to copy passages in pencil, by hand, from Haley's archives. This laborious model of information transferal worked well for monks in the Middle Ages, but seems inappropriate for the age of digital technology.

As luck would have it, several years before Haley's death, he had named researcher Anne Romaine as his "official biographer." Romaine was a white folksinger, trained neither as a historian nor as a biographer. Yet she was apparently diligent and serious about her work. Between the late 1980s until to her death in 1995, Romaine had conducted audiotaped interviews with over fifty individuals, some of whom covered the background to Haley's role in producing the *Autobiography*. The great bulk of Romaine's papers and research materials pertaining to the *Autobiography* were also donated to the University of Tennessee's archives. To my delight, there were absolutely no restrictions on Romaine's papers; everything can be photocopied and reproduced. One folder in Romaine's papers includes the "raw materials" used to construct Chapter Sixteen of the *Autobiography*. Here, I found the actual mechanics of the Haley–Malcolm X collaboration. Malcolm X apparently would speak to Haley in "free style"; it was left to Haley to take hundreds of sentences into paragraphs and then appropriate subject areas. Malcolm also had a habit of scribbling notes to himself as he spoke. Haley learned to pocket these sketchy notes and later reassemble them, integrating the conscious with subconscious reflections into a workable narrative. Although Malcolm X retained final approval of their hybrid text, he was not privy to the actual editorial processes superimposed from Haley's side. Chapters the two men had prepared were sometimes split and restructured into other chapters. These details may appear mundane and insignificant. But considering that Malcolm's final "metamorphosis" took place in 1963–65, the exact timing of when individual chapters were produced takes on enormous importance.

These new revelations made me realize that I also needed to learn much more about *Haley*. Born in Ithaca, New York in 1921, Alex Haley was the oldest of three sons of Simon Alexander Haley, a professor of agriculture, and Bertha George Palmer, a grade school teacher. Haley had been raised as a child in Henning, Tennessee. As a teenager, in 1939, Haley enlisted in the U.S. Coast Guard as a mess boy. During World War II, he had come to the attention of white officers for his flair as a talented writer. During long assignments at sea, Haley had ghost-written hundreds of love letters for sailors' wives and sweethearts back at home. While Haley's repeated efforts to gain print publication for his unsolicited manuscripts failed for eight long years, his extracurricular activities gained the approval and admiration of his white superiors. By the late 1940s, Haley was advanced into a desk job; by the mid-1950s he was granted the post of "chief journalist" in the Coast Guard. After putting in twenty years' service, Haley started a career as a professional freelance writer. Politically, Haley was both a Republican and a committed advocate of racial integration. He was not, unlike C. Eric Lincoln or other African-American scholars who had studied the NOI's activities during the late 1950s, even mildly sympathetic with the Black group's aim and racial philosophy.

To Haley, the separatist Nation of Islam was an object lesson in America's failure to achieve interracial justice and fairness. As Mike Wallace's controversial 1959 television series on the Black Muslims had proclaimed, they represented "The Hate That Hate Produced." Haley completely concurred with Wallace's thesis. He, too, was convinced that the NOI was potentially a dangerous, racist cult, completely out of step with the lofty goals and integrationist aspirations of the civil rights movement. Haley was personally fascinated with Malcolm's charisma and angry rhetoric, but strongly disagreed with many of his ideas. Consequently, when Haley started work on the *Autobiography*, he held a very different set of objectives than those of Malcolm X. The Romaine papers also revealed that one of Haley's early articles on the NOI, co-authored with white writer Alfred Balk, had been written *in collaboration with the FBI*. The FBI had supplied its information about the NOI to Balk and Haley, which formed much of the basis for their *Saturday Evening Post* article that appeared on January 26, 1963, with the threatening title, "Black Merchants of Hate."[5]

I then began to wonder, as I pored through Romaine's papers, what Malcolm X really had known about the final text that would become his ultimate "testament." Couldn't I discover a way to find out what was going on inside Haley's head, or at Doubleday, which had paid a hefty $20,000 advance for the *Autobiography* in June 1963? And why, only three weeks following Malcolm X's killing, had Doubleday canceled the contract for the completed book? The *Autobiography* would be eventually published by Grove Press in late 1965. Doubleday's hasty decision would cost the publisher millions of dollars.

The Library of Congress held the answers. Doubleday's corporate papers are now housed there. This collection includes the papers of Doubleday's then–executive editor, Kenneth McCormick, who had worked closely with Haley for several years as the *Autobiography* had been constructed. As in the Romaine papers, I found more evidence of Haley's sometimes weekly private commentary with McCormick about the laborious process of composing the book. These Haley letters of marginalia contained some crucial, never previously published intimate details about Malcolm's personal life. They also revealed how several attorneys retained by Doubleday closely

5. Alfred Balk had contacted the FBI in October 1962, seeking the Bureau's assistance in collecting information about the Nation of Islam for the proposed article he and Haley would write for the *Saturday Evening Post*. The Bureau gave Balk and Haley the data they requested, with the strict stipulation that the FBI's assistance not be mentioned. The Bureau was later quite pleased with the published article. See M.A. Jones to Mr. DeLoach, FBI Memorandum, October 9, 1963, in the Anne Romaine Papers, Series 1, Box 2, folder 16, University of Tennessee Library Special Collections. Also see Alfred Balk and Alex Haley, "Black Merchants of Hate," *Saturday Evening Post* (January 26, 1963).

monitored and vetted entire sections of the controversial text in 1964, demanding numerous name changes, the reworking and deletion of blocks of paragraphs, and so forth. In late 1963, Haley was particularly worried about what he viewed as Malcolm X's anti-Semitism. He therefore rewrote material to eliminate a number of negative statements about Jews in the book manuscript, with the explicit covert goal of "getting them past Malcolm X" without his co-author's knowledge or consent. Thus the censorship of Malcolm X had begun well *prior* to his assassination.

A cardinal responsibility of the historian is to relate the full truth, however unpleasant. In the early 1960s, the Nation of Islam had been directly involved with the American Nazi Party and white supremacist organizations—all while Malcolm X had been its "national representative." This regrettable dimension of Malcolm's career had to be thoroughly investigated, yet few scholars, Black or white, had been willing to do so. In 1998, in my book *Black Leadership* (New York: Columbia University Press, 1998), I had described Farrakhan's anti-Semitic, conservative, Black nationalism as an odious brand of "Black Fundamentalism." Farrakhan had been Malcolm's prime protégé, and the question must now be posed whether Malcolm X was partially responsible for the bankrupt political legacy of Black anti-Semitism and Black Fundamentalism. The whole truth, not packaged icons, can only advance our complete understanding of the real man and his times.

The Romaine papers also had provided clear evidence that the lack of a clear political program or plan of action in the *Autobiography* was no accident. Something was indeed "missing" from the final version of the book, as it appeared in print in late 1965. In Haley's own correspondence to editor Kenneth McCormick, dated January 19, 1964, Haley even described these chapters as having "the most impact material of the book, some of it rather lava-like."[6] Now my quest shifted to

6. On January 9, 1964, Haley wrote to Doubleday Executive Editor Kenneth McCormick and his agent, Paul Reynolds, that "the most impact material of the book, some of it rather lava-like, is what I have from Malcolm for the three

finding out what the contents of this "impact material" were. The trail now led me to Detroit attorney Gregory Reed. In late 1992, Reed had purchased the original manuscripts of the *Autobiography* at the sale of the Haley Estate for $100,000. Reed has in his possession, in his office safe, the three "missing chapters" from the *Autobiography*, which still have never been published. I contacted Reed, and after several lengthy telephone conversations, he agreed to show me the missing *Autobiography* chapters. With great enthusiasm, I flew to Detroit, and telephoned Reed at our agreed-upon time. Reed then curiously rejected meeting me at his law office. He insisted instead that we meet at a downtown restaurant. I arrived at our meeting place on time, and a half hour later Reed showed up, carrying a briefcase.

After exchanging a few pleasantries, Reed informed me that he had not brought the entire original manuscript with him. However, he would permit me to read, at the restaurant table, small selections from the manuscript. I was deeply disappointed, but readily accepted Reed's new terms. For roughly fifteen minutes, I quickly read parts from the illusive "missing chapters." That was enough time for me to ascertain without doubt that these text fragments had been dictated and written sometime between October 1963 and January 1964. This coincided with the final months of Malcolm's NOI membership. More critically, in these missing chapters, Malcolm X proposed the construction of an unprecedented, African-American united front of Black political and civic organizations, including both the NOI and civil rights groups. He perhaps envisioned something similar in style to Farrakhan's Million Man March of 1995. Apparently, Malcolm X was aggressively pushing the NOI beyond Black Fundamentalism, into open, common dialogue and political collaboration with the civil rights community. Was this the prime reason that elements inside both the

---

essay chapters, 'The Negro,' 'The End of Christianity,' and 'Twenty Million Black Muslims.'" See Alex Haley to Kenneth McCormick, Wolcott Gibbs, Jr., and Paul Reynolds, January 19, 1964, in Anne Romaine Collection, the University of Tennessee Library Special Collection.

NOI and the FBI may have wanted to silence him? Since Reed owns the physical property, but the Shabazz estate retains the intellectual property rights of its contents, we may never know.

With each successive stumbling block, I became more intrigued. The complicated web of this man's life, the swirling world around him, his friends, family, and intimate associates, became ever more tangled and provocative. The tensions between these at times feuding factions, the innuendos, the missed opportunities, the angry refusals to speak on the record, the suppression of archival evidence, the broken loyalties and constant betrayals, all seemed too great. It required of me a difficult journey of many years, even to possess the knowledge of how to untangle the web, to make sense of it all. What I acquired, however, by 2003–2004, was a true depth of understanding and insight that was surprising, and much more revelatory than I had ever imagined. I finally learned that the answer to the question—why was this information about Malcolm X so fiercely protected—because the life, and the man had the potential to become much more dangerous to white America than any single individual had ever been.

Malcolm X, the *real* Malcolm X, was infinitely more remarkable than the personality presented in the *Autobiography*. The man who had been born Malcolm Little, and who had perished as El-Hajj Malik El-Shabazz, was no saint. He made many serious errors of judgment, several of which directly contributed to his murder. Yet despite these serious contradictions and personal failings, Malcolm X also possessed the unique potential for uniting Black America in any unprecedented coalition with African, Asian, and Caribbean nations. He alone could have established unity between Negro integrationists and Black nationalists inside the United States. He possessed the personal charisma, the rhetorical genius, and the moral courage to inspire and motivate millions of Blacks into unified action. Neither the *Autobiography* nor Spike Lee's 1992 movie revealed this powerful legacy of the man, or explained what he could have accomplished. What continues to be suppressed and censored also tells us something so huge about America itself, about where we were then, and where we, as a people, are now. Malcolm X was potentially a new type of world leader, personally drawn up from the "wretched of the earth," into a political stratosphere of international power. Telling that remarkable, true story is the purpose of my biography.

Credits

Grateful acknowledgment is made for permission to reprint excerpts from the following copyrighted works:

"Four Convicts Turn Moslems, Get Calls Looking to Mecca," *Boston Herald*, April 20, 1950. Reprinted with permission of the *Boston Herald*.

"Local Criminals in Prison, Claim Moslem Faith Now: Grow Beards, Won't Eat Pork; Demand East-Facing Cells to Facilitate 'Prayer to Mecca,'" *Springfield Union*, April 20, 1950. © The Republican Company. All rights reserved. Reprinted with permission of the publisher.

Amsterdam News: "Riot Threat as Cops Beat Muslims" by James Hicks, issue of May 4, 1957. "Malcolm X in Detroit for 2 Weeks," August 31, 1957. "Malcolm X Making Hit in Detroit, September 7, 1957. "Malcolm X Returns; Detroit Moslems Grow," October 26, 1957. "Malcolm X Wed; It's a Surprise," January 25, 1958. "Moslems Accuse Cops; Bring Their Own Steno to Court" by Al Nall, March 14, 1959. "Moslems Ten Day Trial; Lawyer Breaks Down in Tense Courtroom," March 21, 1959. "Moslems Fight Back; Bar White Press," August 1, 1959. "Separation-Or-Death Muslim Watchword," July 1, 1961. "Muslims and Police," May 12, 1962. "Malcolm X: 'Why I Quit and What I Plan Next'" by James Booker, March 14, 1964. "Telegram to Muhammad" by Malcolm X, March 14, 1964. "In the Middle, Editorial Cartoon" by Melvin Tapley, March 14, 1964. "Ex-Sweetheart of Malcolm X Accuses Elijah," July 11, 1964. "Ossie Davis' Stirring Tribute to Malcolm X," March 6, 1965. Reprinted with permission of *Amsterdam News*.

Pittsburgh Courier: "Malcolm X Married!," issue of August 15, 1959. "Arabs Send Warm Greetings" by Malcolm X, August 15, 1959. "Malcolm X Explains Wee-Hour Visits," October 1, 1960. "Muslim Malcolm X Out as Howard University History Speaker," February 25, 1961. "What Courier Readers Think: Muslim vs. Moslem!" by Malcolm X, October 6, 1962. "What Courier Readers Think: A Blast at Muhammad" by Yahya Hawari, October 27, 1962. Reprinted with permission of the *Pittsburgh Courier* Archives.

"Going Upstairs—Malcolm X Greets Fidel" by Ralph D. Matthews, Jr., *New York Citizen-Call*, September 24, 1960. Reprinted by permission of author.

Bayard Rustin, Oral History, 1987. Used by permission of the Columbia Center for Oral History, Columbia University.

"2 Negroes with Opposing Views Debate Segregation-Integration," by Joe Matasich, the *Ithaca Journal*, March 8, 1962. © 1962 Gannett. All rights reserved. Used by permission and protected by the copyright laws of the United States. The

The Militant: "L.A. Negro Community Unites in Defense of Black Muslims," issue of May 21, 1962. "How Malcolm X Viewed March," April 16, 1963. "2,000 Hear Malcolm X," April 13, 1964. Reprinted with permission of *The Militant*, 306 W. 37th St., New York, NY, 10018.

Title Unknown, *State News*, January 24, 1963. Reprinted by permission of the *State News* (East Lansing, Michigan).

Rochester Democrat and Chronicle: "Racial Tension Causes Aired by 3 Panelists," issue of March 7, 1963. "The Rochester Image Two-Faced?" by William Vogler, March 13, 1963. © 1963 *Rochester Democrat and Chronicle*. All rights reserved. Used by permission and protected by the copyright laws of the United States. The printing, copying, and redistribution or retransmission of this content without express written permission is prohibited.

"Trial Set for 15 on Riot Charge," *Rochester Times-Union*, February 28, 1963. © 1963 *Rochester Times-Union*. All rights reserved. Used by permission and protected by the copyright laws of the United States. The printing, copying, and redistribution or retransmission of this content without express written permission is prohibited.

Peter Goldman interview, Malcolm X Project, July 12, 2004. Used by permission of Peter Goldman.

"Malcolm X Tells Negroes: Quit Integrating, 'Get Off Welfare'" by James Dufur, *Fresno Bee*, October 5, 1963. By permission of the *Fresno Bee*.

Hartford Courant: "Malcolm X Tells About White Fox," issue of October 13, 1963. "Rights Groups Give Malcolm X Cool Reception," March 11, 1964. "Stores Told to Close for Malcolm X Funeral," February 26, 1965. Used with permission of The Associated Press Copyright © 1963, 1964, 1965. All rights reserved.

Excerpts from "Message to the Grass Roots" and "The Ballot or the Bullet" from *Malcolm X Speaks: Selected Speeches and Statements,* edited by George Breitman. Copyright © 1965, 1989 by Betty Shabazz and Pathfinder Press. Reprinted by permission of Pathfinder Press.

"Miami Notebook: Cassius Clay and Malcolm X" by George Plimpton, *Harper's Magazine*, June 1964. Used with permission of the Estate of George Plimpton.

"It's Ballots or Bullets Answers Malcolm X," *Cleveland Plain Dealer*, April 4, 1964. © 1964, *The Plain Dealer*. All rights reserved. Reprinted with permission.

"Malcolm X Home Is Bombed," *Chicago Tribune*, February 15, 1965. Used with permission of The Associated Press Copyright © 1965. All rights reserved.

"Negro Leaders Express Dismay Over Slaying," *Los Angeles Times*, February 22, 1965. Used with permission of The Associated Press Copyright © 1965. All rights reserved.

Gerry Fulcher, Oral History Interview, October 3, 2007 (transcript). Used by permission of Gerry Fulcher.

Index